CONFIGURATIONS OF SENTENTIAL COMPLEMENTATION

The investigation of sentential complementation focuses on properties of sentences that are embedded in other sentences. This book brings together a variety of studies on this topic in the framework of generative grammar.

The first part of the book focuses on infinitival complements. The author provides new perspectives on raising and control, longstanding problems in infinitival complementation. He then examines the problem of clitic ordering in infinitives in Romance languages.

The second part of the book addresses various aspects of *wh*-sentences: extraction from negative and factive islands, agreement in relative clauses, and the relation between French relative and interrogative *qui* and *que*.

Throughout the work, the author compares properties of complementation in French and other Romance languages with such properties in the Germanic languages. He assumes Chomsky's Principles and Parameters framework, but also integrates insights from the Minimalist Program.

Drawing on some of Johan Rooryck's most innovative work, this study forms a valuable illustration of the interaction between syntax and semantics where matrix and embedded sentences meet.

Johan Rooryck is currently Professor of French Linguistics at Leiden University. He previously held positions at the Pennsylvania State University and Indiana University. Mainly from the perspective of Romance and Germanic languages, his research interests focus on the syntax–semantics interface, ranging from lexical decomposition to Binding.

ROUTLEDGE LEADING LINGUISTS
Series editor Carlos Otero

CONFIGURATIONS OF SENTENTIAL COMPLEMENTATION

Perspectives from Romance Languages

Johan Rooryck

London and New York

First published 2000
by Routledge
11 New Fetter Lane, London EC4P 4EE

Simultaneously published in the USA and Canada
by Routledge
29 West 35th Street, New York, NY 10001

Routledge is an imprint of the Taylor and Francis Group

Typeset in Garamond 3 by Stephen Wright-Bouvier of
The Rainwater Consultancy, Faringdon, Oxfordshire.
Printed and bound in Great Britain by
TJ International Ltd, Padstow, Cornwall

British Library Cataloguing in Publication Data
A catalogue record for this book is available
from the British Library

Library of Congress Cataloging in Publication Data
Configurations of sentential complementation: perspectives from
Romance languages / Johan Rooryck.
p.   cm.
Includes bibliographical references and index
1. Romance languages–Complement 2. Romance languages–syntax.
I. Title.
PC207.R66   1999
440' . 045—dc21   99–18881
CIP

ISBN 0–415–18779–6

Je dédie ce livre à la mémoire
de Anne Vanderseypen

Assim em cada lago a lua toda
Brilha, porque alta vive.
(Fernando Pessoa, *Odes de Ricardo Reis*)

CONTENTS

PREFACE

The generative inquiry into sentential complementation has made explicit a set of theoretical and empirical questions bearing on the relations that are established between a matrix and an embedded clause. On the one hand, there is a set of questions relating to the way in which properties of the embedded sentence are determined by elements from outside. In the case of control verbs, for example, the question arises as to how semantic properties of the matrix verb determine the controller of the subject of the embedded infinitive. Similarly, factive matrix verbs or the matrix negation influence sentential complements in such a way that they turn into weak islands for extraction. Even in relative clauses, the way in which agreement information from the head noun passes into the relative clause can be shown to involve problematic aspects.

On the other hand, there is the related problem of how the structure of embedded sentences interacts with the matrix sentence. How exactly do the sentential complements of raising verbs differ from those of control verbs so as to allow the subject of the infinitive to move to the matrix subject position? How can it be that infinitival clitics climb to the matrix verb? Finally, there is the issue of the elements that are active at the left edge of the embedded sentence: the syntactic and semantic properties of complementizers, and the morphological make-up of interrogative and relative *wh*-elements.

In this book, I try to provide some answers to these classical problems. The first three chapters of the book tackle traditional issues in the area of infinitival complements involving raising and control, but also the less traditional case of apparent raising (pseudo-raising) out of tensed clauses. The two following chapters focus on enclitic ordering and clitic climbing in Romance. In a final set of three chapters, aspects of *Wh*-sentences are examined: extraction out of negative and factive islands, feature theory and agreement in French relative clauses, and the morphology of French interrogative and relative *qui* and *que.*

With the exception of the sections on control and on interrogative/relative *qui/que,* the chapters contained in this book have been previously published in various journals and proceedings. I have chosen not to make these chapters crucially different from the original published versions. As a result, they are self-contained, and this means that there is some redundancy in places.

Since these chapters were written at various stages over the last ten years, there is no perfect theoretical unity from cover to cover. The analyses are couched in terms of the Principles and Parameters framework (Chomsky 1981, 1986a, 1986b), and many are inspired by the more recent Minimalist framework (Chomsky 1995). For many problems, new or obscure data are shown to shed new light on old theoretical problems. As a result, the analyses often seem to go into the nitty-gritty details of linguistic puzzles, carefully carving out the empirical details of theoretical proposals. As always, the truth is in the details.

In the remainder of this preface, I will try to show that the chapters fit into each other like pieces of a puzzle at various levels. More particularly, they illustrate various ways in which syntactic and semantic configurations are related to interpretation in the domain of sentential complementation. Before illustrating the unity of this volume, I will give an overview of the subjects and analyses proposed.

In chapter 1, arguments are proposed to the effect that raising-to-subject with *seem*, *appear*, and raising-to-object (ECM) with *believe*-type verbs first requires an independently motivated movement operation of the embedded AGR_SP to SpecCP. This movement of AGR_SP to SpecCP is argued to be independently motivated by a [+Focus] property of $C°$. Moving AGR_SP to SpecCP as a first step before raising of the embedded subject allows for a unified CP complementation of such verbs, while voiding improper movement effects. In addition, Postal's (1974) Focus-related Direct Object Constraint (DOC) effects are shown to find a natural explanation. Another important aspect of this analysis is that *seem* and *believe* in their raising contexts can be viewed as two sides of the same coin: adapting Freeze's (1992) and Kayne's (1994) analysis for *have* and *be*, it is argued that *believe* is the accusative counterpart of *seem*. As a result, (the raising uses of) *seem* and *believe* can be eliminated as separate items in the lexicon. Finally, this analysis accounts rather elegantly for the crosslinguistic variation between French and English as regards raising-to-object with *believe*-type verbs.

The analysis of pseudo-raising in Chapter 2 can be considered an extension of the analysis of Raising predicates to tensed clauses. It is argued that sentences such as *Sandy$_i$ seems like she$_i$ is happy* or *Kim believes of Sandy$_i$ that she$_i$ is happy* do not involve raising proper, but Strong Binding between *Sandy* and *she* after movement of the embedded AGR_SP to SpecCP.

Because of the strong resemblance to raising out of infinitival complements, this construction is dubbed pseudo-raising. The Strong Binding relation between the subject of *seem* and the object of *believe* in such sentences is similar to that observed in *easy-to-please* constructions. The different properties of pseudo-raising in English and Portuguese, as well as the absence of the construction in other Romance languages, are shown to derive from independent restrictions in those languages.

From the perspective of the types of infinitival complementation, Chapter 3 on Control naturally fits with the chapters on raising. The chapter tackles the old problem of why and how the choice of the controller of PRO in the matrix clause is determined by the semantic properties of the matrix verb. In other words, how can it be explained that the infinitival complement of *promise* requires subject control and that of *coerce* object control, without stipulating such properties in the lexicon? I argue that control of PRO, or more precisely of anaphoric AGR_S (Borer 1989), can be derived from the way in which the temporal interpretation of the infinitival complement is determined by the matrix verb. The interpretation of the infinitival complement of a verb is dependent on the type of matrix verb: for a verb such as *coerce*, the infinitive is interpreted with respect to the future of the forcing event, while the infinitival complement of a verb such as *regret* can lie in the past of the regretting event. It is proposed here that the temporal interpretation of infinitives is determined via the selectional restrictions of the matrix verb. More specifically, this selection is argued to take place via identification of the [– realized] temporal feature of the infinitive with the [– realized] subevents represented in the aspectual subevent structure of control verbs. This identification takes care of the temporal interpretation of infinitival complements. Coming back to control now, the anaphoric infinitival AGR_S is coindexed with the infinitival $T°$, which in turn is identified with the [– realized] subevents of the matrix verb. This chain of syntactic coindexation and selectional identification then restricts access of the infinitival anaphoric AGR_S to all and only those arguments that are represented in the [– realized] subevents of the matrix control verb. This analysis effectively excludes the subject of *coerce*-type verbs from the set of possible controllers, because the subject of *coerce* is not represented in a [-realized] subevent. An analysis of the aspectual subevent structure of various control verbs is proposed and related to the specific control properties involved. The interaction between the temporal interpretation of the infinitive and the aspectual subevent structure of the matrix verb determines control. As a result, control properties are derived from independently needed mechanisms at the interface between syntax and the lexicon. Importantly, the control module assumed in Chomsky (1981) can be eliminated from the grammar, a most welcome result from the perspective of the Minimalist program.

At first sight, the analyses of raising and control differ widely in solutions and results. However, this is only true on the surface: in both cases, configurations are crucially related to meaning. In the case of raising, the syntactic configuration involving movement of AGR_SP to SpecCP is related to the comparative meaning inherent in *seem*. In the case of control, the configurational aspects of the subevent structure of control verbs are shown to ultimately determine control properties: only arguments present in [– realized] subevents can control the anaphoric AGR_S. In both cases, the selectional properties imposed on $C°$ by the matrix verb trigger the specific characteristics of raising and control in combination with other modules of the grammar.

In Chapter 3, it is assumed that the infinitival AGR_S is an anaphor with a 'default' pronominal interpretation, much like Romance *si/se* (Burzio 1992; Pica 1991). This assumption is crucial in chapters 4 and 5 where an explanation is proposed for enclitic ordering in imperatives and infinitives and for clitic climbing. In Chapter 4 it is argued that enclitic ordering in imperatives and infinitives in Romance languages is the result of clitics being left behind by the verbal complex as it moves to a higher functional projection. This excorporation applies to prevent the application of Relativized Minimality (Rizzi 1991). It is argued that imperative and infinitival AGR are respectively pronominal and anaphoric in nature. As such, they can intervene as potential governors in a chain relating a (pronominal or anaphoric) clitic to its trace. When a clitic is moved along with the verb to an anaphoric or pronominal AGR head, the only way to prevent Relativized Minimality from applying is to leave the clitic behind. As a result, positive imperatives which involve a pronominal AGR_C, and Romance infinitives moving as high as AGR_S will feature enclitic ordering. In Chapter 5, the consequences of this approach for clitic climbing are discussed in detail. It is shown that Kayne's (1991b) claim that clitic climbing always involves movement to the matrix clause of both the clitic and the embedded Tense cannot be maintained, and an alternative is proposed that is in line with the analysis of Chapter 4.

Chapter 6 takes up the theme of semantic selection by the matrix verb that was instrumental in chapters 1–3, but with a different slant. It is argued that the restrictions on extraction out of negative and factive islands can be derived from the selectional restrictions that the matrix factive verb and the matrix negation impose on the $C°$ head of the CP they select. Various arguments are put forward to show that the $C°$ heading negative and factive islands receives a negative or a universal value respectively that is incompatible with the *Wh*-properties of elements passing through the specifier of that C. Although other analyses have recently been proposed for negative and factive islands (Szabolcsi and Zwarts 1993; Barbiers 1998), I do think that the explanation proposed in Chapter 6 addresses a number of facts that these analyses do not account for.

Chapters 7 and 8 focus on properties of *Wh*-elements in $C°$ and SpecCP. Like the preceding chapters, chapter 7 is concerned with the way in which information from outside a sentential complement is passed on to elements inside that clause. In French, there is dialectal variation with respect to agreement in $C°$ when a subject is relativized. In Standard French, the noun heading the relative clause fully agrees with the verb in the relative clause, 'transporting' all its [person, number, gender] features into the relative clause. In other dialects of French, this 'feature transfer' takes place partly, or does not occur at all. The question arises as to how feature theory can accommodate such agreement types. It is argued here that such facts constitute evidence for two types of underspecification, involving 0-features and α-features. It is shown that the notion of underspecification is neither specific to phonology nor to syntax, and that it should be viewed as an independent module of feature representation in the language faculty which is accessible to both syntax and phonology.

Chapter 8 offers a unified morphological analysis of French relative *qui*/*que* and interrogative *qui?*/*que?*. Despite their formal identity, these relative and interrogative elements have often been treated as homonyms in view of their many different morphosyntactic properties. It is shown that both relative and interrogative *qui* and *que* are bimorphemic, consisting of a $C°$ *qu-* and the $D°$s *i(1)* and *(1)e*, respectively. Their interrogative or relative use is entirely determined by whether it is $C°$ or $D°$ that projects in the configuration. The different morphosyntactic properties can be derived from the interaction of the underspecified properties of *qui* and *que* with the configuration resulting from projection of $C°$ or $D°$.

The links between these various chapters are indicative of recurring themes. An important topic is the way in which syntactic properties of sentential complements are determined by the semantic properties of the matrix verb through selection. In the case of raising, I argue that a raising verb such as *seem* selects a $C°$ with a [+Focus] property, triggering a particular configuration by which a comparative relation is established between AGR_SP in SpecCP and its trace. This comparison then satisfies the interpretive relation established by *seem*. In the case of control, it is proposed that the aspectual subevent structure of the control verb determines the temporal interpretation of the infinitive through semantic selection of the infinitival $C°$. This semantic selection in turn restricts the choice of a controller for the anaphoric AGR_S, hence for PRO. The analysis of factive and negative islands likewise involves selectional properties of the embedded $C°$ that are determined by the matrix verb. The solutions proposed all explore to what extent semantic properties play a role in syntax, the way in which these semantic properties can be represented, as well as exactly how these properties come to determine syntactic properties of sentential complements.

The relevance of semantics in syntax also comes to the fore in the chapters on enclitic ordering and clitic climbing. It is argued that Rizzi's (1991) notion of 'potential intervening governor' should incorporate a semantic restriction. More precisely, it is proposed that a potential governor Z intervening between X and Y must be semantically definable in the same terms as X and Y. Similarly, in the chapter on clitic climbing, great attention is given to the precise temporal interpretation of clitic climbing constructions.

In terms of the Minimalist Program, these issues can be considered Interface problems involving the relation between (morpho)syntax and lexical semantics. A central question that runs through all chapters concerns the minimal array of lexical structure that is needed in syntax. This line of inquiry shows up in the chapters on raising, where it is argued that the main semantic contribution of *seem* to the syntax is that it requires a configuration in which comparison between events can be licensed. It also appears in the analysis of control, where the aspectual subevent structure of control verbs is argued to determine control of PRO. In a different vein, the view of underspecification exploited in chapters 7 and 8 also raises the question as to what is minimally needed to account for the representation of morphosyntactic properties in the lexicon and in the syntax, respectively.

In this book, the relation between structural representation of semantic properties and its influence on syntactic configurations is argued to be a bidirectional one. On the one hand, configurations of meaning influence syntactic properties: aspectual subevent structure determines control, the semantic notion of comparison is crucial for the syntactic configuration of raising, a matrix factive verb or the matrix negation selectionally influences the C° head of its complement CP in such a way that configurations of movement through SpecCP are affected.

On the other hand, syntactic configurations build meaning as well: the raising configuration creates an interpretive object relating an event type to an event token, the configurational projection of the morphological complex consisting of *qu-* and *-i(1)* as either C° or DP determines the meaning and function of the resulting element, configurations of features in C° determine agreement possibilities in the relative clause. Of course I use the term 'configuration' here more loosely than its usual syntactic meaning allows. But I think that ultimately the term refers to what makes linguistics fun: finding new structure in the apparent chaos of data.

ACKNOWLEDGEMENTS

I would first like to thank the people who have guided my serendipitous journey in linguistics over the years. Karel Van den Eynde, Beatrice Lamiroy, Ludo Melis, and Pierre Swiggers initiated me into Romance linguistics at the KU Leuven in the early 1980s and stimulated my love for linguistic puzzles. Yves D'Hulst, Richard Kayne, Nicolas Ruwet, Liliane Tasmowski, and especially Pierre Pica pushed me to go beyond. In 1988, Dick Frautschi and Phil Baldi gave me the opportunity to work for two years at the Pennsylvania State University. Subsequently, Albert Valdman and Emmanuel Mickel offered me a position in the Department of French and Italian at Indiana University, where I worked for three happy years with great colleagues: Albert Valdman, Laurie Zaring, and Alice ter Meulen, to name a few. Jan Kooij and Teun Hoekstra were instrumental in my joining Leiden University and the Holland Institute for Generative Linguistics (HIL) in 1993. There I was fortunate enough to collaborate with a slew of the finest and most creative syntacticians: Sjef Barbiers, Hans Bennis, Marcel den Dikken, Teun Hoekstra, Gertjan Postma. Back in Brussels, with the small but fine library of the KU Brussel just around the corner, Guido Vanden Wyngaerd and Dany Jaspers made sure 'our' Vanderborghtstraat maintained the highest concentration of generative linguists in Belgium.

I also have to thank my undergraduate and graduate students in the various universities I worked in. Their so-called 'basic' questions often provided me with my best ideas, and forced me to make them more explicit.

I would like to specially thank Carlos Otero, who invited me to put this book together. Thanks to the editorial team at Routledge, and especially Liz Brown for her swift answers to my queries.

Over the years I made quite a number of friends in linguistics on both sides of the Atlantic. They are too numerous to name here. Their help in shaping my ideas is all too inadequately acknowledged in the first footnote of every chapter. I am sure I forgot many; my apologies to them.

Finally, I would like to thank my closest friends, most in faraway places: they know who they are and why. And Anna, for making our lives together and apart into a fascinating experience.

Chapter 1 first appeared in *Studia Linguistica* 1997, 50, 1–49 and is reproduced here with the kind permission of Blackwell Publishers, Oxford. Chapter 4 first appeared in *The Linguistic Review* 1992, 9:3, 219–50 and is reproduced here with the kind permission of Mouton de Gruyter, Berlin. Chapter 5 first appeared in Mike Mazzola (ed.), *Issues and Theory in Romance Linguistics: Selected Papers from the Linguistic Symposium on Romance Languages XXIII* (1994) and is reproduced here with the kind permission of Georgetown University Press, Washington, DC. Chapter 6 first appeared in *Journal of Linguistics* 1992, 28:2, 343–74 and is reproduced here with the kind permission of Cambridge University Press, Cambridge. Chapter 7 first appeared in *Probus* 1994, 6, 207–33 and is reproduced here with the kind permission of Mouton de Gruyter, Berlin.

Leiden/Brussels
Summer 1998

1

RAISING

1 Introduction: the alternation between *seem* and *believe*·

Recapturing insights and arguments of Postal (1974), Chomsky (1995) and Lasnik (1994) argue that the subject of the infinitival AGR_SP in the complement of *believe*-type verbs raises covertly to the $SpecAGR_OP$ position of the matrix verb to check or license accusative case. As a result, Exceptional Case Marking ceases to be exceptional. This analysis allows for a generalization with respect to raising out of sentential complements. Overt raising-to-subject ($SpecAGR_SP$) out of the sentential complement of verbs such as *seem* (1) is mirrored by covert raising-to-object ($SpecAGR_OP$) out of the sentential complement of *believe* (2).

(1) a. It seems [CP that Alfred eats his veggies]

b. Alfred seems [$_{AGRSP}$ t_{Alfred} to eat his veggies]

(2) a. Sue believes [$_{CP}$ that Alfred ate his veggies]

b. Sue believes [$_{AGROP}$ – AGR_O [$_{AGRSP}$ Alfred to have eaten his veggies]]

                             LF movement

Raising-to-subject for *seem* and raising-to-object for *believe* proceed in a parallel fashion: in both cases, a case-feature in the matrix sentence is checked by an NP that originates in the embedded AGR_SP.

This syntactic parallelism becomes even more interesting when it is acknowledged that it corresponds to a semantic correspondence. With respect to their thematic roles, *seem* and *believe* can be analyzed as converses of each other. The internal PP Experiencer argument of *seem* shows up in *believe* as an external argument:

(3) a. It seemed *to all of us* that this was wrong

b. *We all* believed that this was wrong

The sentence *we believe XP* should then be viewed as *to-us seems XP*. Similarly, the raising-to-subject verb *appear* has a semantic raising-to-object counterpart in *find* and *acknowledge*.[1]

(4) a. It appeared *to all of us* that this was wrong

b. This appeared *to all of us* to be wrong

(5) a. *We all* found/acknowledged that this was wrong

b. *We all* found/acknowledged this to be wrong

This semantic correspondence is expressed morphologically in some languages. In Dutch, the verb *denken* 'believe' can be considered the accusative counterpart of the morphologically related *dunken* 'seem' which requires a dative:[2]

(6) a. Ik denk [$_{CP}$ dat Jan ziek is]
     'I think that Jan is sick'

b. Me   dunkt   [$_{CP}$ dat Jan ziek is]
     to-me$_{DAT}$ think$_{3SG}$ that Jan sick is

'It seems to me that Jan is sick'

These semantic and morphological correspondences can be made syntactically explicit if Kayne's (1993) and Hoekstra's (1993) analyses of possessive *have* and *be* are taken into account. Formalizing ideas first put forward by Benveniste (1960), and following Freeze (1992), Kayne (1993) analyzes 'possessive' *be* with a dative possessor like Latin *esse* 'be,' and English *have* in essentially the same way. The structure of *have/be* includes a DP, the D° head of which can assign dative case. In Kayne's (1993) analysis, the D° either does not incorporate and assigns dative case to the possessor *we* (Hungarian, Latin), or it incorporates and does not assign case to the possessor *we*, which moves up to be the (nominative) subject of *have* (English 8b). The structure in (7b) is a simplified version of the structure Kayne assumes for *be* in Hungarian, which has a dative possessive construction like the one illustrated here for Latin. The structure (8b) represents Kayne's analysis of English *have*, which corresponds to *be* with an incorporated D°.

2

(7) a. Sunt nobis mitia poma

Are us$_{\text{DAT}}$ ripe apples$_{\text{NOM}}$
'We have ripe apples'

b. sunt [DP nobis [D°$_{\text{DAT}}$] mitia poma]

(8) a. *e*   be [DP we D°$_{\text{DAT}}$ [DP ripe apples]]

b. We have$_{\text{be+D° –DAT}}$ [$_{\text{DP}}$ $t_{\text{D° –DAT}}$ [$_{\text{DP}}$ ripe apples]]

Hoekstra (1993) shows that this analysis has another consequence. It ensures that incorporation of the case-assigning dative D°/P° into *be, ergo have,* provides that resulting *have* with an accusative case-feature that must be checked in SpecAGR$_{\text{O}}$P of *have* by its 'possessee' NP complement. The 'possessor' NP checks nominative case in SpecAGR$_{\text{S}}$P. The resulting structure is as in (9c). Incorporation of the dative D°/P° thus has two consequences: it adds an accusative feature to the verb *be*, which turns into *have*, and it allows the internal possessor argument to externalize as the subject of *have,* as illustrated in the resulting (9c).

(9) a. <nom> BE   [$_{\text{DP}}$ NP$_{\text{possessor}}$ D°/P°$_{\text{DAT}}$ NP$_{\text{possessee}}$]

  are   us$_{\text{DAT}}$ ripe apples

b. <nom> HAVE   <acc> [$_{\text{DP}}$ NP$_{\text{possessor}}$ D°/P°$_{\text{DAT}}$ NP$_{\text{possessee}}$]
    (BE+DAT)

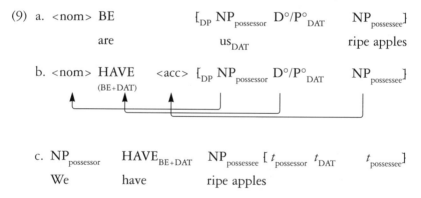

c. NP$_{\text{possessor}}$ HAVE$_{\text{BE+DAT}}$ NP$_{\text{possessee}}$ [$t_{\text{possessor}}$ t_{DAT} $t_{\text{possessee}}$]

  We   have   ripe apples

The same analysis can now be applied to *seem* and *believe* in (3), and *appear* and *find* in (4–5). *Seem* is like *be* in that the Experiencer (possessor) is the internal complement of a dative D°/P°. Assuming the *have / be* analysis proposed by Hoekstra (1993) and Kayne (1993), incorporation of the dative D°/P° into *seem* again has the two consequences described above: it adds an accusative feature to the verb *seem*, which turns into *believe*, and it allows the internal Experiencer argument to externalize as the subject of *believe*. The same analysis applies, *mutatis mutandis*, to *appear* and *find*.

(10) a. <nom> SEEM [$_{DP}$ NP$_{EXP}$ D°/P°$_{DAT}$ [CP]]

     It   seemed   to all of us   [that this was wrong]

   b. <nom> BELIEVE <acc> [$_{DP}$ NP$_{EXP}$ D°/P°$_{DAT}$ [CP]]
      (SEEM+DATIVE)

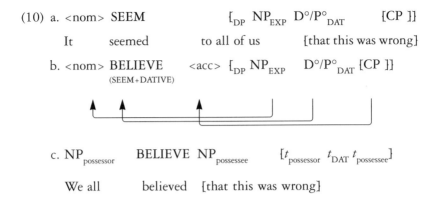

   c. NP$_{possessor}$ BELIEVE NP$_{possessee}$ [$t_{possessor}$ t_{DAT} $t_{possessee}$]

     We all   believed [that this was wrong]

In a language such as Dutch, this process takes place transparently, as illustrated by the alternation in (6).

Assuming that *seem* and *appear* are lexically and syntactically related to *believe* and *find* in the way sketched above, it now becomes clear why both the class of raising-to-subject verbs (*seem, appear*) and the class of raising-to-object verbs (Postal's (1974) B-verbs: *believe, consider, take, find, prove, show*) contain a semantically coherent set of verbs. If the class containing *seem* and *appear* is semantically coherent, it is understandable that the class of verbs with their 'accusative' counterparts (*believe, find*) and the set of 'augmented,' 'causative' forms of *appear* (*show, prove* cf. note 1) is also semantically coherent, since they can be reduced to the same lexical element.

2 The syntax of the complement of *seem/believe*: a critical overview

Let us now turn our attention to the syntax of the sentential complement of *seem/believe*. Exceptional Case Marking constructions as in (11–13) and raising constructions as in (14) have long been a challenge to a uniform approach of sentential complementation that would view all sentential complements as instances of the same type, namely CP. The standard analysis of these cases establishes a radical difference between the infinitival complementation in (11) with *want*-type verbs, and the infinitival complementation in (12–14) with verbs such as *believe, see* and *seem*. For the verb *want* in (11ab), selection is uniform, since the tensed CP alternates with an untensed CP introduced by an optionally overt complementizer *for*. This complementizer assigns case to the NP in SpecAGR$_S$P, independently of the infinitival morphology (Chomsky 1981: 19).

(11) a. Sue wants [$_{CP}$ that Alfred eats his veggies]

   b. Sue wants [$_{CP}$ (for) Alfred to eat his veggies]

4

(12) a. Sue believes [$_{CP}$ that Alfred ate his veggies]

   b. Sue believes [$_{AGRSP}$ Alfred to have eaten his veggies]

(13) a. Sue saw [$_{CP}$ that Alfred ate his veggies]

   b. Sue saw [$_{AGRSP}$ Alfred eat his veggies]

(14) a. It seems [$_{CP}$ that Alfred eats his veggies]

   b. Alfred seems [$_{AGRSP}$ to eat his veggies]

For the complementation of *believe-* and *see-*type verbs as in (12–13), the answer is not that simple. Chomsky (1981) suggested weakening the categorial unity of the sentential complement of *believe-*type verbs: a rule of S′ deletion was introduced, which allowed the matrix verb to assign case to the subject of the infinitive, thereby licensing its presence by what was called Exceptional Case Marking. In later work and especially in the Minimalist framework (Chomsky 1995), reference to a special rule of S′ (CP) deletion is dropped, and *believe-*type verbs are simply assumed to involve two categorial types of complementation, AGR$_S$P (IP/S) and CP. Following Postal (1974), Chomsky (1995) and Lasnik (1994) argue that the subject of the infinitival AGR$_S$P complement of *believe-*type verbs raises covertly to the SpecAGR$_O$P position of the matrix verb to check or license accusative case.

Crucially, it is the presence of a 'reduced' sentential complement that allows the subject of the infinitive to move at LF to the matrix SpecAGR$_O$P for case-checking. Movement of the NP *Alfred* to the SpecAGR$_O$P of *believe* in (12b) cannot proceed through a SpecCP. Moving the NP from the lower A-position to the higher A-position via the SpecCP A′-position would involve a case of 'improper movement' (Chomsky 1986a, 1995). In the same way, raising verbs such as *seem* must alternate between CP complementation as in (14a) and IP complementation as in (14b): raising to SpecAGR$_S$P of *seem* in (14b) may not take place via SpecCP, again to avoid 'improper movement.'

The alternation between CP complementation and AGR$_S$P complementation is not simply an alternation of tensed (CP) versus untensed (AGR$_S$P) complementation. Unlike English *believe* and *seem*, the French verbs *croire* 'believe' and *sembler* 'seem' allow for untensed CP complements involving control (15b–16b), besides the raising-to-subject (15a) or ECM (16a) construction:[3]

(15) a. Alfred semble [$_{AGRSP}$ manger assez de légumes]
      'Alfred seems to eat enough vegetables'

b. Il lui$_i$ semblait [$_{CP}$ [$_{AGRSP}$ PRO$_i$ avoir mangé assez de légumes]]
   'It seemed to him to have eaten enough vegetables'

(16) a. Voilà une personne [O$_i$ que je crois [$_{CP}$ t'_i [$_{AGRSP}$ t_i avoir mangé assez de légumes]]]
      'This is a person who I believe to have eaten enough vegetables'

   b. Alfred$_i$ croyait [$_{CP}$ [$_{AGRSP}$ PRO$_i$ avoir mangé assez de légumes]]

In Chomsky's (1995) and Lasnik's (1994) analysis, AGR$_S$P selection seems to be linked in a rather arbitrary way to raising to SpecAGR$_O$P (*believe*) or SpecAGR$_S$P (*seem*). In essence, AGR$_S$P selection is needed because otherwise an additional projection would 'get in the way' of raising to a case-checking position. The alternation between untensed (controlled) CP and untensed (raising) AGR$_S$P as complements of *believe* and *seem* verbs is a mere stipulation that has to be recorded in the lexical entry of these verbs. Moreover, why would it be the case that only untensed sentential complements can be either selected as, or 'reduced' to, AGR$_S$P? It thus appears that this rather arbitrary difference in selection of the type of sentential complement is the only thing that drives raising to AGR$_S$P or AGR$_O$P: AGR$_S$P selection by *believe* or *seem* necessarily triggers raising.

For *believe*-type verbs, an alternative analysis has been proposed that does not make use of AGR$_S$P complementation. Kayne (1981b) argues for an analysis of ECM with *believe*-type verbs that is close to the analysis proposed for *want*-type verbs. Kayne (1981b) proposes that (2b) involves a CP with a zero P-like C° that assigns case to the infinitival subject. French does not have such a case-assigning C°, forcing the infinitival subject to *Wh*-move to the embedded SpecCP where V° assigns case across CP. As a result, French does not display ECM with the subject of the infinitive in the embedded SpecIP position, since in that case the NP subject of the infinitive is too low to receive case from the governing V°.

(17) a. Voilà la linguiste [O$_i$ que je crois [$_{CP}$ t'_i [$_{IP}$ t_i avoir été mal comprise]]]
      'This is the linguist who I think to have been misunderstood'

   b. *Je crois cette linguiste avoir été mal comprise
      'I believe that linguist to have been misunderstood'

Updating Kayne's analysis in a Minimalist framework proves quite diffi-cult. Accusative case-assignment to the right by V° has been reduced to case-checking in a Spec–Head configuration after movement to SpecAGR$_O$P. If Kayne's (1981b) analysis were to be adopted in a Minimalist framework, movement of the subject of the infinitive to $SpecAGR_OP$, an A- position, would have to transit through SpecCP, an A´-position, resulting in improper movement.

Assuming that this problem can be solved, a Minimalist perspective requires Kayne's (1981b) case-assignment by V° to the embedded subject to be reinterpreted as movement to $SpecAGR_OP$. This predicts both object agreement on the matrix V° and the possibility of further movement to $SpecAGR_SP$ in matrix passives where AGR_O is 'defective.' Let us briefly investigate both predictions.

It is well known that the presence of a trace in $SpecAGR_OP$ can trigger overt agreement on the participle in French in the relevant dialects, while LF movement of an NP does not trigger participle agreement (Kayne 1985a, 1989a; Chomsky 1991, 1995).

(18) a. La voiture que j'ai prise
'The car that I have taken.FEM'

b. J'ai pris(*e) la voiture
'I have taken.(FEM) the car'

As Ruwet (1982) first pointed out, the dialects that obligatorily trigger agreement on the participle in (18) never allow agreement of the infinitival subject with the matrix verb in ECM contexts:

(19)   Voilà la candidate qu'on a dit(*e) être la meilleure de toutes
'This is the candidate that they have said to be the best of all'

Bouchard (1987) has pointed out that in SC contexts, the relevant agreement does obtain:

(20)   Voilà la femme qu'on a dite la plus intelligente de son époque
This is the woman that they have said the most intelligent.
FEM of her time
'This is the woman who was considered the most intelligent of her time'

This suggests that the problem only involves the infinitival construction with *believe*-type verbs, and not ECM in general.

A second indication that the subject of the infinitive in French does not move to $SpecAGR_OP$ at any point in the derivation comes from passive. Unlike in English, the subject of the infinitive in French cannot be passivized in ECM constructions with *believe*:

(21)   *Cette candidate était dite/crue être la meilleure de toutes
         'This candidate was said/believed to be the best of all'

The simplest analysis for the ungrammaticality of this sentence is that the subject of the infinitive never raises to SpecAGR$_O$P in French. As a result, it can never be sensitive to the 'defective' character of AGR$_O$P in passives which triggers movement to the matrix SpecAGR$_S$P position. The absence of agreement on the passive participle and the absence of passive can then be related in a straightforward way: the subject of the infinitive does not move to the matrix SpecAGR$_O$P at any point in the derivation. The question then of course arises as to how the *Wh-* moved or restrictively-focused subjects of the infinitives in (17a) and (19) acquire case in French. I will come back to this problem in section 6.

Rizzi (1990a: 52) provides a recent update of Kayne's analysis by assuming that the acceptability of (17a) is related to an infinitival AGR$_C$° that can properly govern and assign case to the trace in the infinitival SpecIP if it is licensed by an appropriate specifier. Rizzi's (1990a) reinterpretation of Kayne's analysis escapes some of the problems pointed out: since case is assigned inside the CP by AGR$_C$°, the subject of the infinitive will never have to move through the matrix SpecAGR$_O$P. As a result, improper movement is avoided, and the analysis predicts the absence of participle agreement and passive in the matrix clause. However, in a Minimalist framework, all structural case must be assigned in a Spec–Head configuration. This means that AGR$_C$° would have to assign case to the subject of the infinitive in SpecAGR$_C$P. Although this analysis is not unlikely (cf. *infra*, section 6), Rizzi (1990a) does not offer any independent evidence for this claim. As a result, the case-assigning properties of AGR$_C$° amount to a mere stipulation in Rizzi's account.

Both Kayne's and Rizzi's analyses are also empirically inadequate. Pollock (1985) has shown that infinitival subjects can stay downstairs under restrictive Focus (see also Postal 1993). The same seems to be true for 'heavy' NPs without overt restrictive Focus:

(22) a. Je crois n'avoir été condamnés que trois de mes amis
                                                         (Pollock 1985)
        'I believe only to have been condemned three of my friends'

     b. Je crois avoir été condamnés plusieurs des amis qui avaient été
        arrêtés en même temps que moi
        'I believe to have been condemned several of the friends that had
        been arrested at the same time I was'

Pollock (1985) also shows that the embedded CP in (22a) actually involves an impersonal construction where the NP *trois de mes amis* receives a non-nominative case. Lasnik (1992) argues that the case assigned to objects in impersonal constructions is a partitive case which is checked by a passive functional head (see also Rooryck 1995). Such an analysis is confirmed by data such as (23), which show that the 'heavy' NP displays indefiniteness effects typical of impersonal constructions:

(23)   *Je croyais avoir été condamnée ma tante préférée de Besogne-en-Semoule
        'I believed to have been condemned my favorite aunt from Besogne-en-Semoule'

In the framework of Kayne's (1981b) and Rizzi's (1990a) analyses, one would be forced to say that the impersonal subject *pro* in these constructions has to be *Wh-* moved in order to acquire case from the higher $V°$ or the embedded $AGR_C°$. Besides the fact that such a solution would be quite unlikely, the question is why constructions such as (22) are allowed in this context.[4]

More importantly, the Focus-related restrictions on the subject of ECM constructions in French reported by Kayne (1981b) and Pollock (1985) are very similar to restrictions that occur with a specific subset of English ECM verbs. Postal (1974) was the first to point out that there are a number of verbs in English that are semantically very close to *believe* and *find*, but nevertheless syntactically behave in a startlingly different way. Postal (1974) observes that a number of verbs in English such as *estimate, assume, assure, admit, concede, demonstrate, determine, discover, reveal, think, know, guess, feel* etc. can support ECM constructions if the subject of the infinitive is Focused by either left dislocation, heavy NP shift to the right, or *Wh-* movement. Postal terms this restriction on ECM the *Derived Object Constraint* (DOC). The ECM construction is sharply ungrammatical if the subject of the infinitive remains in its canonical subject position as in (27). I will therefore call the construction with *estimate*-type verbs the ECM-with-Focus construction. Examples in (24) through (27) come from Postal (1974: 298–9 (20–32)).

(24)   Bill's dinosaur, I estimate to be 175 feet long

(25)   I estimated to be over 175 feet long all the dinosaurs which we caught yesterday in Central Park

(26)   Which dinosaur did you estimate to be 175 feet long?

(27)   *They estimated Bill's dinosaur to be 175 feet long

Interestingly, English speakers report a great deal of variation with respect to the exact set of verbs that observe the DOC-type/ECM-with-Focus pattern, or the *believe* pattern without Focus.[5] Moreover, the English verbs that support the ECM-with-Focus construction are in some cases semantically very close to the verbs that have ECM constructions without Focus effects. According to Postal (1974), a verb such as *think* supports ECM with Focus effects, while its synonym *believe* has no such Focus effects. Similarly, Postal (1974) has *find* as a *bona fide* ECM verb, while its semantic near synonym *discover* only supports ECM with Focus effects.

(28) a. Philomène thought/discovered to have been overrated all the novels that had been written after Proust

b. Philomène believed/found/*thought/*discovered all those novels to have been overrated

This of course raises the question as to what property *believe* and *find* have that English *think*, *discover*, and French *croire* 'believe' do not possess. From a slightly different perspective, the question arises why Focus interferes with raising-to-object in the first place. More generally, one might also wonder what property licenses ECM for the entire class of verbs displaying ECM, with Focus effects or not.

Summing up this review, it must be concluded that ECM with verbs such as *believe* is adequately described neither by an analysis in terms of AGR_SP selection (Chomsky 1981, 1995), nor by an approach in terms of empty case-assigning complementizers (Kayne 1981b). Nevertheless, both analyses have some attractive properties that should be maintained in any explanatory account of sentential complementation with *believe* and *seem*. Kayne's (1981b) analysis rightly insists on the idea that selection of sentential complements should be uniform CP selection. Postal's (1974), Chomsky's (1995), and Lasnik's (1994) analysis allow for a generalization with respect to raising out of the sentential complements of *seem* and *believe*, an analysis that is all the more attractive since *seem* and *believe* arguably are lexically related in the way sketched above. Finally, *believe*-type verbs in both French and English seem to display intricate Focus effects on the subject of their sentential complement that cannot be explained by the standard analyses.

As a result, there are two important problems that have to be investigated with respect to raising out of sentential complements of *seem*/*believe*-type verbs:

(29) i. If sentential complementation uniformly involves CPs, how can raising out of CP complements to the matrix $SpecAGR_{S/O}P$ of *seem* and *believe* be achieved in a parallel fashion without producing 'improper movement'?

ii. What does Focus have to do with raising-to-object (= SpecAGR$_O$P)? Why does ECM require the subject of the infinitive to be Focused either generally (French *croire, dire*) or with a large, variable subset of DOC verbs (English *think, discover, estimate* etc.)? Why is there a contrast between ECM with Focus (*think, discover, assure*) and 'Focusless' ECM (*believe, take, consider, find*) in the first place?

In the remainder of this chapter, I will show that both problems are much more closely related than has hitherto been assumed.

3 Two-step raising: IP moves to SpecCP before subject movement

At least technically, the problem in (29i) can be solved quite easily. In order to maintain uniform CP complementation, it can be proposed that English raising constructions involve movement of the infinitival AGR$_S$P to SpecCP. This analysis is quite reminiscent of Baker's (1988) analysis of French causatives, where VP is moved to SpecCP of the CP complement of *faire* 'make.' Once AGR$_S$P is in SpecCP, the infinitival subject can move out of the sentential complement to SpecAGR$_S$P. This yields the following configuration:

(30)

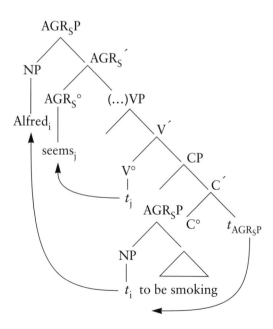

The configuration for *believe* should be identical to (30) as far as overt movement of the embedded AGR_SP to SpecCP is concerned. The exact nature of the subsequent movement of the embedded subject is more controversial. Following Chomsky (1995) and Lasnik (1992), the embedded subject covertly moves to $SpecAGR_OP$ in order to check case. This movement will only take place when the verb moves to AGR_O at LF to check its own features, for reasons of equidistance.[6]

However, there is cogent evidence that ECM constructions actually involve overt movement to $SpecAGR_OP$. Postal (1974) has shown convincingly that the subject of the infinitive can be placed before adverbs referring to the matrix verb:

(31) a. They found Germany recently to have been justified in sinking the *Lusitania*

b. I don't find Mary anymore to be foolish

c. I've believed John for a long time now to be a liar (Kayne 1985b: 114(70))

If the subject of the infinitive were to stay inside the CP before LF, it would be very difficult to account for the fact that the adverbs modifying the matrix verb somehow show up in this embedded CP. Vanden Wyngaerd (1989) argues that the subject of the infinitive in (31) moves overtly to $SpecAGR_OP$ in English. This straightforwardly derives the facts in (31). The matrix adverbs in (31) are arguably adjoined to the matrix VP, and the subject of the infinitive overtly moves beyond them to $SpecAGR_OP$. This account requires the additional assumption that the matrix verbs *find* and *believe* in (31) (and verbs generally) move to a functional $X°$ position beyond $AGR_O°$. One argument for movement of verbs in English beyond $AGR_O°$ was put forward by Pesetsky (1989) and Costa (1994). Pollock (1989) justifies the low position of verbs in English by the fact that adverbs occur in front of them and cannot intervene between the verb and the direct object. However, Pesetsky (1989) shows that adverbs can intervene between verbs and PPs:

(32) a. *Mickey visited quietly his parents

b. Mickey talked slowly to Gary

(33) a. *Chris hit quickly the dog

b. Chris walked quickly down the street

This suggests that the absence of adverbs between verbs and their direct object is due to an adjacency requirement. This adjacency requirement can

(34)

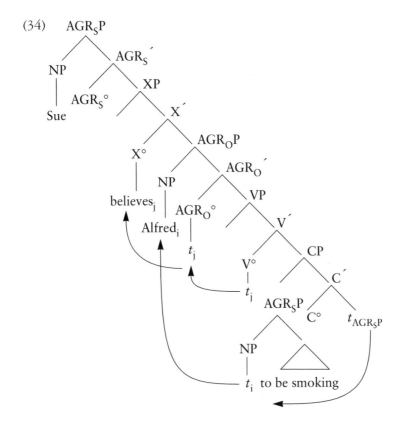

be derived from the fact that objects in English always move overtly to SpecAGR$_O$P, with the verb sitting in a functional head, provisorily labeled X°, sitting directly above AGR$_O$P. Costa (1994, 1998) offers various arguments to justify the existence of this position. The structure of ECM *believe* then must be represented as in (34):

It can be concluded that both raising-to-subject (SpecAGR$_S$P) and raising-to-object (SpecAGR$_O$P) involve overt movement. In section 5, it will be shown that this analysis allows for an explanation of the DOC facts adduced by Postal (1974, 1993).

Nothing in the Minimalist framework prevents movement out of the SpecAGR$_S$P in SpecCP. The movement involved here very much resembles the extraction out of a *Wh-* NP in SpecCP cited by Torrego (1985). Chomsky (1986a: 26) states that a matrix verb must be allowed to L-mark the specifier in a structure such as (35) in order to explain sentences such as (36):

(35)   V [$_{CP}$ *Wh-* phrase C IP]

(=Chomsky 1986a: (50))

(36) a. Éste es el autor [del que]$_i$ no sabemos [$_{CP}$ [qué libros t_i] leer]
'This is the author by whom we don't know what books to read'
(= Chomsky 1986a: (48a), citing Torrego 1985)

b. ¿De qué autora no sabes qué traducciones han ganado premios internacionales?
'By which author don't you know what translations have won international awards?'
(= Chomsky 1986a: (49b), citing Torrego 1985)

Chomsky (1986a) states that if the verb *saber* 'know' in (36) does not L-mark the *Wh-* element in SpecCP, the sentences should be ruled out by subjacency, since the *Wh-* element in SpecCP, and by inheritance CP itself, would then be Barriers to movement. The sentence (36a) contrasts with (37), where the NP *varias traducciones* is not in SpecCP, hence cannot be L-marked by *saber* 'know,' and does not allow for extraction:

(37) *Ésta es la autora [de la que]$_i$ [$_{IP}$ [varias traducciones t_i] han ganado premios internacionales]
(= Chomsky 1986a: 26(49a))

'This is the author by whom several translations have won international awards'

The same analysis remains valid in a Minimalist context. Chomsky (1995) crucially appeals to LF extraction out of SpecCP in the context of Binding. LF movement of *self* (LF cliticization or CL_{LF}) out of the *Wh-* NP accounts for the fact that the anaphor can be bound by the matrix subject in (38):

(38) John wondered [which pictures of himself] Bill saw t
(= Chomsky 1995: ch. 3(36))

The configurations proposed in (31–34) suggest that this type of extraction is also relevant in raising contexts. Extraction of the subject NP out of the infinitival CP is possible only after AGR$_S$P moves to SpecCP in (31–34). Importantly, improper movement of the subject of the infinitive is avoided, since the subject does not itself move from an A′-position back into an A-position. Consequently, it is predicted that the subject of an infinitive cannot be extracted from an infinitival CP unless AGR$_S$P moves to SpecCP. Uniform CP complementation with both raising-to-subject (*seem*) and raising-to-object (*believe*) verbs can be maintained, while allowing the subject of the infinitive to move out of the infinitival CP to respectively SpecAGR$_S$P and SpecAGR$_O$P in a parallel fashion.

However, as the analysis stands now, it seems to violate the Minimalist principle of Greed, which stipulates that an element cannot move just for the sake of another element. In this case, movement of the embedded AGR_SP to SpecCP seems to be invoked for the sole purpose of allowing the subject NP of the infinitive in (31–34) to escape to the higher $SpecAGR_{S/O}P$ position. In other words, the analysis proposed does not independently motivate movement of the embedded AGR_SP to SpecCP.

I would nevertheless like to argue that movement of the embedded AGR_SP to SpecCP is independently motivated by a [+ Focus] feature of $C°$ that must be checked by AGR_SP via movement to SpecCP. More precisely, I want to argue that *seem* and *believe* select a [+ Focus] $C°$ in raising contexts which involves event-focus rather than argument-focus. This [+ Focus] feature is an optional feature of $C°$, in the same way that [+ Wh-] is an optional feature on the $C°$ selected by verbs such as *know* and *ask* (*I know that X/I know how X*). For now, I have to stipulate that this feature is only active in the case of infinitival CPs. I will come back to this stipulation later.

That this type of event-focus exists should be relatively uncontroversial. English displays Focus constructions which at first sight involve movement of VP to the higher SpecCP.

(39) a. Eat an apple, I was told that Sue will/can/should/must

b. *Eaten an apple, I was told that Sue has

In (39a), it can be assumed that the projection being focused is in fact an infinitival projection that moves to the [+ Focus] CP of the higher clause. This type of movement is only licensed if infinitival projection is governed by a $T°$ that involves modal auxiliaries such as *will, can, should*. The combination of a [+ Focus] $C°$ in the higher clause, and a [+ Modal] $T°$ governing the infinitival projection seems to be the driving force behind movement of this projection to the higher SpecCP.

The question now arises as to whether the same type of movement could apply to infinitival AGR_SP if it is governed by an appropriate [+ Modal] head. Indeed, it is not likely that focus as in (39a) is an exclusive property of the infinitival projection, but rather a property of English infinitival projections in general. The question then becomes: when does a $C°$ governing AGR_SP have [+ Modal] properties such that it can govern the trace of infinitival AGR_SP, thereby allowing AGR_SP to move? I would like to suggest that the untensed $C°$ governed by *believe* has this licensing property. First of all, if the infinitival complement of *believe* has a $C°$, this $C°$ must be untensed since it is well known that tensed and untensed $C°$s are in complementary distribution with tensed and untensed $T°$. Now an untensed $C°$ already involves some modal property, namely 'unrealized' tense (Guillaume 1929; Bresnan 1972; Stowell 1982). This property is of course not a sufficient condition to license the trace of AGR_SP, otherwise control contexts could always license ECM, which is of course not the case. Clearly, selection of C° by *believe* plays a role in 'reinforcing' the modal property of C°. The [+ Focus] selection of the complement C° by *believe*, together with the [– tensed] modal property of C°, might be sufficient to license the trace of AGR_SP in the same way modal auxiliaries license the trace of the infinitival projection in (39a).

If it is accepted that a 'strong' [+ Focus] feature in C° is what motivates movement of AGR_SP to SpecCP, it is possible to provide an explanation for the questions formulated in (29ii): why does ECM require the subject of the infinitive to be Focused either generally (French *croire, dire*) or with a large subset set of ECM verbs (English *think, discover, estimate*) and why does only a small subset of ECM verbs have 'non-Focus' ECM (*believe, take, consider, find*) with the subject of the infinitive in its canonical position between the matrix verb and the infinitive. The tentative answer to these questions is that Focus is what ECM with *believe-* and *seem-*type verbs is all about. The generalization we are led to is that all ECM verbs seem to have the property of focusing on elements of the embedded CP via a [+ Focus] C°. French *croire, dire* and English *think, discover, estimate* must have Focus on the subject of the embedded infinitive. The apparently 'Focusless' *bona fide* ECM verbs such as *believe, take, consider, find*, and *seem, appear, be likely* in fact do display a 'hidden' type of Focus, namely event Focus, on AGR_SP, which moves to SpecCP and thereby enables subsequent movement of the subject of the infinitive into the matrix $SpecAGR_{O/S}P$.

Reference to a [+ Focus] feature to motivate movement of AGR_SP to SpecCP seems to allow for a first rough answer to the question what Focus and raising-to-object (= raising-to-$SpecAGR_OP$) have in common. However, the fact that the trace of AGR_SP can be licensed by a [+ Focus] C° in the same way as the trace of the infinitival projection in the modal context of (39a) is not enough evidence to conclude that Focus-movement to SpecCP indeed occurs in raising to SpecAGRP contexts with *believe* and *seem*. What does it mean to have Focus on the event in ECM contexts with *believe*? It is not immediately clear what the semantic difference is in terms of Focus between the tensed 'unfocused' sentential complement in (40a) and (41a), and the 'focused' ECM sentential complement in (40b) and (41b).

(40) a. Sue believes [$_{CP}$ C$_{-FOC}$ [$_{AGRSP}$ that Alfred ate his veggies]]

b. Sue believes [$_{CP}$ [$_{AGRSP}$ Alfred to have eaten his veggies] C$_{+FOC}$ t_{AGRSP}]

(41) a. It seems [$_{CP}$ that C$_{-FOC}$ [$_{AGRSP}$ Alfred ate his veggies]

b. Alfred seems [$_{CP}$ [$_{AGRSP}$ to have eaten his veggies] C$_{+FOC}$ t_{AGRSP}]

As a result, the analysis proposed seems highly counterintuitive, despite the generalization it allows for. If the analysis advocated here is to be maintained, the type of Focus involved in AGR_SP movement to SpecCP and its relation to the semantics of *seem* and *believe* must be investigated more closely. In other words, the first step leading to subsequent raising of subject NPs out of infinitival complements must be further motivated.

4 The likeness of *seem*: comparison and Focus

In order to motivate Focus movement of AGR_SP to SpecCP, I would like to take a closer look at the the morphology and the semantics of the verb *seem*. The principal semantic feature of *seem* seems to be comparison. In many languages, the verb stem of verbs of comparison and *seem* are identical: Dutch *lijken* 'seem' and *vergelijken* 'compare,' French *sembler* 'seem' and *ressembler* 'resemble,' *paraître* 'seem' and *comparer* 'compare,' Spanish *parecer* 'seem' and *comparar* 'compare.' In English, the raising verb *be likely* is derived from *like* which also yields the adjective *alike*, and the comparative verb *liken*. *Like* also shows up as the obligatory complementizer of the verb *look* in a usage that is semantically close to *seem*:[7]

(42)   It looks like/as if/*that Alfred has eaten his veggies

Even English *seem* has a syntactic relation to *like*: *seem* might be the only verb that can select the complementizers *that*, *as if*, and the complementizer *like*: the analysis of *like* as a complementizer is supported by the fact that it cannot cooccur with *that*.

(43) a. It seems that/like/as if Alfred has eaten his veggies

b. *It seems that like/like that Alfred has eaten his veggies

Also note the use of comparative *as* in the complementizer *as if*.[8] *As if* by itself, in combination with the verb *be*, is more or less equivalent to *seem* as shown in (44a). Interestingly, similar considerations apply to expressions expressing the meaning of *believe* as in (44bc):

(44) a. It is as if Alfred has eaten his veggies

b. I was, like: they are really good   (Valleyspeak)

c. Ik heb zoiets van: Jan moet maar oprotten   (Dutch)
I have such-something of: Jan should hit the road
'I think that Jan should hit the road'

The sentences (44bc) involve a sentential complement expressing direct speech. Whatever their exact syntactic representation, it is important to note that they overtly involve the verbs *be* or *have*, and an element of comparison, *like* in (44b), and *zo* in Dutch (44c). The Dutch sentence in (44c) also seems to involve the object expletive *iets*. Importantly, these cases provide further evidence for the analysis put forth in section 1 that *believe* is the accusative counterpart of *seem*.

In more traditional accounts of raising with *seem*-type verbs, this morphological relation of *seem* with verbs of comparison is systematically disregarded. The morphological evidence strongly suggests that the semantics of *seem* should involve comparison at some level. In this analysis, I would like to syntactically represent the comparative semantics of *seem*. If this is correct, there must be two items to be compared. In a structure like (43a), this is relatively simple. Following Bennis (1986), and Moro (1992), I argue that subject *it* in (43a) is not a dummy element marking the subject position. Moro (1992) analyzes *it* as the predicate of the SC complement of *seem* (cf. Moro (1992) for arguments and discussion). The pronoun *it* is necessary for Full Interpretation, and moves to the SpecIP position of *seem* as an instance of predicate inversion. Under the analysis developed here, the pronoun *it* should be analyzed as a deictic pronoun, referring to an event at hand that is compared to the event expressed by the sentential complement of *seem*. The sentence (45a) then can be semantically glossed as (45b):

(45) a. It *seems* that/like/as if Alfred has eaten his veggies
    b. There is a contextually salient event (= it) that *is similar to* or *resembles* a (typical) event in which Alfred has eaten his veggies

The pronoun *it* functions as a *pro*-CP. This property can probably be derived through the predicative nature of the SC, which mirrors the event properties of the CP onto *it*. Moro's SC analysis can now be viewed as a case of predicate Focus.[9] Following Partee (1991), Focus can informally be taken to involve implicit reference to a set of which one member is given saliency. In the case of *seem*, I argue that the set referred to consists of two members, one of which is given saliency by predicate inversion/Focus, namely deictic *it*. It is crucial to emphasize that predicate inversion/Focus is triggered by an element in the matrix clause in this case. *Pro*-CP *it* is not a dummy, but an essential element for the interpretation of *seem* which compares two overt elements. As a result, this analysis immediately explains why *it* cannot be replaced by the CP complement (* *That Alfred has eaten his veggies seems*): such a replacement would eliminate an essential member of the comparison set.

A similar analysis can be given of *appear*. I would like to argue that *appear* also involves a comparison between two events, but that it does so on a different plane. *Appear* basically says that the event the *pro*-CP *it* refers to is about to manifest itself as a true case of the CP complement. Sticking more closely to the analysis of both *seem* and *appear* in terms of comparison, one might say that *appear* means 'resemble to the point of becoming identical with'. However, *appear* should not be viewed as an aspectually imperfective marker of predication: *appear* is not quite to *seem* what *become* is to *be*, since *appear* does not allow for the progressive. In this, *appear* is like *seem*, but unlike *become*. Rather, both *seem* and *appear* are stative, but while *seem* is just stative, *appear* should be viewed as referring to a resultative endstate. In keeping with the gloss given in (45b), an appropriate semantics for *appear* could be represented as in (46bc):

(46) a. It *appears* that Alfred has eaten his veggies

　　 b. There is an event that *resembles to the point of becoming identical with it* an event in which Alfred has eaten his veggies

　　 c. There is an event that *has reached the endstate of being identical to* an event in which Alfred has eaten his veggies

Again, there is some morphological evidence for a semantics in which *appear* receives an analysis close to that of *seem*. Dutch *blijken* 'appear' seems to be composed of *lijken* 'seem' and the morpheme *be-*, which has been described as a resultative marker by Mulder (1992). Dutch *blijken* 'appear' then quite literally is 'resemble to the point of resulting in CP.' Similarly, justifying gloss (46c), French *s'avérer* 'appear' includes a stem identical to that in *vérité* 'truth,' and a morpheme *a*. The morpheme *a* diachronically derives from Latin *ad* 'towards, at' and marks direction and the endpoint to be reached. Interestingly, English *turn out* (*Alfred turned out to have eaten his veggies*) can be equally considered a periphrastic counterpart of *appear*, overtly marking resultativity in the preposition *out* (den Dikken, personal communication).

If this semantic analysis of *seem* and *appear* as involving the comparison of situations or events is on the right track, how can it be extended to those cases where raising out of the sentential complement has occurred? That is, if *seem* and *appear* involve comparison, what are the two events being compared in (47)?

(47)　 Alfred seems/appears to have eaten his veggies

In a traditional analysis that takes the sentential complement of raising verbs to be of the type AGR_SP, there is no answer to this question. However, I have tried to argue above that the analysis of raising in (47) involves the more complex structure in (41b), repeated here as (48), where AGR_SP has raised to SpecCP.

(48)   Alfred seems $[_{CP} [_{AGRSP}$ to have eaten his veggies$]$ C$_{+FOC}$ $t_{AGRSP}]$

Assuming this analysis, I would like to suggest that this configuration satisfies the comparative interpretation required by *seem*. The configuration in the embedded CP in (48) is an instance of an operator–variable relation between the AGR$_S$P in SpecCP and its trace in the complement of C°. Movement of AGR$_S$P in SpecCP is triggered by the fact that C° is a comparative Focus operator, whose comparative properties are acquired via selection under government by matrix *seem*. The morphological form of the complementizers in tensed sentences demonstrates that the C° selected by *seem* can be overtly comparative. It might be argued that this comparative selection establishes the background set which is required for Focus. Movement of AGR$_S$P to SpecCP allows the comparative Focus C° to establish a comparative relation between the AGR$_S$P in SpecCP and its variable left behind after movement. This is therefore an operator–variable relation. Formally speaking, the configuration is strictly identical to an operator–variable relation of the *Wh*- type. In (49), there is an operator establishing a set, and a relation between the set and the variable. Another way of expressing this would be to say that (49a) involves a type–token distinction, where type stands for the set of elements such that they are books, and token for the specific token of that type that is questioned. This is represented in (49c).

(49) a. $[_{CP} [_{NP}$Which book$]$ did $[_{AGRSP}$John read $t_{NP}]]$

   b. Which x, x an element of the set S of books, is such that John read x

   c. Which x, x a token of the type X, X = book, is such that John read x

Similarly, the operator–variable relation in the CP complement of seem may be paraphrased as in (50b), with a slightly more formal semantic interpretation as in (50cd):

(50) a. Alfred seems $[_{CP} [_{AGRSP}$ to have eaten his veggies$]$ C$_{+FOC}$ $t_{AGRSP}]$

   b. This instance of Alfred eating his veggies resembles the 'typical' instance of Alfred eating his veggies (this is not quite a full-fledged version of Alfred eating his veggies)

   c. For S the set of situations resembling a situation in which Alfred eats his veggies, there is an x such that x is an element of the set S

   d. For S the situation type which involves Alfred eating his veggies, there is an x such that x resembles the type S

20

The representations in (50b–d) reflect the interpretation of the embedded CP, in which the [+ Focus] C°, which is selected by *seem*, is the element that establishes the resemblance between x and X. The paraphrase in (50b) is a more intuitive representation of the comparative meaning of (50a). The representations in (50cd) offer a translation of this insight into LF-style interpretations in which an element/token of the set/type of situations is included/compared to its set/type, establishing an operation of resemblance between the element/token and the set/type.

If these representations are on the right track, there are two configurational ways in which comparative Focus can be established with *seem*. Focus in the matrix clause may trigger movement of predicative *it* into SpecIP by predicate inversion (Moro 1992), yielding sentences such as (43a). In these cases, the comparative relation is established by *seem* itself between the NP *it* (the *pro*-CP) in its subject position and the CP in its complement position. In these cases, *seem* itself functions as an operator relating the (raised) variable/token *it* to the set of situations/type denoted by the CP complement. In raising contexts such as (50), the comparison is established 'one notch down' in the complement clause: the elements compared involve the AGR_SP operator in SpecCP on one hand, and the variable of this AGR_SP on the other. The requirement of the verb *seem* for comparative Focus can be satisfied either way.[10]

The net result of this analysis is twofold. First, *seem* and *appear* can be analyzed straightforwardly as involving a configurationally expressed comparison of events or situations both in raising and nonraising contexts. Second, I have advanced independent motivation for the Focus movement of AGR_SP to SpecCP in raising contexts, corroborating an analysis of sentential complementation as uniform CP complementation. As suggested before, it is this AGR_SP movement to SpecCP that enables movement of the subject of the infinitive to the matrix $SpecAGR_OP$. In the next sections, I will show that an extension of this analysis of *seem* to *believe* allows for the derivation of a large number of hitherto unexplained facts involving ECM in English.

5 *Believe* and Focus

Turning our attention from *seem* and *appear* to *believe*- and *find*-type verbs, the same semantic analysis can be proposed for Focus movement of AGR_SP to SpecCP in the CP complement of *believe* and *find*. Recall that *believe* and *find* simply are the 'accusative' counterparts of *seem* and *appear*, respectively. The only difference lies in the position to which the subject of the infinitive raises, $SpecAGR_OP$ for *find* and *believe* rather than $SpecAGR_SP$ for *seem* and *appear*.

(51)   Sue [$_{XP}$ believes[$_{AGROP}$ Alfred $t_{V°-AO°}$] [$_{VP}$ $t_{V°}$ [$_{CP}$ [$_{AGRSP}$ t_{Alfred} to be smoking] C° t_{AGRSP}]]]

(52)   To Sue, Alfred seems to be smoking

[$_{AGRSP}$ Alfred [[seems]AGR$_S$] [$_{VP}$ $t_{V°}$ [$_{CP}$ [$_{AGRSP}$ t_{Alfred} to be smoking] [$_C$ C° t_{AGRSP}]]

The sentences (51) and (52) have the same semantics, roughly meaning something like: to the (dative or subject) Experiencer Sue, this event of Alfred's smoking only resembles an event in which Alfred smokes.

The analysis proposed suggests that there should be other differences between ECM complements and tensed CPs of *believe*-type verbs that are triggered by movement of AGRSP to SpecCP in ECM cases and the absence of this movement in tensed CPs. An important argument for such an additional difference comes from negation. Besides their ECM complementation, *believe*-type verbs also have particular properties with respect to negation. First of all, verbs such as *believe* create negative islands (Ross 1984; Rizzi 1990a; Rooryck 1992a):

(53) a. This is the person who I believe likes my book

b. (?) This is the person who I do not believe likes my book

c. *How don't you believe that I selected the article?

Second, verbs such as *believe* have the property of being Neg-raising verbs (Horn 1978): the sentences (54a) and (54b) seem to be equivalent.[11]

(54) a. Fred believes that God does not exist

b. Fred does not believe God to exist

Rooryck (1992a, this volume Ch 6) proposes that both properties can be derived if negation in the matrix clause in (54b) is allowed to have scope over the embedded sentence by binding the embedded C° as a variable.[12] As a result, any *Wh-* element passing through the embedded SpecCP on its way to the matrix SpecCP receives the property of being a variable for negation.

Movement to the matrix SpecCP then moves the *Wh-* element beyond the negation operator binding it, resulting in a violation of principles governing operator–variable relations.

This analysis of negative islands is relevant to the present purposes, because *believe* does not give rise to the slight negative island effect on subject extraction in the context of ECM:

(55)   This is the person who I do not believe to have liked my book

The admittedly slight contrast in English appears more strongly in French. For reasons that are not entirely clear, extraction of the subject out of the tensed CP complement in (56a) triggers a negative island effect that is stronger than that in English (53). However, with ECM complements of negated *croire* 'believe,' where the subject has to be *Wh-* moved or otherwise focused, negative island effects disappear as shown in (56b).

(56) a. *Voilà la personne que je ne croyais pas qui a été arrêtée
       'This is the person I didn't believe has been arrested'

     b. Voilà une personne que je ne crois pas avoir jamais été arrêtée
        'This is a person who I do not believe to have ever been arrested'

Recall that sentential complementation of *believe/croire* always involves CPs in the analysis advocated above. In this context, the facts about negative islands provide interesting evidence that the value of C° is crucially different in tensed CP complements and in CP complements with ECM.

Following Rooryck (1992a, this volume Ch 6), it can be assumed that C° in tensed CPs acts as a variable for negation. According to the analysis developed here, the [+ Focus] C° triggering AGR_SP movement to SpecCP functions as an operator. The C° head of the CP selected by *believe* can simply have two different values, one for negation with tensed CPs, and another one for Focus with untensed CPs. It is natural to assume that the functional head C° cannot have both values at the same time.[13] The Focus operator value of C° in untensed CPs and its negation variable value in tensed CPs are mutually exclusive: they both involve an operator–variable structure, and an element cannot be both an operator and a variable at the same time. Focus and negation arguably belong to the same set of phenomena.

We are now in a position to explain why negative islands are lifted in ECM contexts. Rooryck (1992a, this volume Ch 6) argues that negative islands such as (56a) are only triggered by the presence of a C° functioning as a variable for negation. In the analysis assumed here for ECM contexts, C° cannot have such a negative value, since it is a Focus operator that is incompatible with negative variablehood. As a result, negative island effects disappear in

ECM contexts because C° cannot function as a variable for the matrix negation if it has to carry a [+ Focus] value.

Not only do ECM contexts seem to lift negative island effects, they also seem to have interesting effects on Neg-raising. If both the matrix and the embedded tensed clause of *believe* are negated, both negations seem to cancel each other out: (57a) is equivalent to (57b):

(57) a. Sue cannot believe that Clara was not a composer

b. Sue believes that Clara was a composer/Sue believes Clara to have been a composer

This 'canceling out' of both negations is due to the fact that *believe* is a Neg-raising verb. In Rooryck's (1992a, this volume Ch 6) terms, the matrix negation can extend its scope into the embedded clause by binding the embedded C° as a negative variable.

If the ECM construction were a simple variant of its tensed counterpart, it would be expected that double negation in ECM contexts cancels out as well. According to the native speakers I consulted, this does not seem to be the case: (58a) is not equivalent to (57b). If it is interpretable at all, it means something closer to (58b), where both negations are preserved.[14]

(58) a. Sue cannot believe Clara not to have been a composer (she'd rather not pronounce herself on the matter)

b. The beliefs of Sue about Clara do not include that she has not been a composer

The fact that both negations are preserved is due to the fact that the matrix negation does not have scope over the embedded clause. In our view, negation cannot have scope over the embedded clause since the embedded C° is [+ Focus]. Since the matrix negation cannot bind this C° as a negative variable, it cannot extend its scope into the embedded clause. As a result, the negations in the matrix and embedded clauses of (58a) do not cancel out.

6 On more differences between French and English

6.1 *Reexamining the data*

We still have to tackle the problem stated in (29ii), concerning the relation between ECM and Focus on the subject with French *croire*, *dire* and with a large subset of verbs (English *think*, *discover*, *estimate* etc.). Recall that these verbs cannot have ECM with an overt subject in SpecAGR$_S$P position of the infinitive, as the sentences (59b) and (63) show. Instead, the subject of the infinitive has to be Focused by Focus movement to the left, *Wh*- movement, or Heavy-NP-shift to the right.

(59) a. Voilà la linguiste [O$_i$ que je crois [$_{CP}$ t'_i [$_{IP}$ t_i avoir été mal comprise]]]
'This is the linguist who I think to have been misunderstood'

    b. *Je crois cette linguiste avoir été mal comprise
'I believe that linguist to have been misunderstood'

(60)   Je crois n'avoir été condamnés que trois de mes amis

                                  (Pollock 1985)

       'I believe only to have been condemned three of my friends'

(61)   Je crois avoir été condamnés plusieurs des amis qui avaient été arrêtés en même temps que moi
'I believe to have been condemned several of the friends that had been arrested at the same time I was'

(62) a. Bill's dinosaur, I estimate to be 175 feet long

    b. I estimated to be over 175 feet long all the dinosaurs which we caught yesterday in Central Park

    c. Which dinosaur did you estimate to be 175 feet long?

(63)   *They estimated Bill's dinosaur to be 175 feet long

Until now, I have only been able to give a very rough answer to this problem, suggesting that even apparently 'Focusless' verbs such as *believe* and *find* actually do involve a 'hidden' Focus movement of AGR$_S$P to SpecCP.

In Minimalist terms, these observations might be explained in the following way. From a purely descriptive point of view, it might be argued that English *believe* differs from French *croire* and English *estimate* in the target of Focus (AGR$_S$P or the subject) and in the overt or nonovert nature of the Focus movement involved ('strong' vs. 'weak' features). First, we might say that the target of Focus with *believe*-type verbs is AGR$_S$P, while the target of movement in the embedded CP of French *croire* and English *estimate* is the infinitival subject. Second, movement of AGR$_S$P to SpecCP with *believe*-type verbs is the result of a 'strong' Focus feature in C°, forcing overt movement. The [+ Focus] C° selected by *croire* 'believe' in French and *estimate* in English is a 'weak' feature in the sense of Chomsky (1995) which can only be licensed at LF by the infinitival subject.[15] The 'weak' character of [+ Focus] C° explains why subjects must either move all the way up to the higher SpecCP (59, 62c), or must stay downstairs if restrictively focused or heavy- NP- shifted as in (60, 61, 62ab). The Focused infinitival subject in (60, 61, 62b) only moves at LF to be licensed by 'weak' [+ Focus] C°, while the *Wh-* moved infinitival subject in (53, 56c) and the extraposed subject in (56a) license the 'weak' [+ Focus] feature in the lower C° at LF by the operation Form–Chain (Chomsky 1995). In all grammatical cases, 'weak' Focus prevents infinitival subjects from surfacing in SpecCP at spellout as in (59b–63).

This analysis raises, however, the nontrivial question why 'strong' Focus only triggers movement of the entire AGR_SP, while 'weak' Focus only attracts the subjects of the embedded CP. As it stands, the Minimalist account given cannot explain this correlation. Moreover, the analysis is not entirely consistent with the full range of data in English and French. Postal (1974) observes that verbs such as *estimate, allege, acknowledge, affirm, demonstrate, know, guess, think, figure* etc. not only allow for ECM with Focus as in (62), but that they also display ECM without Focus if the subject of the infinitive is an expletive NP such as *it* or *there*. Moreover, these verbs allow for passives as in (65) which do not involve Focus either. Examples and judgments are from Postal (1974: 298(21, 25, 28)).

(64) a. I estimate there to be two million people in that valley

b. I estimate it to be raining

c. *I estimate it to be six inches long

(65) Bill's dinosaur was estimated to be 175 feet long

These data show that licensing the subject of the infinitival complement cannot simply reduce to Focus movement. The curious difference between expletive and referential NPs in subject position of the infinitive suggests that there is a difference in the way the Case of expletive and referential subjects is licensed. I will investigate this question shortly.

A closer look at the French data also suggests that Focus is not always necessary to license the subject of the infinitive of ECM verbs, although in a different and surprising way. A number of ECM constructions in French involve movement of a clitic which is subject of the infinitive to the matrix clause. Obviously, the clitic subject of the infinitive cannot be focused in these cases. However, clitic ECM seems to be subject to a hitherto overlooked constraint with respect to focus. Two sets of examples seem to be relevant. The first set of verbs involves predicative verbs in the embedded clause. If the infinitive consists of *être* 'be'/*devenir* 'become' followed by an AP or NP complement, movement of the clitic is only possible if the predicate is contrasted or focused:[16]

(66) a. ?Je le crois être le plus intelligent de tous

(Kayne 1981b: 361fn.15(v))

'I him believe to be the most intelligent of all'

b. *Je le crois être malade/au lit avec la fièvre jaune
'I believe him to be sick/in bed with yellow fever'

c. *Je la croyais être rentrée chez elle/avoir été nommée directrice
'I believed her to-be at home/to have been appointed a director'

d. *Je le considère être sans importance
'I consider him/it to be without interest'

(67) Ce peintre était son Dieu parce qu'elle le savait être le plus pur parmi les purs
'That painter was her God because she knew him to be the purest among the pure'

(Georges Michel, *Les Montparnos*, 43, in Sandfeld 1943: 187)

(68) * Je les nie être de quelque importance que ce soit
'I deny them to be of any interest at all'

(Kayne 1981b: 357fn.12(ii))

(69) a. ?Louis la croyait être sans aucun doute la plus grande chanteuse qui ait jamais vécu
'Louis believed her to be without question the greatest singer that ever lived'

b. *Louis le croyait être un inconnu
'Louis thought him to be a stranger'

All felicitous examples need a comparative or superlative predicate. Guéron (1981) has argued that comparatives involve LF movement to SpecCP. A second set of examples involves nonpredicative verbs. Very few examples involving clitic ECM can be found with such verbs. Nevertheless, those attested examples that can be found, quoted by Sandfeld (1943: 187–8) and Grevisse (1980: §2600) share the characteristic that movement of the clitic subject of the infinitive is dependent on *Wh*- movement of a complement of the infinitive to the SpecCP of the matrix clause. The variety of French that allows for this strategy is quite literary. The generalization here seems to be that clitic climbing of the subject of the infinitive is in some sense parasitic on *Wh*- movement of another element out of the embedded clause. This strategy is also available to predicative verbs as shown by (72). Native speakers report contrasts between clitic ECM with and without accompanying *Wh*- movement of another element.

(70) a. 'ce genre de jeunes gens (. . .) auxquels Swann me croyait
          ressembler'
          the type of young persons to-whom Swann me-believed to-
          resemble
          'the kind of adolescent whom Swann believed that I resembled'
          (M. Proust, *A l'ombre des jeunes filles en fleur*,
          57, Sandfeld 1943: 188)

      b. *Swann me croyait ressembler aux jeunes gens peu scrupuleux
          'Swann believed me to resemble the unscrupulous adolescents'

(71) a. 'L'emplacement de la vraie maison où on le sait avoir vécu'
          The site of the real house where one him-knows to-have lived
          'The site of the real house where he is known to have lived'
          (E. Henriot, *Le Monde*, 20 janvier 1960,
          quoted by Grevisse 1980: §2600)

      b. *Nous le savions avoir vécu dans une maison en banlieue
          'We knew him to have lived in a house in the suburbs'

(72) a. '[ils] prenaient tout simplement la femme mystérieuse pour
          They took very simply the woman mysterious for
          ce qu'elle était ou du moins pour ce qu'ils la croyaient être'
          what she was or rather for what they her-believed to-be
          'They simply took the mysterious woman for what she was or,
          rather, for what they believed her to be'
          (Richepin, *Contes sans morale*, 258,
          quoted by Sandfeld 1943: 188)

      b. *Ils la croyaient être la chanteuse qui avait le rôle de doña Anna.
          'They believed her to be the singer with the role of doña Anna.'

Both sets of examples involving clitic ECM constructions with *croire* 'belie-
eve'-type verbs share the property that either a complement of the infinitive
must be overtly focused via *Wh-* movement, or the predicate following the
infinitive must be (comparatively or superlatively) contrasted.

6.2 *Capturing English*

Recapitulating the relevant data from French and English, it appears that
English verbs such as *estimate* do not require Focus on expletive subjects of
their ECM constructions, nor on any other element of these ECM constructions. In French, by contrast, Focus properties seem to be required at all times
in ECM complements of *croire* 'believe'-type verbs. When the subject of the
infinitive cannot bear Focus because of its clitic properties, it appears that

28

Focus has to be expressed on another element of the sentential complement of *croire* 'believe.' In other words, Focus only surfaces in some cases in English, but it is a constant in French ECM constructions quoted in the literature.

This apparent puzzle can be solved if the mechanism of case-checking in these constructions is examined more closely. I would like to relate these facts to the well-known observation that the subject of the infinitive in French cannot be passivized in ECM constructions with *croire* 'believe'-type verbs, contrary to both English *believe*-type verbs and *estimate*-type verbs:

(73) a. Voilà la linguiste qu'on a cru/dit avoir été mal comprise
'This is the linguist who they believed/said to have been misunderstood'

b. * Cette personne était dit(e)/cru(e) avoir été mal comprise
'This person was said/believed to have been misunderstood'

(74)   Bill's dinosaur was estimated/believed to have been 175 feet long

I will try to show that the entire range of differences between French and English can be derived from the fact that English always licenses the subject of the infinitive in the matrix SpecAGR$_O$P, while French never licenses the subject of the infinitive in the matrix SpecAGR$_O$P. French will be argued to license case internally to the CP complement in ECM constructions with *croire* 'believe'-type verbs.

English *estimate*-type verbs allow for the subject of the infinitive to become the subject of a passive matrix clause as in (74). This shows that the subject of the infinitive is sensitive to the 'defective' nature (the absence of accusative) of the matrix AGR$_O$. It moreover suggests that the subject of the infinitive should be licensed in this matrix SpecAGR$_O$P position in all other instances of ECM with *estimate*-type verbs, that is both the cases of ECM with Focus on the subject as in (62), and the cases of ECM with expletive subjects (64). How can this peculiar double restriction of DOC verbs with respect to the NP subject of ECM constructions, which must be either expletive, Focused or passivized, be explained?

Recall it was argued that in ECM constructions with *believe*-type verbs, the embedded infinitival AGR$_S$P overtly moves to SpecCP, and that this movement enables the NP subject of the infinitive to overtly move to the matrix SpecAGR$_O$P. Let us now assume that all English ECM verbs, both *believe*-type and *estimate* (DOC)-type verbs, always display AGR$_S$P movement to SpecCP. The only difference between both types of verbs would involve the overt or covert nature of this movement: movement of AGR$_S$P to SpecCP with *believe*-type verbs is overt, while *estimate*-type verbs have covert movement of AGR$_S$P to the embedded SpecCP. The structure for *believe* with overt movement of AGR_SP to SpecCP therefore differs minimally from the structure assumed for *estimate*-type verbs presented in (75):

(75)   They estimated

$[_{AGROP}\, e\; AGR_O\, [_{CP}\, e\; C°\; [_{AGRSP}\, Bill's\; dinosaur\; to\; be\; 175\; feet\; long]]]$

         ↑ LF-movement of   ↑ LF-movement of

         Bill's dinosaur   AGRSP

Covert movement of AGR_SP to SpecCP immediately entails that the NP subject of the infinitive (*Bill's dinosaur* in (75)) cannot move overtly to the the matrix $SpecAGR_OP$, but will only be allowed to move covertly to this position at LF. Now it was assumed that NP subjects of infinitives with *believe*-type verbs have to move overtly to $SpecAGR_OP$ to check case-features. The absence of overt AGR_SP movement with *estimate* (DOC)-type verbs therefore entails that the NP subject of the infinitive does not move overtly and fails to check its case-features before LF, as it should. As a result, sentences with *estimate*-type verbs where the NP subject of the infinitive is in the $SpecAGR_SP$ position of the infinitive will be ungrammatical, and the sentences in (76), repeated here, are correctly excluded.

(76) a. *They estimated Bill's dinosaur to be 175 feet long

    b. *I estimate it to be six inches long

How can sentences with expletive, Focused, and passivized subjects of the ECM infinitive be licensed? Expletive subjects can of course check their case-features overtly like referential NPs. This is at least the case in raising-to-subject ($SpecAGR_SP$) contexts as *It seems to have rained.*

There is however some evidence that in raising-to-object ($SpecAGR_OP$) contexts, expletive subjects do not move overtly. Kayne (1984) shows that although adverbs may appear after the NP subject of the infinitive with *believe* constructions (Postal 1974), they cannot appear after expletive subjects of the infinitival complement. This suggests that the NP *John* in (77a) moves overtly out of the infinitival complement, beyond the adverb *for a long time now*, while the expletive *there* in (77b) and the idiom chunk *advantage* in (77c) cannot do so.[17] This evidence strongly suggests that expletives and nonreferential NPs generally only move to $SpecAGR_OP$ at LF: (our (77) = Kayne 1985b: 114(70, 71, 73)).

(77) a. I've believed John for a long time now to be a liar

    b. *I've believed there for a long time now to be no solution to this problem

c. *I've believed advantage for a long time now to have been taken of me

Now if expletive subjects of infinitival complements do not move to SpecAGR$_O$P overtly with *believe*-type verbs, they must also move covertly out of the complement of *estimate*-type verbs. Recall now that LF movement of the infinitival AGR$_S$P to SpecCP with *estimate*-type verbs prevents referential NP subjects of this AGR$_S$P from checking its case-features overtly. Expletive subjects of the infinitival AGR$_S$P in the complement of *estimate*-type verbs cannot and must not move overtly to the matrix SpecAGR$_O$P. However, LF movement of AGR$_S$P to SpecCP will feed LF movement of the expletives to SpecAGR$_O$P. As a result, the sentences in (78) are predicted to be grammatical, with a derivation as in (79):

(78) a. I estimate there to be two million people in that valley

b. I estimate it to be raining

(79) I estimate [$_{AGROP}$ e AGR$_O$
[$_{CP}$ e C° [$_{AGRSP}$ there to be 2M people in that valley]]]

——LF——>

I estimate

[$_{AGROP}$ there AGR$_O$
[$_{CP}$ [$_{AGRSP}$ t_{there} to be 2M people in that valley] C° t_{AGRSP}]]

The results of this analysis can be recapitulated as follows. Covert movement of AGR$_S$P to SpecCP has the side effect of preventing movement of referential NP subjects out of the sentential complement and into SpecAGR$_O$P as in (75–76). Covert movement of AGR$_S$P to SpecCP ensures that further movement out of AGR$_S$P will only be allowed if this movement is also covert.[18] This situation entails that only nonreferential subjects, which are the only subjects that move covertly to the matrix SpecAGR$_O$P, can be licensed as subjects of the infinitival complement of *estimate*-type verbs.

For sentences with Focused/*Wh*-moved subjects of infinitives as in (62), I will assume that a *pro*-variable in the sense of Cinque (1991) is inserted in SpecAGR$_S$P position of the infinitive. This *pro*-variable is licensed at LF via movement to SpecAGR$_O$P in the same way as expletives, and is related to the Focused/*Wh-* moved element via Form–Chain.

(80)   Bill's dinosaur,

I estimate [$_{AGROP}$ *e* AGR$_O$
[$_{CP}$ *e* C° [$_{AGRSP}$ pro$_{var}$ to be 175 feet long]]]

—— LF ——>

Bill's dinosaur,

I estimate [$_{AGROP}$ pro$_{var}$ AGR$_O$
[$_{CP}$ [$_{AGRSP}$ *t*$_{pro}$ to be 175 feet long] C° *t*$_{AGRSP}$]]

The same analysis is valid for cases where the subject of the infinitive is right-dislocated, since this NP is arguably outside of the infinitive (Postal 1993):

(81)   I could assure you *e*$_y$ to be one of the world's ten best cars, and hereby do assure you *e*$_y$ to be one of the world's ten best cars – [the 1992 model De Soto that you see standing in front of you]$_y$

Postal's (1993) *e*$_y$ in (81) can thus be taken to be a *pro*-variable in the sense of Cinque (1991).

It is important to point out that this analysis accounts for the variation noted among speakers of English with respect to the verbs that display the ECM with Focus pattern of *estimate* verbs, or the 'Focusless' *believe* pattern (cf. note 3). In the analysis presented here, the only difference between both dialects involves overt vs. covert movement of AGR$_S$P to SpecCP. In a Minimalist framework, this is exactly the kind of dialectal parameter one might expect. Nevertheless, as was observed before, this small difference has serious consequences for the types of NPs that can be licensed as subjects of the infinitival complement.

I still have to explain the existence of passive sentences with *estimate*-type verbs as in (74), repeated here as (82).

(82)   Bill's dinosaur was estimated to be 175 feet long

The logic of our analysis should exclude these sentences, since it was assumed that covert movement of AGR$_S$P to SpecCP prevents the overt movement of the subject of the infinitive into the higher clause, be it to SpecAGR$_O$P or SpecAGR$_S$P as in (82). Only overt movement of AGR$_S$P to

SpecCP can license overt movement of the subject of the infinitive to the matrix SpecAGR$_S$P in (82). It is not likely that overt movement of AGR$_S$P to SpecCP depends on the passive morphology of the matrix verb. How can such sentences be explained in our analysis?

I would like to suggest that the passive morphology of the matrix verb is the key to understanding passive sentences with *estimate*-type verbs. Passive morphology 'deactivates' the accusative case features of AGR$_O$, preventing case-checking of the infinitival subject in SpecAGR$_O$P. Recall now that *believe*-type verbs have been analyzed as the accusative counterparts of *seem*. Verbs such as *estimate* are also accusative counterparts of *seem*. In the analysis presented here, the only difference between *estimate*-type verbs and *believe*-type verbs concerns covert/overt movement in the CP complement of AGR$_S$P to SpecCP. If the matrix AGR$_O$ of *estimate*-type verbs is deactivated, *estimate* in a sense becomes *seem* again, which has no "accusative" feature. Now *seem* has overt movement of AGR$_S$P to SpecCP, feeding overt movement to the matrix SpecAGR$_S$P. If passive *estimate* is configurationally equivalent to *seem*, it is natural to assume that movement of AGR$_S$P to SpecCP is also overt, feeding overt movement of the infinitival subject to the matrix SpecAGR$_S$P:

(83)   Bill's dinosaur was estimated
       [$_{CP}$ [$_{AGRSP}$ $t_{B's\ dino}$ to be 175 feet long] C° t_{AGRSP}]

Recapitulating the main points of the analysis, I assume that *estimate*-type verbs involve LF (covert) movement of AGR$_S$P to SpecCP if the matrix verb has active morphology (cf. *supra*). Passive morphology on the matrix verb 'deactivates' AGR$_O$°. This makes *estimate*-type verbs configurationally equivalent to *seem*-type verbs, and forces overt movement of AGR$_S$P to SpecCP.

The analysis of passive *estimate*-type verbs presented here crucially depends on the assumption that the functional configuration of matrix verbs partially determines the syntax of their complement. There is some independent evidence for this analysis: in a number of languages, certain verbs only behave as raising verbs if they are passivized:

(84)   Brutus   mihi   videtur   venisse   (Latin)
       Brutus   to-me   see.PASS   to-have-come
       'Brutus seems to have come'

(85) a. Jan werd geacht/verondersteld te komen   (Dutch)
'John was supposed to come'

b. *Ik achtte/veronderstelde Jan te komen
'I supposed John to come'

c. *Wie achtte/veronderstelde jij te zullen komen?
'Who did you suppose to come?'

(86) a. Jean était censé/supposé venir   (French)
'John was supposed to come'

b. *J'ai censé/supposé Jean venir
'I supposed John to come'

c. *Qui avais-tu censé/supposé venir?
'Who did you suppose to come?'

In Latin, passive *videre* 'see' is used to express English *seem*,[19] and in Dutch and French only the passivized forms of certain verbs expressing belief syntactically display raising behavior, while having a meaning close to modal raising verbs such as epistemic *devoir* 'must/should'. These facts show that passive *believe*-type verbs have in many languages a special 'accusatively deactivated' status that makes them 'revert' to nominative *seem*-type verbs. It is our contention that the passive use of *estimate*-type verbs participates in the mechanism that makes (84–86) possible. Admittedly, this is not yet an explanation of why these verbs behave this way. It is only our purpose to establish a correlation between a special set of 'accusatively deactivated' verbs as in (84–86) and the passive *estimate*-type verbs which remain as a problem for the analysis presented above. The exact implementation of the idea that syntactic configuration of matrix verbs influences the syntax of the complement of these verbs is a problem I will leave for further research.

6.3 Capturing French

Let us now turn our attention ot the French data. It was observed above that Focus properties seem to be required at all times in ECM complements of *croire* 'believe'-type verbs. At the same time, I want to make the assumption that Case is licensed internally to the CP complement of *croire* 'believe' verbs in French. In other words, the overt subject of the infinitive in the complement of *croire* 'believe' does not move to the matrix $SpecAGR_OP$ in French. This assumption was motivated by the absence of agreement on matrix participles (9), the absence of passives with ECM constructions (11).

As a result, two questions have to be solved:

(87) i. Why is Focus always present in ECM complements of *croire* 'believe'?

    ii. How is Case on the subject licensed internally to the ECM complement?

I would like to propose that Case on the subject in ECM infinitives is linked to Focus in French. French seems to have the property of independently licensing a case for the subject of infinitives if the event is focused. This can be seen in root infinitives such as (88):

(88)   Et les linguistes de s'engueuler tout le temps
        And the linguists of each-other-yell all the time
        'And the linguists did nothing but yell at each other'

The sentence in (88) involves restrictive Focus on the event. Following Kayne (1981b, 1994), I take *de* in (88) to be C°. The presence of an overt subject in front of *de* forces us to conclude that this configuration licenses a case in SpecCP.[20] Case is overtly checked and therefore 'strong' in the sense of Chomsky (1995).

There is one case in which the root infinitive construction quoted in (88) shows up in ECM contexts:[21]

(89) a. On soupçonne cette histoire d'avoir été inventée de toutes pièces
        'They suspect that story to have been entirely made up'
                              (Ruwet 1983: 23n.18, 19)

     b. Je soupçonne ces bouteilles d'avoir plus de trente ans de cave
        'I believe those bottles to be over thirty years old'

In this case, it can be assumed that the verb *soupçonner* 'suspect' selects a [+ Focus] C° which licenses a case feature that has to be checked overtly by the subject of the infinitive.

In (59–61), repeated here as (90–92), case is a 'weak' feature associated with [+ Focus] C°. Therefore, it may not be licensed overtly. As a result, the subject of the infinitive has to move all the way up to the matrix SpecCP, licensing Case and Focus in the embedded SpecCP at LF by Form–Chain as in (90a). Another possibility is for the subject to stay overtly 'downstairs' under restrictive Focus expressed by *ne . . . que* or by Heavy-NP-shift, only to covertly raise to the embedded SpecCP at LF, checking Case and Focus. This is what happens in (91–92).

(90) a. Voilà la linguiste [O$_i$ que je crois [$_{CP}$ t'_i [$_{IP}$ t_i avoir été mal comprise]]]
'This is the linguist who I think to have been misunderstood'

b. * Je crois cette linguiste avoir été mal comprise
'I believe that linguist to have been misunderstood'

(91) Je crois [$_{CP}$ e C° [$_{AGRSP}$ n'avoir été condamnés que trois de mes amis]]

LF movement

'I believe only to have been condemned three of my friends'

(92) Je crois [$_{CP}$ e C° [$_{AGRSP}$ n'avoir été condamnés plusieurs des amis

LF movement

qui avaient été arrêtés en même temps que moi]]
'I believe to have been condemned several of the friends that had been arrested at the same time I was'

Checking of case and Focus can be dissociated: in the cases of clitic ECM quoted in (66–69) above and repeated here as (93–94). In these cases, the clitic checks 'weak' case at LF, thanks to its trace in the embedded C°. The [+ Focus] feature is checked covertly by movement of the comparatively focused AP in the infinitive, as in (93a). Following Guéron (1981), I assume that comparative/superlative APs must move to SpecCP at LF. The [+ Focus] feature can also be checked by *Wh-* movement to the matrix CP of another element in the clause, as in (94a), (70a), and (72a). This *Wh-* moved element will check Focus in the embedded SpecCP by Form–Chain at LF.

(93) a. ?Je le crois être le plus intelligent de tous
(Kayne 1981b: 361fn.15(v))
'I him believe to be the most intelligent of all'

b. *Je le crois être malade/au lit avec la fièvre jaune
'I believe him to be sick/in bed with yellow fever'

(94) a. 'L'emplacement de la vraie maison où on le sait avoir vécu'
The site of the real house where one him-knows to-have lived
'The site of the real house where he is known to have lived'
(E. Henriot, *Le Monde*, 20 janvier 1960, quoted by Grevisse 1980: §2600)

b. *Nous le savions avoir vécu dans une maison en banlieue
'We knew him to have lived in a house in the suburbs'

It is now possible to formulate an answer to the question in (87i), i.e. why Focus is always present in French ECM constructions with *croire* 'believe.' French *croire* 'believe'-type verbs do not allow movement of AGR_SP to SpecCP, contrary to *sembler* 'seem'-type verbs which require this type of movement.[22] As a result, the 'weak' [+ Focus] feature of $C°$ must always be licensed by some other element in the embedded clause.

The dissociation between [+ Focus] and case for the subject of the infinitive also accounts for the dialectal variation reported for French ECM. As noted in section 2, Pollock (1985) pointed out the existence of two dialects with respect to French ECM constructions. One dialect restricts the embedded ECM infinitives of *croire* verbs to impersonal passives and ergatives, while another dialect does not manifest such a restriction. Recall it was shown above that the constructions in (95a) involve impersonal constructions with an impersonal *pro* subject.

(95) a. L'homme que je croyais être arrivé/entré/avoir disparu
'The man who I thought to have arrived/come in/disappeared'

b. (*) L'homme que je croyais avoir téléphoné/toussé/plongé dans l'eau
'The man who I thought to have telephoned/coughed/dived into the water'

It should be noted that those speakers of French who do not have a restriction on the type of infinitives in ECM constructions are usually speakers of a more conservative dialect of French (CF), while speakers who only accept embedded impersonal constructions speak a less conservative, 'advanced' dialect of French (AF). Importantly, the bare infinitive construction with an overt, case-marked subject in (87) is only featured in Conservative French. This correlation holds the key to understanding the variation between CF and AF. If AF does not have bare infinitives which case-mark an overt subject such as (88), our analysis predicts that ECM infinitives selected by *croire* 'believe' in this dialect should not be able to case-mark their subjects either. The options for the subject of the infinitive in AF are thus extremely limited: the subject cannot move out of the embedded CP to be licensed by the matrix case-features, and the infinitive itself does not provide case-features either. The only infinitival constructions that may occur in the complement of *croire* 'believe' are those in which the subject does not need the case of an overt NP. It can be assumed that the impersonal *pro* of impersonal passives and ergatives fits this profile, and does not need case. As a result, AF only allows these impersonal infinitives in the CP complement of *croire* 'believe' as in

(95a). Of course, the CP complement of *croire* 'believe' still has a [+ Focus] feature that needs to be licensed: the only difference between CF and AF concerns the case-marking potential of infinitives, not the 'weak' [+ Focus] property which in embedded contexts is a function of the matrix verb. This 'weak' [+ Focus] feature in the embedded SpecCP of (95a) will be licensed at LF by Form–Chain, after the subject of the infinitive has moved overtly to the higher SpecCP.

The other dialect of French, Conservative French, has the case-marking bare infinitive (88), and therefore its ECM infinitives can assign case to the subject of any infinitive. As a result, there are no restrictions on the type of infinitives that may occur in the complement of *croire* 'believe' in CF.

There is a final question with respect to the analysis proposed here for French *croire* constructions with pseudo-ECM. Recall it was assumed for *seem/sembler* that in a raising structure such as *Alfred seems to have eaten his veggies*, the CP complement contains an operator–variable structure, with AGR_SP in SpecCP (the operator) and a trace of the AGR_SP (the variable), both necessary for the comparative interpretation required by *seem*. I have assumed that English *believe*-type verbs and *estimate*-type verbs in ECM constructions can be considered 'accusative' counterparts of 'nominative' *seem*. As a result, movement of AGR_SP to SpecCP in the complement of *seem* and *believe* could both be motivated in terms of comparative Focus. For French *croire* constructions closely resembling English *believe* constructions with ECM, I have argued that there is no ECM and no movement of AGR_SP to SpecCP in the complement of *croire*. As a result, there is no way in which two events can be compared in an operator–variable structure. It is therefore predicted, contrary to fact, that Full Interpretation is violated in French *croire* constructions, since the requirement of comparison inherent in *croire*, the 'accusative' counterpart of 'nominative' *sembler*, cannot be satisfied.

However, this conclusion is unwarranted. I have indeed assumed that the subject of the infinitive in the complement of *croire* constructions does not get its case in the matrix $SpecAGR_OP$, contrary to raising to $SpecAGR_OP$ in English, both overt (*believe*) and covert (*estimate*). This means that the AGR_O of *croire* still has an accusative case-feature that must be discharged. The only argument that can license this feature is the infinitival CP complement itself, moving to $SpecAGR_OP$ at LF. It has been argued extensively in the literature that Romance infinitival complements fall under Case theory in the same way as ordinary NPs (cf. Contreras 1985; Picallo 1985; Raposo 1987; Plann 1986). This movement then creates the necessary relation between operator and variable, the CP complement of *croire* having operator status via its Focus on the event (cf. the discussion of (88)).

7 Conclusions and conjectures

7.1 *Results*

Let us summarize the results of the previous sections. I have argued that all raising constructions, both raising-to-subject (SpecAGR$_S$P) with *seem*-type verbs and raising-to-object (SpecAGR$_O$P) with *believe*-type verbs, involve CP complementation. This claim allows for a simplification of the types of sentential complements verbs can select for. The consequence of this assumption is that there must be movement of the infinitival AGR$_S$P to SpecCP, feeding movement of the subject of the infinitive to the SpecAGR$_O$P of the matrix verb. If AGR$_S$P failed to move to SpecCP, movement of the subject of the infinitive to the matrix SpecAGR$_O$P would result in improper movement. AGR$_S$P movement to SpecCP is motivated by a [+ Focus] feature in C°.

The configuration of the complement CP with a chain relating the AGR$_S$P in SpecCP to its trace was further motivated by the semantics of *seem*, which was argued to involve a comparison between a token of the event and its type. Other differences between ECM and control constructions of *believe*-type verbs, such as the absence of negative islands, can also be advantageously explained by analyzing the complement of *believe*-type verbs in ECM constructions as a CP.

CP complementation of *believe*-type verbs also allowed us to reduce the spectacular syntactic differences in English between *believe*-type verbs and *estimate*-type verbs in ECM contexts to a single parameter: overt or covert movement of AGR$_S$P to the embedded SpecCP. The variation between English speakers with respect to the verbs following the syntactic *believe*-type pattern or the *estimate*-type pattern can be reduced to this parameter.

With respect to French, CP complementation of *believe*-type verbs effectively prevents movement of the subject of the infinitive to SpecAGR$_O$P. I have argued that [+ Focus] infinitives in one variety of French (CF) have the possibility of independently licensing Case for the subject of the infinitive inside CP. The other variety of French (AF) was argued to only allow impersonal *pro* subjects in the infinitival complements of *croire* 'believe'-type verbs.

7.2 *Conjectures*

In the analysis presented here, the difference between raising and control verbs does not lie in the categorial type of sentential complement these verbs select for (AGR$_S$P or CP, respectively). The configurational properties of raising and control CPs are nevertheless radically different. Raising of a subject out of its infinitival CP requires that the infinitival AGR$_S$P first move to SpecCP. In control contexts, such AGR$_S$P movement to SpecCP never obtains.

In the analysis presented here, this configurational difference gives rise to an interpretive semantics for raising CPs, which require operator–variable relations ranging over events. The question now arises as to how this analysis can be extended to the complementation of other raising verbs. Barbiers (1993, 1995) shows how the epistemic and deontic uses of modal verbs such as *moeten* 'must' and *kunnen* 'can' are influenced by Focus particles in Dutch. It is likely that these Focus particles determine the [+ Focus] feature on C° which triggers movement of AGR$_S$P to SpecCP, feeding overt movement of the subject of the infinitive to the matrix SpecAGR$_S$P of *moeten* 'must' and *kunnen* 'can.'

The very same idea might be extended to aspectual raising verbs such as *begin, stop, resume, keep, continue, finish*.[23] In a loose sense, these verbs focus on a part of the internal temporal structure of the event expressed in their untensed complement, comparing as it were a subset of the event to the event itself. The analysis presented here allows for a configurational representation of this intuition, although a bit more work is required as to the exact semantics of the operator–variable relation in these cases.

Further research questions in this area include the problem of ECM with verbs of perception as in (3b), especially in the light of their relation with raising verbs of the *seem* type in languages such as English and Latin (cf. note 13). In this context, it is interesting to note that raising verbs of the *seem* type are often derived from the semantic converse of *see*: Persian *be næzær residæn* 'seem' literally means 'reach to view' (Hajati 1977), and Dutch *schijnen* 'seem' also means 'shine' as in *the sun shines on us*, allowing for an interpretation of *Het schijnt dat Jan ziek is* 'It seems that John is sick' along the lines of 'That John is sick shines on me' (Hoekstra, personal communication). Similar considerations apply to English *appear*.

Finally, the idea that raising verbs turn the embedded C° of their CP complement into an operator quantifying events might also offer new insights into the problem of those verbs which can be used either as control verbs or as raising verbs. These include verbs such as *promettre* 'promise' and *menacer* 'threaten,' *risquer* 'risk,' *faillir* 'escape,' verbs of movement such as *aller* 'go' and *venir* 'come' (Ruwet 1983; Rooryck 1992c). The use of these verbs as control verbs involves realizing one internal argument projected by the verb as an infinitive, while the raising use does not project any arguments at all.

(96) a. Louis nous a promis [un livre]/   (thematic, control)
          [de lire ce livre]
          'Louis promised us a book/to read that book'

      b. Il (*nous) promet de pleuvoir   (nonthematic, raising)
          'It promises to rain'

(97) a. Louis nous a menacé [du poing]/[de tout dire au doyen]

                                                 (thematic, control)

      'Louis threatened us with his fist/to tell everything to the dean'

  b. Il (*nous) menace de pleuvoir   (nonthematic, raising)

      'It threatens to rain'

(98) a. Il risque [sa vie]/[de se faire tuer]   (thematic, control)

      'He takes the risk (of losing) his life/of getting killed'

  b. Il risque de pleuvoir   (nonthematic, raising)

      It risks to rain

      'It is probable that it will rain'

(99) a. Il faillit [à son devoir]/[à faire son devoir] (thematic, control)

      'He has failed at (carrying out) his responsibilities'

  b. Il a failli pleuvoir   (nonthematic, raising)

      It has barely-escaped to rain

      'There was a possibility of rain/it almost rained'

(100) a. Elle est allé [à la poste]/[chercher des livres] (thematic, control)

      'She went to the post office/to look for books'

  b. Elle va avoir un enfant   (nonthematic, raising)

      'She is going to have a baby'

  c. Elle aura un enfant

      'She will have a baby'

(101) a. Elle est venu [de la poste]/[chercher des livres] (thematic, control)

      'She came from the post office/to look for books'

  b. Elle vient d'arriver à Bruxelles   (nonthematic, raising)

      She comes from to-arrive in Brussels

      'She just arrived in Brussels'

As pointed out by Ruwet (1983), the existence of such verbs is a challenge for a principle such as the theta-criterion. Any analysis based on a radical distinction between raising and control verbs is forced to assume homonymous pairs of verbs in these cases. But it should be clear that this only restates the problem. For one thing, it is striking that the nonthematic raising use of these verbs is semantically very restricted: it can be shown that these verbs involve an epistemic modal meaning of necessity or possibility.

Before making an attempt at explaining the dual nature of these verbs in a nonstipulative fashion, I would like to adequately illustrate the modal properties of the verbs involved. The epistemic modal 'possibility' reading of *risquer* and *avoir failli* is sufficiently clear from the glosses and translations in (98–99). The necessity reading of the so-called 'futur proche' *aller* can be deduced by comparing the contextual implications of the inflectional future in (100c) with those of the periphrastic future *aller* in (100b): (100b), but not (100c), implies that one is pregnant. (100c) can be said of a seven-year-old (she will have a baby when she is a grown up), but saying (100b) referring to a seven-year-old would be distinctly odd under normal assumptions about childbearing age. This shows that *aller* carries the meaning of an 'inescapable,' 'imminent' future. This interpretation of 'imminence' should be viewed as a result of the epistemic modal necessity inherent in *aller*: the sentence (100b) says that the necessary conditions for having a baby are present. Since one of these necessary conditions includes pregnancy, the interpretive difference between the future of *aller* 'go' and the inflectional future is accounted for if *aller* in (100b) carries not only the meaning of future but also that of necessity.[24] Interpretive notions such as 'inescapable' future and the traditional term *futur proche* then follow from the combination of the modal and the temporal characteristics yielding a property of 'future necessity' inherent in *aller*.

Another indication that modal necessity is involved in *aller* is that as a raising verb, *aller* cannot be used with a perfective aspect (102a). This is unexpected because inflectional future tense (102b) and the 'possible' periphrastic future *risquer* can cooccur with perfective aspect (102c): if *aller* simply expressed a future, it should be combinable with perfective aspect, expressing a future perfective.[25]

(102) a. *Il est allé pleuvoir (demain matin)
It is gone to rain (tomorrow morning)
'It went to rain (tomorrow morning)'

b. Il aura plu (demain matin)
'It will have rained (tomorrow morning)'

c. Hier soir, il a risqué de pleuvoir à un moment donné
'Yesterday evening, there was a risk of rain for a moment'

Now, it is generally the case that objective epistemic necessity is incompatible with perfective aspect. In (103a), the necessity of a raining event can only involve objective epistemic necessity,[26] and perfective aspect is excluded:

(103) a. Il doit absolument/*a absolument dû pleuvoir pour
It must absolutely/have must absolutely to-rain in-order-to
assurer les besoins en eau potable
ensure the needs in water drinkable

'Rain is/was necessary to satisfy the needs for drinking water'

b. La pluie a été nécessaire pour assurer les besoins en eau potable
'The rain has been necessary to satisfy the needs for drinking water'

The sentence (103b) shows that objective epistemic necessity is not intrinsically incompatible with perfective aspect. Therefore, it is not clear to us why there is this aspectual constraint on objective epistemic necessity expressed by *devoir* 'must.' What is clear, however, is that the restriction that is responsible for ruling out the combination of *devoir* 'must' and perfective aspect can also be invoked to rule out the combination of *aller* and perfective aspect, if it is assumed that *aller* involves a modal epistemic operator of necessity.

Finally, this idea must be extended to the recent past *venir de* in (101). I would like to suggest that it involves past necessity in the same way *aller* involves future necessity. The argument for this analysis is harder to make than for *aller*, and needs a little more work. This may be due to the fact that *venir de* also involves an aspectual feature of punctuality as observed by Ruwet (1983). However, like *aller* in (102) and *devoir* 'must' in (103a), *venir de* cannot be combined with perfective aspect:

(104) Elle vient/venait/*est venu d'arriver à Bruxelles
She comes/came/has come from to-arrive in Brussels
'She just arrives/arrived in Brussels'

I would like to suggest that the incompatibility of *venir de* with perfective aspect is due to the same restriction that applies to *aller* in (102) and *devoir* 'must' in (103), namely the general incompatibility of perfective aspect with objective epistemic necessity.

Similar considerations extend to *promettre* 'promise,' and *menacer* 'threaten.' From a temporal and modal perspective, the raising construction of *promettre* 'promise' seems to be closely related to *aller*, carrying an additional positive connotation, while *menacer* 'threaten' seems to be basically a variant of *risquer* 'risk,' with pejorative import. Note that *promettre* 'promise' does not allow for a perfective tense, like *aller* 'go', while *menacer* 'threaten' does, like *risquer* 'risk.'

(105) a. Il promet/*a promis de faire beau
It promises/has promised to do nice (weather)
'The weather promises to be nice'
(= the necessary conditions for nice weather are present')

b. Il menace/a menacé de pleuvoir
'It threatens/has threatened to rain' (= it will possibly rain)

The modal necessity present in *promettre* 'promise' and the modal possibility implied in *menacer* 'threaten' in (106a–107a) can be deduced from the interpretation of these sentences in (106b–107b):

(106) a. Cette maison menace de s'écrouler
      'This house threatens to collapse'

   b. It is possible/*?necessary that this house will collapse
      'Certain conditions are present for this house to collapse'

(107) a. Cette maison promet d'être un havre de paix
      'This house promises to be a haven of peace'

   b. It is *?possible/necessary (inevitable) that this house will be a haven of peace
      All conditions are present for this house to be a haven of peace

The following chart illustrates the combinations of tense and modality in French raising verbs expressing Tense:

(108)

	objective epistemic necessity	*objective epistemic possibility*
future	aller/promettre	risquer/menacer
past	venir de	avoir failli

These epistemic modal properties of raising verbs expressing Tense are rather unexpected: why isn't it the case that at least some raising verbs simply express a nonmodal Tense similar to those expressed by inflectional bound morphemes in French? For instance, why is there not a raising verb with a nonmodal meaning similar to the past or future tense? The verbs under discussion function as control verbs when they project their canonical thematic structure, without modal properties, and they function as raising verbs when their thematic structure disappears in favor of a combination of temporal and modal properties. This complementary distribution leads us to formulate the following generalization:

(109)   Verbs which 'lose' their canonical thematic structure to function as raising verbs receive a meaning which combines temporal properties with epistemic modality

The question thus arises as to how this generalization can be explained. Recent thought-provoking work by Postma (1994, 1995) may provide a tentative answer to this problem. Postma raises the novel problem as to how the interpretation of NPs arises. He observes that (110a) involves the perception of an actual ball or dog, while (110b) has two interpretations. The first, and less interesting, interpretation of (110b) is one in which the sentence simply refers to the fact that one doesn't see an actual ball or dog (110b.i). In the second interpretation (110b.ii), the nouns *ball* and *dog* have lost their fully referential meaning to function as negative polarity items with universal meaning.[27] To use Postma's (1994) terms, the nouns lapse into zero-semantics. Postma (1994) shows that this second interpretation does not allow the nouns to take plural morphology: (110c) can only refer to actual balls and dogs.

(110) a. Ik zie een bal/hond
'I see a ball/a dog'

   b. Ik zie geen bal/hond
     i. 'I don't see a ball/dog'
     ii. 'I don't see anything/anyone'

   c. Ik zie geen ballen/honden
     'I don't see balls/dogs'/'*I don't see anything/anyone'

A similar process is operative in coordinations such as (111), where the lexical meaning of the elements disappears in favor of a universally quantified meaning (Postma 1994):

(111) a. Het schip verging met man en muis
'The ship went down with man and mouse (= with everyone on it)'

   b. Zij deed haar werk met hart en ziel
     'She did her job with heart and soul (= with all her heart)'

Postma (1994) shows that the process by which nouns lose their lexical meaning to function as quantificational elements is extremely productive in natural language. He observes that there is a complementary distribution between lexical and quantificational meaning. He proposes an interpretive mechanism by which nouns are assigned quantificational or lexical meaning configurationally. I refer the reader to Postma (1994, 1995) for the details of this far-reaching hypothesis.

What is important to us in this context is an issue that is not yet fully addressed by the interpretive mechanism Postma (1994) proposes. It is striking that the nouns in (110–111) do not entirely lose their meaning in favor of universal quantification, but seem to retain some basic syntactico-semantic features. In (110) *hond* 'dog' retains the feature [+ animate], referring to 'any person' in zero-semantics, while *bal* 'ball' retains the [− animate] feature, referring to 'anything.' The same is true in (111), as is clear from the glosses and translations.

Let us now come back to the verbs under study, which can function both as 'thematic' control verbs and 'nonthematic' raising verbs. These verbs lose their lexical 'fully thematic' meaning in favor of a meaning combining epistemic modality and temporal properties. It is well known that epistemic modality can be described as involving universal quantification. I therefore claim that the verbs described above function exactly like *bal* 'ball,' *hond* 'dog,' *man en muis* 'man and mouse,' and *hart en ziel* 'heart and soul' in (110–111). In the same way as these nouns, the verbs mentioned lose their lexical semantics in favor of universal quantification (= epistemic modality), while at the same time retaining some of their syntactico-semantic features. More particularly, in the same way nouns such as *bal* 'ball' and *hond* 'dog' retain their [±animate] features, these verbs retain their lexical features of referring to past and future.[28] In other words, the raising use of *aller* 'go,' which involves both modal or universally quantified meaning and the feature [future], receives its (quantificational) zero-semantics through the same interpretive mechanism proposed by Postma (1994) for the universally quantified, [+ animate] *hond* 'dog' in (110b.ii). *Mutatis mutandis*, the same applies to the other verbs schematically represented in (108) with the semantic features characterizing their raising use. The complementary distribution between the control use and the raising use of these verbs can thus be explained by independent principles operative in the grammar.

From a purely syntactic point of view, it must be noted that both the control and the raising use of the verbs under investigation involve a CP complement. In the context of the ideas developed in this chapter, the switch from control to raising does not entail some process of CP deletion. The only change concerns the interpretation of the CP complement. The modal property acquired by the verb imposes a modal interpretation on the $C°$ head of CP, triggering movement of AGR_SP to SpecCP, and subsequent raising of the infinitival subject to the matrix $SpecAGR_SP$. The interpretation of the CP as a full argument in a thematic structure does not trigger such movement, and a control configuration ensues.

Notes

* A slightly different version of this chapter was first published as Rooryck (1997). I would like to thank Sjef Barbiers, Rose-Marie Déchaine, Denis Delfitto, Marcel den Dikken, Colin Ewen, Yves d'Hulst, Claire Foley, Teun Hoekstra, Victor Manfredi, René Mulder, Gertjan Postma, Guido Vanden Wyngaerd, and two anonymous reviewers of *Studia Linguistica* for various comments and discussions. I also would like to thank audiences at *Going Romance* 1994, Rijksuniversiteit Utrecht; LSRL 1995, University of Washington, Seattle; and GLOW 1995, Universitetet i Tromsø, where many ideas included in this paper were presented. The usual disclaimers apply.

1 There is also a causative lexical relation between raising-to-subject *appear* and raising-to-object verbs such as *show* and *prove*. *Show* and *prove* can be equated with 'make appear'. In these cases, it is unclear why the internal dative Experiencer, which can be expressed with tensed complements (*I showed/proved to Bill that Rousseau was wrong*), is completely impossible in an ECM context (*I showed/proved (*to Bill) Rousseau to be wrong*).

2 It should be noted that *dunken* 'seem' selects infinitival complements, and features raising-to-subject: *Jan dunkt mij een aardige jongen te zijn* 'Jan seems to me to be a nice guy.' *Denken* 'think' can be used as a control verb: *Jan denkt weg te gaan* 'Jan thinks to go away – Jan thinks of going away.' A similar construction is possible in certain dialects of English for *think*, without a corresponding morphological change: *Methinks that you are wrong*. In Icelandic, the verb corresponding to *think* may show up in ECM contexts with a dative Experiencer subject, while the subject of the infinitive is marked with Nominative case by the matrix verb (Sigurdsson 1989). In Swedish, the verb *tycka* 'believe,' which is diachronically related to the Icelandic form in (i), has a nominative subject as in (ii):

i. Mér   þykir/-ja   þeir   vera gáfaðir   (Icelandic)
    I_{DAT} think$_{3sg/3pl}$ they$_{NOM}$ be gifted$_{NOM}$
    'I think they are gifted'

ii. Jag tycker att de är begåvade   (Swedish)
    'I think that they are gifted'

3 In this chapter, I will use both the terms 'ECM' and 'raising-to-object.' ECM will be used as a descriptive term to refer to infinitival constructions with an overt subject in the complement of a matrix verb. It will be shown that such constructions do not always involve raising-to-object position (SpecAGR$_O$P), as e.g. in French. Therefore, the term 'raising to object' will be restricted to those infinitival constructions with an overt subject which uncontrovertibly involve this movement operation.

4 Pollock moreover shows that there are actually two dialects in French with respect to this construction. One dialect restricts the ECM construction to CPs in which the extracted (17a) or restrictively focused (22) subject is an internal argument of the embedded verb. A large number of French speakers have the following contrasts (examples from Pollock 1985: 298(24)):

i. L'homme que je croyais être arrivé/entré/avoir disparu
    'The man who I thought to have arrived/come in/disappeared'

ii. *L'homme que je croyais avoir téléphoné/toussé/plongé dans l'eau
    'The man who I thought to have telephoned/coughed/dived into the water'

Other speakers report no contrast between the two types of sentences. It is clear that an appropriate analysis of ECM in French must provide an account for this variation. We will come back to this issue in section 6.

5 Kayne (1981b: 360n.15) reports that he accepts almost all the verbs cited by Postal (1974: 305) in a nonfocused *believe*-type construction such as (i):

i. I believe/acknowledge/have determined John to be the most intelligent of all

Kayne (1984: 5) nevertheless observes the DOC with the verb *assure* (see also Postal 1993):

ii. John, who I assure you to be the best/*I assure you John to be the best

Postal lists *assume*, as a verb which only supports ECM-with-Focus. Nevertheless, the following example can be found:

iii. 'In childhood, when we assume the world to have been elaborately arrayed for our own benefit (. . .)'

(John Updike, *The Afterlife and other stories,* 46)

One reviewer for this article emphatically sides with Kayne's judgments, urging me to disregard Postal's data as 'not robust enough to include in an article.' I think this is beside the point: even if variation were limited to a difference between *assure* on one hand and all other *believe*-type verbs on the other, as for Kayne and the reviewer, the facts still need to be accounted for. Moreover, the question would still remain as to why Postal speaks his variety of English. Marginalizing Postal's variety of English will not make the facts go away. Whatever the verb-specific variation among speakers, the basic facts are clear for most speakers: one set of verbs allows for 'normal' ECM (*believe*), while an additional, more speaker-specific, set of verbs supports the ECM-with-Focus construction (*assure*). In this chapter, an analysis will be pursued which not only accounts for both types of data, 'Focusless-ECM' and 'ECM-with-Focus,' but which also derives the individual variation among speakers on this point from a single syntactic difference (cf. also Postal 1993: 349fn.4).

6   In Italian, the difference between a controlled CP and the raising construction is morphologically marked by the obligatory presence of a complementizer in the control construction (Kayne 1984):

i. Gianni sembra (*di) essere partito
'Gianni seems (di) to have left'

ii. Mi$_i$ sembra [$_{CP}$ *(di) PRO$_i$ aver capito]
To-me it seems to have understood
'It seems to me that I have understood'

In Romanian, raising out of tensed subjunctive complements requires the absence of the subjunctive complementizer *ca*, while its nonraised counterpart requires the presence of *ca* (Motapanyane 1994):

iii. Studenţii   par   (*ca) să organizeze   o grevă
students-the seem$_{3PL}$ that organize$_{SUBJ.3PL}$ a strike
'The students seem to organize a strike'

iv. Se   pare   că   studenţii organizează   o grevă
Self   seems$_{3SG}$ that   students organize$_{IND.3PL}$ a strike

Such alternations are usually taken to be an indication that CP deletion/AGR$_S$P selection has occurred. The idea that raising constructions involve movement of the infinitival AGR$_S$P into SpecCP allows for another explanation. The absence of the complementizer in raising constructions simply is an instance of the well-known (but poorly understood) restriction against lexically filling both C° and SpecCP, the so-called 'doubly filled COMP filter.'

7   Cf. also Latin *videre* 'seem', expressed as passive: *Mihi videtur* 'to-me (it) is-seen' (cf. infra).

8   The possibility of using 'comparative' complementizers such as *as if* seems to be subject to crosslinguistic variation. Dutch allows for it while French does not:

i. Het lijkt wel alsof Alfred zijn groenten opgegeten heeft   (Dutch)

ii. Il semble *comme si/que Alfred a mangé ses légumes   (French)
'It seems as if Alfred has eaten his veggies'

9 In the analysis of *seem* advocated here, I will remain noncommittal as to the exact relative positions of the CP and *it* within the SC. Moro (1992) argues that *it* is in the complement position of the SC. Heycock (1992) advances arguments showing that *it* might be in the subject position of the SC. If *it* is the subject of the SC and the CP its predicate, the semantic interpretation of the CP complement in (45) as a type, i.e. a *typical* event, may be derived from the fact that predicates denote properties, not individuals (tokens).

One reviewer raises a more compelling question for this analysis. If *it* is not an expletive, but a pronoun referring to the situation or event at hand, why can *it* not be replaced by any other expression? For example, if *It seems that John is sick* has the same structure as *It looks like the flu*, comparing referential elements (situations, things), why is there a contrast between **This seems that John is sick* and *This looks like the flu*? The answer to this question is not entirely clear to me at this point. However, the following should be observed. The analysis proposed here assumes that 'expletive' *it* is coreferential with the CP in complement position of *seem*. In cases where *it* is coreferential with NPs, as in *John read the book and Mary read it too*, it is rather difficult to replace *it* by another expression as well. I suggest that these facts are related.

10 At this point, the perspicuous reader might wonder why the strategy of an operator–variable relation at work in raising constructions such as (50) could not be used in the case of tensed CP complements as well. Why wouldn't it be possible to raise the CP complement to the subject position of *seem*, leaving out the expletive, as in (i)?

i.   It seems [$_{CP}$ that John is sick]

ii. *[$_{IP}$ [$_{CP}$ that John is sick] seems t_{CP}]

Arguably, this movement would create a relation between the moved CP and its trace. I would like to argue however that this movement does not comply with the interpretive requirements of *seem*. The relation between the CP in SpecIP position and its trace is neither an operator–variable relation as in (50), nor a relation between an event-token (the *pro*-CP *it*) and an event-type (CP) as in (i). As a result, the comparative relation required by the semantics of *seem* cannot be satisfied in (ii). The sentence (ii) therefore is ungrammatical because it is uninterpretable.

11 Note that *seem* also is a Neg-raising verb. This supports our analysis of *seem* and *believe* as essentially the same verb with *believe* the 'accusative' counterpart of 'nominative' *seem*:

i.   It does not seem to have rained

ii. It seems not to have rained

12 Rooryck (1992a) shows that Rizzi's account of negative islands based on Relativized Minimality cannot hold since there are cases where negation can intervene in between a *Wh*- chain:

i.   Qui ne veux-tu pas qui vienne encore ici?
     'Who don't you want that still comes here?'

These cases are ruled grammatical since the C° selected by *vouloir* 'want' cannot function as a variable for negation, *vouloir* 'want' not being a Neg-raising verb.

13 One reviewer observes that there are elements that can both be Focus and negative variables, like anyone in *There isn't anyone in the room*. This fact does not undermine the analysis proposed, however. In the case of *anyone*, the entire NP carries Focus, while the negative variable is only a part of the NP, namely *any*. In the case of C° as a variable, I claim that Focus and negation compete to attribute a value to the same element.

14 A similar contrast was noted by Postal (1974: 236):

    i.   I couldn't believe none of the sailors kissed Sally

    ii.   *I couldn't believe none of the sailors to have kissed Sally

However, Postal relates this to the fact that when the negative object is raised, there would be two negations in the matrix clause, an illicit situation.

15 I assume here that 'strong' and 'weak' values of the feature [+ Focus] can be selected for by a matrix verb. This selection should be likened to whatever selection mechanism ensures a 'strong' [+ Wh-] feature in the C° head of the CP complement of verbs such as *wonder*.

16 See Kayne (1981b: 361fn.15) for further references on this construction which seems to be subject to a certain amount of subtle variation among speakers. Kayne (1981b: 357fn. 12) insists on the fact that these examples are formed by analogy with the SC construction of these same verbs. In other words, the grammaticality of (i) is due to the fact that this verb also has (ii):

    i.   Je le crois être *?(le plus) intelligent
         'I consider him to be the most intelligent'

    ii.   Je le crois (le plus) intelligent
         'I consider him the most intelligent'

This analogy is supported by the fact that verbs such as *nier* 'deny,' and *constater* 'consider,' which do not have the SC construction, do not have the clitic ECM construction either:

    iii. *Je le constate être le plus intelligent
         'I consider him to be the most intelligent'

    iv. *Je le constate (le plus) intelligent
         'I consider him the most intelligent'

Although the analogous influence might play a role, it does not provide an explanation for the additional contrastive constraint that is operative in CP complements, but not in SC complements.

17 As noted, movement to SpecAGR$_S$P of nonreferential subjects must take place overtly: *it seems to be raining, advantage seems to be taken of me*. It is not immediately clear why there should be this difference between movement to SpecAGR$_S$P with *seem* and to SpecAGR$_O$P with *believe*. It might simply be that in the case of movement to SpecAGR$_S$P with *seem*, another requirement, besides pure case considerations, plays a role in forcing overt movement. We might here think of a general requirement of predication or (a version of) the Extended Projection Principle.

18 There is a potential objection to this analysis. It could be argued that it is possible for the NP subject of the infinitive to move overtly to the higher SpecAGR$_O$P in one fell swoop, this long movement being licensed at LF by covert AGR$_S$P movement to SpecCP, where the trace of the NP subject in SpecAGR$_S$P position could be licensed by Form–Chain. If such a derivation were permitted, overt or covert movement of AGR$_S$P to SpecCP would entail no difference between *believe*-type verbs and *estimate*-type verbs: in both cases, referential NPs could be licensed as subjects of the infinitival complement.

    However, this scenario violates the shortest move condition built into the Minimalist Program: of two derivations, the one with the fewer steps and the shorter moves will be selected as the only derivation possible, by economy of derivations (Chomsky 1995). In the derivation adopted in the text, AGR$_S$P moves to SpecCP and feeds subsequent NP movement to SpecAGR$_O$P in the ECM complements of both *believe*- and *estimate*-type verbs. This derivation involves two steps. The derivation in which the NP first undergoes long movement to the matrix $\text{SpecAGR}_O\text{P}$, while its trace is licensed later by covert movement of AGR_SP, likewise involves two steps. In both cases, AGR_SP movement to SpecCP is equally long. However, the latter derivation is ruled out via the shortest move condition: the step involving long NP movement out of $\text{SpecAGR}_S\text{P}$ to the matrix $\text{SpecAGR}_O\text{P}$ is longer than the same step of NP movement in the other, more economical derivation, where it takes place out of the AGR_SP in SpecCP. As a result, the analysis in the text can be fully maintained. As pointed out to me by Marcel den Dikken, this argument provides an empirical basis for favoring the derivational approach outlined in Chomsky (1995) over a purely representational view of syntax.

19   Note that this analysis of passive *videre* 'see' might throw a new light on the well-known English alternation between active and passive *see* with respect to the presence of *to* on the infinitive:

   i.   Zigomar saw Zénobie (*to) cross the street
   ii.   Zénobie was seen *(to) cross the street

The analysis proposed here suggests that passive *see* in English simply involves the syntactic configuration of *seem*, which also involves a *to-* infinitive. This analysis is corroborated by the often noted observation that passive *see* as in (ii) can have a 'psychological' meaning close to *believe* (= *seem*) that (i) lacks.

A similar problem shows up in a curious difference between *want* and *expect*. Both verbs select a CP, with an optional complementizer *for* assigning case to the subject of the infinitive:

   iii. Zigomar wanted/expected (for) Zénobie to cross the street

Nevertheless, *want* does not allow for passivization while *expect* does:

   iv. Zénobie was *wanted/expected to cross the street

Under the analysis where the subject of the infinitive receives case inside the infinitive by the C° *for*, there is no reason for that subject to ever leave the CP, moving to the matrix $\text{SpecAGR}_S\text{P}$ position. The case-assigning properties of the complementizer *for* do not change depending on active or passive morphology in the matrix clause. According to this view, passives of *want*-type verbs should always be ungrammatical. The grammaticality of the example with *expect*, therefore, is quite unexpected. Note, however, that passives of certain verbs in Dutch and French (*veronderstellen*, *supposer* 'suppose') can be used with the raising configuration of *seem*-type verbs (cf. *infra*). The passive of *expect* is very close semantically to these cases: passive *expect*, *veronderstellen*, 'suppose,' *supposer* 'suppose' have an epistemic meaning close to 'should.' This meaning might be derived along the lines of the 'zero-semantics' analysis presented in section 6.2 for verbs that are ambiguous between control and raising. We will therefore assume that the passive of *expect* in (iv) licenses the raising configuration of *seem*-type verbs, independently of its ECM construction of the *want*-type.

20   The presence of the subject in SpecCP, and its adjacency to C° *de*, can be tested by the impossibility of inserting adverbs between *de* and the subject (*Et les linguistes de (?toujours) remplir leurs verres/Et les linguistes (*toujours) de remplir leurs verres*).

21   Two other verbs, *empêcher* 'prevent,' and *permettre* 'allow' also display the construction exemplified in (89) with *soupçonner* 'suspect' (Ruwet 1983):

   i.   Cet attentat a empêché la linguistique d'être discutée au dernier congrès
       'That terrorist attack prevented linguistics from being discussed at the last congress'

   ii.   Le plastique troué a permis à l'eau de s'échapper
       'The punctured plastic allowed the water to escape'

iii. Louis soupçonnait cette histoire d'être montée de toutes pièces
'Louis suspected that story to have been completely invented'

All constructions share the same structural properties. Although all three verbs can select three arguments in their 'standard' use as control verbs (*prevent someone from doing something, suspect someone of doing something, allow someone to do something*), the constructions with an inanimate indirect object behave as if both postverbal arguments were a single sentential complement, corresponding to the single complement NP in (iii) and (iv):

iv. Cet attentat a empêché la discussion de la linguistique
'That terrorist attack prevented the discussion of linguistics'

v. Le plastique troué a permis la contamination du terrain
'The punctured plastic allowed for the contamination of the site'

vi. Louis soupçonnait une histoire montée de toutes pièces
'Louis suspected a made-up story'

This analysis is confirmed by the fact that the infinitives in (i–iii), being part of a larger constituent, cannot be pronominalized on the matrix verb, while the infinitives in control constructions, which are independent arguments of the matrix verb, can be pronominalized. Another piece of evidence that (i–iii) and (iv–vi) involve uses of the relevant verbs with a single complement, CP in (i–iii) and NP in (iv–vi), comes from their behavior with respect to temporal modification: the sentences (i–vi) cannot be modified by verbs testing punctuality such as *venir de* 'just have.' The 'standard' use of *empêcher* 'prevent,' *permettre* 'allow,' and *soupçonner* 'suspect' as control verbs, on the contrary, quite freely allows for modification by *venir de* 'just have.'

In the text, *soupçonner* 'suspect' is analyzed as a *believe*-type verb in disguise that selects a [+ Focus] CP. The uses of the verbs *empêcher* 'prevent,' *permettre* 'allow' with a [+ Focus] CP should be related to ECM with the causative *faire*: in a sense, these verbs are causatives in disguise.

22 It is not clear to me why there is this difference between *seem*-type verbs and *croire*-type verbs in French. It might be due to the fact that *seem*-type verbs always seem to impose a 'strong' [+ Focus] feature on the C° head of the CP they select, while *believe*-type verbs can select either a 'strong' [+ Focus] feature (triggering AGR_SP movement as in English) or a 'weak' [+ Focus] feature, triggering movement of an element in the embedded clause at LF as in French. The fact that *seem* always selects a 'strong' [+ Focus] feature might be due to the fact that *seem* always requires the comparison of the event and its trace (cf. *supra*). However, this still leaves us without an answer for the question why 'weak' Focus cannot trigger covert AGR_SP movement to SpecCP at LF in the complement of French *croire* 'believe'-type verbs. I will leave this question for further research.

23 Cf. Meulen (1990) for a description of aspectual verbs as Generalized Quantifiers in a three-dimensional square of oppositions which allows for an explanation of various semantic relations between aspectual verbs.

24 It might be noted that something similar is the case for English *will* ('possible' future, *she will have two girls and two boys*) as opposed to *be going to* ('necessary' future: *she is going to have two girls and two boys*). Crosslinguistically, the necessity meaning is nevertheless not always linked up with the counterparts of *go/aller*. In Swedish, the auxiliary *ska* 'will' expresses necessary future in the context cited, whereas the auxiliary *kommer att* 'go' expresses the 'neutral' possible future.

25 Note that perfective aspect for the counterpart of *aller* 'go' and of epistemic *moeten* 'must' seems to be perfectly possible in Dutch:

i. Het is gaan regenen

It is go rain
'it started raining'

ii.   Het had moeten regenen om de oogst te redden
It had must rain to the crop to save
'It should have rained to save the crops'

However, in these cases the usual perfective participle marked by *ge-* has been replaced by the infinitival form, a possibility that also exists in other complementation – even raising – structures where well-known word order differences are correlated with it:

iii.   Jan is begonnen/beginnen een boek te lezen
Jan is begun a book to read
'Jan started to read a book'

iv.   Jan is een boek beginnen/*begonnen te lezen
Jan is a book begin to read   (Southern Dutch)
'Jan started to read a book'

Importantly, in (i) the perfective participle is impossible:

v.   *Het is gegaan regenen
It is went rain
'It has started to rain'

vi.   *Het had gemoeten regenen om de oogst te redden
It had must rain to the crop to save
'It should have rained to save the crops'

It seems then that the structures in (i) are saved by the switch of participial morphology to infinitival morphology. I have no further explanation for this intriguing fact.

26   Lyons (1977) makes the distinction between objective epistemic necessity and subjective epistemic necessity: the latter is necessity related to the world of the speaker as in (i).

i.   Il doit/a dû faire chaud dans le Kalahari aujourd'hui
'It must be/have been warm in the Kalahari today'

Subjective epistemic necessity involves probability. Importantly, this subjective epistemic meaning of *devoir* 'must' can be combined with perfective aspect.

27   English has something similar: the NP *shit* in *I didn't see shit* does not usually refer to actual excrement, but means 'anything.'

28   It is also remarkable that the beneficiary/maleficiary interpretation for the Goal argument in the 'thematic' use of verbs such as *promettre* 'promise' and *menacer* 'threaten,' as well as the negative connotation of 'risk' in *risquer* 'risk,' seem to be retained in the 'nonthematic' use of these verbs in raising contexts. In these cases, the meaning is slightly changed to the positive (*promettre* 'promise') or negative (*menacer* 'threaten,' *risquer* 'risk') consequences of the possible or necessary situation.

2

PSEUDO-RAISING

(in collaboration with João Costa)*

In this chapter, a number of consequences of the raising analysis for *seem* and *believe* in chapter 1 are explored in further detail. In particular, apparent cases of raising out of tensed complements with *seem* and *believe* will be given an analysis that does not involve raising proper, but that nevertheless is entirely parallel to raising out of infinitival complements. Crosslinguistic variation with respect to this construction is shown to derive from independent properties. The results of this analysis confirm the account presented in chapter 1, and raise new questions for the complementary distribution between finite and infinitival complements of raising verbs.

1 Apparent raising out of tensed CPs in Portuguese

Besides the typical cases of raising exemplified in (1) and (2), (spoken) European Portuguese displays a construction which seems to involve raising out of a tensed CP as shown in (3):

(1)   *pro*_{imp} parece que tu estás doente
      it   seems that you are sick

(2)   Tu pareces estar doente
      you seem$_{2SG}$ to be sick

(3) a. Tu pareces que estás doente
       you seem$_{2SG}$ that (you) are$_{2SG}$ sick

    b. Os meninos parecem que estão doentes
       the children seem$_{3PL}$ that (they) are$_{3PL}$ sick

    c. Nós parecemos que estamos felizes
       we seem$_{1PL}$ that (we) are$_{1PL}$ happy

In (3), both the matrix and the embedded verb exhibit agreement with the matrix subject. This suggests that the subject of the embedded tensed

CP has raised out of this clause to the matrix subject position, agreeing successively with both the embedded and the matrix AGR_S. In this respect, it is important to point out that the sentences in (3) are substantially different from cases like (4):

(4) Tu, pro_{imp} parece   que estás doente
     you, it   seems   that you are sick

Here, the sentence initial subject is clearly left-dislocated, since the matrix verb exhibits no agreement and the sentence degrades significantly without comma intonation.

However, if the sentences in (3) were indeed to involve raising from the embedded to the matrix subject position, they constitute a clear case of improper movement (Chomsky 1981, 1986a, 1995), since the embedded subject would have to move from its A-position to another A-position via the intermediate and unavoidable SpecCP A´-position. Moreover, raising out of tensed CPs violates the uniqueness requirement on case-assignment to chains (Chomsky 1981), since the extracted NP is moving from a case-position to another case-position which is known to be an illegitimate movement. Finally, analyzing the cases in (3) in the same way as *bona fide* raising in (2) immediately raises the question why such sentences are generally excluded across languages, as in English, French, and Spanish (5), which only display raising out of untensed complements:[1]

(5) a. *You seem that (you) are sick You seem to be sick   (English)

     b. *Tu sembles que tu es malade Tu sembles être malade (French)

     c. *Pareces que estás enfermo   Pareces estar enfermo   (Spanish)

The phenomenon in (3) will henceforth be referred to as pseudo-raising. Indeed, it will be argued below that closer scrutiny falsifies the first impression that *bona fide* raising is involved in these cases.

The data are nevertheless slightly more complex. Despite the data in (5a), English also seems to display sentences similar to those of Portuguese (3) if the selected complementizer is *like*, *as if*, or *as though*. To our knowledge, these data were first noted by Lappin (1983, 1984) as a problem for the raising analysis of *seem*:

(6) a. The cows seem {like as if/as though/*that} they have eaten too much grass

     b. The cows look/sound {like/as if/as though *that} they have eaten too much grass

    c.   It looks {like/as if/as though/*that} the cows have eaten too much grass

    d.   *It looks {that like/like that} the cows have eaten too much grass

In (6ab), the pronominal subject of the embedded sentence *they* is obligatorily coreferential with the subject of the matrix clause *the cows*. At first sight, the pronoun looks like a resumptive pronoun spelled out after raising of *the cows* out of the embedded clause. Clearly, these sentences strongly resemble the Portuguese cases of pseudo-raising. The sentence (6c) shows that pseudo-raising is not obligatory: the matrix subject can be an expletive. Strikingly, the complementizers involved in these constructions have comparative properties. The complementizer status of *like*, *as if*, and *as though* can be illustrated by their complementary distribution with other complementizers. Verbs such as *look* and *sound* only select *like* as a complementizer (cf. (6bc)). Moreover, *like* is in complementary distribution with other complementizers (cf. (6d)), which may be explained if the two forms in (6d) are competing for the same position (Rooryck 1997, Ch 1 this volume).

These data raise two questions. First, why do Portuguese and English have apparent raising-to-subject out of tensed CPs?[2] Second, why is the phenomenon restricted to certain types of complementizers in English? In the next section, some other properties of these contructions will be investigated which correlate with exceptional raising-to-subject out of tensed CPs in Portuguese and English.

2 Similarities and differences between Portuguese and English

2.1 Definiteness effect on the matrix subjects

In both English and Portuguese, pseudo-raising constructions display definiteness effects. This is shown in the contrast between (7a) and (7b) in Portuguese. In English, the same restriction applies, as is clear from the fact that a bare plural may only appear in these structures if an adverb such as *always* is present, yielding a generic reading (cf. (7c)). The function of the adverbs is to unselectively bind the bare plural, assigning it a universal (hence, definite) reading. A truly indefinite reading as in (7d) seems to be unavailable (Lappin 1983, 1984).

(7) a. *Umas meninas parecem que estão doentes
        a few girls seem$_{3PL}$ that they are sick

      b. As meninas parecem que estão doentes
        the girls seem that they are sick

      c. Cows *(always) seem like they have eaten too much grass

d. *Few cows seem like they have eaten too much grass

2.2 Restrictions in the complement of seem/parecer

A second difference between these constructions in European Portuguese and English concerns the type of complements licensed by *seem/parecer*. In Portuguese, only predicative verbs may appear in these constructions, as the contrast with the transitive verb in (8c) illustrates:

(8) a. Tu pareces que estás parvo
     you seem$_{2SG}$ that you are stupid

 b. Tu pareces que continuas parvo
     you seem$_{2SG}$ that you continue stupid

 c. *Tu pareces que comes o bolo
     you seem$_{2SG}$ that you eat the pastry

In English, such a restriction does not apply:

(9) a. The cows seem like they are happy

 b. The cows seem like they have eaten too much grass

 c. The cows seem like they continue to be happy

2.3 Restrictions on the bound pronoun

Another difference between English and European Portuguese has to do with the feature specification of the pronoun which surfaces as subject of the matrix and embedded sentences. In English, only the second person pronoun (*you*) or the third person plural (*they*) may appear:

(10) a. The cows seem like they have eaten too much grass

 b. You seem like you have been happy all your life

 c. *We seem like we have eaten too many quails

 d. *This cow seems like it has been eating too much grass

 e. *I seem like I have eaten too many quails

Portuguese lacks such a restriction on person. All the pronouns may appear, as (11) shows:

(11) a. Eu pareço que estou feliz

I seem$_{1SG}$ that I am happy

b. Tu pareces que estás feliz
you seem$_{2SG}$ that you are happy

c. Ele parece que está feliz
he seems$_{3SG}$ that he is happy

d. Nós parecemos que estamos felizes
we seem$_{1PL}$ that we are$_{1PL}$ happy

e. Vocês parecem que estão felizes
you seem$_{3PL}$ that you are$_{2PL}$ happy

f. Eles parecem que estão felizes
they seem$_{3PL}$ that they are$_{3PL}$ happy

The questions raised by the data in (1) to (11) can be summarized as follows:

(12) i. Why does pseudo-raising occur in Portuguese and English, but not in e.g. French?

ii. What is the role of the comparative complementizers in English pseudo-raising?

iii. What is the reason for the definiteness effect on the subject?

iv. Why are pronouns restricted to second and third in English pseudo-raising, but not in Portuguese?

v. Why are the sentential complements in Portuguese pseudo-raising restricted to predicative verbs?

3 Pseudo-raising and Strong Binding

We would like to claim that sentences involving pseudo-raising are reducible to an analysis along the lines of that proposed for *easy-to-please* constructions (Chomsky 1977, 1995).

(13)   John$_i$ is easy [$_{CP}$ O$_i$ [$_{IP}$ to please t_i]]

It has been argued that in these constructions the subject NP is base-generated in the matrix subject position, getting its theta-role by means of Strong Binding with the operator moved to SpecCP.

In section 2.3, it was observed that the pronouns which may function as variables for the matrix NP are *you* and *they* in English, and *pro* in Portuguese. A closer look reveals that exactly these pronouns may have a quasi-universal interpretation. As suggested by Cinque (1988), quasi-universal interpretation arises when the pronouns are bound by a universal operator. In the examples (14adef), generic tense is the binder of the variables:

(14) a. In France, they drive like madmen

   b. They say that it's going to rain

   c. They announced that the war is over, but I don't think so

   d. You never know . . .

   e. How do you say that in English?

   f. In Holland, you don't drink good coffee

The claim that Strong Binding is the mechanism behind pseudo-raising can be easily tested. If the embedded sentence contains no bindee, as in (15), it is ungrammatical. Since a full NP is not part of the pronouns able to bear a quasi-universal interpretation, it will not be able to function as a variable for the matrix subject. Therefore, the matrix subject will not be able to get a theta-role, and the sentences will be ruled out as violations of the theta-criterion. Note that the test is even more convincing if the embedded subject is an epithet as in (15c). In this case, it might be expected that an epithet could establish coreference with the matrix subject from an interpretive point of view, since in topic constructions as (15d) such coreference is possible.

(15) a. *Tu pareces que o Paulo está doente
      you seem$_{2SG}$ that Paulo is sick

   b. Kim$_i$ seems like she$_i$/*Sandy is happy

   c. *The cows seem like the poor things have eaten too much grass

   d. As for the cows, it seems that/like the poor things have
      eaten too much grass

If the construction involves Strong Binding, there is no reason why it should be limited to subject bindees. This prediction is confirmed. Lappin (1983) notes that the bindee need not be the subject itself, as illustrated in (16):

(16) a. Kim$_i$ seems as if Sandy likes her$_i$/*Bill

   b. Mary$_i$ appears as if her$_i$/*Bill's job is going well

An analysis based on Strong Binding also easily explains the definiteness effects on the subject of pseudo-raising constructions in both English and Portuguese (cf. (7) above). Cinque (1988) proposes that only universal operators may function as binders for pronouns capable of receiving a quasi-universal interpretation. It follows straightforwardly that only definite strong NPs may appear in the matrix subject position, since only this type of NP can function as a universal operator. As a result, the question (12iii) is solved.

The difference between English and Portuguese with respect to the feature specification of the pronouns which may appear in the embedded subject position (cf. (10) and (11), question (12iv)) is now derived by the types of pronouns that are available in English and Portuguese for a quasi-universal interpretation. In English, only *they* and *you* may receive such a quasi-universal interpretation, while in Portuguese *pro* is the relevant pronominal form. Since *pro* is underspecified with respect to features, it will get the number and gender features of any matrix NP it is coindexed with. The language-specific restrictions on the feature specification of the subjects in pseudo-raising are therefore related to the type of pronouns available for a quasi-universal interpretation in those languages.

Summing up, the pseudo-raising construction can be viewed as an instance of Strong Binding interacting with the pronouns which may receive a quasi-universal interpretation. This allows for an explanation of the fact that there can be only one subject in these constructions (cf. (15)) lest a violation of the theta-criterion ensue. Moreover, the subject which may appear has to be definite, otherwise the embedded pronouns would not be bound. Finally, the different set of pronouns available in English and Portuguese for a quasi-universal interpretation also explains the difference in the kind of subjects each language permits in pseudo-raising.

Comparing the pseudo-raising construction with the *easy-to-please* construction, it is admittedly the case that *easy-to-please* constructions do not display the definiteness effects and person specification restrictions of pseudo-raising constructions. However, this situation is not a result of Strong Binding itself. It should be pointed out that the nature of the variable in both cases is radically different: in the case of *easy-to-please* constructions, the variable is a *Wh-* operator, while pseudo-raising constructions involve a pronominal variable that must be bound by a quasi-universal operator. Although it is not clear why this is so, the data seem to point to the correctness of this hypothesis.

4 How does Strong Binding come about?

Before the other questions raised in (12) can be answered, it is necessary to enquire how Strong Binding can come about in sentences such as (3). From the point of view of binding, *they/pro* in (3) and (5) cannot be bound by their antecedent, since pseudo-raising clearly involves a CP barrier. In order to circumvent this problem, two hypotheses can be advanced. Under the first hypothesis, the bound pronoun raises to SpecCP in the same way as the empty operator raises to SpecCP in *easy-to-please* constructions. However, it is not clear why the pronoun would raise to SpecCP, since it would not raise to license properties of its own, but only for the sake of licensing the matrix subject by Strong Binding. In addition, the bound pronoun would have to be raised to SpecCP from various positions in the embedded clause: the sentence (16b) above involves binding of the possessor inside a DP. Such a construction-specific type of raising would be highly unlikely. A second hypothesis is that a constituent containing the bound pronoun would move to SpecCP. Chomsky (1986a, 1995), has argued, based on arguments advanced by Picallo (1985) and Torrego (1985), that constituents can move into the matrix clause out of a larger constituent sitting in the embedded SpecCP. As a result, it can be assumed that NPs in the matrix clause can also bind antecedents in a constituent sitting in an embedded SpecCP.

With respect to pseudo-raising, the question arises as to which constituent containing the bound pronoun could be a candidate for moving to SpecCP in order to enable these pronouns to be bound by the quasi-universal operator in the matrix clause of (3) and (5)? Rooryck (1997, Ch 1 this volume) has argued that raising verbs such as *seem* and *believe* involve overt raising of the embedded AGR_SP to SpecCP, and that this movement feeds further movement of the subject of AGR_SP to the higher $SpecAGR_SP$ (*seem*) or $SpecAGR_OP$ (*believe*, cf. Postal 1974, Chomsky 1995). This analysis is represented in (21ab):

(17) a. To Sue, Alfred seems to be smoking

$[_{AGRSP}$ Alfred [[seems]AGR_S] $[_{VP}$ $t_{V°}$ $[_{CP}$ $[_{AGRSP}$ t_{Alfred} to be smoking]$_C$ $C°$ t_{AGRSP}]]

b. Sue believes Alfred to be smoking[3]

Sue $[_{XP}$ believes
$[_{AGROP}$ Alfred $t_{V°-AO°}$] $[_{VP}$ $t_{V°}$ $[_{CP}$ $[_{AGRSP}$ t_{Alfred} to be smoking]$_k$ $C°$ t_{AGRSP}]]

Rooryck (1997) argues that this analysis allows for a simplification of the types of sentential complementation. Recall that Chomsky (1981) had to allow for a rule of S′-deletion, reformulated in later frameworks as a difference between CP and AGR_SP selection. The ill-motivated distinction between these two types of complementation is made superfluous by the analysis in (16). The property-motivating movement of AGR_SP to SpecCP is argued to involve a [+Focus] property in the C° selected by raising verbs. Rooryck (1997) shows that such an analysis allows for an explanation of both the focus-related restrictions on ECM constructions observed for French by Kayne (1981b) and Pollock (1985), and the focus-related Derived Object Constraint formulated by Postal (1974). In order to further clarify the motivation for this [+Focus] feature, let us briefly examine the way in which Rooryck (1997) explains its interpretive import in raising constructions with *seem*. Traditional analyses of *seem*-type verbs have mostly overlooked the fact that these verbs are often related to verbs of comparison. In many languages, the verb stem of verbs of comparison and *seem* are identical: Dutch *lijken* 'seem' and *vergelijken* 'compare,' French *sembler* 'seem' and *ressembler* 'resemble,' *paraître* 'seem' and *comparer* 'compare,' Spanish *parecer* 'seem' and *comparar* 'compare.' In English, the raising verb *be likely* is derived from *like* which also yields the adjective *alike*, and the comparative verb *liken*. *Like* also shows up as the obligatory complementizer of the verb *look* as in (5). Following Bennis (1986), and Moro (1992), Rooryck (1997) argues that the subject *it* in (18) is not a dummy element marking the subject position. Moro (1992) analyzes *it* as the predicate of the SC complement of *seem* (cf. Moro (1992) for arguments and discussion).

(18)   It seems that John is sick

Under Rooryck's (1997) analysis adopted here, the pronoun *it* should be analyzed as a deictic pronoun, referring to an event at hand that is compared to the event expressed by the sentential complement of *seem*. The sentence (19a) then can be semantically glossed as (19b):

(19) a. It *seems* that/like/as if John is sick

b. There is a contextually salient event (= it) that *resembles* a (typical) event in which John is sick

The pronoun *it* functions as a *pro*-CP. This property can probably be derived through the predicative nature of the SC, which mirrors the event properties of the CP onto *it*. Moro's predicate inversion analysis can now be viewed as a case of predicate Focus. Following Partee (1991), Focus can informally be taken to involve implicit reference to a set of which one member is given saliency. In the case of *seem*, it is argued that the set referred to consists of two members, one of which is given saliency by predicate inversion/Focus, namely deictic *it*. It is crucial to emphasize that predicate inversion/Focus is triggered by an element in the matrix clause in this case. *Pro*-CP *it* is not a dummy, but an essential element for the interpretation of *seem* which compares two overt elements. As a result, this immediately explains why *it* cannot be replaced by the CP complement (* *That Alfred has* *eaten his veggies seems)*: such a replacement would eliminate an essential member of the comparison set.

This analysis of *seem* as involving the comparison of situations or events is extended to those cases where raising out of the sentential complement has occurred. Rooryck's (1997, Ch 1 this volume) analysis immediately raises the question as to what are the two events being compared in (20)?

(20) Alfred seems/appears to have eaten his veggies

Assuming the analysis in (17a), Rooryck (1997) argues that this configuration satisfies the comparative interpretation required by *seem*. The configuration in the embedded CP in (17a) is an instance of an operator–variable relation. Via selection under government, *seem* turns $C°$ into a comparative Focus operator. The morphological form of the complementizers in tensed sentences suggests that the $C°$ selected by *seem* can be overtly comparative (cf. (5)). It is argued that this comparative selection establishes the background set which is required for Focus. Movement of AGR_SP to SpecCP allows the comparative Focus $C°$ to establish a comparative relation between the AGR_SP in SpecCP and its variable left behind after movement. This is therefore a reflexive operator–variable relation. Formally speaking, the configuration is strictly identical to an operator–variable relation of the *Wh*-type. In (21), there is an operator establishing a set, and a relation between the set and the variable. Another way of expressing this would be to say that (21a) involves a type-token distinction, where type stands for the set of elements such that they are books, and token for the specific token of that type that is questioned. This is represented in (21c).

(21) a. $[_{CP} [_{NP}$ Which book] did $[_{AGRSP}$ John read t_{NP}]]

   b. Which x, x an element of the set S of books, is such that John read x

   c. Which x, x a token of the type X, X = book, is such that John read x

Similarly, Rooryck (1997, Ch 1 this volume) translates the reflexive operator–variable relation in the CP complement of *seem* as in (22b), which is rendered more transparent in (22cd):

(22) a. Alfred seems $[_{CP} [_{AGRSP}$ to have eaten his veggies] C_{+FOC} t_{AGRSP}]

   b. This is an x, x an element of the set X of Alfred's veggie-eating situations, such that x resembles the set X

   c. This is an x, x a token of the type X, which involves Alfred's
      veggie-eating situations, such that x resembles the type X

   d. This instance of Alfred eating his veggies resembles the 'typical'
      instance of Alfred eating his veggies, (this is not quite a
      full-fledged version of Alfred eating his veggies)

In all of these representations, the LF-style interpretation takes an element/token of the set/type of situations and compares it to the others of that set/type, establishing an operation of resemblance between the element/token and the set/type. Rooryck (1997) also offers independent tests based on the analysis of negative islands developed in Rooryck (1992a) to show that the $C°$ involved in raising constructions involves a [+Focus] property.

Coming back to the analysis of pseudo-raising, the relevance of this analysis may be clear: it independently motivates raising a constituent (AGR_SP) containing the pronominal variables *they/pro* to SpecCP. Only in this position can these pronouns receive a quasi-universal interpretation, since they can be Strongly Bound by the matrix subject functioning as a quasi-universal operator. It can be assumed that in pseudo-raising, movement of AGR_SP to SpecCP takes place covertly. Such covert movement of AGR_SP to SpecCP is by no means limited to pseudo-raising: Rooryck (1997, Ch 1 this volume) argues that it also takes place in the ECM constructions of those verbs that are subject to Postal's Derived Object Constraint.

Note that this analysis establishes a correlation between covert movement of a finite AGR_SP and the presence of bound variables in this AGR_SP. This correlation in itself is not explained. That is, it remains unclear why the mere movement of AGR_SP to SpecCP is associated with the obligatory presence of bound variables in that AGR_SP. One possible explanation is that the presence of bound variables allows for the CP to be interpreted as a predicate, much in the way the infinitival CP in *easy-to-please* constructions is converted into a predicate by movement of the *Wh-* operator to SpecCP (den Dikken & Mulder 1992). However, such an analysis does not explain why this conversion to a predicate is only possible in the context of *seem*.

Importantly, this analysis offers an insight as to the role of the comparative complementizers *like, as if, as though* in the English pseudo-raising constructions (question (12ii)). The comparative nature of these complementizers must be related to the configuration of comparison that is necessarily established for Strong Binding to take place. It is interesting to note that overt raising with *seem*, as in (17a), does not require an overt comparative complementizer in the infinitival complement, while the Strong Binding cases in (6) must overtly mark the comparative nature of the complementizer in the finite CP with *like, as if,* or *as though*.

The strictly parallel analysis of raising and pseudo-raising raises a number of additional questions with respect to the distribution of finite and infinitival complements in comparative configurations. Under the terms of this analysis, it appears that overt raising only occurs with infinitival complements after overt movement of the infinitive to SpecCP, while Strong Binding (pseudo-raising) is limited to finite CPs moving covertly to SpecCP. This parallelism clearly needs an explanation. I will leave it for further research.

5 Restrictions on movement of AGR$_S$P to SpecCP

So far, most of the similarities and differences between English and Portuguese pseudo-raising have been derived (cf. section 3). Pseudo-raising is a case of Strong Binding of a pronoun by an NP functioning as a universal operator. This derives the fact that the binder in the matrix clause must be definite (question 12iii). The restriction to second and third person in English, which is absent in Portuguese (question 12iv), can be attributed to the fact that only second and third pronouns in English may have a quasi-universal interpretation. Finally, the role of the comparative complementizers (question 12ii) can be related to the idea that the tensed IP moves to SpecCP in order to establish a comparative semantic relation between that IP interpreted as an event-type and the IP-trace, interpreted as a variable event-token. Movement of IP into SpecCP is a precondition for Strong Binding of pronouns contained in that IP by the matrix subject.

Two questions remain to be answered: why does the construction occur in English and Portuguese, but not in e.g. French? (question 12i), and why are there restrictions on the complement of *seem parecer* (question 12v)? Recall the pattern from (8) and (9), repeated here as (23) and (24):

(23) a. Tu pareces que estás parvo
you seem$_{2SG}$ that you are stupid

b. Tu pareces que continuas parvo
you seem$_{2SG}$ that you continue stupid

c. *Tu pareces que comes o bolo
you seem$_{2SG}$ that you eat the pastry

(24) a. The cows seem like they are happy

b. The cows seem like they have eaten too much grass

c. The cows seem like they continue to be happy

While in Portuguese these constructions are restricted to small clause complements, in English such a restriction does not occur.

At first sight, the complement restriction suggests that the difference between English and Portuguese is due to the type of constituent that can be moved to SpecCP. If covert movement to SpecCP applies to AGR_SPs in English, and is restricted to small clause complements in Portuguese, the contrast in (23) is explained. However, this analysis is very unlikely. The sentences (25) and (26) show that both English and Portuguese can move infinitival complements to the left periphery of the sentence.

(25) a. Eat too much grass, I'm sure the cows will

b. Drive that car, John can

c. Try those quails, you must

(26) a. Pastar demasiado, tenho a certeza de que as vacas vão

b. Conduzir aquele carro, o Paulo pode

c. Provar aquelas codornizes, tu deves

If the difference between English and Portuguese were related to the type of constituent moving to SpecCP, we would expect this difference also to show up in other types of movement of clausal complements to the left periphery, contrary to fact.

Another analysis for the crosslinguistic difference illustrated in (23–24) can be proposed, however. More specifically, it appears that covert movement of AGR_SP to SpecCP in pseudo-raising is restricted to C°s that are fully comparative. In English, only *like* is a fully comparative C°, and this C° does not impose any restrictions on the type of clause selected:

(27) a. Eating {like *that} she ate . . .

b. Talking {like *that} she talked . . .

c. Intelligent {like *that} he is . . .

d. Sick {like *that} he is . . .

In Portuguese, *como* 'how/as' is comparative, but it is not a C°. Rather, it should be viewed as an element in SpecCP, since it occurs in positions occupied by Wh-constituents. The element *que* is a C° complementizer. Interestingly, the contrast between (28ab) and (28cd) shows that it only functions as a comparative complementizer if its complement includes small clauses:

(28) a. Comer {como/*que} ela comeu . . .
eat {like/that} she ate . . .

b. Falar {como/*que} ela falou . . .
talk {like/that} she talked . . .

    c. Inteligente {como/que} ele é
       intelligent {like/that} he is

    d. Doente {como/que} ele está
       sick {like/that} he is

Since *como* is not a $C°$, it is not expected to appear in pseudo-raising constructions:

(29) a. The cows seem {*that/like} they have eaten too much grass

      b. As vacas parecem {que/*como} estão felizes
        'The cows seem {that/like} they are happy'

Importantly then, the Portuguese complementizer *que* only functions as a comparative $C°$ in the context of small clauses. Now recall that pseudo-raising in Portuguese is restricted to CPs containing a small clause (question 12v). In the cases of (28cd), there is overt movement of AGR_SP to a Focus position. It can now be argued that the same movement operation that takes place in (28cd) with comparative *que*, is covertly operative in the cases of pseudo-raising. As a result, only small clause complements allow for movement of AGR_SP to SpecCP, be it covert or overt. Therefore, only small clauses create the configuration permitting Strong Binding. This now answers the question (12v) as to why the sentential complements in Portuguese pseudo-raising are restricted to predicative verbs.

This explanation, which is dependent on the nature of $C°$, also explains the cross-linguistic limitations: if Portuguese is compared to the closely related Romance languages French and Spanish, it appears that only Portuguese *que* has this comparative function, as illustrated by (30) through (32). Therefore, it is expected that pseudo-raising only exists in Portuguese.

(30)   *Portuguese:*

     Inteligente {como/que} és, podes fazer o que quiseres
     'Intelligent as you are, you can do what you want'

(31)   *French:*

     Intelligent {comme/*que} tu es, tu peux faire ce que tu veux
     'Intelligent as you are, you can do what you want'

(32)   *Spanish:*

     Inteligente {como/*que} eres, puedes hacer lo que quieras
     'Intelligent as you are, you can do what you want'

An interesting confirmation of this hypothesis was brought to our attention by two speaker linguists of Argentinian Spanish, Claudia Borgonovo and Ana Arregui, for whom both pseudo-raising and comparison with *que* have an equally marginal status:

(33)   *Argentinian Spanish:*

 a. Inteligente {como ??que} eres, puedes hacer lo que quieras
  'Intelligent as you are, you can do what you want'

 b. ??Vos pareces que estás enfermo
  You seem$_{2SG}$ that you are sick

The fact that pseudo-raising occurs in English and Portuguese, but not in e.g. French (question (12i)), can thus be reduced to the language-specific extent to which complementizers can have a comparative function.

6 Pseudo-raising in *believe* contexts

In the previous sections, it was shown that Strong Binding (pseudo-raising) into finite complements of *seem* involves a configuration that is parallel to that required for raising out of infinitival complements. In both cases, AGR$_S$P moves to SpecCP before Strong Binding or raising-to-subject takes place. The question now arises whether pseudo-raising also occurs with other verbs related to *seem*. More specifically, Rooryck (1997, this volume Ch 1) has argued that there is a complementarity between *seem* and *believe* in that *believe* should be taken to be the accusative counterpart of nominative *seem*, in the same way accusative *have* is the counterpart of nominative *be* (Freeze 1992; Kayne 1994). This relation between *seem* and *believe* can be expressed as follows (Rooryck 1997):

(34) a. <nom> **SEEM** $[_{DP}$ NP$_{EXP}$ D°/P°$_{DAT}$ [CP]]
   It   seemed   to all of us [that this
                     was wrong]

 b. <nom> **BELIEVE** <acc> $[_{DP}$ NP$_{EXP}$ D°/P°$_{DAT}$ [CP]]
      (SEEM+DATIVE)

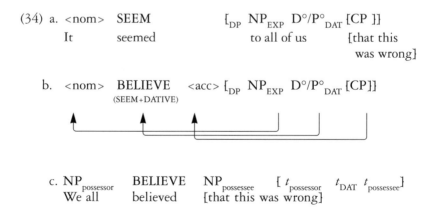

 c. NP$_{possessor}$ **BELIEVE** NP$_{possessee}$ $[$ $t_{possessor}$ t_{DAT} $t_{possessee}]$
   We all   believed [that this was wrong]

68

The complementarity between *seem* and *believe* translates in their possibility of selecting the same sentential raising configurations: both *seem* and *believe* allow for CPs in which AGR_SP moves to SpecCP before the subject of the infinitive moves on, respective to the matrix subject ($SpecAGR_SP$) of *seem*, or the object ($SpecAGR_OP$) position of *believe*. The question now arises whether this complementarity between *seem* and *believe* also shows up with respect to the selection of sentential configurations involving Strong Binding. In other words, if *seem* allows for a CP complement involving Strong Binding, Rooryck's (1997) analysis predicts that the same should be true of *believe*.

In this section, it will be shown that this is indeed the case. Khalaily (1997) discusses a construction of *believe*, which he terms the *believe of* construction, illustrated in (35):

(35)   Kim thinks/knows of $Sandy_i$ that she_i is intelligent

Khalaily (1997) offers a thorough and interesting discussion of many properties of this construction. In his analysis, the surface complement of *of* in (35), *Sandy*, is raised overtly out of the tensed CP, leaving behind a resumptive pronoun. I will not adopt this analysis here. I would like to show that the properties of this construction are very similar to those of pseudo-raising with *seem*, warranting an analysis of the bound variable reading in (35) in terms of Strong Binding.

A first similarity between the *seem as if* and the *believe of* construction is that both require a bindee in the embedded CP:[4]

(36) a. $Sandy_i$ seems as if she_i/*Pat is happy

b. $Sandy_i$ seems as if Kim likes her_i/*Pat

c. $Sandy_i$ appears as if her_i/*Pat's job is going well

(37) a. Kim believes/knows of $Sandy_i$ that she_i/*Pat is intelligent

b. Kim believes/knows of $Sandy_i$ that flowers make her_i extremely happy

c. Kim believes/knows of $Sandy_i$ that her_i grandparents were Russian

Secondly, the binders in both constructions are subject to a definiteness effect:

(38) a. The/*few students seem like they are happy

b. Kim believes/knows of the/*few students that they are intelligent

Thirdly, Khalaily (1997) observes that the CP complement in the *believe of* construction is an island for extraction. The same is true for the *seem as if* construction:

(39) a. *Which book$_j$ does Kim believe/know of Sandy$_i$ that she$_i$ likes t_j?

b. *Which book$_j$ does Sandy$_i$ seem like/as if/as though she$_i$ likes t_j?

All these properties can be derived under a uniform analysis in terms of Strong Binding of the bindee in the embedded CP by the binder occurring in the subject position of *seem as if* or in the PP complement of *believe of*. It was claimed above that Strong Binding requires the AGR$_S$P of the embedded CP to move to SpecCP at LF so that the bindees present in AGR$_S$P can be bound by the definite subject of *seem*. The same analysis now applies to the CP in the *believe of* construction. The extraction data offer additional evidence in favor of this analysis: if SpecCP must be available for movement of AGR$_S$P into it at LF, SpecCP cannot be used for prior, overt, movement of elements out of the embedded CP. As a result, the embedded CP effectively becomes an island for extraction, as illustrated in (39).

The similarities between the *seem as if* and the *believe of* construction clearly warrant an analysis in the same terms. This conclusion supports Rooryck's (1997) analysis of *seem* and *believe* as each other's converses. Both *seem* and *believe* do not only select infinitival CPs in which AGR$_S$P-to-SpecCP movement applies before raising of the subject to a position in the matrix clause, but they also select finite CPs where AGR$_S$P-to-SpecCP movement licenses a process fairly similar to raising, i.e. Strong Binding.

A number of questions remain. There are the differences between both constructions: *seem* requires an overtly comparative complementizer which is absent in the *believe of* construction; and the CP in the *believe of* construction, but not in the *seem as if* construction, is subject to a constraint stipulating that it must express a characteristic property of the binder. Furthermore, the exact syntactic status of the PP and the CP with respect to *believe* is not entirely clear.[5, 6] I will leave such questions for further research, since my purpose here was only to show that there are sufficient grounds for analyzing both constructions in the same way.

7 Conclusion

Recapitulating briefly, pseudo-raising can be reduced to a case of Strong Binding of pronouns by a quasi-universal operator. Strong Binding of the subject of the embedded clause by the matrix subject over and above a CP Barrier is made possible by covert movement of the embedded AGR$_S$P to SpecCP. Differences between English and Portuguese are largely a function of the difference in lexical properties of the elements involved: the feature specifications of pronouns available for a quasi-universal interpretation in both languages, and the independent properties of comparative complementizers. What look like quixotic differences between Portuguese and English in an apparently theory-defying construction such as pseudo-raising are entirely reducible to the interaction of independent principles of the grammar with language-specific lexical properties. In addition, the properties of Strong Binding displayed by *seem* have been shown to be shared by a special construction of *believe*, the so-called *believe of* construction, confirming Rooryck's (1997, this volume Ch 1) analysis of *seem* and *believe* as syntactic and semantic converses.

Notes

*   A previous version of this chapter including most of sections 1–5 was published as Costa & Rooryck (1996). I would like to thank João Costa for his collaboration and for his permission to use the material of our joint paper here.

1   Romanian (Motapanyane 1994) and Greek display a construction similar to that of Portuguese and English, although with different characteristics:

Romanian:

i.   Studenţii   par   să organizeze   o grevă
ii.   *Studenţii   par   că organizeze   o grevă
     students-the $seem_{3PL}$ MOOD organize $_{3PL.SUBJ}$ a strike
     'The students seem to organize a strike'

Greek:

iii.   ?I fitités fénonte na organónun apoxi'
     the students $seem_{3PL}$ MOOD organize $_{3PL.SUBJ}$ a-strike

iv.   *I fitités fénonte oti organónun apoxi'
     the students $seem_{3PL}$ that organize $_{3PL.IND}$ a-strike

In this chapter, we will not address these constructions in these languages, not only because the distinction between subjunctive and infinitives is not clear, but more specifically because they have been argued to involve a canonical case of raising (cf. Dobrovie-Sorin 1991).

2   Lappin (1984) cites similar cases of pseudo-raising from Cree and Hebrew.

3   In the representation of (17b), movement to $SpecAGR_OP$ is represented as involving overt movement. The distribution of adverbs shows that nominal objects do indeed move overtly to $SpecAGR_OP$ in English (cf. Costa 1996; Johnson 1991).

4   Khalaily (1997) claims that the bindee must occur in subject position on the basis of sentences like the following:

i.   *John knows/thinks of Mary$_i$ that Bill is proud of her$_i$ (Khalaily 1997: 88(25ab))

ii.   *Kim thinks of Mary$_i$ that Pat likes her$_i$

However, a comparison of these cases with (37bc) shows that the ungrammaticality of (i–ii) is due to an independent factor. It appears that the CP containing the bindee must be construable as a characteristic, i.e. generic, property of the binder. This is the case in (37bc), but not in (i–ii). This property of the construction also shows up in (37a):

Khalaily (1997) notes that there is an individual-level restriction on predicates in the CP:

iii.   Kim believes/knows of Sandy$_i$ that she$_i$ is intelligent/*ill

This restriction can be reduced to the more general constraint that the CP in the *believe of* construction must involve a characteristic or generic property of the binder.

5   Khalaily notes that the complement of *of* in English cannot be extracted in the *believe of* construction, an odd fact in view of the extractability of the DPs in (ii), and the fact that the complement of *van* in Dutch can be extracted in the same construction:

i.   *Which student$_i$ do you know/think of t_i that she$_i$ is intelligent?

ii.   Which persons did you know/think of?

iii.   Dit zijn de studenten waarvan ik dacht dat ze intelligent waren
     'These are the students of whom I thought that they were intelligent'

The syntactic status of the CP as a complement of *believe* can be ascertained through a comparison with Dutch, which allows Focused DPs or pronouns in the position of the CP:

iv.   Kim weet van Marie$_i$ dat ze$_i$ intelligent is *(alleen/zelfs) haar$_i$ adres
     'Kim knows of Mary only her address/that she is intelligent'

v.   Kim wist/geloofde het niet van Marie (dat ze directeur geworden was)
     'Kim didn't know/believe it of Mary (that she had become a director)'

6   Khalaily (1997) also notes a number of other properties of this construction, such as the fact that the complementizer *that* is obligatory in the *believe of* construction, but not in other *believe* constructions:

i.   John thinks/knows (that) Mary is intelligent

ii.   John thinks/knows of Mary *(that) she is intelligent

This property may have two possible explanations, one semantic, the other syntactic. Syntactically, the obligatory character of *that* might be due to the status of the embedded CP as an adjunct, or at least as a non-complement. Since only complement clauses have the possibility of dropping *that* in English, the embedded CP in (ii) may be argued to occupy an adjunct position. Semantically, the obligatory presence of *that* may be linked to the specific interpretation of *believe* in this context. It is well known that the presence of *that* is influenced by modal properties modifying the matrix verb (cf. Bolinger 1972; Pica and Rooryck 1995):

iii. a. John believes (that) the winner is Greek
     b. John disbelieves *(that) the winner is Greek

iv. a. John believes (that) the winner is Greek
     b. John probably believes ? ??(that) the winner is Greek

Interestingly, the *believe of* construction reflects a 'permanent' or 'timeless' belief on behalf of the subject, as indicated by the contrast in (v–vi):

v.   I (*just now) thought of Mary that she is intelligent

vi.   I (just now) thought that Mary is intelligent

I would like to suggest that the 'permanent' or 'timeless' property of the *believe of* construction should be viewed in the same way as the negation in (iii) and the adverb in (iv), i.e. it involves a modal property that makes the presence of *that* obligatory.

3

CONTROL

1 Introduction[*]

Ever since the program of fully explicit grammars was initiated in the early 1960s, control has been a serious challenge for the explanatory adequacy of the theory of grammar. In the 1980s, control was partially reduced to Binding theory: PRO behaves as an anaphor which has the matrix clause as its governing category. However, control is different from Binding in that there seem to be semantic restrictions on controller choice which are absent for anaphoric Binding. These semantic restrictions have long been viewed as part of a poorly understood control module. In this chapter, it will be argued that there is no separate module for control ('control theory') in the grammar. Instead, control results from the modular interaction of independently motivated principles and modules of the grammar: Binding theory, lexical event structure, and government. The idea is developed that control is largely determined by the interaction between Binding theory on the one hand, and an explicit theory of semantic selection by the matrix $V°$ which properly governs the infinitival $C°$ on the other. I claim that the selectional mechanisms that determine the temporal interpretation of an infinitive also determine control of this infinitive. It is argued that the temporally [− realized] infinitival morphology in $C°$ is identified and coindexed with temporally [− realized] subevents lexically represented in the aspectual subevent structure of the matrix $V°$. The subevent coindexed with $C°$ determines the temporal interpretation of the infinitive. More importantly, the lexical coindexation of $C°$ with the [− realized] subevent in $V°$ severely restricts the possible Binding antecedents of anaphoric PRO which is coindexed with the infinitival $C°-T°$ temporal morphemes. PRO can only be bound by arguments in the matrix clause which are lexically represented in the subevent with which $C°$ is lexically coindexed. The explanatory adequacy of this idea will be illustrated by the analysis of the event structures defining various coherent semantic classes of control verbs.

2 A modular analysis of control or a control module?

Most proposals concerning the syntax of control in the last decade have concentrated on the way control is related to Binding (Manzini 1983; Koster 1984; Bouchard 1985; Borer 1989, Vanden Wyngaerd 1990, 1994). Simplifying somewhat, this discussion has led to the insight that the infinitival subject PRO or the infinitival AGR_s° (Borer 1989) is basically anahoric in nature, since the controller is to be found in the local domain in which the controlled infinitive is a complement.

(1) Pat_k claims that Kim_i promised $Sandy_j$ $PRO_{i/*j/*k/*arb}$ to do the dishes

These proposals partially reduce control theory to Binding. This insight is a necessary, but nevertheless insufficient, step towards a full understanding of obligatory control in infinitival complements. If Binding alone were responsible for control, any three-argument verb with two arguments besides the controlled sentential complement should allow PRO to be bound by either argument in the matrix clause. This is not the case: the subjects of verbs expressing influence such as *force* or verbs of 'judgment' such as *accuse* or *praise* cannot function as controllers:

(2) a. Kim_i forced $Sandy_j$ $PRO_{*i/j/*arb}$ to do the dishes

b. Kim_i praised $Sandy_j$ $PRO_{*i/j/*arb}$ for doing the dishes

As observed by Chomsky & Lasnik (1991), control is very different in this respect from Binding. Control of PRO in (2) seems to be provided by a specifically designated argument in its governing category. Binding of an anaphor does not face such a restriction: in (3), even though Binding is obligatory, the anaphor can be 'freely' bound by any argument in its governing category.

(3) Kim_i talked to $Sandy_j$ about $herself_{i/j}$

Chomsky & Lasnik (1991: 72–3) view this thematic uniqueness restriction on the antecedent for PRO as an argument in favor of a control module in the theory of grammar.

However, 'free' control of PRO by any argument in the matrix clause is attested. Obligatory Binding/control of PRO by any argument of the matrix clause is restricted to some verbs of transfer, sometimes involving more delicate patterns of control shifts (Růžička 1983a, 1983b; Larson 1990). Verbs of the *propose, offer, suggest* class allow for free control (4), verbs such as *promise* and *guarantee* involve preferential subject control (5ab), and verbs of asking involve preferential object control (5cd):

(4)   Kim$_i$ offered Sandy$_j$ PRO$_{i/j/i+j/*arb}$ to do the dishes

(5)   a.   Kim$_i$ promised Sandy$_j$ PRO$_{i/*j/*arb}$ to do the dishes

    b.   Kim$_i$ promised Sandy$_j$ PRO$_{*i/j/*arb}$ to be allowed to do the dishes

    c.   Sandy$_i$ asked Kim$_j$ PRO$_{*i/j/*arb}$ to do the dishes

    d.   Sandy$_i$ asked Kim$_j$ PRO$_{i/*j/*arb}$ to be allowed to do the dishes

'Free' control of PRO in the matrix clause of (4) then is on a par with 'free' Binding of the anaphor in (3). It is clear that lexical properties of the matrix predicates somehow determine why the subject in (4–5) is available for control, but not in (2). More precisely, the set of possible controllers in (2) is restricted to the object, but in (4–5) it includes both the subject and the object. This much is admitted by Manzini (1983), who shoves these problems under the lexical rug, a temporarily justified but ultimately unsatisfactory solution. Note that purely thematic accounts of control along the lines of Jackendoff (1972, 1987) would be unable to account for the variation in (4–5): the thematic 'grid' of the class of verbs such as *offer* (*propose, suggest*) (2) and the class of *promise, guarantee* (5ab) involve exactly the same Source–Theme–Goal structure, but the control properties exemplified by the verbs in these classes are different. Other traditional solutions include registering these control properties as idiosyncratic features of the matrix verb (Rosenbaum 1967; Chomsky 1981), or as purely pragmatically determined properties (Postal 1970; Sag & Pollard 1991). Both types of solutions to the control problem are ultimately circular: *promise* is a subject control verb because it belongs to the class of events expressing a promise. We may conclude that there is a lexical residue of control theory which is unreducible to Binding and which needs to be explained by independently motivated semantic factors.

It can of course be claimed that these semantic factors are the object of a separate module in the grammar: control theory. However, in a modular framework, the minimal hypothesis would be to assume that Binding of PRO in the matrix clause is somehow further constrained by these lexical properties. How can such a modular analysis of control be achieved? It is the purpose of this contribution to solve this puzzle. The problem can be subdivided into four basic questions:

(6)   i.   What is the semantic representation allowing for an accurate distinction between the different classes of control verbs? (the force-type class, the offer-type class, the promise-type class, the ask-type class).

ii. What properties of this semantic representation determine control?

iii. How do these properties determine control given standard assumptions about semantic selection of C° by V° under proper government?

iv. How can these properties be integrated in a modular way with the insight that PRO is an anaphor subject to Binding theory? How does proper government of C° further restrict Binding of PRO?

These questions will be treated in good order. With respect to (6i), I would like to claim that the event structure of control verbs is the semantic representation which is relevant for distinguishing control verb classes (sections 3 and 6). With respect to question (6ii), it will be proposed that the aspectual subevents which can be defined in terms of the temporal feature [– realized] are involved in defining control. These [– realized] subevents of the matrix V° determine control (6iii) via semantic selection of the infinitival C°. Since the infinitival C° can be defined in terms of the feature [– realized] (Stowell 1981), there is a lexical identification between the [– realized] aspectual subevent properties in V° and the temporally [– realized] properties of C° (section 4). This temporal identification of the infinitival C° in V° determines the temporal interpretation of the infinitive. It will be shown that this temporal interpretation of the infinitive by the matrix control V° effectively reduces the number of Binding possibilities for PRO (section 5). Control of the infinitival subject is determined by the temporal interpretation of the infinitive. In this way, the lexical residue of control theory can be derived. As a result, a truly modular explanation of control is reached, and the need for a control module in the grammar is eliminated. In section 6, an analysis of the event structure of the control verb classes in (2–5) will illustrate how their control properties can be derived.

3 Fine-tuning lexical semantics: event structure and control

It is claimed here that the semantic properties determining controllerhood are to be found in the aspectual event structure of each class of control verbs. The event described by a particular verb or class of verbs can be represented as developing through time. In this section, I would like to briefly introduce Pustejovsky's (1988) framework which will be used to represent the event structure of semantic verb classes, though augmented with some additional descriptive devices.

Pustejovsky (1988) distinguishes three event-types ε: States are of the type $[_S e]_S$, Processes are of the type $[_P e_1 \ldots e_n]_P$, and Transitions are of the type $[_T \varepsilon_1 \ldots \varepsilon_2]_T$. A State is represented as an event without internal development. Processes contain an undetermined succession of subevents translating a progressive change through time. Transitions contain two variable event-types, and their structure allows for the representation of the change of one event-type to another. They correspond to Vendler's (1967) accomplishments and achievements. These event-types allow for complex compositional structures in which thematic roles can be expressed on the events and subevents. Importantly, then, thematic roles in this framework are not simply an unordered list or 'theta-grid' of thematic role labels as for e.g. Stowell (1981), but they are ordered and embedded in the temporal development of the event. Some concrete examples may make this compositional framework for *Aktionsarten* more transparent.

Verbs of creation are represented as Transitions consisting of two subevents, one of which is a Process expressing the incremental action of creating, and the other represents the state of what is created after the time of verbal action. The event structure of a 'creation' verb such as *build* can be represented as follows:

(7) a. John built a house

b. $[_T [_P e_1 \ldots e_n]_{P_{act\ (John,\ x)}} e_{house\ (x)}]_T$

(= Pustejovsky 1988: (3))

In this representation, x is a variable representing the object being created, and e represents the subevents into which the event of building can be subdivided (Pustejovsky (1988: 25)).[1] In plain English, (7b) states that the event of John building a house involves two subevents: the first subevent is a Process of building which starts at a moment e_1 and goes on until an undetermined moment e_n. This Process subevent is associated with a predicate expressing causation which is predicated of the subject *John*: the agent *John* exerts an action upon the object x which is being created. The second subevent translates a stative subevent at which the object x being created is identifiable as a house. This representation then translates the conceptual notion of 'incremental creation' (Dowty 1991) into aspectual subevent structure. Agentive properties are integrated in the aspectual event structure of verbs as predicates (*act*) attached to temporal subevents. In Pustejovsky's (1988) terms, the external structure of a verb such as *build* is a Transition, whereas the internal structure of the verb consists of the combination of a Process and a State.

Some observations can be added to Pustejovsky's (1988) representation which will prove useful for the discussion of control. Notice that both the Process and the State subevents are nonpunctual and in a sense 'unrealized' in (7): the 'future' State subevent does not have temporal boundaries delimiting the event. A Process only has a starting point e_1. The Process event-type then also is 'unrealized' in the sense that it is undetermined with respect to a particular temporal point: a Process does not have an intrinsic endpoint. In (7b), it is the Transition structure which 'stops' the Process subevent, not the properties of the Process subevent itself. The State subevent in (7b) is also 'unrealized,' since it takes place in an undetermined future with respect to the Process of building.

This representation also allows for a temporal analysis of 'transfer' verbs. Pustejovsky (1988) analyzes verbs such as *give* as a Transition consisting of two events, the punctual agentive State of transfer and the resulting nonpunctual, temporally undetermined State of possession. The asterisk represents the fact that the event structure is headed by the first event.

(8) a. Mary gave the book to Bill

   b. $[_T \; e^*_{1 \; act \; (Mary) \; \& \; move \; (Mary, \; book)} \; e_{at \; (book, \; Bill)} \;]_T$

   (= Pustejovsky 1988: (2a))

In the representation (8b), the first subevent states that at a punctual moment e_1, the subject Mary is agentive and moves the book. The second subevent translates the implication that Bill comes into a State of possession of the book for a stretch of time that is undetermined with respect to the punctual moment at which the first subevent takes place. The external Transition structure of *give* translates the temporal relation of one subevent being linked to another on the time axis. Notice that the subevent e_1 is punctual. From a temporal point of view, e represents event-types that can be true at a specific, punctual, moment (e_1), at an undetermined, 'unrealized,' moment in the future (e_{house} in (7b)), or during an undetermined, 'unrealized,' time period (e_{at} in (8b)). It is implicit in Pustejovsky's (1988) framework that the event-type e can be further subdivided by the [± realized] feature. Punctual 'realized' States can be represented by numerical indexes (e_1). 'Unrealized' States may be represented without an index by Pustejovsky (1988) if the subevent extends over a (future) time-period without temporal boundaries, as in (8b), and by e_n if the Stative subevent takes place at an undetermined moment (cf. (7b)).

Beyond the representational problem, it is crucial to define more precisely the notion of 'unrealized' subevent. 'Unrealized' (sub)events can be defined by their relative independence with respect to the temporal development of the event. This temporal independence of the subevent with respect to the temporal development of the event can be realized in two ways. First of all, a (sub)event can be independent of the time axis because it is not delimited with respect to past or future relatively to the time set by the temporal morpheme it is linked to. These subevents can also be represented as e_n. Examples of such a nonpunctual, 'temporally unrealized' event would be the Stative verbs *deserve, sit, regret, love* and the like. A Stative verb in a present tense presupposes that the event did not start or end with that present tense: on the contrary, the event is presented as extending before and after the event time of the temporal morpheme.[2] In the same way, it will be shown later on that in the more complex Transition event structures, a subevent can be temporally independent with respect to past or future relatively to the subevent e_1 which is linked to the temporal morpheme.

There is a second way in which (sub)events may be temporally independent or 'unrealized' with respect to the temporal development of the event. It has already been observed above that subevents can be temporally undetermined with respect to the future development of the event. These 'unrealized' (sub)events, then, are only partly independent from the temporal development of the event. This is the case for Process (sub)events as in (7b),which have no internal future boundary, but also for (sub)events which take place at an undetermined moment (7b) or time period (8b) in the future. The term 'unrealized' subevent here refers to a 'possible future' subevent, which can be represented as e_{n+1}. The term temporally 'unrealized' then can be defined as follows:

(9)   A (sub)event is temporally 'unrealized' ([−realized]) iff (i) or (ii):

    i.   The (sub)event is not linked to a specific point on the time axis representing the temporal development of the verb; it is temporally undefined with respect to the past and future of the event time e_1 which is linked to the temporal morphemes in T°. This type of subevent is represented as e_n.

    ii. The (sub)event includes at least one point or period on the time axis that lies in the future with respect to the event time e_1 linked to the temporal morphemes in T°; the (sub) event refers to a 'possible future,' and is represented as e_{n+1}.

Both parts of the definition are of course conceptually related: the term temporally 'unrealized' refers to (sub)events that are *not* temporally realized on the past/future time axis, and to 'possible future' (sub)events that are *not yet* temporally realized on the time axis. The relation between the two parts of the definition then has to do with the traditional grammarian's category of 'Mood.' The 'atemporal' character of a State can be considered a 'modal' property. Lyons (1977: 677) has observed that the expression of futurity in language never involves an exclusively temporal concept, but necessarily includes an element of prediction or a modal notion. For mnemonic purposes, it is important to keep in mind that the subscript $_{(n)}$ will consistently be used in the subevent structures proposed to indicate all types of [– realized] subevents. The importance of this definition for the control problem will become clearer later on. Before going back to the analysis of control proper, it is important to discuss the way in which thematic roles are represented and derived in Pustejovsky's (1988) framework.

An interesting property of Pustejovsky's compositional representation is that it integrates two types of semantic structures that are essential for the semantics of verbs: the 'theta-grid' (Stowell 1981) of the verb on the one hand, and the temporal-aspectual, internal development of the verbal event on the other. Both aspects of the lexical semantics of verbs will be shown to be essential for control. Moreover, the flexibility of the representation allows for a large number of combinations of the event-types State, Process, and Transition. Notice that in this framework, thematic roles are embedded in a complex subeventual frame representing the temporal development of the verb. The subeventual representation of transfer verbs allows Pustejovsky to view thematic roles of the Source–Theme–Goal type as notions derived from a temporal structure, and not as basic elements of a theory of thematic roles. Presumably, the same analysis can be applied to the class of verbs expressing the same type of transfer as *give,* such as *grant, lend, hand, donate.* The representation provides for more fine-grained distinctions among thematic roles than that of classical thematic roles, allowing for a representation of the distinction between *give* and *throw* (Pustejovsky 1988).

It is clear that representations similar to that of (8b) can be used to determine the semantic specificity of each class of control verbs expressing 'transfer': the verbs of the *propose, offer* type, the verbs of asking, and the verbs of the *promise* type. In this way, the different conceptual structures associated with each verb class can be mapped into different event structures. This representation will make it possible in section 6 to make the minimal semantic differences between these verb classes fully explicit, given some additional specifications of the thematic properties present in the event structure. As already observed, Pustejovsky's (1988) framework allows for the integration of causation properties in the aspectual event structure of verbs. In the analysis of control verbs presented here, these agentive thematic predicates will be described in terms of the (Proto-) Agent properties introduced by Dowty (1991). Attempting to explain subject selection principles by a reduction of thematic roles to the basic notions of (Proto-)Agent and (Proto-)Patient, Dowty uses the characteristics of agency put forth by Keenan (1976, 1984) to redefine Agent and Patienthood as clusters of properties. (Proto-)Agent is thus viewed as a cluster of properties such as *volition, sentience, causation* and *movement.* All of these properties do not have to be realized at the same time on an agentive argument. For instance, the subjects of control verbs with the minimal internal structure of States such as *want* or *love* may only be characterized by the properties of, respectively, Volition and Sentience. Interestingly, this 'cluster' view of Agent–Patient properties entails that all agentive properties do not have to be realized on the external argument: internal arguments may also have agentive properties. The importance of this enrichment of Pustejovsky's representation of event structure will become clear in the semantic description of control verbs and the explanation of their control properties. At this point, it is important to observe that this framework enables us to express the semantics of verbs expressing 'transfer' (*propose/promise/give/ask*) and verbs not expressing 'transfer' (*love, want*) with the same basic tools of semantic representation. I claim that the semantics of event structure is the semantic representation which allows for distinguishing each class of control verbs from the other (cf. section 6). This is the answer to question (6i).

However, the semantic representations of each class of control verbs do not explain anything about control by themselves. Question (6ii) still needs to be addressed: which properties in this semantic representation determine control? How can Pustejovsky's (1988) descriptive formalism offer us an insight into the way in which PRO obtains its reference? I would like to claim that control is determined by the temporal sub-event structure of the matrix verb along the lines of the following descriptive principle:

(10)   The aspectual restriction on controller assignment (ARCA)

A. Only arguments embedded in temporally unrealized subevents (States or Processes) as co-arguments of the infinitival argument are controllers of the unexpressed PRO subject of the infinitival argument.

B. If the set of possible controllers determined by A is greater than one, a thematic hierarchy determines that the (Proto-)Agent argument must be the controller of PRO.

ARCA.A is responsible for singling out the set of possible controllers among the arguments of the matrix verb. In section 6, this principle will be shown to predict that both the subject and the indirect object are possible controllers for the unexpressed subject of the infinitival argument of verbs such as *propose, promise,* and *ask* (3–5), and that only the object is a possible controller for verbs of 'influence' such as *force* and verbs of 'judgment' such as *praise* (2). ARCA.B only applies if the event structure of a control verb with three argument slots contains two temporally 'unrealized' subevents, each embedding a different argument besides the infinitival argument. ARCA.B is instrumental for certain types of subject control verbs, variable control (4) and the control shifts displayed by verbs of promising (5ab) and asking (5cd). Notice that ARCA.B introduces an Agent–Patient hierarchy into the determination of controllerhood, similar to the one first proposed by Foley & van Valin (1984: 304–10). However, in our approach the application of this thematic hierarchy is limited to the set of possible controllers of a control verb: the thematic hierarchy is crucially dependent on ARCA.A, which will be reduced to a precise formulation of semantic selection under proper government.

Let us take a concrete example to see how this descriptive principle works. In French, a number of 'transfer' verbs of the *give* type can function as object control verbs in the same way as *force* (2). Although this sentence has a rather literary flavor, its control properties are clear. The sentence (11a) can be represented in (11b) by changing the variables of the representation (8b):

(11) a. Que les dieux lui donnent/accordent de réussir sa traversée de l'Atlantique
'May the Gods give/grant him to succeed in his crossing of the Atlantic'

b. $[_T \; e^*_{1 \; \text{act (Gods) \& move (Gods, succeed)}} \; e_{n+1 \; \text{(succeed, him)}} \;]_T$

Both subevents contain a referential argument and the infinitival Theme argument. The first subevent including the 'Source' argument is linked to a punctual moment indicated here by the numerical subscript. This subevent can be considered a 'realized' subevent, since it 'starts' the event: it is linked on the time axis to a specific point in time which coincides with the tense of the temporal morphemes in $T°$. Only the 'Goal' argument is embedded with the infinitival argument in a Stative subevent which refers to a temporally extended period after the punctual moment of giving. According to the definition (9), only this second subevent is a temporally 'unrealized' subevent, since it refers to the future with respect to the subevent e_1. The 'unrealized' property of the subevent is represented by the subscript $_{(n)}$ in the subevent e_{n+1} of (11b). ARCA.A correctly predicts that only the argument embedded in the second Stative subevent, the 'Goal' argument, can be a controller.

The question now arises as to why there would be a relation between [– realized] aspect (ARCA.A) and control. Why would a principle such as ARCA.A be relevant for control? Relating this question to our question (6iii), the problem can be reformulated as follows: how can ARCA.A be reduced to semantic selection under proper government? The next section will offer a solution to this problem, and further outline the syntactic underpinnings of an analysis relating aspect and control in our answer to question (6iv).

4 Temporal identification of the infinitival C°

The constraint in ARCA restricting control to [– realized] subevents can be linked to the untensed character of the embedded infinitive. It is usually assumed that untensed verbs have an INFL node that does not realize an independent temporal reference. Infinitives are said to have a feature [– Tense]. In this respect, Bresnan (1972) notes that infinitival complements refer to 'something hypothetical or unrealized.' Guillaume (1929) already defined the infinitival tense as a tense 'in posse': it expresses 'potential' time, or eventuality, which is opposed to tense 'in esse,' a 'real' or finite time reference linked to the time axis. Stowell (1982) makes a similar observation stating that the tense of infinitives must be semantically interpreted as unrealized or as a 'possible future.' Stowell (1981) challenges the idea that infinitives are [– Tense] and suggests instead that they are [+ Tense], but lack a [± Past] feature. This translates the idea that infinitives are not linked to a specific moment on the time axis with respect to future or past, they express 'possible time.' Carlson (1984) appropriately proposes to view untensed verbs semantically as eventualities, an epistemic modal notion. Following these authors, we think that it is appropriate to semantically interpret the infinitival morphology as temporally 'unrealized': an infinitive is not linked to a specific point on the time axis: it is undetermined for a specific moment realizing the event. The infinitival morphology denotes a temporally 'unrealized' tense that can be modally interpreted as an eventuality.

ARCA.A restricts controllerhood to those arguments that are part of a temporally 'unrealized' subevent. The relation between a temporally 'unrealized' subevent of the matrix control verb and an infinitival eventuality could then be viewed as formal identification between identical or mutually identifiable features. This identification could then ensure, in a way to be further specified, that only the argument linked to the temporally 'unrealized' subevent is available for Binding by the unexpressed anaphoric infinitival subject.

Is there any evidence independent of control that there actually is such a temporal identification of the infinitival morphology by the semantics of the matrix verb? It has long been noted that the temporal reference of infinitives is determined by the semantics of the matrix verb. Among other verb classes, Palmer (1974) distinguishes between verbs of 'futurity' and verbs of 'effort and achievement,' Infinitives selected by verbs of 'futurity' (*wish, decide, persuade, expect, promise*) refer to the future, whereas infinitives selected by verbs of 'effort and achievement' (*manage, try, remember*) do not refer to the future (Palmer 1974: 195–206). Lasnik & Fiengo (1975) observe that a control verb imposes selectional restrictions on its infinitival complement: a verb such as *force* does not normally select Stative verbs such as *resemble*. Moreover, Rooryck (1987) has shown that there is a remarkable correspondence between temporal and aspectual restrictions on the infinitive on the one hand and control properties on the other: a semantically homogeneous verb class shares both homogeneous control properties and the same aspectual and modal restrictions setting it apart from any other control verb class. An adequate theory of control should explain this close correspondence between control on the one hand and the temporal-aspectual restrictions of the infinitival argument on the other hand. Let us therefore briefly develop the idea of the temporal determination of the infinitive by the matrix verb.

Stowell (1982) was the first to try to formalize the temporal determination of gerunds and infinitives by the matrix verb. He argues that there is a difference between infinitives and gerunds in the way their temporal reference is determined. The tense of gerunds is determined externally by the semantics of the control verb. The tense of infinitives is not so determined according to Stowell: infinitives have an independent tense in the same way as tensed clauses, their tense is internally determined as 'unrealized.'

(12) a. Jenny remembered to bring the wine

b. Jenny remembered bringing the wine

(13) a. Jenny tried to lock the car

b. Jenny tried locking the car

Stowell observes that the tense of sentences such as (12a,13a) is specified as unrealized with respect to the tense of the matrix verb: Jenny has not yet brought the wine when she remembers to do so and she has not yet locked the car when she tries to do so. In (12b, 13b), the gerund is interpreted with respect to the semantics of the matrix verb: since remembering is about the past, the gerund is interpreted with respect to the past, and in (13b) the gerund is ambiguous between an unrealized and a present interpretation. Stowell suggests that there is a tense operator in COMP to link the 'unrealized' tense of infinitives to the tense of the matrix verb. Gerunds do not have such a tense operator: they depend for their temporal interpretation on the meaning of the governing verb (Stowell 1982).

However, there are a number of arguments against the idea that the tense of the infinitive is dependent on the matrix tense. A first problem for this approach is that it predicts that the tense of the infinitive should always be interpreted with respect to the future of the matrix verb. This prediction is not carried out: verbs such as *like* select an infinitive that is not necessarily interpreted with respect to the future of the matrix verb *like*:

(14) Jenny likes to go to the movies

Sentence (14) means that at the time of the present tense, Jenny likes her experiences of going to movies, both past and present. Stowell's analysis predicts that the only relevant interpretation is one where Jenny likes her future experience of going to the movies.

A second argument against Stowell's analysis comes from French. In French, argument CPs with a [– realized] tense feature are always expressed by infinitives. As in English, the infinitive selected by *se souvenir* 'remember' is interpreted as future with respect to the moment of remembering.

(15)   Jenny s'est souvenu à temps de prendre le vin
        'Jenny remembered in time to take the wine'

This suggests that the French infinitive is temporally on a par with the English infinitive rather than with the gerund. Similarly, object control verbs of the *persuade, force* type impose an interpretation of the infinitive that is situated at an undetermined point in time after the moment of persuading or forcing. However, object control verbs of the 'judgment' type such as *punir* 'punish,' *féliciter* 'congratulate' allow for an interpretation of the infinitive that is situated at an undetermined point which may be past or future with respect to the time of the judging or congratulation event.

(16) a.   Isidore m'a imposé de/invité à/permis de venir à la fête
           'Isidore imposed coming to the party on me/invited me/allowed
           me to come to the party'

     b.   Basile a puni/félicité/plaint Mylène d'avoir écrit/écrire cet article
           'Basile punished/congratulated/pitied Mylène for having written/
           writing that article'

The analysis of (15) shows that French infinitives pattern with English infinitives rather than with gerunds with respect to their temporal interpretation. The temporal interpretation of the infinitive in (16b) preferentially refers to an event that has occurred before the moment of congratulating or punishing. As a result, (16b) clearly shows that the temporal interpretation of embedded infinitives must be determined by the matrix verb rather than by the matrix tense. The temporal interpretation of the infinitive by the matrix verb can only take place via proper government by the matrix verb of the embedded C° heading the CP complement. I would like to propose an analysis for the temporal interpretation of infinitives and gerunds in which only the matrix verb determines the tense of the infinitive or the gerund, rather than the matrix tense.

There is ample evidence in the literature for the temporal character of C°. It has often been noted that tensed and untensed C° always correlate with tensed and untensed T°: in English the infinitival T° contains the infinitival morpheme *to*, while tensed CPs have an optional *that* complementizer. In French, the tensed complementizer *que* and the untensed complementizers *de*, *à*, and Ø are in complementary distribution (Long 1974; Kayne 1981b; Huot 1981). It can be assumed that T° and C° are nondistinct in features. Nondistinctness of features between C° and T° also allows C° to transmit features to T° by virtue of their being coindexed. I will assume that the [– realized] C° head of the embedded infinitive mediates the selectional restrictions exercised by the matrix verb on the embedded infinitive with respect to the temporal interpretation of this infinitive. The *-ing* morphology of the gerunds (in the embedded T° or V°) is also [– realized]. It may be identified by the matrix verb in a slightly different way, since it is not identical to the infinitival morphology.[3] Both C° and the temporal morphology of the gerund receive the temporal interpretation for the embedded clause from the matrix V°.

But how should the selectional restrictions expressed in (14) and the interpretive constraints noted in (12–13) and (15) be conceived of? One could, of course, simply encode in the lexical entry of both verbs the fact that *try* selects a C° with a future interpretation, and that *remember* selects a C° that can refer to both a past and a future event. This information could be encoded as part of an unordered set of lexical features, following Chomsky (1965). However, it seems highly unlikely that the temporal restrictions on the infinitive selected by a verb would be independent of its temporal event structure. Consequently, it might be interesting to make these restrictions follow from the semantic structure of the selecting verb. This now allows a further clarification of the idea that the [– realized] morphology of the infinitive is identified with the [– realized] features of the event structure of the matrix verb. In order to do this, it simply has to be shown that the temporal restrictions on the [– realized] gerund or infinitive follow from the event structure of the matrix verb. In addition, the different temporal interpretations of English infinitives and gerunds have to be explained by showing that both are temporally identified by the matrix verb, but in different ways.

Let us take up again Stowell's examples *remember* and *try*, and try to derive both his observations about the temporal interpretation of the infinitive and the gerund, and our own remarks about infinitival selection. The verb *remember* can be represented as follows:

(17) a. Jenny remembered the wine

b. $[_T e_{n \text{ sent (Jenny, wine)}} \; e^*_{1 \text{ sent (Jenny, e)}}]_T$

The verb *remember* can be represented as a Transition verb: from the point of view of its internal temporal development, it intuitively represents a change between a State of knowledge or experience of something, represented here by the predicate *sentience* on the first subevent e_n, and the punctual moment of remembering that knowledge or experience which heads the event structure. Since *remember* does not involve any agentivity on behalf of the subject, we represent the predicate as a punctual *sentience* predicate that should be distinguished from the one on the first subevent. Recall that these predicates express relatively abstract relations between the arguments. Notice that the nonpunctual State of knowledge or experience is temporally independent of the second punctual subevent on the time axis. This is because the State of knowledge or experience extends on the time axis both before and after the punctual moment of remembering: the experience or knowledge is not temporally limited by the punctual subevent of remembering it. Since the first Stative subevent in (17b) is not linked to the time axis with respect to the past or the future of the second subevent, it should be viewed as temporally 'unrealized' in the sense of (9i). Recall the subscript $_{(n)}$ is used in the subevent structures to indicate all types of [– realized] subevents.

When the argument realized by *the wine* in (17) is realized as an infinitive or a gerund as in (12), the [– realized] morphology of both the infinitive and the gerund is identified with the [– realized] subevent e_n. Since this subevent translating knowledge or experience is not temporally limited with respect to past or future, [– realized] morphemes that are identified with it can in principle refer to a time period before (past) or after (future) the second punctual subevent of remembering it. Besides their temporal [– realized] feature, infinitives as in (12a) have a modal 'possible future' or eventuality interpretation. This 'eventuality' feature of the C° head of the infinival CP is identified in the time frame of the durative state of knowledge or experience with the 'future' period after the punctual moment of remembering which matches this 'eventuality' feature of the infinitive. For the past interpretation of gerunds (12b), I would like to propose a solution in the same spirit. The *-ing* morphology of the gerund, while lacking the temporal 'eventuality' property of infinival C°s, has the feature [+ durative]. This feature also needs to be interpreted with respect to the subevent structure of *remember*. The feature [+ durative] presupposes that the event has already started its temporal progress. As a result, the [+ durative] feature has to be identified with respect to any part of the first Stative subevent in the time frame of *remember* that occurs before the punctual subevent of remembering: anything taking place before the remembrance inherently implies duration, while anything taking place after the remembrance does not (yet) have duration. The temporal identification of the feature [+ durative] with the 'past' part of the Stative subevent in (17) thus results in a past interpretation of the gerund.[4] Both the past interpretation of the gerund and the future interpretation of infinitives then arise through the interaction between the Stative subevent represented in the event structure of the matrix verb and the morphological features ('eventuality'/'durative') of the infinitives and gerunds themselves.

Most importantly, this analysis now also derives the control properties of *remember* according to ARCA.A: both the infinitival argument and the controller are related to the argument variables in the temporally 'unrealized' first subevent of (17b). Consequently, the subject ends up as the controller of the infinitival subject PRO. Importantly, the control properties of the infinitive are derived from its temporal interpretation.

The selectional and interpretive temporal properties of *try* are much simpler to explain. This verb can be analyzed with a simple Process event structure of the following type:

(18) a. Jenny tried to lock the door

    b. $[_P \, e_1 \ldots e_n \,]_{P \; act \; (Jenny, \; lock)}$

Since this event structure does not contain a subevent potentially referring to the past, gerunds cannot receive a past interpretation (13b). The possibility for the gerund to have either a present or an unrealized interpretation can be linked to the way in which the gerund is identified with the temporally 'unrealized' Process event, whose [− realized] property is indicated by the subscript $_{(n)}$.[5] In a Process event, the present tense does not just coincide with the first subevent e_1 of the Process, but with the entire Process event. The durative [− realized] *-ing* morphology can either identify with the entire Process to coincide with it, yielding the present interpretation for the gerund, or it can identify with a stretch of moments after the moment e_1 which starts the event to yield the unrealized interpretation. Again, the control properties of *try* can be derived following ARCA.A, since both the untensed complement and the controller occur together in a temporally 'unrealized' (sub)event.

It is interesting to come back now to the temporal interpretation of the infinitival argument of the *give*-type verbs in French in its relation to control. In (11a), the temporal interpretation of the infinitive with respect to the event of the matrix verb takes place in an undetermined future: when the Gods grant the traveler to arrive safely, he has not yet arrived safely. This future interpretation of the infinitive can be derived, since the [− realized] second subevent in (11b) must be identified by the infinitival [− realized] C°. It has already been shown that following ARCA.A, only the 'Goal' argument occurring with the infinitival argument in this second subevent can end up as the controller. In section 6, it will be argued that the temporal interpretation of *force*-type verbs and judgment verbs in (2) is linked to their event structure in a similar way. For now, it seems that the analysis presented here can integrate most of Stowell's (1982) observations and circumvent its limitations. To conclude, I have shown that both control according to

ARCA.A. and the temporal interpretation of [– realized] clauses can be derived from the event structure of the matrix verb, and that there is a strong link between these two phenomena.

5 Lexical coindexation of C° in V° and Binding of AGR$_S$°

The important question that comes to mind now is exactly how this identification of [– realized] features present in both the matrix event structure and the embedded infinitives or gerunds should be formally realized. The simplest way to formally express the idea that the [– realized] morphology of the infinitive or the gerund is selectionally identified by the event structure of the matrix verb would be to assume that selectional identification involves coindexation between aspectual [– realized] properties of the event structure of the matrix V° and the temporal [– realized] features of the embedded infinitives or gerunds under proper government. Obviously, this coindexation cannot simply involve referential coindexation of the infinitival C° and the V°. Coindexation of the infinitival C° with elements of the matrix event structure must be a partial coindexation of the [– realized] C° with a temporally 'unrealized' subevent in the event structure of the matrix V°. Identification of [– realized] features via coindexation then involves the following syntactic configuration:

(19) $[_{V}^{\circ} e_i (e_j)]_{V}^{\circ} \ldots C_i \ldots \text{AGR}_i \ldots T_i \ldots \text{Vinf}_i \ldots$
  where the index i refers to temporally [– realized]

This means that a temporally [– realized] C° is coindexed with a temporally 'unrealized' subevent of the verb in the matrix clause, rather than with the whole V°–T°–AGR$_S$° complex of the matrix verb. How should the notion of partial coindexation of C° in V° be conceived of in the grammar?

I would like to suggest that identification of temporally [– realized] features via partial coindexation is an instance of semantic selection by a V° head on the X° head of its XP complement. Since Chomsky (1965), selectional restrictions have mainly been thought of as applying to NP complements: a verb such as *eat* only selects NPs with semantic features that are specified in the lexical entry of the verb:

(20) Louise eats raspberry pies/*? sincerity

This type of selection can be conceived of as a type of identification: the semantic properties of the selected N° must match those of the lexical specification. Now the head C° is also selected by the governing V° head: interrogative verbs select interrogative C°s (Bresnan 1972). Alternatively, one might say interrogative C°s match the lexical specification of the governing verb. The idea of selection of C° by identification can now be extended to the temporal feature [– realized] of the infinitive: a [– realized] C° is identified by V° in exactly the same way as a [– abstract] N° is identified by the V° governing it. To make the notion of coindexing more precise, the following principle can be proposed as a general condition on selectional coindexation:

(21)   *Principle of maximal identification of features*
       Coindexation under government involves the maximal
       identification of features between the coindexed elements.

With respect to the requirement of maximal identification of features, the temporally [– realized] eventuality feature of C° will be identified and coindexed with a feature of the matrix V° which governs it, if nothing prevents V° from governing C°. There is a further restriction on this identification which is present in the formulation of ARCA.A, and which can be derived from more general principles. ARCA.A states that the infinitival argument, or rather the argument variable representing the infinitive, must be a co-argument of the controller in the temporally 'unrealized' subevent. In terms of coindexation of C°, this means that the infinitival CP must itself be lexically represented in the 'unrealized' subevent in order for identification and coindexation of C° to come about. This restriction in itself is intuitively reasonable: the infinitival [– realized] C° cannot 'recognize' temporally 'unrealized' subevents with which its CP has no semantic relation. Nevertheless, the restriction stipulating that the infinitival CP should be lexically represented in the subevent with which C° is coindexed should follow from general principles.

This restriction can be derived if we take into account Stowell's (1981) discussion about proper government. Stowell (1981: 376) wonders why proper government by a lexical head is equivalent to coindexing with an antecedent. He suggests that if these two types of government form a natural class, there should be an underlying property unifying them. This underlying property lies in the way thematic roles are assigned, according to Stowell (1981: 381–4). He views the 'matching' between projected A-positions and the θ-'slots' in the lexical representation of the verb as the assignment of the referential index of the subcategorized object to the slot in the thematic grid. θ-role assignment is the identification of the arguments of the verb by relating their indices to the 'slots' in the thematic grid (Stowell (1981: 382). The arguments of the verb are then coindexed with subparts of the verbal structure.

In the event structure analysis advocated here, thematic roles are represented as ordered variables (with subcategorization specifications) embedded in the temporal event structure of the verb. In the analysis presented here, Stowell's (1981) idea can be easily integrated: we will assume that the CP argument identifies its variable in the θ-grid or event structure by assigning its index to it, and thus enables the [– realized] head $C°$ to identify the temporally [– realized] properties of the subevent. The first identification is thematic, and the second has to do with selectional restrictions. In the same way, the NP *a raspberry pie* is identified with the internal θ-role of *eat* in (20), and the $N°$ head *pie* identifies its features with the selectional features ([– abstract]) linked to the internal θ-role. The head of a subcategorized complement can only identify its features with those of the matrix $V°$ if this subcategorized complement has identified and coindexed its θ-role in the event structure of the matrix verb. This hierarchy of identification is in line with Jackendoff's (1987) assumption that selectional restrictions are part of a subvocabulary of conceptual argument structure or θ-theory, that is nevertheless distinct from θ-theory. The lexical coindexation of the temporally [– realized] $C°$ can only take place if the CP is first identified and coindexed in the event structure. In this context, the only subevent the $C°$ head can coindex with is the subevent in which the CP is lexically represented by an argument variable to which it assigns its index. As a result, the restriction limiting coindexation of $C°$ to those subevents in which CP is embedded as an argument can be derived from general assumptions about the relation between thematic roles and selectional restrictions.

In (6iii), part of the control problem was formulated as the question of how the semantic representation of control verbs can determine control respecting standard assumptions about selection by a verbal head. The answer proposed here is that the embedded $C°$ is coindexed with the temporally [– realized] subevent in the event structure of the matrix verb. In this way, the descriptive aspectual restriction of ARCA.A can be reduced to the temporal coindexation of temporally [– realized] $C°$ and the temporally [– realized] subevent in $V°$. This identification in terms of coindexation is necessary for reasons independent of control: the temporal interpretation and selectional restrictions on the infinitive, which also depend on the event structure of the matrix verb, are equally determined by this coindexation. Observe that the part of ARCA.A which links [– realized] subevents to control still needs to be derived. Hitherto, ARCA.A still has been a merely descriptive statement about controllerhood. Reformulating question (6iv), the question arises as to how the coindexation of $C°$ in the event structure of $V°$ further restricts Binding of PRO by an element in the matrix clause, so that ARCA.A may be completely reduced to independent principles of the grammar.

The control relation can be viewed as a consequence of the interaction of this highly structured temporal–aspectual coindexation mechanism with the Binding properties of the unexpressed infinitival subject. First of all, Borer's idea will be adopted, that the embedded $AGR_S°$ is the element that is instrumental in establishing the referential link of PRO with the controller in the matrix clause. Borer analyzes AGR_S° as an anaphor which moves to C°. In this way, the Binding domain of this AGR_S° is extended to the matrix clause, eliminating the need for the notion of Domain-governing category proposed by Manzini (1983).[6] In addition, Borer proposes that AGR_S° is the element subject to Binding rather than PRO.[7] In addition, I would like to adopt Kayne's (1991a) idea; he takes advantage of the revision of Binding theory proposed in Chomsky (1986b: 170ff.) to suggest that the governing category of an anaphor in subject position cannot be the X^{max} of that anaphor, but rather the next category up, since the subject position of that X^{max} is not a potential binder for the anaphor. The anaphor cannot be bound in its own X^{max} because there is no position that might contain a potential binder (Kayne 1991a). Kayne intended these remarks for PRO as an anaphor, but it is clear that they carry over to AGR_S° as an anaphor in Borer's (1989) sense. In this way, no special devices are necessary to extend the governing category of AGR_S° to the matrix clause. PRO gets its reference via Spec–Head agreement with the anaphor AGR_S°. The fact that AGR_S° is an anaphor entails that in principle it can get the reference of any argument in the matrix clause.

Our proposal is now that this essentially free Binding of AGR_S° in the matrix clause is constrained by the index which the infinitival C° (and hence T°) receive under government from the matrix V°. The AGR_S° node of the embedded infinitive is governed by and coindexed with the infinitival C° and T° nodes which have the index of the temporally [– realized] subevent. The AGR_S° node of course does not inherit the [– realized] reference of C°: AGR_S° has only nominal features [αperson, αnumber, αgender] and cannot receive a [– realized] reference, since this is a temporal feature. Only the embedded T° fully shares the [– realized] feature of the infinitive. Nevertheless, coindexing of the infinitival T° and AGR_S°, and perhaps C°, is made obligatory by their functional status with respect to V°: the temporal and nominal reference of the subject which is expressed on the verb must coincide. Let us represent this by provisorily assuming that the 'outer shell' of the AGR_S° node (but not its features) takes on the index of C° and T°. In the preceding paragraphs, it was argued that the head C° of CP is identified by the temporally 'unrealized' subevent in the matrix V° by identification under proper government. This indexation of the infinitival functional nodes can be represented in the following scheme with the index $\mathbf{n}$, which is used throughout to refer to both [– realized] subevents and tenses. The structure (22) is a more detailed version of (19):

(22) $\quad \mathbf{X}[_{V^\circ} e_{n\ (x,CP)}\ e_{m\ (y,CP)}]_{V^\circ} Y [_{CP} C^\circ_n \ldots AGR_{S\ (n(x/*y))}^\circ \ldots$
$\qquad T^\circ_n \ldots V^\circ inf_n \ldots]$

where (i)   X, Y, and CP are the projected arguments of the verb.

(ii) x, y, and *CP* represent the argument variables in the event structure of the matrix verb coindexed with their projected arguments.[8]

(iii) The index **n** represents a (sub)eventual (e_n) or morphological (C°_n) temporally [− realized] feature, and the index *m* a 'realized' subeventual feature.

What does it mean now for AGR_S° to receive the 'same' index as C° and T°? Of course there cannot be an indexation of AGR_S° as indicated in (22) with nominal indexes contained in the temporal index imposed by C° and T°. It is more likely that the nominal index of AGR_S°, which is obtained by Binding with an argument in the matrix clause, simply must be *referentially compatible* with the index **n** of C° and T°. To be referentially compatible with the index **n** of C° and T°, the nominal index of AGR_S° simply must be contained in the lexical reference of **n**. The lexical reference of **n** is the temporally [− realized] subevent which contains both the CP and another argument. Consequently, this referential compatibility between the lexically determined reference of C°–T° and the Binding of AGR_S° can only be achieved if AGR_S° is bound by the projected argument which is also lexically represented in the subevent with which C° is coindexed. Only the noninfinitival argument in the subevent with which C° is coindexed can be the antecedent of the anaphor AGR_S°. The nominal indexing on AGR_S° in (22) then represents the only licit configuration for control. It is the lexically determined index of C° and T° which narrows down the choice of the anaphor AGR_S° in the matrix clause. If AGR_S° took the index of an argument embedded in a subevent that is not coindexed by C° and T°, there would be a referential conflict in the functional categories of the infinitival clause. In this event, the index of AGR_S° obtained by Binding would be completely incompatible with the temporal reference identified by C° in the matrix V°, since on the level of the event structure the antecedent of AGR_S° would not be contained in the subevent identified by C°. Binding of AGR_S° in the matrix clause is heavily restricted, since it must take an antecedent which is lexically identified in the subevent e_n. Only this coindexation of AGR_S° will ensure a coherent indexation of the (C°)–AGR_S°–T° string in the infinitival argument. The requirement of strict coindexing on the infinitival C°–AGR_S°–T° complex is satisfied by the compatibility of the lexical indexes of C°–T° with the Binding index of AGR_S°. Notice that this analysis completely derives the effects of ARCA.A, which can now be viewed as a purely descriptive generalization. So-called control theory reduces to an explicit theory of semantic selection under proper government which interacts in a modular fashion with Binding theory. In fact, the identification and coindexation of C° with (sub)events of the matrix verb functions as a semantic filter for Binding of the anaphor $AGR_S°$. If this line of reasoning is correct, the temporal identification of the infinitive with the matrix verb is ultimately responsible for the control relation as well. This determination of control by aspectual factors then explains Rooryck's (1987) observation on the correspondence between control properties and aspectual selectional restrictions displayed by control verbs.

6 Event structure, Binding, and control: some examples

6.1 Object control

An adequate analysis of object control has to explain why the object is the only argument that can function as a controller. Stated differently, an analysis of object control should account for the fact that the subject of object control verbs can never be the controller of the infinitival subject PRO. Previous syntactic and semantic approaches do not adequately explain the remarkable semantic cohesion of object control verbs that has been noticed by several authors establishing exhaustive lists of these verbs for French (Gross 1975) and English (Visser 1972, 1973, 1978; Wierzbicka 1987; Rudanko 1985, 1989). Object control verbs can be divided into two major semantic categories: the first includes Transition verbs which could be termed verbs of 'influence': *force, impose, invite, order, allow, prevent.* A second important semantic class of object control verbs involves Transition verbs of 'evaluation' such as *praise, punish, accuse.*[9]

(23) Kim_i forced $Sandy_j$ $PRO_{*i/j/*arb}$ to do the dishes

(24) Kim_i praised/punished $Sandy_j$ $PRO_{*i/j/*arb}$ for doing the dishes

Let us now analyze the event structures of these verbs and relate these to their control properties. The basic event structure of 'influence' verbs such as *force* can be represented as follows:

(25) $[T\ e_1^*{}_{act\ (Kim,\ (Sandy,\ do\ dishes))}\ e_{n+1\ do\ dishes\ (Sandy)}]T$

The first punctual subevent represents the fact that the agentive subject *Kim* is involved in establishing a relation between the Patient *Sandy* and the argument *do the dishes*.[10] This is why the three arguments are embedded under the same causation predicate. The second subevent translates the fact that the relation between the Patient 'influencee' and the argument *do the dishes* can come about at any given moment after e_1. In other words, the relation between the 'influencee' and that which is imposed on the 'influencee' can come about at any future moment after the punctual moment of 'influence': the event of doing the dishes can take place at any given moment in the future of the forcing subevent. The temporal interpretation of this infinitive can only refer to the future of the 'influencing' subevent as in (26). Verbs of 'influence' do not select infinitives referring to a moment before the punctual 'influencing' event:

(26)   *Kim$_i$ forced Sandy$_j$ to have done the dishes yesterday

The second subevent with its undetermined future temporal reference can be considered a temporally [– realized] subevent in the sense of (9ii), since it clearly refers to a 'possible future.' The temporal interpretation and the selectional properties of 'influence' verbs show that the infinitival C° is coindexed with this [– realized] subevent.

Object control can be derived from the event structure. The infinitival AGR$_S$° can only be bound by the object argument which is represented in the [– realized] subevent. Only this Binding of AGR$_S$° can ensure coherent coindexing of the infinitival C°–AGR$_S$°–T° complex. The agentive subject is embedded in a punctual 'realized' subevent and cannot be a controller, since the infinitival temporally 'unrealized' C° cannot be identified by and lexically coindexed with this subevent by the Principle of Maximal Identification of Features. If AGR$_S$° were bound by the matrix subject, AGR$_S$° would end up with an index which is incompatible with the lexically determined temporal index of C° and T°. The lexical index of C° and T° and the index obtained by Binding of AGR$_S$° in the matrix clause have to be referentially compatible, and this can only be achieved if AGR$_S$° is bound by a matrix argument which is lexically represented in the subevent C° and T° are coindexed with.

The event structure of the 'evaluation' verbs is related to object control properties in a similar manner. Transition ('achievement') verbs such as *punish* can be represented with a punctual subevent heading the Transition event structure as in (27a). Transition verbs such as *praise* should be represented as in (27b) with an event structure headed by a Process subevent, since they can extend over time. In both cases, the subevent heading the event structure establishes a relation between the agentive subject and the subevent which is evaluated. The reason for this is that it is not so much *Sandy* which is being evaluated, but the relation of *Sandy* to his doing the dishes.

(27) a. punish $[_T\, e_{n\ \text{do dishes (Sandy)}}\ e_{1*\text{act (Kim, } e)}]_T$

b. praise $[_T\, e_{n\ \text{do dishes (Sandy)}}\ [_P\, e_1 \ldots e_x\,]_{P*\text{act (Kim, } e)}]_T$

The first, Stative, subevent translates the fact that this subevent may be true of Sandy at any given time with respect to the past or future of e_1. The evaluation takes place at a point in time which is independent of that nonpunctual Stative subevent: one can be praised or punished for a past or a future property or event. This subevent then can be characterized as [– realized] according to (9i). This temporally 'free' character of the subevent can be checked by the past (28a) and future (28b) interpretation of the infinitives:

(28) a. Kim punished/praised Sandy for having written/writing that article yesterday

b. Kim punished/praised Sandy for leaving so soon tomorrow

This temporal interpretation of the infinitive is due to the fact that the infinitival C° is coindexed with the Stative [– realized] subevent. With respect to control, the coherent coindexation of the infinitival C°–AGR$_S$°–T° complex requires that the infinitival AGR$_S$° have a Binding index which is compatible with the index of C°. Only arguments that are lexically represented in the [– realized] subevent can comply with this requirement. Consequently, only the object argument *Sandy* in (28), which is embedded in the [– realized] subevent in the representations (27) together with the argument variable representing the infinitive, can be coindexed with the infinitival AGR$_S$°, and end up as the controller of the unexpressed infinitival subject. As a result, 'evaluation' verbs can only be object control verbs.

6.2 *Variable and preferential control*

We have already observed that verbs of the *propose, offer, suggest* class allow for free control (29), verbs such as *promise* and *guarantee* involve preferential subject control (30), and verbs of asking involve preferential object control (31):

(29) Kim$_i$ offered Sandy$_j$ PRO$_{i/j/i+j/*arb}$ to do the dishes

(30) a. Kim$_i$ promised Sandy$_j$ PRO$_{i/*j/*arb}$ to do the dishes

b. Kim$_i$ promised Sandy$_j$ PRO$_{*i/j/*arb}$ to be allowed to do the dishes

(31) a. Sandy$_i$ asked Kim$_j$ PRO$_{*i/j/*arb}$ to do the dishes

b. Sandy$_i$ asked Kim$_j$ PRO$_{i/*j/*arb}$ to be allowed to do the dishes

These sets of verbs show a remarkably fine-grained semantic cohesion. The specific control properties of these verbs and their semantic coherence have been repeatedly noted for German *anbieten* 'offer' and *vorschlagen* 'propose' (Abraham 1982, 1983, (Růžička 1983a, 1983b; Siebert-Ott 1983, 1985; Wegener 1989), but they have never been adequately explained in relation to other semantically coherent sets of control verbs implying 'transfer.'

We think that a proper analysis of the event structure of these verbs can achieve a coherent explanation of both their semantic cohesion and their 'variable' control properties. In terms of 'Source–Recipient' relations, these verbs are identical to the object control 'transfer' verbs. If the semantic unity of these variable control verbs is to be analyzed in intuitive terms with respect to the *give*-type (11) verbs, we might say that the *propose, offer, suggest* class represents a type of 'transfer' that does not necessarily come about, and that may be 'resisted' by the 'Recipient.' Let us replace the infinitive in (29) by a nominal argument to make the thematic structure of 'transfer' clearer:

(32)   Kim offered Sandy an apple

In the subevent structure of this verb class, the transfer involved in *propose, offer, suggest*-type verbs takes place at an undetermined moment in time after the time of the proposal. In terms of the entailments of the event of proposing/offering something, the event structure of these verbs should at least incorporate the following structure:

(33) $[_T\ e_{1^*\ \text{vol (Kim, T)}}$

$[_T\ e_{n+1\ \text{act (Kim)}}\ \&\ \text{move (Kim, apple)}\ e_{n+2\ \text{act (Sandy, en+1)}}\ \&\ \text{at (Sandy, apple)}\ ]_T\ ]_T$

The first subevent represents the punctual time of the proposal which is expressed as a volitional act of the subject to undertake a transition. This expresses the idea that *propose* involves the intention of a future giving event. The event time e_n of the embedded Transition is of course 'unrealized,' since it is restricted to the 'future' time period after the time e_1 of the proposal. The index $n+1$ refers to a [– realized] 'giving' subevent that follows the punctual subevent e_1, and the 'receiving' subevent takes place at an undetermined moment e_{n+2} after the subevent e_{n+1}. In plain English, (33) says that Kim has the intention of transferring something, that this transfer is to be executed by Kim at an undetermined moment in the future, that Sandy decides on whether Kim's transfer comes about, and thus can come into possession of the transferred 'Theme' at the final moment in the development of the event. Notice that both the 'Source' and the 'Recipient' argument are described with agentive properties: this reflects the fact that the 'transfer' is in some sense subject to an active intervention of the 'Recipient' who can resist or accept the 'transfer' expressed in the first subevent of the embedded Transition.[11] This notion of 'resistance/acceptance' is crucial in the semantic description of *propose*-type verbs, since it allows them to be distinguished from verbs such as *promise*. In the next paragraph, we will show that the event structure of *promise* also involves a 'future transfer,' but it is intuitively clear that no notion of 'resistance/acceptance of transfer' is involved in the semantic description of the Recipient in the event of promising. This intuitive notion of 'possible resistance' can be represented in the event structure if it is accepted that both arguments have agentive properties. The idea that different arguments of the same verb can share (Proto-)Agent properties is due to Dowty (1991). For *offer/propose*-type verbs, we would simply like to say that the 'Recipient' argument is characterized by an agentive property, thus translating the intuitive notion of 'resistance/acceptance of transfer' in agentive terms. This does not mean that both agentive arguments have the same thematic properties: unlike the 'Recipient' argument, the 'Source' argument also has the (Proto-)Agent property of volition.

The event structure of *propose/offer*-type verbs in (33) can now be related to their variable control properties when the direct object of these verbs is realized as an infinitive. The temporal interpretation of the embedded infinitive shows that the coindexation of [– realized] $C°$ must be with a subevent referring to a 'possible future,' since infinitives referring to a moment before the punctual subevent 'starting' the offer are ruled out:

(34)   * Kim offered Sandy to have done the dishes yesterday

In terms of the event structure in (33), the coindexation of [– realized] $C°$ is possible with either subevent of the embedded Transition. Both the 'Source' and the 'Recipient' arguments of *propose/offer*-type verbs are embedded with the infinitival Theme argument in the temporally undetermined [– realized] subevents of the embedded Transition in (33). Embedding in such a 'nonrealized' subevent is the most important condition for achieving the status of possible controller: as noted before, the Agentive external argument of *force*-type verbs is only embedded in a punctual subevent and therefore does not meet the principal condition for possible controllerhood. The [– realized] $C°$ head of the CP selected by *propose*- and *offer*-type verbs can now be coindexed either with the first or with the second subevent of the embedded Transition, triggering Binding of the infinitival $AGR_S°$ by either the 'Source' or by the 'Goal' argument. Either Binding of $AGR_S°$ can achieve coherent coindexing of the infinitival $C°–AGR_S°–T°$ complex. In ARCA.B (10), we stated that a thematic hierarchy should designate the agentive argument as a controller in case there is more than one possible controller. However, since both arguments are agentive in the case of *offer/propose*-type verbs, no particular controller will be chosen. Since the thematic hierarchy cannot apply, the 'Source,' the 'Recipient,' or both arguments can freely function as controllers.[12] In this case, there are no lexical restrictions on Binding of the infinitival $AGR_S°$ in the matrix clause, and the thematic hierarchy ARCA.B cannot apply since both arguments have agentive properties.

Given the event structure proposed for variable control verbs of the *propose/offer* type, we would like to analyze preferential subject (*promise*) or object (*ask*) control verbs in a similar way. As we already suggested, *promise* minimally differs from the *propose/offer*-type verbs in the agentive properties of the argument associated with the nonpreferential controller. Contrary to the 'Recipient' argument of the *propose/offer* verbs, this argument should be viewed as nonagentive. Hence, the event structure of *promise, guarantee* in (35) involves the subevents expressed in (36):

(35)   Kim promised Sandy an apple

(36) $[_T \, e_{1* \text{ vol (Kim, T)}} \, [_T \, e_{n+1 \text{ act (Kim) \& move (Kim, apple) \& at (Sandy, apple)}} \,]_T \,]_T$

As can be seen from the event structure of *propose/offer*-type verbs, the only difference between the event structure of *propose/offer* and *promise/guarantee* lies in the absence of agentive 'resistance' to the 'transfer' for *promise/guarantee*. An event of promising involves a punctual subevent e_1 translating the volition of the subject to undertake a future 'transfer.'

Verbs of asking can be given an event structure that is the thematic converse of verbs of the *promise* class. The 'Source–Goal' relations of these verbs are linked to exactly the opposite arguments. The subject 'Source' of *promise*-type verbs resembles the object 'Source' of *ask*-type verbs in that both arguments must be represented in the event structure as initiating the possible 'transfer' of the 'Theme' argument.

(37)   Kim asked Sandy for an apple

(38) $[_T \, e_{1* \text{ vol (Kim, T)}} \, [_T \, e_{n+1 \text{ act (Sandy) \& move (Sandy, apple) \& at (Kim, apple)}} \,]_T \,]_T$

The event structure of verbs of asking may be paraphrased as follows: at a punctual moment e_1, the subject *Kim* expresses volition with respect to a future 'transfer.' The 'Source' *Sandy* may initiate the 'transfer' of the 'Theme' *apple* at an undetermined time e_{n+1} after the time e_1 of asking, and the subject *Kim* may come into possession of the *apple* at an undetermined moment e_{n+2} ($=e_{at}$) after the initiation of the transfer. This event structure is almost identical to that of *promise/guarantee* in (36), with the exception that the order of subject and indirect object in the second subevent is reversed.

In the same way as for the *offer/propose*-type verbs, the 'transfer' associated with *promise* and *ask* can[13] be carried out at an undetermined time e_{n+1} after the time of promising or asking, and the 'State of possession' of the 'Recipient' is established at a time e_{n+2} ($=e_{at}$) after the initiation of the 'transfer.' Again, there are two [– realized] subevents in this event structure. When the 'Theme' is realized as an infinitive, the infinitival [– realized] $C°$ must be coindexed with one of these 'possible future' [– realized] subevents. This can be checked by the fact that *promise/guarantee* and verbs of asking cannot select an infinitive referring to the past:

(39)   * Thérèse promised/guaranteed/asked her friends to have left yesterday

How can the event structures (36) and (38) be linked to 'preferential' control properties? Recall that the coherent indexing of the infinitival $C°–AGR_S°–T°$ complex requires $AGR_S°$ to have an index compatible with that of $C°$: this requires the argument binding $AGR_S°$ to be lexically represented in the subevent $C°$ is coindexed with. As for *propose/offer*-type verbs, both the subject and object arguments of *promise* and *ask* are embedded in temporally undetermined and hence [– realized] subevents with the 'Theme' infinitival argument. Since coindexation of $C°$ can be either with the subevent embedding the 'Source' or with the 'Recipient' argument, $AGR_S°$ can be coindexed with either argument. Binding of the infinitival $AGR_S°$ in the matrix clause is not restricted to any particular argument, both subject and object belong to the set of possible controllers. In the case of *offer/propose*-type verbs, the thematic hierarchy ARCA.B did not apply because of the fact that both the 'Source' and the 'Recipient' arguments bear agentive properties. This is not the case for *promise/guarantee*-type verbs: the 'Recipient' is not characterized by agentive properties. The thematic hierarchy in ARCA.B thus ensures that the agentive subject of *promise/guarantee* ends up as the preferential controller, as in (30a).

Sentence (31a) clearly shows that the 'Source' argument of verbs of asking is the preferential controller. How can this argument be characterized as the agentive argument? In the event structure (38) of verbs of asking, the subject bears the (Proto-)Agent property *volition* with respect to the Transition expressed in the second subevent. However, the 'Source' argument is characterized by more (Proto-)Agent properties: the properties of *causation* and *movement* translate the initiation of the 'possible future transfer.' Following Dowty (1991), this 'Source' argument, then, is the most agentive argument in the event. Consequently, the thematic hierarchy ARCA.B will designate it as the preferential controller. The event structure of verbs of 'asking' then not only is the converse of the event structure of *promise*-type verbs in terms of 'Source-Recipient' relations, but also with respect to control properties.

Control shifts occur in modal and passive contexts through a thematic mechanism interacting with Binding and ARCA.B. Whenever the preferential controller of *promise* and *ask* coincides with the implicit agent of the embedded passive (*to be allowed (by X)*), the controller is interpreted as both subject and implicit agent of the infinitive. Such structures are ruled out independently (*Jane$_i$ is allowed to leave (by Xi)*). Consequently, the preferential controller becomes unavailable for control. According to ARCA.A, both the

Source and the Goal arguments of *promise* and *ask* are possible controllers, with the Source argument the preferential controller following ARCA.B. When the preferential controller is unavailable for control, the controller with less agentive properties (Goal) will be selected as the controller of the infinitive by the interaction of Binding and ARCA. The same explanation applies to those contexts in which modals trigger control shifts in French, and interrogative infinitives which trigger control shifts when selected by verbs such as *ask*:

(40) a. Théophile$_i$ a promis à Théodore$_j$ de PRO$_{i/*j}$ lire/PRO$_{*i/j}$ pouvoir lire le journal
'Théophile promised Théodore to read/to be allowed to read the paper'

b. Eulalie$_i$ a demandé à Euphrasie$_j$ de PRO$_{*i/j}$ lire/PRO$_{i/*j}$ pouvoir lire le journal
'Eulalie asked Euphrasie to read/to be allowed to read the paper'

(41)   Bill$_i$ asked Bob$_j$ how PRO$_{i/*j}$ to shave himself

Interrogative infinitives trigger a deontic interpretation for the infinitive: *how to shave himself* here means *how he should/could shave himself*, not *how he is/will be shaving himself*. This deontic interpretation, which seems to be linked to the interaction of *Wh-* movement and [– realized] tense, has the same effect as overt modals such as *pouvoir* 'can': if the preferential controller (Source) is interpreted as the instance behind the permission/obligation expressed in the embedded infinitive, this preferential controller becomes unavailable for control, and controllerhood shifts to the Goal argument.

6.3 'Split' control

Until now, it was only noted cursorily that for certain control verbs, the 'Source' and the 'Recipient' argument can jointly control the PRO subject of the infinitival argument. This type of 'split' control becomes clearer when the interpretation of the infinitive requires a plural subject. This interpretation can be forced by adding an element such as *together* to the infinitive as in (42).

(42)   Kim$_i$ offered/promised/asked Sandy$_j$ PRO$_{i+j}$ to go to the movies together

Verbs of variable control and preferential subject or object control seem to allow for 'split' control as well. This observation should not come as a surprise: since both arguments are lexically embedded in 'unrealized' subevents, both are available for control, in compliance with ARCA.A.

It is more surprising that some verbs of the *force* type expressing 'influence' also allow for 'split' control if the infinitive requires a plural interpretation for its subject. These data have hitherto gone unnoticed in the literature. There is a minimal contrast between the (b) sentence of (43), which does not allow for 'split' control, and the (b) sentences of (44–46), which do:

(43) a. Kim$_i$ told/coerced Sandy$_j$ [PRO$_{*i/j}$ to do the dishes]

    b. Kim$_i$ told/coerced Sandy$_j$ [PRO$_{*i+j}$ to do the dishes together]

(44) a. Kim$_i$ forced Sandy$_j$ [PRO$_{?i+j}$ to do the dishes together]

    b. Kim$_i$ cajoled Sandy$_j$ into [PRO$_{i+j}$ doing the dishes together]

(45) a. Kim$_i$ made Sandy$_j$ get used to [PRO$_{i+j}$ doing the dishes together]

    b. Kim$_i$ nagged/browbeat Sandy$_j$ [PRO$_{i+j}$ to do the dishes together]

(46) a. Kim$_i$ convinced/persuaded Sandy$_j$ [PRO$_{j/*i}$ to do the dishes]

    b. Kim$_i$ convinced/persuaded Sandy$_j$ [PRO$_{i+j}$ to do the dishes together]

The difference between the verbs in (43) and those in (44–46) is that the exertion of influence over the Patient argument *Sandy* is progressive and spread out over time in verbs such as *cajole*, *nag*, or *persuade*, while the way in which influence is exerted over the Patient in verbs such as *tell* or *coerce* is punctual and immediate. The relevant generalization thus seems to be that 'split' control is possible if the matrix verb expresses 'progressive' exertion of influence over the Patient. Importantly, these cases irrefutably demonstrate the interaction between lexical aspect and control, which is the main thesis of this chapter.

How can these cases of 'split' control be explained by the subevent structure of the verbs involved? More particularly, a representation in terms of subevent structure should explain why the 'Agent' argument of object control verbs only becomes available for control if the infinitive requires a plural interpretation. I would like to propose that 'progressive' object control verbs such as *cajole*, *nag*, or *persuade* only differ from 'punctual' object control verbs such as *tell* or *coerce* by the nature of the first subevent. First of all, the first subevent of *cajole*, *nag*, or *persuade* involves a Process, while the first subevent of *tell* or *coerce* is punctual. This reflects the idea that the relation between Patient and Theme is brought about progressively by the Agent in verbs such as *cajole*, *nag*, or *persuade*. The relevant representations are thus as in (47) and (48):

(47) a. Kim_i nagged/cajoled/persuaded $Sandy_j$ $[PRO_{i+j}$ to do the dishes together]

    b. $[_T [_P e_1 \cdots e_n]_{P \text{ act (Kim, (Sandy, do dishes))}} e_{n+1 \text{ do dishes (Sandy)}}]_T$

(48) a. Kim_i told/coerced $Sandy_j$ $[PRO_{*i / j / *i+j}$ to do the dishes together]

    b. $[_T e_1^{*}{}_{\text{act (Kim, (Sandy, do dishes))}} e_{n+1 \text{ do dishes (Sandy)}}]_T$

These representations now allow for an explanation of 'split' control. In order to provide this, the definition of 'unrealized' subevent in (9) above needs to be expanded to include Process subevents. This is not unintuitive, since the Process subevent contains an undefined final subevent e_n, which refers to the fact that Processes are 'not yet realized.' If this extension is granted, the [– realized] Process subevent becomes available for coindexation with the [– realized] $C°$ head of the infinitive. Notice however that such coindexation makes both arguments of the verb jointly available for control. In other words, $AGR_S°$ cannot pick an argument in the Process subevent at its convenience: coindexation of $C°$ with the Process subevent forces coindexation of $AGR_S°$ with both arguments embedded in that subevent. As a result, coindexation of $C°$ with the Process subevent will only come about if the infinitive accommodates a plural interpretation for its subject. In all cases where a singular interpretation for the infinitive is possible, coindexation of $C°$ will only be possible with the second [– realized] subevent, e_{n+1} in (47–48). The analysis thus explains rather elegantly why the 'Agent' argument of object control verbs is only available for control if the infinitive requires a plural interpretation.

7 Control in infinitival subjects and adjuncts

The behavior of infinitival subjects in subject and adjunct sentences has not yet been addressed.[14] In these cases, infinitives are not complements of the verb and hence lack theta-marking. As a result, there is no Binding domain for the infinitival $AGR_S°$. In these cases, it is expected that the infinitival clause will not only act as a Barrier for extraction, but also for Binding. In principle, this would mean that the infinitival $AGR_S°$ cannot be bound at all, contrary to fact. To gain a better understanding of the behavior of anaphoric $AGR_S°$ in contexts where no Binding domain is available, it is useful to look at the behavior of other anaphors in contexts where they have no access to an appropriate Binding domain.

Burzio (1992) and Pica (1987, 1991) propose that the absence of ξ-features is a morphological defining property of anaphors. Burzio (1992) moreover proposes that impersonal *si* 'self' in Italian is equally featureless, but lacks an antecedent since there is no governing category for it. Burzio proposes that impersonal *si* 'self' therefore receives a 'default' first person plural interpretation as in (49a). The impersonal *si* 'self' can, however, also refer to the third person if context is supplied (49b).

(49) a. Si è contenti in Italia
   SELF is happy$_{PL}$ in Italy
   'One is happy in Italy'

   b. Tutti lo dicevano. Si è contenti in Italia
   All it$_{cl}$ said. SELF is happy$_{PL}$ in Italy
   'Everyone said it. One is happy in Italy'

I would like to claim that the same is true for anaphoric AGR$_S$° in sentential subjects and infinitival adjuncts. In the cases where the infinitival clause is a complement of a matrix verb, the infinitival anaphoric AGR$_S$° is bound in its Binding domain, the matrix clause. In sentential subjects and infinitival adjuncts, the anaphoric AGR$_S$° receives a 'default' first or second person interpretation, or a third person interpretation if context is supplied. The sentential subject in (50) is preferably interpreted as *our/your making noise*.

(50)   PRO making noise at midnight will frighten Sue

The fact that PRO in these sentences is preferably interpreted as first or second person has been pointed out by Thompson (1973: 377) for adjectival arguments as in (51):

(51)   'Bill, tearing up my new paper dolls was mean,' cried Sue

This referential property of PRO in sentential subjects has led Van Haaften (1982: 118) to claim that arbitrary PRO in these cases cannot be interpreted as third person. Bresnan (1982) and Vanden Wyngaerd (1990: 216) have pointed out that the infinitival subject can be interpreted as referring to a third person if context is supplied:

(52) a. Tom felt sheepish. Pinching those elephants was foolish.
   He shouldn't have done it

   b. Frankly, I'm worried about Mary. What has she gotten herself into?

Don't get me wrong: I think it was fine to join the group. But getting herself photographed with those starving wolves was dangerous

It is important to underscore that control of the infinitival subject in all these cases is not subject to locality restrictions. Despite examples such as (52), it is striking that the unexpressed subject PRO in infinitival and gerundial subjects is preferably interpreted as a discourse first or second person referent. The same is true in infinitival adjuncts when the subject of the infinitive does not correspond to the matrix subject. Clark (1985) has claimed on the basis of (53) that control in infinitival adjuncts is subject to locality. However, it appears that this claim is based on a rule of prescriptive grammar stipulating that the subject of the matrix clause should be a controller in infinitival adjuncts and gerunds.[15,16] When making abstraction of this prescriptive reflex, sentences such as those in (54) can be construed which show that a nonlocal argument can control the unexpressed subject of a lower adjunct if it is second person, or properly introduced in the discourse:[17]

(53) a. John felt old after seeing himself/*oneself in the mirror
(= Clark 1985: 292(55))

b. John kissed Mary after seeing himself/*herself in the mirror
(= Clark 1985: 293(57))

c. Mary thought that Bill had died after seeing *herself/himself in the mirror

(54) a. So you think now that Bill might have died right after shaving yourself on June 6. Why would that be?

b. We have interviewed several people living in the neighborhood of the robbed bank. One person claimed the bank was attacked right after shaving himself at eight o'clock.

c. Bill will only come home after calling him repeatedly

d. Mr Freckletweeter$_i$ was a very disorderly person at times. I$_j$ see you$_k$ have realized now that without PRO$_{i/j/k}$ classifying them properly, his$_i$ papers would have been irremediably lost for posterity.

The interpretation of impersonal *si* 'self' in (49) is very close to the preferential interpretation of PRO in subject sentences and infinitival adjuncts: in both cases, the interpretation of the subject involves a discourse referent, but it can refer to third person given an appropriate context. The reflexive/

impersonal *si* 'self' and the AGR_S° in subject sentences and infinitival adjuncts also share a syntactic context: in both cases, the anaphor does not have a governing category. I will assume here that gerunds and infinitives have the same type of anaphoric AGR_S°. The similarity between the overt reflexive/impersonal *si* 'self' and the infinitival AGR_S° warrants an analysis of this infinitival AGR_S° along the same lines: the infinitival AGR_S° is anaphor which can receive a 'default' pronominal interpretation if there is no governing category for it.

The fact that the infinitival AGR_S° takes on a 'default' pronominal interpretation in subject infinitival sentences predicts that there should be a difference between control of PRO in base-generated subjects and control in derived subjects. Subject sentences that originate as complements must at least allow for anaphoric control by an argument of the matrix verb, whereas base-generated sentential subjects only allow for pronominal control. Since pronominal control can pick up any NP in the context, this type of control easily masks anaphoric control. The only way to tell pronominal control and anaphoric control apart in these cases is that only pronominal control is subject to the discourse restrictions discussed above: the 'default' pronominal interpretation of AGR_S° is restricted to first and second person, third person antecedents need to be discursively introduced, as noted in (51–52) above. Such a restriction does not apply to anaphoric control in complement sentences.

The difference between anaphoric and pronominal control introduced by the above analysis allows for an explanation of some long-standing problems with respect to restrictions on the reference of PRO in untensed subject sentences of Psych- predicates. It has often been noted that the subject-contained PRO in (21) must be bound by the Experiencer object:

(55)   Playing/to play basketball is fun for/pleases/disturbs John

The untensed subject sentence is never interpreted as the playing of some unspecified person. Notice, however, that pronominal control is not excluded. Pronominal control is possible if the controller is properly introduced in the discourse:

(56) a.   We$_i$ thought that [PRO$_i$ to play/playing] basketball may be fun for/please/disturb John

   b.   John$_i$ thought that PRO$_i$ to play/playing basketball might be fun for/please/disturb us.

The interpretation of (55) with the 'Experiencer' object then certainly cannot involve pronominal control. If (55) involved pronominal control, it should involve the discourse restrictions noted above on pronominal control of third person coreferents. Since (55) is perfectly acceptable out of context, it must involve anaphoric control. The problem then arises as to how this can be the case: at first sight, the 'Experiencer' antecedent which binds the anaphoric AGR_S° contained in the untensed subject sentence is not located in the immediately superordinate binding domain of the infinitive, and does not c-command it.

Vanden Wyngaerd (1990) points out that an analysis of Psych- predicates such as the one proposed by Belletti & Rizzi (1988) or Pesetsky (1990, 1994) allows for an explanation of these anaphoric control properties. Belletti & Rizzi (1988) analyze Psych-predicates as unaccusative verbs where the surface subject is base-generated as a complement Theme. Psych-verbs then are projected as follows:

(57) a. [[V Theme] Experiencer]

b. [[please [to play basketball]] John]

Vanden Wyngaerd (1990) then assumes that the anaphor PRO may be bound by the c-commanding Experiencer argument when the untensed complement containing PRO is in its base position. Consequently, anaphoric control is possible. Similarly, in the analysis developed here, the infinitival anaphor AGR_S° contained in the untensed complement has the matrix clause of the Psych-verb as its governing category. Crucially, however, control by the Experiencer in the matrix clause is possible because of the lexical coindexation of the infinitival C° with the Stative [– realized] event of the matrix verb. Since Psych- predicates are Stative verbs, their event structure is [– realized] because it is not linked to a specific point on the time axis (cf. the definition in (9i)). The agentive predicate inside the subevent structure translates the fact that the Theme of Psych-verbs is causative (cfr. Pesetsky 1990 for discussion):

(58) $[_S e_{n\ \text{act (playing/to play basketball, John)}}]_S$

The Stative event with which the infinitival C° is coindexed then is temporally [– realized] in the sense of (9i). Since the [– realized] infinitival C°, or the [– realized] tense of a gerund, are coindexed with an aspectually [-realized] event in which the Experiencer is lexically represented, this Experiencer can bind the infinitival AGR_S° without giving rise to a coindexing conflict in the infinitival C°–AGR_S°–T° complex.

But this is not all. Anaphoric control is not the only possibility for the AGR_S° contained in the untensed complement of Psych-predicates. Moving the untensed sentence to subject position affords its anaphoric AGR_S° another option: anaphoric AGR_S° can receive a pronominal default interpretation at LF, since it has no governing category. This explains the cases of pronominal control in (56). In other words, Psych-verbs allow both anaphoric and pronominal control of the infinitival AGRS° contained in the subject infinitival sentence. Anaphoric control is determined in the base position of the infinitive, while pronominal control is fixed in the derived subject position that the infinitive ends up in.

In Minimalist terms (Chomsky 1995), this situation resembles that of the cases in (59). Chomsky argues that LF movement of *self* (LF cliticization or CL_{LF}) out of the *Wh*-NP in SpecCP accounts for the fact that the anaphor can be bound by the matrix subject in (59), while reconstruction of the anaphoric part of the *Wh*-NP downstairs accounts for the reading in which the anaphor is bound by the embedded subject.

(59)   John$_i$ wondered [which pictures of himself$_{i/j}$] Bill$_j$ saw t

(=Chomsky 1995: Ch 3(36))

The difference between anaphoric control and pronominal control in the case of Psych-verbs can be viewed in a similar way: anaphoric control is obtained by reconstruction of the anaphoric part of the infinitival CP (the anaphoric $AGR_s°$) in complement position of the Psych-verb, while pronominal control is obtained by interpreting the anaphoric $AGR_s°$ inside the infinitival CP upstairs, where it will receive a 'default' pronominal interpretation because of the lack of a higher Binding domain.

The difference between anaphoric and pronominal control in the case of Psych-verbs now explains why the following sentence is awkward:

(60)   * PRO$_i$ shaving himself$_i$ is fun for/pleases/disturbs John$_i$'s girlfriend

It has been observed by Mohanan (1983: 671) that this type of sentence is ungrammatical if *John* is not previously introduced in the discourse, and grammatical if *John* is discursively salient.[18] This discourse restriction suggests that pronominal control is involved. In fact, anaphoric control with *John* as the antecedent for the anaphoric infinitival $AGR_s°$ is excluded, since the controller *John* does not c- command the infinitival anaphor $AGR_s°$, and since the controller is not an argument occurring in the subevent structure of the matrix verb. The $AGR_s°$ contained in the sentential subject in (60) can only corefer with *John* through its 'default' pronominal interpretation.

Finally, the analysis of pronominal and anaphoric control with Psych-predicates proposed here can solve some issues in the long-standing debate over Super Equi-NP deletion (Grinder 1970, 1971; Kimball 1971). In fact, the analysis predicts that leaving the sentential complement in its base position only allows for anaphoric Binding of the infinitival $AGR_s°$ by the matrix 'Experiencer,' since in that case the untensed sentential complement has the matrix clause as its governing category. This prediction is carried out. Grinder (1970: 301) notes that impersonal constructions of Psych- verbs do not allow for what he calls Super Equi, namely control by the subject of the superordinate clause:

(61) a. Harry$_i$ believes that [PRO$_i$ to make a fool of himself in public] disturbed/pleased Sue

b. * Harry$_i$ believes that it disturbed/pleased Sue$_j$ [PRO$_i$ to make a fool of himself in public]

c. Harry$_i$ believes that it disturbed/pleased Sue$_j$ [PRO$_j$ to make a fool of herself in public]

Grinder explains these sentences in terms of the Intervention Constraint. Adapted to modern usage, this constraint stipulates that control between *Harry* and PRO in (61b) is blocked because of the intervening possible controller *Sue*.[19]

In the analysis adopted here, the untensed sentential complement in (61b) is in its base position where it is L-marked by the matrix verb. If the sentential complement in (61b) were extraposed from a subject position to some A′-position, ECP violations are expected with respect to extraction. This is not the case; extraction out of the sentential complement is fine, as illustrated in (62):

(62)   This is the kind of good cause which it never bothers/always pleases Sue to give money to

Extraction shows that the sentential complement is not an extraposed subject in an A′-position. The complement CP is not a barrier to extraction because it is L-marked by the matrix Psych-verb. The impersonal construction of Psych- verbs only allows for anaphoric Binding of the infinitival AGR$_S$° in its governing category, the matrix clause, as in (61c). Coindexing AGR$_S$° with the subject of the superordinate clause in (61b) is incompatible with its anaphoric nature. This indexing is perfectly possible as the result of pronominal control when the untensed complement has moved to subject position as in (61a).

Now let us compare the sentences in (61) with the following:

(63) a. Harry$_i$ believes that PRO$_i$ behaving himself in public would help Sue$_j$

b. Harry$_i$ believes that it would help Sue$_j$ PRO$_i$ to behave himself in public

c. Harry$_i$ believes that it would help Sue$_j$ PRO$_j$ to behave herself in public

Interestingly, control by the subject of the superordinate clause seems to be possible in the impersonal construction (63b), which minimally contrasts with (61b). The sentence (63b) then is an exception to Grinder's (1970) Intervention Constraint: *Sue* is a possible controller in (63b), as evidenced by (63c), but the fact that this NP intervenes between *Harry* and PRO does not prevent control of PRO by *Harry*. In the analysis developed here, the control properties exemplified in (63) seem to indicate that pronominal control is involved. Arguably, the untensed sentential subject in (63a) is base-generated as a subject sentence. As a result, anaphoric control is impossible, since the infinitival AGR$_S$° is never governed by the matrix verb. Moreover, the anaphoric AGR$_S$° does not have a governing category in which it can be bound at any level of representation. The only remaining possibility then is pronominal control: the anaphoric AGR$_S$° receives a 'default' pronominal interpretation and can corefer freely. This analysis is again sustained by extraction phenomena. Extraction out of the untensed sentences construed with verbs such as *help* gives rise to ECP violations:

(64)   * This is the kind of good cause which it often helps Sue to give money to

These extraction phenomena show that the infinitive in (63–64) is a barrier to extraction, a sentential complement that is not L-marked by the matrix verb, and that it is extraposed from its base-generated subject position to an A´-position. Since the extraposed subject involves a barrier, the matrix clause cannot function as the governing category for the infinitival AGR$_S$°. The anaphoric infinitival AGR$_S$° does not have a governing category and as a result receives a 'default' pronominal interpretation.

8 Conclusion: 'out of control'

The lexical residue of control theory can be derived given an explicit theory of event structure which interacts with other modules of the grammar: government-selection of C°, Maximal Identification of Features, Binding of the infinitival AGR$_S$° in the matrix clause. The interaction between the semantic contents of both the infinitival morphology and the matrix verb is crucial to a proper understanding of control. The temporal interpretation of infinitives, which is determined by the matrix verb, constrains the Binding possibilities of the anaphoric subject of infinitives in their Binding domain. In other words, the selectional mechanisms which determine the temporal interpretation of an infinitive also determine control of this infinitive. Subcategorization of the infinitival C° by the matrix control V° should be viewed as an instance of semantic identification of the [– realized] temporal features in C° with the [– realized] subevents represented in the event structure of the matrix control verb. This allows for restricting the set of possible controllers to the object of object control verbs and to both the subject and the object in variable (*propose*) and preferential (*promise / ask*) control verbs.

It was shown that the grammar needs a lexical specification of aspectual information under the form of lexical event structures along the lines of Pustejovsky (1988). Semantic properties which are relevant in the syntax must be lexically represented. The lexical representation of arguments is mediated through lexical aspect. The analysis of control presented here provides evidence for Tenny's (1987, 1988) Aspectual Interface Hypothesis which states that aspectual structures mediate the mapping between thematic structures and syntactic structures.

Notes

* I want to thank Philip Baldi, Yves d'Hulst, David Dowty, Dirk Geeraerts, Richard Kayne, Béatrice Lamiroy, Ludo Melis, Pierre Pica, Nicolas Ruwet, Pierre Swiggers, Liliane Tasmowski, Alice ter Meulen, and Guido Vanden Wyngaerd, and an anonymous but exceptionally thoughtful reviewer of this article for various comments, discussions and constructive criticism. I also would like to thank audiences at the Universitaire Instelling Antwerpen, the 1989 LSA Winter Meeting in Washington DC, the Pennsylvania State University, Indiana University, the Université du Québec à Montréal, the Graduate School of the City University of New York, the Ohio State University, the *séminaire de syntaxe avancée* of the Université Paris VIII, and the *Workshop on lexical insertion and lexical specification* at the Rijksuniversiteit Utrecht, where I had a chance to present various versions of the ideas expressed here.

1 There may be other formalisms than Pustejovsky's (1988) to express these insights, but the formalism itself is not what is under discussion here. The aim of this chapter is to show how the internal temporal structure of verbs is related to control, independently of the exact formal representation of their event structure.

2 This is not trivially true of all verbs. For Achievement verbs such as *arrive*, tense delimits the 'lower bound' of the event, namely when it is realized, as in *John arrives*.

3 Contrary to the infinitival morphology, the *-ing* morphology also has a [+ durative] feature, and, though it is 'unrealized,' it does not have the interpretation of a 'possible future,' an eventuality. The [– realized] feature only applies to the fact that the event is not linked to a specific moment on the time axis. The [+ durative] feature in addition specifies that this event is 'spread out' over different unspecified moments of the time axis.

4 It seems that Stowell (1982) is not entirely correct in stating that the gerund in (12b) is interpreted with respect to the period before the punctual event because of the fact that one usually remembers things about the past. Contrary to the infinitive of *remember*, the infinitive selected by the verbs in (16b) refers preferentially to the past of the moment of punishing or congratulating. Like *remember*, the verb *punish* seems to have an event structure that is characterized by both a Stative and a punctual subevent as in (27a). The Stative subevent of *punish* can extend both before and after the punctual subevent of punishing. The punctual event of punishing does not say anything with respect to

the temporal interpretation of the infinitive: one can very well be punished for something that extends before, during, and after the moment of punishing: in (16b) there is no reason to assume that the writing stops after the congratulation or the punishment. The only requirement is that the Stative subevent is partly realized at the moment of punishing, as predicted by the analysis of the temporal interpretation of gerunds presented here. The fact that *remember* imposes a past interpretation only for the gerund can be attributed to the fact that one cannot remember something while at the same time experiencing it: there can be no overlap between the Stative subevent and the punctual remembrance event.

5   A similar analysis is possible for *like* in (14). *Like* has a Stative event structure. An infinitive or a gerund can only be interpreted with respect to the entire State. As a result, the infinitive selected by *like* gets an interpretation in which the event expressed by the infinitive is in a sense 'coextensive' with the State. This temporally 'coextensive' relation between the matrix State and the infinitive or gerund is why *Jenny likes to go/going to the movies* refers to all of Jenny's moviegoing experiences, past and present.

6   See also Koster (1984), Lebeaux (1984), Vanden Wyngaerd (1994) for alternative proposals to extend the governing category of PRO to the matrix clause. In addition to the syntactic arguments for the anaphoric nature of PRO / infinitival AGRS°, there are classical semantic arguments to the same effect. Castañeda (1966), Fodor (1975), Helke (1979, and Higginbotham (1989) have argued that infinitival subjects receive an interpretation corresponding to 'self' or 'he himself.' Fodor (1975: 133–4) uses the scope properties of *only* to claim that (i) is equivalent to (ii), but not to (iii–iv). Fodor convincingly argues that to remember giving the speech entails what he terms an 'epistemic privacy': only the person giving the speech can remember doing so, whereas remembering his/Churchill's giving the speech can be done by anyone who heard the speech.

i.   Only Churchill remembers giving the speech about blood, sweat, toil and tears
(= Fodor 1975: 133(9))

ii.   Only Churchill remembers himself giving the speech . . .
(= Fodor 1975: 133(10))

iii. Only Churchill remembers his giving the speech.
(= Fodor 1975: 133(11))

iv.   Only Churchill remembers Churchill('s) giving the speech
(= Fodor 1975: 133(12))

7   I will take no position as to whether the Binding domain for AGRS° is extended by moving AGRS° to C°.

8   From the representation in (27) which is close to that of 'transfer' verbs, the argument CP seems to be identified in both subevents: this is only a consequence of the representation, and it is not a real problem for the analysis.

9   The PP complement of *praise* and *punish* is clearly an argument theta-governed by the verb, as attested by the fact that it can be extracted out of a *Wh-* island:

i.   This is a crime for which I wonder how hard the policemen will be punished

10 It is important to view the CP *do the dishes* as a single argument, the action of which should not be confused with the event of the matrix verb. This point can be more clearly made with a verb such as *impose* which allows for both NPs and gerunds:

i.   Géraldine imposed that party/going to that party on François

The subevent structure of a verb such as *impose* is identical to that of *force*. The construction with a nominal argument in (i) makes clear that the event structure should simply specify a 'future' relation between the Patient argument and *party*, without specifying that there is an 'action' to be carried out by the Patient: this would be to confuse the events of the matrix and the embedded verbs.

11   One might ask at this point whether expressing two *act* predicates on two different arguments would not involve a violation of the θ-criterion. In a framework with clusters of Proto-Agent properties (*sentience, volition, movement, causation*, Dowty 1991), it could be argued that two arguments belonging to the same event structure cannot be characterized by exactly the same Proto-Agent properties. The θ-criterion is preserved since every argument is uniquely determined by (Proto-)Agent/Patient properties. This interpretation of the θ-criterion allows for two arguments with *causation* properties as in the case of *propose*-type verbs, if at least one of the arguments also bears another Proto-Agent/Patient property.

12   It might be objected that the possibility of split antecedents for the infinitival anaphoric $AGR_S{}^\circ$ suggests that control is not a true form of anaphoric binding. This is only true if $AGR_S{}^\circ$ is identified with anaphors of the type *himself*. Anaphors such as *each other* do allow for split antecedents. The claim implicit in this article, then, is that the infinitival anaphoric $AGR_S{}^\circ$ has properties of both *himself* and *each other*: it is nonreciprocal like *himself*, but at the same time allows for split antecedents like *each other*. The objection that this would not be a 'true' form of anaphoric binding presupposes that the range of coreferential relations relevant to Binding is restricted to anaphors such as *himself*. There is nothing inherent in Binding theory that would validate this restriction.

13   The necessary character of the notion of 'obligation' in the definition of *promise* has been discussed by Searle (1969), Bogusławski (1983), and Wierzbicka (1987). Note that the notion of 'obligation to give in the future' (*promise*) is semantico-pragmatic rather than thematic in nature: the notion of obligation may disappear in insincere promises. Our discussion of control does not make reference to this 'cancelable' notion of 'obligation.'

14   For the issue of quantified 'arbitrary' PRO, as in sentences such as (i), see Lebeaux (1984). Vanden Wyngaerd (1990, 1994) has shown that most cases of arbitrary control, as in (ii), involve control by an unexpressed or empty argument.

   i.   [PRO$_i$ to know her] is [PRO$_i$ to love her]
   ii.   It is difficult (for X) [PRO$_x$ to remain calm]

15   Numerous exceptions to this prescriptive rule can be noted, see Harmer (1979) for French.

   i.   'Peu d'instants après avoir quitté l'autostrade, le ciel entier prit une teinte grise'
         'A few moments after having left the highway, the entire sky took on a gray color'
                                      (P. Fisson, *Voyage aux horizons*, 58, quoted by Harmer (1979: 146))

   ii.   'Moreover, Ms Tamposi said the search was begun by one of her assistants Carmen DePlacido, acting director of the passport office, without consulting her'
                                      (Robert Pear, *New York Times,* 1, November 14, 1992)

16   I will not go into the intricacies of control into purpose clauses. For a discussion of control into rationale and purpose clauses in terms of thematic hierarchies, see Faraci (1974), Nishigauchi (1984), and C. Jones (1985, 1988). For some criticism on the relevance of these thematic hierarchies for control, see Bach (1982) and Ladusaw & Dowty (1988). Within the logic of the analysis developed here, I assume that, purpose clauses being adjuncts, AGR-S° becomes pronominal and can in principle freely corefer with arguments of the matrix clause. This free coreference must in some way be further constrained by the semantics of purpose clauses. I will leave this problem for future research.

17   It should be added that the sentences in (54) receive quite diverging acceptability judg-

ments from various speakers. The contrast between the sentences in (53) and (54) is more difficult to explain. Descriptively speaking, it seems that PRO in temporal adjuncts is subject to a constraint that has often been noted for the binders of so-called logophoric uses of anaphors, namely that the controller needs to be the 'subject of consciousness' or the 'speaker' (cf. (54c) of the sentence (cf. Kuno 1972; Zribi-Hertz 1989; Tancredi 1997). Clearly, the starred sentences in (53) correspond to cases in which the controller cannot be construed as the 'subject of consciousness.' I will not go into this problem here.

18   Note that within a single sentence, nominal constructions can introduce coreferential arguments in the discourse when their head noun is not animate. This is also true for derived and nonderived subject sentences:

i.   Shaving himself would be good for John's career/*friends

ii.   To behave himself in public would help Bill's development/*friends

19   See also Jacobson & Neubauer (1976) and Chierchia & Jacobson (1986) for discussion.

4

ENCLITIC ORDERING IN IMPERATIVES AND INFINITIVES

1 Introduction[*]

In all Romance languages,[1] clitics have to follow a non-negated imperative. This is illustrated for French, Italian, Spanish, and European Portuguese in (1):

(1)   a. Fais-le! (Fr.)/Falo! (It.)/Hazlo! (Sp.)/Fá-lo! (Port.)
          Do$_{2SG}$ it$_{cl}$!

      b. * Le fais!/*Lo fa!/* Lo haz!/*O faz!
          Itcl do$_{2SG}$!

The observation also holds for Catalan, Romanian, Sardinian (Jones 1988: 337), Rhaeto-Romance (Haiman 1988: 377), and Corsican (Albertini 1972: 45) in (2):[2]

(2)   a. Fes-ho! (Cat.)/Pune-o! (Rom.)/Píkalu (Sard.)/Do m! (Rh.-Rom.)
          Do$_{2SG}$ it$_{cl}$!/'Set$_{2SG}$. it$_{cl}$!/Take$_{2SG}$ it$_{cl}$!/Give$_{2SG}$ me$_{cl}$!

      b. Dálluli/ Dállilu   (Cors.)
          Give$_{2SG}$ it$_{cl}$ to-him$_{cl}$ / Give$_{2SG}$ to-him$_{cl}$ it$_{cl}$

The enclitic ordering in positive imperatives is not restricted to Romance, but also extends to other, only distantly related, languages: Albanian (3ab) (Newmark et al. 1982, quoted by Rivero 1988), Modern Greek (3c), and Modern Macedonian (Joseph 1983):

(3)   a. Digj-   e !   (Rivero (1988: fn.10(ia)))
          Burn$_{IMP. 2SG}$ it$_{cl}$

      b. Mos e digi!   (Rivero (1988: fn.10(ib)))
          Neg it$_{cl}$ burnimp.$_{2SG}$.

      c. Grapse   to!   (Rivero (1988: (45)))

Write$_{\text{IMP. 2SG}}$ it$_{\text{cl}}$

Surprisingly, the observation holds even for languages which never allow clitics to follow the verb otherwise. In French for instance, the only case where clitics follow the verb is in the positive imperative. It is well known for example that in Spanish and Italian (4a) the clitics follow the infinitive (see Kayne 1991a for an analysis of this phenomenon), but in French this option is excluded:

(4) a. Quiero hacerlo/Voglio farlo
        I want to do it$_{\text{cl}}$

    b. Je veux le faire/*faire le
        I want to it$_{\text{cl}}$ do/ do it$_{\text{cl}}$

This striking generalization is a major puzzle for contrastive linguistics: why do so many languages exhibit this particular ordering of clitics with imperatives? It could of course be claimed that there is a rule postposing clitics in positive imperatives, but such a solution would fall short of explaining why this specific ordering is required across languages in the first place. If the postverbal ordering were rule-governed or subject to some low-level grammatical constraint, one would expect much more variation crosslinguistically than is actually the case. The issue is an interesting one when viewed from the perspective of a modular grammar in which modules and principles interact to generate acceptable sentences. In such a framework, the postverbal ordering of clitics with positive imperatives is likely to involve a very general principle of the grammar. It is likely that the same principle which is responsible for enclitic ordering in imperatives is also responsible for enclitic ordering in Spanish and Italian infinitives.

I would like to show that the position of clitics in both imperatives and infinitives follows from such a very general principle operating in the syntax which involves the core relation of government, Relativized Minimality (Rizzi 1990a). Relativized Minimality can be defined as follows (Rizzi 1990a):

(5) X α-governs Y only if there is no Z such that

    (i)   Z is in a base-generated position

    (ii) Z is a typical potential α-governor for Y

    (iii) Z c-commands Y and does not c-command X

    where α-government ranges over A, A´, and X° government

This means that in a linear syntactic string X–Z–Y, X cannot govern Y if an element Z intervenes which is in the same type of phrase structure position (argument, nonargument, or head position) as X and Y. An example from Rizzi (1990a: 11(24)) can make this clear:

(6) a. They could have left $X°_{could}$ — $Y°_{have}$

     b. Could they t have left $X°_{could}$ — $Y°$ t_{could}— $X°_{have}$

     c. *Have they could t left $X°_{have}$ — $Y°_{could}$ — $Z°$ t_{have}

In (6c), *have* has moved to a position (C°) from which it cannot govern its trace, since another head, the modal *could*, intervenes between *have* and its trace. Since the trace of *have* is not governed, the sentence is ruled out by the Empty Category Principle which states that every trace should be governed. I would like to argue that the grammatical mechanism which excludes (6c) also excludes (1b). It will be shown that a modular theory of syntax can explain the, at first sight, puzzling generalization involving clitic ordering in imperatives. In order to achieve this goal, I will assume the multilayered nature of functional categories (Pollock 1989; Belletti 1990), and the incorporation analysis of clitics (Kayne 1989c). The analysis shows how a modular analysis can capture syntactic generalizations such as the one expressed in (1–3) on the basis of independently motivated principles and properties.

2 Framing the problem

In this section, I will first take a closer look at the variation of clitic ordering in Romance. In addition, I will try to establish how the problem of enclitic ordering has to be formulated. At first sight, two options are open: either the verb moves over the base-generated clitics, or the clitics are left behind by the verb on its way up to the relevant functional categories. I will show that the problem at hand really involves the question of why clitics are left behind by the verb, and that, in principle, nothing seems to prevent the verb from moving up with its clitics. Finally, I will argue that the nature of the AGR° morphemes in imperatives and infinitives forces clitics to be left behind.

Contrary to the generalized enclitic ordering in positive imperatives, Romance exhibits a great deal of variation with respect to clitic ordering in negated imperatives. Kayne (1991b) observes that in Northern Italian, the enclitic ordering in negative imperatives (7b) is by far preferred to the proclitic ordering which is common in the dialects of the Center. This distribution is paralleled in the infinitival negative imperatives (8) of these dialects:

(7) a. Non lo fate!   (= Kayne 1991b: (47))
         Neg it$_{cl}$ do$_{INF}$

117

    b. Non fatelo!   (= Kayne 1991b: (48))
       Neg it$_{cl}$ do$_{2PL}$

(8) a. Non farlo!   (= Kayne 1991b: (4))
       Neg do$_{INF}$ it$_{cl}$

    b. Non lo fare!   (= Kayne 1991b: (5))
       Neg it$_{cl}$ do$_{INF}$

The possibility for clitics to precede or follow the negated imperative is also reported for Rhaeto-Romance (Haiman 1988: 377). Spanish, Catalan, and Portuguese negated imperatives which use the subjunctive morphology do not allow for the enclitic option. The following are from Spanish:

(9) a. Hazlo!/Hágalo!/Hagámoslo
      Do$_{2SG \cdot IMP}$ it$_{cl}$/do$_{2SG \cdot HON. SUBJ}$ it$_{cl}$! (honorific you)/Do$_{1PL}$ it$_{cl}$!
      (exhortative)

    b. No lo hagas!/*No lo haz!
      Neg it$_{cl}$ do$_{2SG \cdot SUBJ}$ (not honorific)

    c. * No hágaslo/*No hágalo
      Neg do$_{2SG \cdot SUBJ}$ it$_{cl}$/Neg do$_{3SG \cdot SUBJ}$ it$_{cl}$ (honorific you)

In Spanish infinitival imperatives, clitics cannot precede the verb in any dialect that I am aware of:

(10) a. No hacerlo!
      Neg to do it$_{cl}$!

    b. *No lo hacer!
      Neg it$_{cl}$ to do!

Outside of the imperative system in Romance, clitics do not necessarily precede the verb either. In Spanish and Italian, clitics can follow infinitives. Besides the variation in clitic ordering in negated imperatives in Romance, the position of the clitics exhibits a great deal of variation even in tensed clauses across Romance languages, despite the fact that the core position is proclitic. In Portuguese, clitics precede or follow the verb in tensed clauses according to a very complex rule system. In European Portuguese, clitics have to follow the verb in root clauses whereas they mostly precede the verb in embedded clauses. However, in root clauses, the presence of quantifiers on the subject or negation forces proclitic ordering. With infinitives, the choice of the embedding preposition seems to be relevant (12) (see Pizzini 1981 for an analysis of these data).

(11) a. Disseram-me que ele te escreveu
    They told me$_{cl}$ that he to-you$_{cl}$ wrote

   b. Contaste-lhe a historia?
    Did you tell him$_{cl}$ the story?

   c. Vi-o
    I saw it/ him$_{cl}$

   d. Não o vi/Ninguem o viu
    Neg it/ him$_{cl}$ saw$_{1SG}$./Nobody it/him$_{cl}$ saw

   e. Todos me disseram que ele te escreveu
    (They) all told me$_{cl}$ that he to-you$_{cl}$ wrote

(12) a. Começou a vê-lo
    He began to see it/him$_{cl}$

   b. Vieram para la escrever
    They came to it$_{cl}$ write

Brazilian Portuguese has different rules for clitic–verb ordering, which mostly indicate a shift towards the proclitic position. These examples may suffice to indicate the variation of clitic ordering in those cases which do not involve positive imperatives.

I do not want to go here into the specifics of clitic ordering outside of the imperative and infinitival system in Romance. The variation in clitic ordering attested in Portuguese must be due to language-specific factors which will not be investigated here (see Rouveret 1989). However, it is not likely that language-specific factors are responsible for enclitic ordering in imperatives, since this ordering seems exceptionless even across language families (cf. *supra* (3a)). In view of the attested variation of clitic ordering in nonimperative contexts, the absence of variation in clitic ordering with positive imperatives is all the more surprising. It seems worthwhile investigating whether this enclitic ordering in imperatives can be made to follow from general principles of the grammar.

Let us first try to show how the problem of enclitic ordering in positive imperatives can be formulated in the framework assumed here. Following Baker (1988) and Kayne (1989c, 1991a), it will be assumed that the core position of clitics in Romance is obtained by adjunction (incorporation) of the $X°$ clitics to the left of a functional projection of the verb. The verb itself moves to its functional projections, adjoining first to the left of $T°$ and subsequently to AGR-S° (Belletti 1990). Adjunction to the left of the functional projections ensures that the verb picks up tense features in $T°$ before receiving agreement features in (14), following Belletti in assuming that AGR-S° selects TP. Furthermore, I will assume with Rivero (1988) that positive imperatives as in (1–2) involve head movement of the V–T–AGR complex to $C°$. This movement to $C°$ can be motivated. First of all, imperatives express a modality (close to the classical grammarian's definition of *irrealis / potentialis*) that can be associated with the temporal/modal $C°$ morpheme. Rivero claims that the imperative $C°$ makes the verb function as a performative operator. Moreover, several languages have specific morphemes for imperatives which differ from indicative or subjunctive morphology and which must be associated with a distinct functional category. Rivero labels this type of imperative 'true' imperatives for the languages of the Balkans, as opposed to 'surrogate' imperatives which correspond morphologically to existing tenses in the system (cf. (3)). This imperative morphology then forces movement of the verbal complex to $C°$ in the case of positive imperatives.

With respect to negative imperatives, Rivero (1988) claims that negation prevents the verb from moving beyond AGR-S° and $T°$ to its specific imperative AGR morphology in $C°$ which lies beyond NegP. This is an important argument in favor of movement to $C°$ in imperatives, since it allows for an explanation of the contrast in (9ab). In (9a), the verb moves all the way to its specific AGR morphology in $C°$. In (9b), however, it does not move any farther than AGR-S°, since negation blocks movement of the verb to $C°$.[3]

(13) a. Hazlo!
'Do it'
$[_{CP}$ Ha - z AGR-C° $[_{IP}$ lo [VP]]]

b. No lo hagas!
'Not do it'
$[_{CP}$ AGR-C°$[_{IP}$ no lo hagas [VP]]]

I would like to assume that the imperative morphology in $C°$, which cannot be expressed in negative imperatives, functions in many Romance dialects as an operator triggering the subjunctive morphology in the lower AGR-S° and $T°$ (9b, 13b). The subjunctive morphology then appears in the same way as in embedded clauses which are governed by a verb ruling the subjunctive: in these cases, the value of $C°$ which is lexically determined by the governing V also triggers the subjunctive in the embedded $T°$. Rivero's (1988) claim that the morphology of 'true' imperatives is located in $C°$ and forces movement of the verbal complex hence seems to be well motivated.

In itself, head movement of the verbal complex to $C°$ cannot explain why clitics have to stay behind in AGR-S°. In principle, the complement clitics should move with the V°–T°–AGR-S° complex to $C°$. After the DP containing the clitic moves to SpecAGR$_O$P to check case, D° incorporates into a left-peripheral position of the V°–T° complex, following Kayne (1991a).

Subsequently, the cl–V°–T° complex moves from T° to AGR-S° without major difficulties, as shown in (14b). The representation in (14b) reflects the fact that, although clitics are more peripheral to the verb than tense and agreement morphemes, they nevertheless form a complex head with the V°–T°–AGR-S° complex. In Roberts' (1991) terms, clitics are moved by adjunction to the X° level, and X° morphemes are moved by substitution to the X⁻¹ level. The sentence (14a) then has the structure in (14b):[4]

(14) a. Nous le regardions
        We it/him_cl watched

b.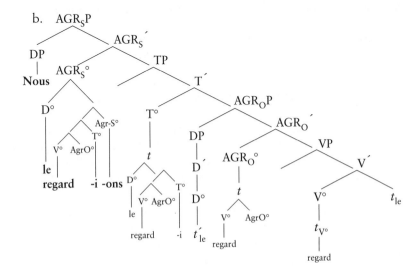

Within the general framework sketched so far, the enclitic ordering in positive Romance imperatives raises the problem of why the verb alone moves to C°, leaving its clitics behind. At first sight, there appears to be no principled reason for splitting the verbal complex from its clitics in the movement operation taking it from AGR-S° to C°.

At this point, it might be objected that the problem should not be framed in this way. Adapting Jaeggli (1986), it might be claimed *contra* Kayne (1989c) that clitics are not base-generated in object position, but in AGR-S°. It would then suffice to say that clitics never move with the verb, and that the Romance verb simply moves beyond the clitics to C° in imperatives. However, this analysis raises serious empirical problems. Let us briefly go into the problem of the position of verbs and adverbs in Romance. The ordering of adverbs with respect to tensed verbs and infinitives has allowed Pollock (1989) to argue that tensed verbs in French move up to AGR-S°

beyond the adverb souvent 'often' in (15a). Infinitives stay put in their base position, or in a position below the adverb (15b).

(15) a. Marie (*souvent) parle (souvent) de lui
'Mary (often) talks (often) about him'

b. Marie prétend [(souvent) parler (*souvent) de lui]
'Mary claims to (often) talk (often) about him'

Belletri (1990) argues that Italian differs from French in that infinitives move up to AGR-S° in the same way as tensed verbs. The main argument for this is the position of adverbs, which is the same in both cases:

(16) a. Maria (*spesso) parlava (spesso) di lui
'Mary (often) talked (often) about him'

b. Maria sostiene di (*spesso) parlare (spesso) di lui
'Mary claims to (often) talk (often) about him'

Let us now see how this analysis of Italian infinitives raises a problem for the base-generation of clitics in AGR-S°. In Romance languages such as Italian and Spanish, clitics are postposed to infinitives as illustrated in (10). If both infinitives and tensed verbs move to the same structural position in Italian, it would be hard to explain why clitics are postverbal in the case of infinitives and preverbal in the case of tensed verbs. This problem would remain even if clitics were base-generated as adjuncts to AGR-S°-P.

It thus appears that the problem of postverbal ordering of clitics in Romance positive imperatives does arise in the way claimed here. The question why the verb complex does not take its clitics with it while moving to C° is a relevant one. It will moreover be shown that this analysis of the postverbal position of clitics in positive imperatives in Romance can be extended to explain the position of clitics in Spanish and Italian infinitives, given the movement of infinitives to AGR-S° in these languages.

If it is accepted with Kayne (1989c) that clitics incorporate into the verbal complex and then move further up with it through the functional projections, the question remains why they do not move up with the verb all the way to C°. I would like to attribute this to the nature of C° in imperatives. Imperatives not only have specific modal (*irrealis* / *potentialis*) properties that are determined by C°, they also have specific agreement properties which are restricted to second person singular and plural (honorific or not), or to first person plural for the exhortative (cf. (9a)). Extending to root clauses Rizzi's (1990a) suggestion that embedded C°s in English can contain either the complementizer *that* or a nonovert AGR-C°, these restricted AGR features can be attributed to an imperative AGR morpheme in C°. In example (13), the imperative $C°$ with agreement features was labeled $AGR-C°$. The fact that $AGR°$ features are present in $C°$ is particularly plausible in view of the observations by Rivero (1988) and Zanuttini (1991) that languages which display specific imperative morphology do not allow this morphology to show up in negative imperatives. Recall that where negation is present the verb is prevented from moving to $C°$ and attaching to the imperative morphology.

Interestingly, the hypothesis that an $AGR°$ morpheme is in some way responsible for enclitic ordering can be extended to the postverbal ordering of clitics in Spanish and Italian infinitives. As pointed out in the preceding section, there is evidence from the position of temporal adjuncts that the verb moves up to $AGR-S°$ in Spanish and Italian, but not in French. This description has been further refined by Kayne (1991a). Kayne claims that in French, $V°$ moves up with its clitics to an INF projection containing the infinitival morphology which is added to the verbal stem. This projection is preceded by adverbs of the *souvent* 'often' type, exemplified in (17b). Sardinian moves the clitic + infinitival $V°$ complex up to $T°$ and has an order clitic + infinitive + adverb as in (17b) (Kayne 1991a). In Italian and Spanish, following Belletti (1990), the infinitival $V°$ moves up to $AGR-S°$, leaving behind its clitics in $T°$ (cf. (4a) and (17c)).

(17) a. $\dots AGR-S° \dots T° \dots ADV \dots [[CL° [V°]] INF°] \dots t_{[cl° [V°]]}$

   (French)

   b. $\dots AGR-S° \dots [[[CL° [V°]] INF°] T°] \dots ADV \dots$
   $t_{[[cl° [V°]] INF°]} \cdots t_{[cl° [V°]]}$

   (Sardinian)

   c. $\dots [[[t_{cl°} [V°]] INF°] T°] AGR-S° \dots t_{[[[CL°_{[V°]] INF°] T°]}} \cdots$
   $ADV \dots t_{[[cl° [V°]] INF°]} \cdots t_{[cl° [V°]]}$

   (Italian, Spanish)

Again, it seems that the infinitival $AGR-S°$ somehow forces clitics to be left behind in Italian and Spanish. In French, the verb does not move up to $AGR-S°$. Consequently, clitics remain in their left-adjoined position to the verb. The following approximative generalization can thus be formulated:

(18)   Whenever a verb is related through movement with the $AGR°$ morphemes associated with imperative or infinitival morphology, it must leave clitics behind.

This formulation captures both the case of Italian-Spanish where clitics follow the verb since the verb has moved up to $AGR-S°$, and the case of

French-Sardinian where the verb has not moved high enough for it to leave its clitics behind. Why is this the case? What properties of this morphology enable it to force clitics to be left behind when the verb moves up? Let us therefore analyze in some detail the feature composition of the functional categories involved in imperatives and infinitives.

3 The anaphoric nature of the infinitival AGR-S° and the imperative AGR-C°

Infinitives and imperatives are similar in many respects: neither imperatives nor infinitives license overt subjects. For Beukema & Coopmans (1989), this is due to the [– tensed] value of the temporal morphemes in imperatives and infinitives which do not allow nominative case to be assigned to the subject position. This claim has to be modified to the extent that the temporal value of imperatives certainly is not characterized by the absence of tense. Contrary to the suggestion by Beukema & Coopmans, it cannot be the case that imperatives have a [– tensed] feature which would be more or less identical to that of infinitives: Latin has a temporal morpheme for the future imperative:

(19) a. ama
   love$_{\text{IMP. 2SG}}$

   b. amato
   love$_{\text{IMP. FUT. 2SG}}$

   c. amate
   love$_{\text{IMP. PRES. 2PL}}$

   d. amatote
   love$_{\text{IMP. FUT. 2PL}}$

It is more accurate to say that the tense of imperatives is restricted to non-past tense. It remains true however that past imperative morphology does not seem to exist. It might therefore be useful to characterize the temporal/modal value of imperatives as [– realized], a temporal/modal value which is compatible with future, but not with past interpretation. This characterization has been proposed for the tense of infinitives by Stowell (1982). This definition of the tense of infinitives is not new. It has long been noted that the semantic interpretation of the infinitival morphology corresponds to a temporal/modal notion. Bresnan (1972) observes that infinitival complements refer to 'something hypothetical or unrealized.' Guillaume (1929) had already defined the infinitival tense as a tense *in posse*: it expresses 'potential' time, or eventuality, which is opposed to tense *in esse*, a 'real' or finite time reference linked to the time axis. Stowell (1982) makes a similar observation stating that the tense of infinitives must be semantically interpreted as unrealized or as a 'possible future.' Reinterpreting Beukema & Coopmans (1989), I then propose that imperatives and infinitives have the temporal feature [− realized] in common rather than the feature [− tensed].

How can this common [− realized] property of infinitives and imperatives be related to the position of clitics in these cases? In order to offer an answer to this question, we have to take a closer look at the AGR° morphemes that are associated with [− realized] T° morphemes. During the 1980s it was repeatedly argued that control theory can be partially reduced to Binding theory, since the infinitival PRO takes the sentence in which the infinitive is embedded as the domain in which its antecedent is to be found. In the following sentence, the infinitival subject (the anaphoric AGR-S°) cannot be bound by the subject of a superordinate clause:

(20)   You said that Harry promised to shave himself/*yourself

Borer (1989) has argued that the AGR-S° of infinitives is what is anaphoric in nature rather than the PRO subject of infinitives. Let us assume that this is indeed the case.[5] To say that the infinitival AGR-S° is anaphoric in nature is tantamount to saying that it is morphologically identical to the overt clitic *se/si*, which is the anaphoric clitic in Romance.

(21)   Giovanni si vede
        Giovanni self$_{cl}$ sees
        'Giovanni sees himself'

It can be concluded that the infinitival T° can be characterized as [− realized], and is associated with an anaphoric AGR-S°.

It is important to point out that tensed AGR-S° should not be defined as an anaphor in terms of the Binding theory: it is neither an anaphor, nor a pronoun, but simply subject to Spec-Head agreement with whatever is the subject at S-structure. Tensed T° can only be associated with an AGR-S° that is not defined in terms of the Binding theory, since embedded tensed sentences are never subject to control in Romance. The absence of control in tensed sentences shows that tensed AGR-S° is fundamentally different from the AGR-S° associated with [− realized] tense. This difference is further corroborated by the difference in the actual morphemes for both types of AGR-S°. Overt agreement morphemes for tensed T° (e.g. 1st person pl. /õ/, 2nd person pl. /e/in French) always appear in the context of tensed T° morphemes (e.g. imperfective /j/for 1st and 2nd person pl. in French *nous mangions* 'we were eating'). These tensed agreement morphemes never cooccur with the infinitive /e/morphology associated with untensed T° of *manger* 'eat.' Conversely, the infinitival AGR°, which remains morphologically unexpressed in Romance, will always cooccur with [– realized] T°. Functional agreement and tense categories with the same 'settings' always cooccur.

Let us now see how the characterization of anaphoric AGR° associated with [– realized] T° can be extended to imperatives. From a formal point of view, it is tempting to say that the imperative agreement morphology is at least partly identical to that of infinitives. The reason for this is simplicity: if T° morphemes with [– realized] temporal features are associated with anaphoric AGR-S° in infinitives, it is conceptually simpler to assume that some anaphoric AGR° morpheme is also associated with the [– realized] T° of imperatives: c-selectional properties between functional categories should be identical. At first sight, this cannot be the case: the imperative morphology is certainly distinct from the infinitival morphology. The imperative agreement morphology lacks a complete inflectional paradigm, but shows first and second person endings, unlike infinitives. The imperative tense morphology does not show [+ past] markings, like the infinitival morphology, but unlike the infinitival morphology it can exhibit morphemes for the future and subjunctive endings. It is likely that the subjunctive agreement and temporal morphemes are present in the imperative AGR-S° and T°. Recall that I have assumed with Rivero (1988) that negation blocks movement of the verb to C°, triggering subjunctive morphology in most Romance languages. Since the verb does not move beyond AGR-S°, AGR-S° and T° must contain the relevant subjunctive and agreement morphemes. Only when the verb moves to AGR-C° can it receive the properly imperative morphology. For reasons of simplicity, it may then be assumed that the imperative AGR-S° and T° are identical in every respect to 'normal' tensed morphology, since the imperative AGR-S° (2nd person sg. and pl., 1st person pl.) and T° (subjunctive) morphemes are identical to the morphology of the verb in a tensed sentence. I would like to propose that it is the imperative AGR-C° which bears the [– realized] tense features in an imperative. This actually allows one to make sense of the fact that the imperative T° can be subjunctive (Spanish, Portuguese, Italian . . .) or future (Latin): both the subjunctive mood and the future tense, but not the past, are compatible with the feature [– realized] in the imperative AGR-C°. In infinitives, however, T° itself bears the temporal [– realized] feature and can never exhibit subjunctive, past, or future morphology. As a result, the syntactic and semantic similarity between the imperative and infinitival tense morphology can be derived.

What is the nature of the agreement features associated with the [– realized] AGR-C°?[6] It is well known that there are specific agreement morphemes for imperatives in some Romance languages (cf. *supra*). Moreover, since it was assumed that the imperative AGR-S° and T° morphemes are identical to those of the tensed morphology, we have to derive the fact that imperatives are restricted to second person singular and plural and first person plural. It is likely that the imperative AGR-C° is responsible for this restriction, but independent motivation for this conjecture is necessary. I would like to claim that the restriction is due to the basically anaphoric nature of the imperative AGR-C°. Let us therefore return to the possible interpretations of clitic anaphors in Romance.

In recent work on the properties of reflexive *se/si* 'self' clitic anaphors in Romance (21), Burzio (1992) and Pica (1987, 1991) suggest that these reflexives are 'defective' morphemes in that they do not have φ features at DS. Burzio (1992) and Pica (1987, 1991) propose that the absence of φ- features is a morphological defining property of anaphors. Burzio moreover proposes that impersonal *si* 'self' in Italian is equally featureless, but lacks an antecedent since there is no governing category for it. Burzio proposes that impersonal *si* 'self' therefore receives a 'default' first person plural interpretation as in (22a). The impersonal *si* 'self' can however also refer to third person if context is supplied (22b).

(22) a. Si è contenti in Italia
SELF is happy$_{PL}$ in Italy
'One is happy in Italy'

b. Tutti lo dicevano. Si è contenti in Italia
All it$_{cl}$ said. SELF is happy$_{PL}$ in Italy
'Everyone said it. One is happy in Italy'

Rooryck (this volume Ch 3) argues that the same is true for anaphoric AGR-S° in certain infinitival clauses. In the cases where the infinitival clause is a complement of a matrix verb, the infinitival anaphoric AGR-S° is bound in its Binding domain, the matrix clause (cf. (20)).

When infinitives are not complements of the verb and hence lack theta-marking, there is no Binding domain for the infinitival AGR-S°. In these cases, the infinitival clause will not only act as a barrier for extraction, but also for Binding. This is the case for sentential subjects and infinitival adjuncts. The sentential subject in (23) is preferably interpreted as *our/your making noise*.

(23)   PRO making noise at midnight will frighten Sue

The fact that PRO in these sentences is preferably interpreted as first or second person has been pointed out by Thompson (1973: 377) for adjectival arguments, as in (24):

(24)   'Bill, tearing up my new paper dolls was mean,' cried Sue

This referential property of PRO in sentential subjects has led Van Haaften (1982: 118) to claim that arbitrary PRO in these cases cannot be interpreted as third person. Bresnan (1982) and Vanden Wyngaerd (1990: 216) have pointed out that the infinitival subject can be interpreted as referring to a third person if context is supplied:

(25) a. Tom felt sheepish. Pinching those elephants was foolish. He shouldn't have done it

b. Frankly, I'm worried about Mary. What has she gotten herself into? Don't get me wrong: I think it was fine to join the group. But getting herself photographed with those starving wolves was dangerous

It is important to underscore that control of the infinitival subject in all these cases is not subject to locality restrictions as in (20). Despite examples such as (25), it is striking that the unexpressed subject PRO in infinitival and gerundial subjects is preferably interpreted as a discourse first or second person referent. The same is true in infinitival adjuncts when the subject of the infinitive does not correspond to the matrix subject. Clark (1985) has claimed on the basis of (26) that control in infinitival adjuncts is subject to locality. However, it appears that this claim is based on a rule of prescriptive grammar stipulating that the subject of the matrix clause should be a controller in adjunct infinitivals and gerunds. When making abstraction of this prescriptive reflex, sentences such as those in (27) can be construed which show that a nonlocal argument can control the unexpressed subject of a lower adjunct if it is second person, or properly introduced in the discourse:[7]

(26)   Mary thought that Bill had died after seeing *herself/himself in the mirror

(27) a. So you think now that Bill might have died right after shaving yourself on June 6. Why would that be?

b. We have interviewed several people living in the neighborhood of the robbed bank. One person claimed the bank was attacked right after shaving himself at eight o'clock

c. Bill will only come home after calling him repeatedly

d. Mr Freckletweeter$_i$ was a very disorderly person at times. I$_j$ see you$_k$ have realized now that without PRO$_{i/j/k}$ classifying them properly, his$_i$ papers would have been irremediably lost for posterity.

Rooryck (this volume Ch 3) points out that the interpretation of impersonal *si* 'self' in (22) is very close to the preferential interpretation of PRO in subject sentences and infinitival adjuncts: in both cases, the interpretation of the subject involves a discourse referent, but it can refer to a third person given an appropriate context. The reflexive/impersonal *si* 'self' and the AGR-S° in subject sentences and infinitival adjuncts also share a syntactic context: in both cases, the anaphor does not have a governing category. I will assume here that gerunds and infinitives have the same type of anaphoric AGR-S°. The similarity between the overt reflexive/impersonal *si* 'self' and the infinitival AGR-S° warrants an analysis of this infinitival AGR-S° along the same lines: the infinitival AGR-S° is an anaphor which can receive a 'default' pronominal interpretation if there is no governing category for it. Importantly, the infinitival AGR-S° is defined in terms of Binding theory.

The simplest hypothesis with respect to the nature of AGR-C° in imperatives, then, is to assume that it is also basically anaphoric in nature. Since imperatives cannot be embedded, there will never be a governing category for the imperative anaphoric AGR-C°, and it will forcibly take a default first or second person pronominal interpretation.[8, 9] In this way, the imperative AGR-C° effectively restricts the normal tensed morphology in the lower imperative AGR-S° and T° to the attested 'defective' imperative morphology: second person singular and plural, and first person plural. This analysis can be reinforced by the observation that infinitives can be used as imperatives in Romance languages and in many languages not directly related to Romance.[10]

(28)   Ne pas faire du bruit!
        'Not to make noise!'

In the analysis developed here, this interpretation arises from the specific feature contents of the functional categories in the infinitive: the tense features of the infinitive are [– realized], and the infinitival AGR-S° receives a default pronominal first or second person interpretation since no governing category is present. The semantic properties of the functional categories in nonembedded infinitives bring them very close to the semantic properties present in the functional categories of imperatives.

As a result, the claim that the imperative AGR-C° is anaphoric seems to be well motivated. The default pronominal interpretation of the anaphoric AGR-C° can explain why imperatives are restricted to first and second person. Moreover, the minimal hypothesis with respect to the distribution of anaphoric and nonanaphoric AGR° in the context of other functional categories suggests that anaphoric AGR° should manifest itself in the context of [– realized] T°. Functional categories have cooccurrence restrictions express-

ible in terms of c-selection. Consequently, an infinitival [– realized] T°
should be accompanied by an infinitival AGR° which I have argued to be
anaphoric in nature. Finally, nonembedded infinitives can receive the interpretation of imperatives, a property which would go unexplained if their
agreement morphemes had nothing in common. This makes it possible to
adopt the strongest hypothesis, and claim that [– realized] T° is always associated with an anaphoric AGR° morpheme. This hypothesis is also the
simplest, since it assumes a minimal set of possible interpretations for AGR°
morphemes in the grammar. AGR° morphemes are only definable in terms
of the Binding theory in the context of [– realized] T° (basically anaphoric
with the possibility of a default pronominal interpretation). They are not
definable in terms of Binding in normal tensed clauses where AGR° is only
subject to Spec-Head agreement. A last question that needs to be answered
in this context is why AGR° morphemes would only be anaphoric in the
case of [– realized] tense. I would like to suggest that this is due to the fact
that [– realized] tense is in some sense an 'anaphoric' tense. Unlike embedded
tensed clauses, embedded infinitives are dependent for the interpretation of
their tense on the matrix verb (cf. Stowell 1982; Rooryck this volume Ch 3).
The properties of the AGR° morphemes associated with T° then simply
mirror this 'anaphoric' nature.

4 Analysis: the anaphoric AGR°(-S/-C°) as an intervening governor for RM

Coming back to (18) and reinterpreting it, I would like to argue that the
definition of the imperative AGR-C° and the infinitival AGR-S° in terms of
the Binding theory is responsible for clitics being left behind in the lower
functional category. I have claimed that the infinitival AGR-S° and the
imperative AGR-C° are anaphoric in nature, and can have a default pronominal interpretation. As such, they are identical in every respect to the
Romance reflexive clitic *se/si*. Since these functional categories are defined in
terms of the Binding theory, they strongly resemble clitics. Clitics are either
anaphors (*se/si* 'self') or pronouns (French *le* 'him/it', *lui* 'to-him/her' etc.).

Let us see what happens if the entire clitic–V–T–AGR complex were to
move to AGR-C°. Within the resulting complex, the imperative anaphoric
AGR-C° would constitute a single complex head with both the clitics and
the V°–T°–AGR-S° complex. The sentence (29b) would thus have the structure in (29c), in which AGRC°[11] would dominate the clitics which are more
deeply embedded in the morphological complex.

(29) a. Regarde-le
       Watch it/him$_{cl}$

b. *Le-regarde
    It/him_cl watch

c.

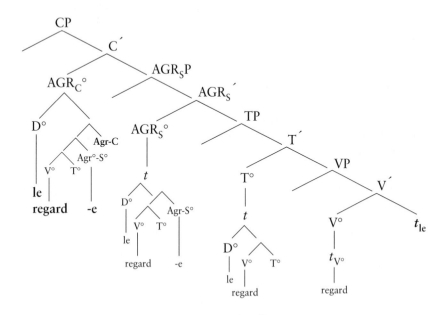

I would now like to argue that in the configuration (29c), AGR-C° is a potential governor in the sense of Relativized Minimality, intervening between the clitic in AGR-C° and the trace of the clitic. As such, AGR-C° interrupts the chain relating the clitic in the verbal complex to its trace. The relevant elements are shown in bold type in (29c), where the anaphoric AGR-C° is a potential X° governor for the trace of the clitic in the nonanaphoric AGR-S°. Consequently, the trace of the clitic in AGR-S° would not be governed by the clitic in the anaphoric AGR-C°, and the structure is ruled out by the Empty Category Principle, since the trace of the clitic is not governed. The only way for the verb to acquire the imperative morphology in C° is to leave its clitics behind in AGR-S° so as to prevent an ECP violation from arising for its clitic subpart.

Exactly the same situation obtains with infinitives in Spanish and Italian (cf. (4a)), but this time it is the anaphoric nature of the infinitival AGR-S° which is involved. As noted before, the verb in these languages moves up all the way to AGR-S° in infinitival constructions (Belletti 1990). Since the infinitival AGR-S° is an anaphor, it acts as an intervening governor for Relativized Minimality, thus forcing the clitics to stay behind in the infinitival T°. Interestingly, exactly the same configuration as with imperatives obtains, with the difference that everything happens 'one notch down.'[12] In French (4b), no such configuration involving Relativized Minimality can arise since the verb stays down in a projection lower than AGR-S°. Consequently clitics are allowed to stay attached to the verb.

The idea that AGR-C° counts as an intervening governor needs further argumentation. First of all, it must be made clear why AGR-C°, but not AGR-S°, would count as an intervening governor for the chain relating the clitic to its trace. The reason AGR-C° counts as an intervening governor in terms of Relativized Minimality is that both clitics and the imperative AGR-C° and infinitival AGR-S° morphology are definable in terms of the Binding theory. Since both these clitics and AGR morphemes are grammatically defined as elements of the same type, the AGR° morphemes are able to function as intervening governors for a relation between verb-adjoined clitics and their traces in a lower functional category.

Secondly, it is not entirely clear how AGR-C° in (29c) would intervene between the clitic and its trace, since the clitic is attached higher in the structure than AGR-C° itself. Rizzi (1990a: 7) characterizes the hierarchical terms of Relativized Minimality stipulating that an α-governor Z intervening between X and Y must c-command Y and not c-command X. In (29c), AGR-C° at first sight does not c-command the clitic in the amalgamated verbal complex in AGR-C°, nor its trace in AGR-S°. It could then be objected that Relativized Minimality cannot apply to this structure, since the hierarchical clause of its definition is not fulfilled. However, it must be the case that hierarchical relations between the elements amalgamated in an X° by adjunction are of a different nature from those expressed outside X° complexes. For one thing, if the most deeply embedded element in (29c), V°, is to c-command its traces out of an X° complex, it must be accepted in any case that it is somehow on exactly the same hierarchical level as the functional X° elements it has adjoined to. Therefore, I would like to argue that all elements in the X° complex in (29c), clitics, V°, and functional affixes, are hierarchically on the same level as the highest functional element, AGR-C°, with respect to the c-command relation they entertain with their traces lower down in the structure. As a result, within the X° complex, the c-command relation in the strong hierarchical sense cannot apply between AGR-C° and the clitic in (29c) in its usual sense. Therefore, I would like to propose that the c-command requirement built into Relativized Minimality is irrelevant when RM applies to a configuration X–Z–Y, where X, and the potential α-governor for Y, Z, are amalgamated in the same X° complex. Since AGR-C° and the clitic are at the same hierarchical level in (29c), AGR-C° can intervene as a potential α-governor for the trace of the clitic. The argument made here takes seriously the intuition behind RM which is that a trace cannot maintain its chain with its antecedent if another potential governor of the same kind intervenes, so that the trace cannot 'tell' which governor, the higher X or the intervening

Z, is the appropriate one. Similarly in (29c), the trace of the clitic cannot 'tell' which of two elements at the same hierarchical $X°$ level, AGR-$C°$ or the clitic, is the appropriate one.

Finally, this analysis requires a slight modification of the definition of Relativized Minimality as it is proposed by Rizzi (1990a), in the sense that the semantic contents of intervening governors are made more prominent than in Rizzi's original account. More specifically, I would like to add the following condition to the definition of Relativized Minimality in (5):

(5) (iv) Z is semantically definable in the same terms as X and Y (where 'semantically defined' refers to the way in which the feature content of X, Y, Z is interpreted by different modules of the grammar).

This means that if a potential governor Z intervenes between X and Y which is not semantically definable in the same terms as X and Y, it will not block government of Y by X. This modification of Relativized Minimality does not change anything for the core cases to be excluded by Relativized Minimality.[13] In (6c), which is also excluded by Relativized Minimality applying to a case of $X°$ antecedent government, the intervening modal *could* clearly shares verbal AUX features with *have* and its trace, and hence counts as an intervening governor. In the case studied here, the semantic referential properties of the Binding theory are involved. The content of both anaphoric AGR-($C°$/$S°$) and clitics is semantically definable in terms of the Binding theory, so the former can count as an intervening governor for the latter.

This approach of further semantically relativizing Relativized Minimality is in line with the modification proposed by Baker & Hale (1990). They argue that a distinction between functional and lexical categories should be built into the definition of Relativized Minimality: only lexical heads block antecedent-government by another lexical head, and only functional heads block antecedent-government by another functional head. The modification of Relativized Minimality proposed here and Baker & Hale's proposal share the intuition that Relativized Minimality should take into account the content of intervening categories.

Crucially, the lower, nonimperative tensed AGR-$S°$ does not have this blocking capacity for government in terms of Relativized Minimality. In the analysis developed here, this is because of the fact that tensed AGR-$S°$ is different from both the imperative AGR-$C°$ and the infinitival AGR-$S°$ in that the 'normal' tensed morphology is not definable in terms of the Binding theory. Tensed AGR-$S°$ only acquires its nominal features through Spec-Head agreement. Since (29) does not apply to tensed AGR-$S°$, tensed AGR-$S°$

does not count as a potential $X°$ governor: that is, tensed AGR-S° is not 'visible' for a chain relating elements definable in terms of Binding their traces.

The analysis developed here claims that the notion 'potential α-governor' within Relativized Minimality crucially involves the distinction between AGR° morphemes definable in terms of the Binding theory, and AGR° morphemes which are not definable as such. This simply means that the contents of potential intervening governors do play a role in Relativized Minimality. The application of Relativized Minimality is restricted by the fact that the semantic content of an intervening head must be sufficiently similar to the content of elements of the chain it interrupts. A similar observation has been made for some exceptions to Rizzi's (1990a) account of negative islands in terms of Relativized Minimality (Rooryck 1992a, this volume, ch.6).

It is important to provide independent evidence that AGR-C° is the relevant head involved here. In languages such as French where the imperative morphology is nondistinct from either the indicative (*regarde* 'watch$_{2SG}$,' *regardez* 'watch$_{2PL}$') or the subjunctive (*sache* 'know$_{2SG}$,' *sachez* 'know$_{2PL}$') morphology, it could be claimed that it is in fact AGR-S° which is the relevant anaphor preventing clitics from moving up with the verb. This solution would then yield the same results in terms of Relativized Minimality without the assumption of AGR-C°, since the whole structure would just be moved one notch down, with the clitics left behind in T° instead of in AGR-S°. This is in fact what happens in infinitives in Italian and Spanish. This hypothesis runs into several problems. First of all, it would be difficult to explain why negative imperatives, which presumably are in AGR-S° since they exhibit the morphological number distinctions, can, and very often must, have the clitics precede the imperative. If AGR-S° is the functional head involved in positive imperatives, it should not behave differently in negative imperatives. In the analysis presented here, this is not a problem since the imperative AGR-S°, being nonanaphoric, cannot function as a potential $X°$ governor for the clitics. Hence, the unmarked position of clitics in front of negative Romance imperatives can be derived. Recall that the verb has to stay in AGR-S°, since the negation prevents it from raising to C° (Rivero 1988). This is what happens in French, Spanish, Portuguese, and Standard Italian. In the marked Northern Italian dialects where clitics can follow the negated imperative cited in (7b) (Kayne 1991a), it can be assumed that AGR-S° has acquired the anaphoric properties of the imperative AGR-C°, and hence behaves as AGR-C° with respect to Relativized Minimality. Consequently, in order to move to AGR-S°, the verb has to leave behind its clitics in T°, exactly as in the case of infinitives (cf. note 4 below).

Moreover, it seems that in languages such as French, the nonovert morphology of the positive imperative in AGR-C° licenses other types of morphophonological changes than those triggered by AGR-S°. Liaison phenomena can be used to illustrate this point. Liaison has been most extensively studied by Tranel (1981). Tranel analyzes verb liaison as the insertion of a phonological connector /z/triggered by certain morphological contexts. Now imperatives followed by clitics do exhibit liaison phenomena with a clitic immediately following the verb, but it might be argued that this is an obligatory instance of a more general liaison rule which is optional in declarative contexts with words starting with a vowel as in (30b):[14]

(30) a. Prends- / z/-en
Take of-it$_{cl}$

b. Tu en prends /z/encore
You of-it$_{cl}$ take more

There is, however, one case of liaison that is uncontrovertibly linked to the imperative morphology. Positive imperatives in French allow for a clitic-internal liaison which is not attested in any other context. More precisely, liaison can apply between a dative *lui* 'to him/her' clitic and an *en* 'of-it' clitic when they follow positive imperatives, but not in declaratives (31b), nor, more importantly, in negative imperatives (31c):

(31) a. Donne lui-/z/-en
Give$_{2SG}$ to-him/her$_{cl}$ of-it$_{cl}$'

b. *Tu lui-/z/-en donnes
You to-him/her$_{cl}$ of-it$_{cl}$ give

c. *Ne lui-/z/-en donne pas
Neg to him/her$_{cl}$ of-it$_{cl}$ give$_{2SG}$ Neg

In other words, positive imperatives are in different syntactic environments in (31a) and in (31bc). For the sake of simplicity, then, it must be assumed that the clitic-internal type of liaison is triggered by the amalgamation of the verb with the nonovert imperative morphology in AGR-C°, but not by the morphology in AGR-S° in declaratives and negative imperatives. In order to make this argument, it is sufficient to assume a phonological theory of liaison which accepts that liaison is sensitive to specific syntactic environments. Tranel's (1981) work on French liaison offers a framework in which such a relation is assumed for various types of liaison in French. For Tranel, French liaison is triggered by various syntactic environments. Since the relevant liaison facts only occur in the syntactic environment of positive imperatives, it can safely be assumed that this environment is a different one from the one involved in tensed clauses and negated imperatives. In the analysis developed here, this is an additional argument that AGR-C°, and not

AGR-S°, is the functional head to which the verb moves in Romance positive imperatives.

The resulting structure of positive imperatives followed by clitics as in (32a) is then as in (32b), where the phonetically realized elements are shown in bold type:

(32) a. Regarde-le
       Watch it/him$_{cl}$

b.

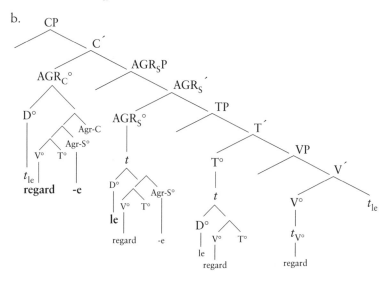

In this structure, the clitic trace in the verb complex in AGR-C° is properly governed by the verb: recall that all elements within an amalgamated X° complex are hierarchically on the same level. A first problem with this representation concerns the status of the element subject to movement in (32). In the representation (32), movement of the verb cluster does not respect the constituent condition on movement, since a part of the verb cluster is left behind. However, recall that there is a difference in connectivity between clitics which are moved by adjunction, and X° morphemes which are moved by substitution (Roberts 1991). Under this analysis, it can be assumed that the part of the verb cluster moved in (32) does comply with constituenthood: in this case, movement only applies to the V°–T°–AGR-S° part of the verb cluster which has arisen through substitution, excluding the adjoined clitic. The analysis presented here, then, actually provides support for Roberts' (1991) analysis of the difference between incorporation of clitics and incorporation into functional categories.

At first sight, this structure also seems to violate Baker's (1988: 73) ban on traces within an X° element, a constraint which he considers a morphological part of the Head Movement Constraint. Baker states this ban as follows:

(33) $*[_{X°} \ldots t_i \ldots]$

(= Baker 1988: 73 (76))

The structure in (32b) clearly does not comply with this constraint. However, the constraint (33) was primarily designed by Baker to prevent a $Z°$ incorporated into $X°$ to successive-cyclically move to a higher $Y°$, as in (34):

(34) $[_{Y°} Z°] \ldots [_{X°} t'_{Z°}] \ldots t_{Z°}$

This configuration clearly does not obtain in (32b). Consequently, it seems justified to weaken Baker's principle by stating that the configuration (33) is allowed if all the elements of the chain of the $Z°$ incorporating into the governing $X°$ are dominated by this $X°$. This is clearly the case in (32b), where the $V°$ in AGR-$C°$ clearly dominates both the clitic and all its traces. This interpretation of Baker (1988: 73) still rules out the relevant structure (34), and is compatible with the exclusion of (34) via the Minimality Condition (1988: 451 fn.9): In this footnote, Baker attributes to Chomsky (p.c.) the idea that (34) may be ruled out by the ECP under an extension of the Minimality Condition, since XP would be a Barrier between $t'_{Z°}$ and its antecedent in $Y°$.

5 Some further problems and consequences

The descriptive generalization that clitics follow imperatives does not extend to cases where the subjunctive is used as an imperative: in these cases, the clitics can precede the verb, as in Italian:

(35)   Gli scriva quella lettera che siamo in ritardo!
        To-him$_{cl}$ write$_{3SG\cdot SUBJ}$ that letter since we are late!

Proclitic ordering with the imperative proper can occur in Albanian, given proper intonation (Aleksander Murzaku, personal communication):

(36)   Ua shkruaj ate leter se jemi vone!
        To-them$_{cl}$ write$_{2SG\cdot IMP}$ that letter since we are late!

However, the forms used for the imperative in Albanian are identical to the first person singular and second person plural forms of the subjunctive for these verbs. It seems that the generalization only applies to those cases where the imperative morphology is independent of the subjunctive. In terms of the analysis developed here, this means that in (36) the verb does not move up to $C°$ whereas in (3a) with enclitic ordering, it does move up to $C°$. These cases are then parallel to the cases of those languages where the subjunctive is used in negative imperatives: in both cases, the imperative value in $C°$ functions as an operator triggering the subjunctive morphology in $T°$. In the case of Albanian, the subjunctive in positive imperatives may move up to the nonovert imperative morphology in AGR-$C°$ which will function as a potential $X°$ governor.

Another apparent exception to the enclitic ordering in positive imperatives seems to be Brazilian Portuguese (Leslie Gabriele, personal communication):

(37)   Dame!/Me da!
        Give$_{2SG}$ me$_{cl}$!/Me$_{cl}$ give$_{2SG}$!

The imperative with clitics preceding the verb has the present indicative morphology and is considered to be more polite. It also often requires the subjunctive morphology. This makes us suspect that these cases involve subjunctive or indicative root sentences which receive the illocutionary force of an imperative, much in the same way as English *You be quiet!*, where it can be assumed that an archaic subjunctive morphology functions as an imperative, perhaps as abbreviations of sentences such as *I demand that you be quiet*. A similar pattern also occurs in French, where the future indicative *Vous nous laisserez tranquilles* 'You will leave us alone' receives the illocutionary force of a polite imperative. Since the languages involved in (35–37) are *pro*-drop, the subject can be left unexpressed. I will disregard these cases here, assuming an explanation along the lines suggested.

Pernot (1934: 189) mentions the existence of two dialect zones in Modern Greek with respect to the placement of personal pronouns, one type of dialects which have preposed pronouns in most forms except imperatives (cf. (3)) and participles, and another type of dialect in which 'weak pronouns' are postposed in all verbal forms except the imperative (Brian Joseph, p.c.). Tsakonian is of the latter type:[15]

(38) a. Eipe mou
         Tell$_{2SG}$ me$_{cl}$

     b. Mou pe
         Me$_{cl}$ tell$_{2SG}$

The distribution of these facts in Tsakonian suggests, however, that if the 'weak pronouns' in (38) are clitics, they are not clitics of the $X°$ type. It may be that these elements are in fact X^{max} pronouns which undergo cliticization at PF, along the lines suggested by Kayne (1983) for French subject clitics and English *it* (**He gave Mary it* vs. *It was given to Mary*). Preposing of clitics in the case of the imperative might be due to movement of the internal argument XP clitic to Spec-CP in order to allow PF cliticization in the domain of C°. This movement triggered by the imperative in C° then resembles V2 phenomena.

A last interesting consequence of this approach is that Kayne's (1991a) analysis of the differences between French, Italian, and Sardinian with respect to both clitic and adverb ordering can be preserved without using V° adjunction to I′. Kayne has formulated the important generalization that Romance languages with infinitive + clitic ordering allow *si* 'if' in C°, whereas languages with clitic + infinitive ordering do not allow this construction:

(39) a. *Marie ne sait pas si aller au cinéma

(= Kayne 1991a: (49))

'Marie doesn't know whether (if) to go to the movies'

b. Gianni non sa se andare al cinema

(= Kayne 1991a: (65))

'Gianni does not know whether (if) to go to the movies'

Kayne (1991a) explains this generalization in terms of adjunction of the verb to the I′-projection, a rather exceptional kind of head movement. The analysis pursued here commits us to an alternative explanation of this generalization. I would like to suggest that in order to be licensed, the *si* 'if' element expressing Eventuality in C° must govern an element that corresponds to this notion. This is merely a selectional requirement imposed by *si* 'if' under government. AGR-P clearly cannot comply with the selectional properties of *si* 'if,' since it is a purely nominal element. Only in languages moving the V–INF–T complex up to AGR-S° will this requirement be met, since only V and temporal/modal morphemes can satisfy the selectional 'Eventuality' requirement of *si* 'if.'[16] The notion 'Eventuality' with respect to infinitives corresponds to the modal interpretation of the temporal feature [– realized] (cf. *supra*). The 'Eventuality' selectional requirement of *si* 'if' can be satisfied by the temporally 'hypothetical/unrealized/*in posse*' properties of the infinitival morphology.

Notice that this does not mean that the infinitive moves to AGR-S° in order to satisfy the selectional requirement, because that would not explain why in French–Sardinian the infinitive doesn't move to AGR-S°. In the analysis presented here, whatever conditions are responsible for moving up the infinitive as far as AGR-S° in Italian–Spanish also allow *si* 'if' to satisfy its selectional properties.

6 Conclusion

The analysis of enclitic ordering in Romance imperatives and infinitives in terms of Relativized Minimality strongly suggests that amalgamated categories are not an unordered bunch of features, but that the morpheme boundaries within the amalgamated complex are preserved. It shows that a purely syntactic principle such as the ECP applies to morphologically amalgamated categories (Baker 1988). Morpheme boundaries are nevertheless different from purely syntactic boundaries in that amalgamated morphemes and their features are visible within the whole complex no matter how many morpheme boundaries intervene.

The analysis of clitic ordering in Romance imperatives advocated here offers strong evidence for Kayne's analysis of $X°$ amalgamation as involving a general left adjunction process. It is also worth while to note that the enclitic ordering in Romance imperatives can be considered a case of reverse excorporation (Roberts 1991): instead of the clitic 'passing through' the V–T–AGR complex, here the verb excorporates into $C°$ because of general principles of the grammar which determine that it cannot take its clitics with it. The analysis presupposes that the grammar makes a distinction between $AGR°$ morphemes that are defined in terms of the Binding theory and $AGR°$ morphemes that are not so defined.

The analysis strongly suggests that Relativized Minimality applies to the morphosyntactic complexes of clitics, verbs, and affixes, and has to integrate a more precise definition of the notion of 'potential $X°$ governor,' taking into account its semantic content. In the next chapter, I will evaluate the consequences of this analysis for clitic climbing.

Notes

* A slightly different version of this chapter appeared as Rooryck (1992b). I would like to thank Judy Bernstein, Denis Bouchard, Marcel den Dikken, Marco Haverkort, Brian Joseph, Richard Kayne, Pierre Pica, Carlos Otero, Raffaella Zanuttini, and a reviewer for *The Linguistic Review* for comments and discussion. The usual disclaimers apply. Thanks also to Leslie Gabriele for the data on Brazilian Portuguese and to Aleksander Murzaku for Albanian. Previous versions of this article were presented at the 1992 LSA Meeting in Philadelphia, January 11, 1992; at the *22nd Annual Linguistic Symposium on Romance Languages,* El Paso, February 20–23, 1992; at the *XVIII Incontro di grammatica generativa*, Ferrara, February 27–29, 1992; and at the *Séminaire de syntaxe avancée* of the Université Paris VIII, Saint-Denis, June 15, 1992.

1 See section 5 for some apparent counterexamples involving imperatives with subjunctive form.

2 The observation also extends to those Romance dialects which are diachronically of the 'langue d'oïl' type. Rézean (1976: 69) gives examples from Vendéen: *dun mœ là* 'give$_{2SG}$ to-me$_{cl}$ it$_{cl}$,' and Remacle (1952: 250) for Walloon: *prinds-è* 'take$_{2SG}$ of-it$_{cl}$,' For Occitan, Sauzet (1986: 153) observes that imperatives display enclitic ordering: *Dona-li de pan* 'Give$_{2SG}$ him$_{cl}$ some bread'. This observation is confirmed for the different Occitan dialects by data attested in the versions of the *Parabole de l'enfant prodigue* cited in Bec (1967), e.g. Auvergnat:

i. Partatjatz vòstre ben   e   bailatz-me   çò que deve aver
    Divide$_{2PL}$ your goods and give$_{2PL}$ me$_{cl}$ that which I should have

For Gascon, these data are confirmed by Rohlfs (1977: 185): *da m'oc* 'give$_{2SG}$ to-me$_{cl}$ it$_{cl}$'. Interestingly, as illustrated in (2b), the respective ordering of accusative and dative clitics in Corsican is free (Albertini 1972: 44–5).

3 Zanuttini (1991: 75–9) argues against Rivero's (1988) analysis of negation blocking movement to C°. Zanuttini argues that if negation were to block movement to C°, negative gerundival adverbial clauses such as (i) in Italian should be out, since they involve V° to C° movement under Rizzi's (1982) classical analysis.

i. Non avendo Mario accettato di aiutarci, non potremo risolvere il problema
    'Mario not having accepted to help us, we won't be able to solve the problem'

However, it might be that the movement-blocking capacity of negation does not apply to the auxiliaries *essere* 'be' and *avere* 'have,' which more closely resemble functional categories. It could be that negation only blocks 'strong' verbs which are fully lexical categories. Restricting our attention to imperatives, it is certainly true that the order *negation + imperative + clitic* exists in Romance, as in (7b). Kayne notes that this order is attested only in those Romance dialects that have the order *infinitive + clitic*. If blocking of V to C by negation were simply constrained language-specifically, there would be no explanation for this correlation. In the analysis adopted below, the correlation INF + CL and IMP + CL can be accounted for (see section 3 for the analysis of this case).

4 In this structure, we assume that movement of complex head clusters leaves behind internally structured traces. This representation simply takes seriously the idea that movement must be completely 'transparent.' In addition, the representation tries to take into account Roberts' (1991) discussion of the difference in incorporation of clitics and verbal affixes. For Roberts, cliticization involves adjunction at the X° level, while affixation takes place at a sublexical level X^{-1}. This difference of incorporation captures the difference of connectivity between clitics and affixes. Roberts' analysis does not have major consequences for the analysis which will be developed here in terms of Relativized Minimality. For Roberts, X^{-1} affixes do count as intervening governors for the trace of incorporated V°. Pursuing the logic of Roberts' analysis, X^{-1} affixes must also be intervening governors for the traces of incorporated X° clitics which are sisters to V°. For our analysis of the postverbal ordering of clitics in imperatives, this means that the AGR-C° imperative morphology can act as an intervening governor for the relation between the clitic incorporated under AGR-C° and the trace of the clitic in AGR-S°.

5 *Contra* Borer (1989), Rooryck (this volume Ch 3) argues that AGR-S° does not move to C° in order to extend its Binding domain to the matrix clause (cf. Manzini 1983). Following Kayne (1991a), Rooryck (Ch 3) assumes that the infinitival AGR-S° (PRO for Kayne) cannot be bound in its own X^{max} because there is no position which might contain a potential binder. Hence, the next category up is the Binding domain for AGR-S°. Extending insights of Stowell (1982), Rooryck develops a modular analysis of control in which the matrix verb determines control via aspectual coindexation of the [– realized] C° with aspectual subevents in the event structure of the matrix verb. This lexical coindexation of the infinitival C° restricts Binding of the anaphoric infinitival AGR-S° in the matrix clause. Since the infinitival AGR-S° is coindexed with the infinitival C°, anaphoric AGR-S° can only be bound by those arguments which are lexically represented in the subevent which the infinitival C° is coindexed with. In other words, partial coindexation of C° with the governing control verb restricts the Binding antecedents for anaphoric AGR-S°. This analysis of control eliminates control theory, since control arises through a modular interaction of general principles of the grammar.

6   We will not go into the question whether the [– realized] temporal/modal features of the imperative AGR-C° and its agreement features are to be dissociated in two distinct projections or not. Since this problem is not relevant for the analysis at hand, we will simply assume that AGR-C° bears both the imperative temporal and agreement features. Beukema & Coopmans (1989) and Zanuttini (1991) have suggested that no nominative case can be assigned to the imperative subject, since the imperative T° is [– tensed]. We would like to reinterpret this suggestion and say that the presence of a [– realized] temporal value in C° prevents case assignment to the SpecIP position.

7   It should be added that these sentences receive quite diverging acceptability judgments from various speakers.

8   The fact that the imperative agreement morphology is restricted to first or second person is by no means a necessary property of the grammar. In fact, the value of the imperative for third person can very well be expressed in French by a root subjunctive clause with a spelled out complementizer:

    i.   Qu'il parte s'il n'est pas content!
        'That he leave, if he is not pleased!'

It should be stressed that these sentences are not to be analyzed as embedded clauses with a suppressed matrix clause, since it is not clear which verb this supposedly suppressed matrix clause should contain. They should be viewed as performative subjunctive clauses. Importantly, in the analysis developed here, the anaphoric status of the imperative AGR-C° allows us to derive this otherwise unmotivated restriction of imperatives to first and second person.

The only element that remains unexplained under this analysis is why imperatives cannot refer to contextually introduced third person referents. This problem might be more general, however. In root sentences with impersonal *si* such as (22), the third person interpretation can only be obtained in context. In imperatives, the performative interpretation may play a role in excluding third person referents.

9   A reviewer for *The Linguistic Review* points out that the referentiality of the anaphoric element in imperatives is more restricted than that of non-sententially bound infinitival AGR and *se*/*si*. In imperatives, it always takes a 'default' first or second person interpretation, but infinitival AGR and *se*/*si* can take either a 'default' interpretation or a generic interpretation.

    i.   En aquél país se trabaja demasiado   (Spanish)
        In that country SELF works too much
        'In that country, people work too much'

    ii. PRO_{arb} to know her is PRO_{arb} to love her

The possibility of a generic interpretation for infinitival AGR and *se*/*si* can, however, be explained independently. Following Lebeaux (1984), we assume that the generic reading of (ii) arises from the presence of generic tense which acts as a universal operator unselectively binding PRO. This generic tense then provides PRO with its generic meaning. This analysis has been extended to unexpressed objects by Authier (1989), and can be equally applied to *pro* in the generic (i). The imperative anaphoric AGR will never be able to receive such a generic reading, since the imperative tense can never be generic.

10 In these cases, we have to assume that the infinitival C° takes on an imperative value in addition to its [– realized] temporal feature. This additional imperative value of C° explains why interrogative infinitives such as *que faire* 'what to do,' with an interrogative C°, cannot be interpreted as imperatives, since imperative and interrogative values are mutually exclusive.

11   I leave out the $AGR_O P$ projection in the representation (29c) for reasons of transparency. Phonetically unrealized morphemes are represented without terminal nodes.

12   This raises a problem for an analysis for clitic climbing along the lines of Kayne (1989c), see section 3 for a possible solution.

13   This approach has a number of consequences for the analysis offered by Rizzi (1990a) of Inner Islands. For Rizzi, negation can intervene between a Wh- element in SpecCP and an intermediate trace in a lower SpecCP to block antecedent-government. Negation being an A´governor, Relativized Minimality rules out a sentence such as (i):

i.   * [$_{CP}$ How didn't you think [$_{CP}$ t_i Mary fixed the car t_i]]

In the approach advocated here, negation would not be able to intervene as an A´ governor because it does not share any semantic features with the Wh-chain it is supposed to block. On the basis of a number of counterexamples to (i) in French, Rooryck (1992a) (this volume ch.6) has shown that negative islands as in (i) should not be explained by Relativized Minimality. Rooryck (1992a) argues that the appropriate principles ruling out (i) have to do with operator–variable scope relations.

14   See Tranel (1981), however, for arguments against such a view. The 'liaison' phenomenon in (15) is reported for at least one other Romance dialect of the 'langue d'oïl' type, Walloon, by Remacle (1952: 250):

i.   Dène-mu-z-è / Dè-m'z-è
     Give$_{2SG}$ to-me$_{cl}$ of-it$_{cl}$

The second form is the abbreviated form of the first one. Thanks to Judy Bernstein for pointing out the Walloon data to me.

15   Brian Joseph furthermore informs me that present-day Tsakonian exhibits the same clitic placement as Modern Greek, probably under the influence of the standard language.

16   With respect to the Projection Principle (selectional properties must be satisfied at each level of representation), this analysis of course entails that it is sufficient for nonthematic selectional properties to be satisfied at S-structure.

5

CLITIC CLIMBING

1 Introduction*

Clitic climbing has received a great deal of attention in recent years. These constructions are not only revealing of the relations between matrix verbs and embedded complements (Rizzi 1982; Burzio 1986; Rosen 1990), but they also allow for an inquiry into the types of head movement (incorporation of clitics vs. incorporation into functional categories, Kayne 1989c; Roberts 1991).

(1)   a. La volevo chiamare ieri
          Her I-wanted to-call yesterday

                                                    (= Roberts 1991: (5a))

      b. Volevo chiamarla ieri
          'Yesterday I wanted to call her up'

Kayne (1989c, 1991a) proposes that clitics incorporate to the embedded $T°$, and that the $cl–T°$ complex then moves up through the embedded $AGR_s°$ and $C°$ to the matrix clause. Roberts (1991) assumes that clitics are different from $V°$ heads in that they involve incorporation by adjunction to a head, whereas a $V°$ head incorporates into functional heads by substitution (see also Rizzi & Roberts 1989).[1] Roberts (1991) argues that clitics, while observing head-to-head movement, move independently through all the embedded functional heads on their way to the matrix verb. Clitic climbing then is a case of excorporation. Crucially, Kayne's (1991a) clitic–$T°$ movement analysis of clitic climbing does not appeal to excorporation of clitics. Kayne (1991a: 661fn.38) argues that Roberts' (1991) view of excorporation of clitics into the matrix clause does not explain the severe limitations on split clitics.[2]

I would like to argue that both approaches to clitic climbing have substantial drawbacks. In both Kayne's (1989c, 1991a) and Roberts' (1991) analyses, clitic climbing involves optional movement: it can, but need not, take place. However, in the narrow Minimalist framework designed by Chomsky (1991,

1995), optional movement is excluded: clitic movement should be expected to be driven by morphological properties. If clitic movement is not necessary for morphological reasons, it does not apply. It is unlikely that (1a) should contain morphological properties forcing clitic or cl–T° climbing which would be absent in (1b). Optional movement for clitic climbing is especially odd to the extent that both analyses assume that the first step in clitic movement involves obligatory incorporation (cf. *Je vois le 'I see it' vs. Je le vois 'I it-see'). An optional clitic movement analysis of (1) thus has to stipulate that once the clitic is incorporated in the lowest verb complex it can, but need not, move further up. This stipulation is quite unattractive, since it is likely that when a clitic is in the structural environment for incorporation, it incorporates automatically. A clitic does not 'know' that it is already incorporated. Notice that Kayne's analysis partially escapes this criticism: for Kayne (1991a), clitic climbing is not just movement of the clitic, but movement of the cl–T complex. However, movement of this cl–T complex must still be conceived of as optional movement, an undesirable result. Therefore, on the basis of Minimalist assumptions, an analysis based on the idea that clitics obligatorily move whenever they are governed by an incorporating head is preferable to one which involves optional movement. The apparent optionality illustrated in (1) then must be derived from properties other than movement.

In this chapter, I would like to develop such an account based on Minimalist assumptions. Throughout, Belletti's (1990) $AGR_S°–T°–V°$ ordering for functional projections in Romance will be assumed. I will develop an argument which supports the view that clitics can move alone to the higher verb, following Roberts' (1991) excorporation analysis. *Contra* Roberts, however, I will assume that clitics do not freely move up through the infinitival functional projections to the matrix clause. Following Kayne (1989c, 1991a), I will accept that clitics are incorporated by adjunction to T° or Infn°. Only morphological heads are triggers for incorporation. This can be stated as in (2):

(2)   Only temporal heads (T°, Infn) properly governing (non-*Wh-*) clitics trigger incorporation by adjunction of these clitics in Romance (Kayne 1991a).[3]

Kayne's (1991a) strong constraint on incorporation is to be preferred to Roberts' (1991) 'free' clitic in/excorporation on Minimalist grounds. Morphological properties triggering movement should be restricted, since it is not likely that every functional category has the morphological property of incorporating clitics by adjunction. Moreover, if clitics were allowed to move up freely through the functional projections as in Roberts' analysis, there is no reason why they would not be allowed to do so in Modern French.

However, French does not have clitic climbing in sentences corresponding to (1). It will be shown that this difference actually derives from (2).

An important consequence of the morphological restriction in (2) is that $AGR_S°$ and $C°$ can never incorporate clitics. In the case of CP complementation, this entails that if the embedded clitic–verb complex does not raise to $C°$, the embedded clitics cannot be properly governed by the matrix $V°–T°–AGR_S°$ complex, and are therefore prevented from excorporating into the matrix clause. Following (2), clitics cannot climb on their own, but must be governed by their excorporation triggers (the matrix $T°$ or $Infn°$) to do so. As a consequence, excorporation into the matrix clause can only take place if the entire embedded cl–T–V complex has moved high enough for the matrix $T°$ or $Inf°$ to govern it. Only when a clitic is carried as high as $C°$ as part of the embedded verb complex will it be governed by the matrix $V°–T°–AGR_S°$ complex which is inserted in the $V°$ position, following Chomsky (1995). The $T°$ of this governing $V°–T°–AGR_S°$ complex then acts as the excorporation trigger for the clitic in the embedded $C°$, making the embedded clitic climb to the matrix clause. Clitics need to hitch a ride from the embedded verb into $C°$ before they can excorporate into the matrix clause. If this ride is not provided, $AGR_S°$ and $C°$ constitute hurdles for clitic climbing: not being able to incorporate clitics on their own, they prevent the matrix $T°$ or $Infn°$ from governing and incorporating the embedded clitics.

In this chapter, two arguments will be developed to show that a Minimalist account of clitic climbing along the lines just sketched is possible and desirable. The first argument comes from a surprising contrast in clitic climbing out of Italian and Spanish *Wh*-infinitives. Kayne's (1989c, 1991a) cl–T° movement analysis predicts that the matrix and embedded verbs will constitute a single temporal domain in all cases of clitic climbing. In the case of clitic climbing out of *Wh*-infinitives, this prediction is not carried out. Therefore, I conclude that clitics can move alone to the higher clause without $T°$ provided the clitics are governed by the matrix $V°–T°–AGR_S°$. The second argument is based on the fact that non *Wh*-clitic climbing constructions do constitute a single temporal domain with the embedded clause, as first argued by Napoli (1981). This property can be linked to $T°$ raising, as assumed by Kayne (1989c, 1991a). However, in view of the fact that $T°$ raising has been shown not to be obligatory in *Wh*-infinitives, it has to be independently motivated. It will be shown that if clitic raising is triggered by a governing $V°$, $T°$ raising is triggered as a last resort effort in order to prevent Relativized Minimality from applying to the chain linking the raised clitic to its trace. The optionality of clitic climbing can ultimately be reduced to the interaction of Relativized Minimality and obligatory $X°$ movement.

2 Clitic climbing out of *Wh*-infinitives

Rizzi (1982) and Kayne (1989c) quote examples of clitic climbing out of *Wh*-infinitives:

(3) a. Non ti saprei che dire
         Neg I to-you would-know what to say

                                        (Kayne 1989c: (16))

         'I would not know what to say to you'

     b. ? Mario, non lo saprei a chi affidare, durante le vacanze
                                        (Rizzi 1982: 36)
         Mario, I him wouldn't know to whom to entrust – during the
         holidays

     c. ?? Un simile problema, proprio non lo saprei come risolvere
         Such a problem, I really wouldn't know how to solve
                                        (Rizzi 1982: 36)

It seems that these cases are very restricted, however. The acceptability of
(3bc) seems to decrease dramatically outside of left dislocation contexts. My
informants rule out the following:

(4) a. *Non ti saprei come dire che la macchina era rotta
         Neg to-you I-would-know how to-tell that the car was broken
         'I would not know how to say that the car was broken'

     b. *Non lo saprei a chi dire
         Neg it I-would-know to whom to-say
         'I would not know to whom to say it'

Therefore, I would like to see the contrast in the preceding examples as
one between (3a) and the unacceptable (4), since these sentences do not
involve a left dislocation context. The examples in (3bc) appear to be
somehow rescued by left dislocation of an NP corresponding to the clitic
climbed. These apparent cases of clitic climbing in the context of left dislocation in Italian (3bc) can be analyzed along the lines of the account for clitic
left dislocation developed by Cinque (1991). Cinque shows that clitics and
their traces in left dislocation contexts have quite different properties, and
analyzes clitics in these contexts as resumptive pronouns. The climbed clitics
in left dislocation contexts might well not be instances of climbed clitics at
all, but resumptive clitics licensed by the left dislocation context in Cinque's
sense. I will not go into this problem here.

Let us now come back to the question as to why (3a) is so much better
than (4). I would like to argue that it is related to the position of the infini-

tives at S- structure in both cases. Bouchard and Hirschbühler (1986) show that French *que* 'what' is a clitic on the verb which forces movement to C° of the clitic–verb complex. It seems that the same is true for the clitic allomorph of Italian *che* 'what,' to the extent that *che* cannot be separated from the verb by the subject in root clauses.

(5) a. [$_{CP}$ Que fait [$_{IP}$ il t_{fait} t_{que}]]
         What does he?
         'What is he doing?'

     b. *Il fait que

(6) a. Mi domando che fa Gianni ?/*che Gianni fa?

     b. Mi domando cosa fa Gianni?/cosa Gianni fa?
         'I wonder what does Gianni/what Gianni does'

In embedded infinitives, the clitic character of *che* cannot be verified by the inversion of the subject, of course. However, elements such as negation cannot intervene between *che* and the verb. If *cosa*, the nonclitic XP allomorph of *che*, is in SpecCP, negation is possible.

(7) a. *Non sapevo che non dirti
         'I didn't know what not to say to you'

     b. Non sapevo cosa non dirti
         'I didn't know what not to say to you'

(8) a. Non ti saprei che dire

     b. Non saprei che dirti
         'I wouldn't know what to say to you'

Clitic *Wh*-elements such as *que/che* in embedded sentences have to move to the embedded C° in order to license their *Wh*-property, in accordance with Rizzi's (1990b) *Wh*-criterion. Belletti (1990) has argued that infinitives in Italian move up to AGR$_S$°. I would like to propose that in Italian movement of *che* to C° takes place via movement of the *che*–infinitive complex to AGR$_S$°, and then on to C° in order to satisfy the [+*Wh*-] properties of *che* 'what' in the way of tensed verbs as in (5–6).[4] Rivero (1988) has suggested that in imperatives, negation prevents the verb from moving to C°, triggering subjunctive morphology. Likewise, I claim that the embedded negation in (7a) prevents the *che*-infinitive complex from moving into C° and thus from verifying its *Wh*-properties. As a consequence, the sentence (7a) is ruled out. In (7b), the nonclitic [+*Wh*-] XP element *cosa* can move alone to [Spec CP], unbothered by negation. In this case, there is no reason for the verb to move to C° since it has no [+Wh-] clitic incorporated into it.

It is now possible to explain clitic climbing in (8a): the *che* + infinitive complex can be assumed to take along the clitic *ti* 'you' to C°. From the position of the *che* + *ti* + infinitive complex in C°, the clitic *ti* 'you' then excorporates to the matrix $V°-T°-AGR_S°$ complex which governs C°. Recall that in Chomsky's Minimalist framework, the matrix $V°-T°-AGR_S°$ complex is inserted in V° and moves only to check features. The temporal morphemes then govern C° from the V° position and obligatorily trigger incorporation of clitics in the same way they would in a root clause where a verb governs the clitic. The embedded clitic *che* 'what' cannot incorporate into the higher verb because it has satisfied its morphological *Wh*-property. This yields the following structure for (8a):

(9)   Non **ti** saprei $[_{CP} [_{C°}$ che - t'_{ti} -$V°$**dire**-$T°$-$AGR°_S$-$C°]$ $[_{AGR\text{-}S\text{-}P} [_{TP} [_{VP}$ t_{dire} $t_{ti}]]]]$

In this way, Kayne's (1991a) assumption that only temporal morphemes T° and Infn° incorporate clitics can be preserved. If clitics are to move to the matrix verb out of a CP, they have to hitch a ride as far as C° on the verb. This analysis explains why clitic climbing out of *Wh*- infinitives is restricted to *che* + infinitive: only in this case, the infinitive is forced to move to C° with the clitic. In case an XP *Wh*-element moves to [Spec CP] as in (4), the verb has no reason to move to C°. Therefore, the clitics will never be high enough to be governed by the matrix verb complex which triggers excorporation.

The analysis proposed now raises the question how (8b) is derived where clitic climbing does not apply. If the *che* + *ti* + infinitive complex moves to C° in (11a), why would it leave behind the clitic *ti* 'you' in (8b)? X° movement to C° surely does not pick at random either *che* + infinitive or *che* + *ti* + infinitive.

An answer to this question can be found if Rooryck's (1992b, this volume Ch 4) analysis of enclitic ordering in Romance imperatives and infinitives is adopted. Rooryck claims that enclitic ordering in infinitives is obtained by the verb leaving its clitics behind in T° before moving to $AGR_S°$. The resulting enclitic ordering is forced by a slightly modified version of Relativized Minimality, adding provision (11) to Rizzi's (1990a) (i–iii) in (10) :

(10)   X α-governs Y only if there is no Z such that:

(i)   Z is in a base-generated position

(ii)   Z is a typical potential α-governor for Y

(iii)   Z c-commands Y and does not c-command X

where α-government ranges over A, A′, and X° government.

(Rizzi 1990a)

(11) (iv) Z is semantically definable in the same terms as X and Y (where 'semantically defined' refers to the way in which the feature content of X, Y, Z is interpreted by different modules of the grammar). (= Rooryck 1992b, this volume Ch 4: (30))

Rooryck (this volume Ch 3) takes seriously Borer's (1989) idea that the $AGR_S°$ of infinitives is what is anaphoric in nature rather than the PRO subject of infinitives. Rooryck (1992b) argues that the anaphoric infinitival $AGR_S°$ can be defined in terms of the Binding theory, contrary to noninfinitival, 'tensed,' $AGR_S°$ which cannot be so defined. Clitics can also be defined in terms of the Binding theory as either pronouns or anaphors. Since both the infinitival $AGR_S°$ and clitics have a semantic feature content which is definable in Binding-theoretic terms, the infinitival $AGR_S°$ can count as an intervening governor for clitics according to (10–11). Exactly this situation arises if the clitics on the infinitive were to be raised with the verb to $AGR_S°$. The following configuration, which adopts Roberts' (1991)

(12)

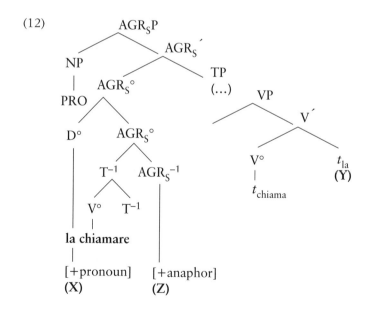

distinction between $X°$ movement by adjunction and substitution, as well as Kayne's (1991a) idea that clitics attach to $T°$, may serve to illustrate this:[5]

One way to avoid this configuration from arising is to leave clitics behind in the lower head, the infinitival $T°$. This means the $V°-T°$ complex moves to $AGR-S°$ without the clitics (Rooryck 1992b). Under this analysis, (8b) has the following structure:

(13)   Non saprei $[_{CP}$ [che - t'_{ti} -$V°$**dir**-$T°$-$AGR°_S$-$C°$] $[_{AGR-S-P}$ $[_{TP}$ **ti** $[_{VP}t_{dire}$ t_{ti}]]]]

In this structure, the (non-antecedent-governed) trace t'_{ti} of the clitic in the infinitival verb complex is properly governed by $V°_{dir}$. Importantly, the structure (13) does not allow the clitic in $T°$ to move to the matrix $V°$ because it is not governed by it.

At first sight, this analysis of (8b) predicts clitic climbing as in (8a) to be impossible, contrary to fact. In the structure (9), the infinitival $AGR_S°$ should also count as an intervening governor for the chain relation between the trace t'_{ti} which is antecedent-governed by the raised clitic, and the lower trace t_{ti}. However, this conclusion is premature. Recall that Rizzi's definition of Relativized Minimality in (10) stipulates that the potential intervening α-governor Z should be in a base-generated position in order to count as a *bona fide* intervening α-governor. If the intervening governor, *in casu* the anaphoric $AGR_S°$, were to move one notch up, the violation of Relativized Minimality is effectively canceled. This is in fact what happens in (9): the entire infinitival $X°$ complex moves to $C°$, voiding the intervening governorhood of $AGR_S°$ with respect to the chain relating the clitic *ti* 'you' and its trace. The clitic *ti* can simply move along with the infinitival complex to $C°$ before excorporating into the matrix verb.

The optionality of clitic climbing illustrated in (8), with the respective structures (9) and (13), then simply boils down to two ways of satisfying Relativized Minimality. In (13), the clitic *ti* 'you' stays down in $T°$, since the intervening governor $AGR_S°$ would be a closer governor for the trace of *ti* if the clitic *ti* were to move to $AGR_S°$ with the rest of the $V°$ complex. Being left behind in $T°$, the clitic is not governed by the matrix verb complex, and therefore cannot excorporate. In (9), the application of Relativized Minimality has been voided via movement of $AGR_S°$ (and the entire infinitival complex) to $C°$. Being properly governed by the matrix verb complex, the clitic must excorporate into the matrix verb. Notice that on the account presented here, movement is never optional. The only optional aspect of the analysis lies in the way Relativized Minimality can be satisfied.

The analysis presented here implies that clitic climbing in *Wh*-infinitives involves just climbing of the clitic, without $T°$ as in Kayne's (1991a) cl–$T°$

movement analysis. Kayne's analysis makes a strong prediction with respect to the interpretation of all sentences involving clitic climbing. If the infinitival cl–T° climbs to the matrix clause in (3a), it must be assumed that it merges with the matrix T°. Kayne's analysis then predicts that every instance of clitic climbing should cause the tenses of the matrix and the embedded clauses to coincide. More precisely, contradictory time adverbs should be impossible in the sentences in (3), or the interpretation of the sentences should require joint completion of the matrix and embedded events. This 'temporal fusion' in clitic climbing constructions has been observed for clitic climbing out of non-*Wh*-infinitives (Napoli 1981; Rosen 1990). For instance, contradictory time adverbs are only possible in the construction which does not involve clitic climbing (14a) (Guasti p.c., quoted by Rosen 1990). Napoli (1981) has observed that in the clitic climbing construction, the actions of the two verbs are tied together in such a way that one must complete both of them (15a). Napoli (1981) also notes that (15c) is ambiguous, but the clitic climbing construction (15d) is not:

(14) a. Oggi, vorrei finirlo domani
Today (I)-would like to finish-it tomorrow

b. ?? Oggi, lo vorrei finire domani
Today, (I)-would like to finish-it tomorrow

(15) a. Ho cercato di finirlo. Ma ho fallito/E ci sono riuscito

b. L'ho cercato di finire. *Ma ho fallito/E ci sono riuscito
'I tried to finish it. But I failed/And I did'

(= Napoli 1981)

c. Voglio di nuovo imprigionarli
'I want once more to imprison them/I want to imprison them once more'

d. *Li voglio di nuovo imprigionare
'I want once more to imprison them/I want to imprison them once more'

The adverb can have scope over either the embedded or the matrix verb, which constitute separate temporal domains in (15c). In (15d), however, the temporal domain of the matrix and the embedded verbs have 'fused' together (Napoli 1981).

Obviously, Kayne's (1989c, 1991a) cl–T° raising analysis would make the correct prediction in the cases (14–15): raising of the clitic–T° complex automatically ensures temporal coindexation of the matrix and embedded clauses. However, the prediction that the same 'temporally fused' interpretation applies to the sentences in (3a) is not carried out. Although judgments vary a lot, at least some Italian and Spanish informants accept the following:[6]

(16) a. % Alle cinque, non gli sapeva ancora che dire (durante la conferenza) (It.)

b. % A las cinco, todavia no le sabía qué decir durante la conferencia (Sp.)
At five o'clock, not to-him/her (he)-knew yet what to tell during the conference
'At five o'clock, he did not know yet what to tell him/her during the conference'

In clitic climbing constructions involving *Wh*-infinitives, the matrix and embedded events clearly are not interpreted as taking place at the same time in the sense specified above: contradicting time adverbs are possible, despite the presence of the climbed clitic on the matrix verb; and even without the adverbial in the embedded clause, speakers who accept (16) have separate temporal interpretations for the matrix and embedded verbs. Therefore, it must be the case that only the clitics in (3) climb to the matrix verb: it is unlikely that the embedded $T°$ would also be raised in (3) without 'fusing' the temporal interpretation of both the matrix and embedded clauses. However, the fact that cl–$T°$ climbing is not involved in the derivation of (3a) does not necessarily mean that cl–$T°$ raising is not involved in the clitic climbing and temporal coindexation of (14–15). If $T°$ climbing is still involved in (14–15), it will have to be motivated independently of clitic climbing, that is, there will have to be a compelling reason for $T°$ to climb to the matrix verb (cf. § 4). The sentences in (16) constitute evidence in favor of an excorporation analysis of clitics in which clitics climb to the matrix clause independently of potential $T°$ movement.

3 Motivating $T°$ climbing independently of clitic climbing

How does clitic climbing take place in non-*Wh*-infinitives such as (1a)? Rochette (1988) and Rosen (1990) argue that these clitic climbing verbs involve VP complementation. However, the position of temporal adverbs modifying the infinitive does not corroborate this analysis. If clitic climbing constructions were to involve VP complementation, VP adverbs should be able to appear between the matrix and the embedded verb. This is not the case:

(17)   Piero ti verrà a (*spesso) parlare (spesso) di parapsicologia
       Piero to-you will-come to (often) speak (often) about
       parapsychology

'Piero will come to speak to you often about parapsychology'

It seems that clitic climbing verbs involve at least AGR_S-P complementation, in keeping with Belletti's (1990) analysis that infinitives in Italian move up to $AGR_S°$.

Rosen (1990) has argued that clitic climbing verbs have two types of complementation. When the verb is 'heavy,' i.e. has an argument structure, its CP complementation does not allow for clitic climbing. The 'light' counterpart of the same verb, which does not have an argument structure, has VP complementation and allows for clitic climbing. In fact, Rosen (1990) analyzes the clitic climbing and the non-clitic climbing constructions as a result of homonymy between 'heavy' and 'light' verbs. This solution is ultimately unsatisfying. It seems hard to believe that the subject in (18) does not bear the thematic role of Theme typical for movement verbs. Similarly, the slight semantic difference noted by Napoli (1981) between *volere* 'want' expressing desire in (1b), but only intent in (1a) does not warrant the radical difference in terms of presence or absence of argument structure advocated by Rosen (1990).[7] Notice also that a homonymy analysis cannot be applied to the cases of clitic climbing out of *Wh*-infinitives.

Following Kayne (1989c: 246), I would like to defend a unitary analysis for the climbing and nonclimbing constructions of (1ab): both the constructions with and without clitic climbing involve the same verb and the same type of complementation. Let us assume that most clitic climbing verbs involve AGR_SP (IP) complementation.[8] This is likely in view of the fact that most clitic climbing verbs are aspectual or modal raising verbs, with a few exceptions such as *volere* 'want,' and *cercare* 'try' (cf. note 7).

The main challenge in analyzing clitic climbing in non *Wh*-infinitives is how to account for the temporal coindexation data observed by Napoli (1981) and Rosen (1990). Recall that it was shown in the previous section that clitic climbing does not automatically entail $T°$ climbing. Kayne (1989c) convincingly shows that the changes in auxiliary selection noted by Rizzi (1982: 19–22) can be explained as a result of the climbing of the embedded $T°$ to the matrix clause:

(18) a. Piero ci è/*ha voluto venire
   Piero there is/has wanted to come

   b. Piero ha/*è voluto venirci
   Piero has/is wanted to come-there

In this way, both the temporal coindexation phenomena and the changes in auxiliary selection can be explained by a single syntactic operation. If this $T°$ raising analysis is to be maintained in order to account for temporal coindexation and auxiliary changes, this movement will have to be motivated independently of the trigger for clitic climbing.

The answer to this question is relatively straightforward in the framework for clitic climbing sketched here. Following Belletti (1990), I have assumed throughout that the embedded clitic–verb complex moves to the $AGR_S°$ node. In this position, the embedded clitic–verb complex will be governed by the matrix verb selecting the AGR_SP, and excorporation of clitics must take place in accordance with (2).[9] Assuming AGR_SP complementation for *volere* 'want' (see note 7), the schematic representation in (19b) summarizes this situation:

(19) a. La volevo chiamare ieri
　　　 her I-wanted to-call yesterday

(= Roberts 1991: (5a))

　　 b. la-$V°$-$T°$-$AGR_S°$ [$_{AGR-S-P}$ [t'_{la}-Vinf-$T°$-$AGR_S°$] [$_{TP}$ . . . T $_{la}$]]

　　 c. la-$V°$-$T°$-$AGR_S°$ - ($T°$-$AGR_S°$) [$_{AGR-S-P}$ [t'_{la}-Vinf-t $_{T°-AGRS°}$] [$_{TP}$ . . . t_{la}]]

Notice that in the structure (19b), the embedded $T°$ has not moved to the matrix clause. In a Minimalist framework, a compelling reason is needed to move $T°$ as in (19c). Such a compelling reason can be found within the analysis outlined above for clitic climbing out of *Wh-* infinitives. Assuming Rooryck's (1992b) analysis, the structure (19b) violates Relativized Minimality: the infinitival $AGR_S°$ counts as an $X°$ governor in a base-generated position intervening between t'_{la} and $t_{la.}$ Recall that if the intervening governor is not in its base-generated position, Relativized Minimality does not apply. In the case of *Wh-* infinitives, this could be done by moving the infinitival complex to $C°$. If the intervening governor $AGR_S°$ were to move to the matrix verb as in (19c), the violation of Relativized Minimality would be canceled.

I would like to claim that the temporal coindexation effects, which only occur in the clitic climbing construction (Napoli 1981; Rosen 1990), indicate that this is indeed what happens. In order to prevent RM from applying to the derivation (19b), the infinitival $AGR_S°$ moves to the matrix verb as in (19c). In view of the auxiliary changes in clitic climbing constructions (18), it can be assumed that movement of $AGR_S°$ also takes $T°$ with it, thereby effectively coindexing the temporal domains of the matrix and embedded verbs.[10] This joint movement of the infinitival $AGR_S°$ and $T°$ can be related to Roberts' (1991) observation that functional categories which incorporate into each other by substitution cannot excorporate independently.

The cases in which the clitic does not climb and remains as an enclitic can of course be accounted for in the manner outlined above for *Wh*-infinitives in (13). In these cases, Relativized Minimality ensures that the clitic does not move up to $AGR_S°$ and remains in $T°$:

(20) a. Volevo chiamarla ieri
       I-wanted to-call-her yesterday

   b. Volevo [$_{AGR-S-P}$ [t'_{la}-V°**chiamare**-T°-$AGR_S°$] [$_{TP}$ **la** [$_{VP}$ t_{la}]]]

Summarizing, whenever there is clitic climbing from AGR_S-P infinitives, temporal coindexation occurs, but the climbing of the clitic and the climbing of the infinitival $AGR_S°$-$T°$ are triggered by different principles. Clitic climbing is triggered by the morphological property of temporal morphemes to incorporate clitics by adjunction (cf. (2)), an obligatory process under a Minimalist approach. Whenever a matrix V°–T°–$AGR_S°$ complex properly governs an embedded cl–V°–T°–$AGR_S°$ complex, incorporation of the clitic into the matrix verb complex obligatorily applies. In that case, the infinitival $AGR_S°$ and $T°$ also move as a last resort effort. If the infinitival AGR_S did not move, it would count as an intervening governor for the chain linking the climbed clitic to its trace, and the structure would be ruled out by RM. Movement of the embedded $AGR_S°$-$T°$ is not triggered by morphological properties, but as a way to prevent RM from applying. In case the clitics do not climb as in (20), I have argued they stay behind in $T°$ rather than moving to AGR_S with the embedded verbal complex where they would violate RM. In this case, clitics cannot move to the higher verb complex because they are not governed by it, and there is no reason for the infinitival AGR_S to move. The optionality of clitic climbing then is determined by two ways of obeying RM: either the infinitival AGR_S moves out of its base position so as to not be an intervening governor for the clitic–trace chain as in (19), or the clitic stays behind in the embedded $T°$ as in (20) to prevent AGR_S from becoming an intervening governor for the chain relating the moved clitic to its trace.

4 Some apparent problems

A few apparent problems for the approach outlined above need to be solved. First of all, it is necessary to explain why clitic climbing does not occur in the French counterpart (21b) of (8a):

(21) a. Je ne sais que lui dire

   b. *Je ne lui sais que dire
      'I don't know what to say to him'

If the clitic–verb complex is in C°, as suggested by the fact that *que* is a clitic on the verb, the *lui* clitic should excorporate into the matrix clause since it is governed by the matrix V°. However, it seems that in certain infinitival clauses in French, the clitic *que* can move to C° without the help of the infinitive. Recall Pollock (1989) has shown that the French infinitive never moves up all the way to AGR_S-P, but stays down in the VP, or in a (possibly modal) Infn head reflecting the infinitival morphology (Kayne 1991a). French infinitives contrast with Italian infinitives which move up to AGR_S° (Belletti 1990). The presence of negation in *que* infinitives in French shows that the infinitive is lower than the projection of negation and T°:[11]

(22) a. ?/?? N'oubliez pas de rappeler à Jean que ne pas leur dire pendant l'interview
'Don't forget to remind John what not to tell them during the interview'

b. (?) Avant de partir, je me demande toujours que ne pas emporter en vacances
'Before leaving, I always wonder what not to take with me on vacation'

In this case, the clitic *que* has moved to T° and subsequently moves to C° alone in order to check its *Wh*-properties. This movement of *que* to C° without the verb is not exceptional: Kayne (1989c, 1991a) has shown that attachment to V° is not an intrinsic characteristic of clitics (cf. note 2). In French, then, the clitic–infinitive complex is not in C°. As a consequence, the clitic *lui* cannot excorporate into the higher clause, since it is not governed by the matrix verb.

The same analysis explains why clitics never climb in non-*Wh*-infinitives in modern French, except in the causative constructions which are irrelevant here (see Guasti 1991 for a recent analysis). As is well known, the counterpart of (1a) is ungrammatical in Modern French. As argued by Kayne (1989c, 1991a) and Haverkort (1993), the lack of clitic climbing in these cases must be linked to the position of the infinitive in French as opposed to Italian/Spanish. Since only proper government of a clitic by a V°–T°–AGR_S° complex triggers clitic climbing, it is predicted that clitic climbing in Modern French will be impossible, because the verb does not move high enough to let excorporation of clitics by the matrix verb take place. Even if clitics adjoin to T°, as in Kayne's (1991a) analysis, they still are not in AGR_S° where they would be governed by the matrix verb. Only the infinitive moving to AGR_S° can take the clitic–T° complex with it into AGR_S°. Clitics will be able to excorporate as far as the embedded T°, but AGR_S° will be an inevitable hurdle, since it is not a trigger for excorporation. As a result, clitic climbing is impossible out of *Wh*-infinitives (CP complements) and non-*Wh*-infinitives which involve AGR_S-P complementation (cf. *supra*).[12] Note that Roberts' (1991) analysis, in which clitics move up freely through all the infinitival projections, predicts that Modern French should have clitic climbing. Pearce (1990) and Martineau (1991) show that in Old and Middle French, which was subjectless like Italian, clitic climbing was very productive. It can be assumed that the infinitive could still move up to $AGR_S°$ and $C°$ at this stage of the language, allowing it to behave like Italian with respect to clitic climbing (cf. also Haverkort 1993).

There is one last objection that might be formulated against the view that the clitic–verb complex must be in $C°$ in order to license clitic climbing. In Aux-to-Comp constructions (Rizzi 1982), infinitival auxiliaries are in $C°$ and can carry clitics. Nevertheless, clitic climbing is not allowed, apparently falsifying the prediction that when a clitic–infinitive complex is in $C°$, clitic climbing is possible.

(23) a. Ritengo [$_{CP}$ aver Lia risolto molti problemi]
I consider have Lia solved many problems

     b. Ritengo [$_{CP}$ averne Lia risolti molti *t*]
I consider have-of+them Lia solved many

     c. *Ne ritengo [$_{CP}$ aver Lia risolti molti *t*]
I of+them consider have Lia solved many

However, I would like to argue that the ungrammaticality of (23c) has to be explained independently. Interestingly, Aux-to-Comp constructions do not allow for successive-cyclic movement of arguments into the matrix clause:

(24)   *Questi sono i problemi che ritengo aver Lia risolti
'These are the problems that I consider Lia to have solved'

This sentence shows that Aux-to-Comp constructions constitute strong islands in the sense of Cinque (1991): the extraction in (24) does not have the flavor of a typical (weak) *Wh*-island violation, but is much stronger. The following are a minimal pair:

(25) a. ?? Questo è il ragazzo a cui mi domando come si possa regalare dei fiori
'This is the boy to whom I wonder how one can give flowers'

     b. * Questo è il ragazzo a cui ritengo aver Lia regalato dei fiori
'This is the boy to whom I consider Lia to have given flowers'

Whatever the explanation for the strong islandhood of Aux-to-Comp constructions, it seems clear that it will also prevent clitics from excorporating into the matrix clause.

5 Conclusion

In this chapter, it has been shown that clitic climbing does not involve 'free' excorporation by adjunction of clitics through all the functional heads of the embedded verb and into the matrix verb. Incorporation by adjunction of clitics is only triggered by temporal heads, following Kayne (1991a). Clitics must excorporate when properly governed by a matrix $V°-T°-AGR_S°$ complex in which $T°$ acts as an excorporation trigger. These minimal assumptions have been shown to be sufficient to account for the range of data involving clitic climbing. Clitic climbing out of *Wh*-infinitives must take place when the *che*–clitic–infinitive complex has moved to $C°$, and cannot take place if only *che* + infinitive moves to $C°$. Whether the clitic moves along with the infinitive to $C°$ or not is determined by two ways of obeying Relativized Minimality. The apparent optionality of clitic climbing thus is derived by means other than optional clitic movement. Clitic climbing, as any type of clitic incorporation, is an obligatory type of movement.

The same conclusion has been reached for clitic climbing out of non-*Wh*-infinitives. I have argued that clitic climbing is independent of $T°$ climbing, and that $T°$ climbing is triggered by a last resort movement to prevent Relativized Minimality from applying. In this case, RM again ensures the apparent optionality of clitic climbing. RM either forces the clitics to stay down in $T°$, ungoverned by their excorporation trigger, or it forces the intervening infinitival $AGR_S°$ governor to move up to the matrix clause taking $T°$ with it, in case clitics have climbed out of the infinitival $V°-T-AGR_S°$ complex under government from the matrix $V°-T°-AGR_S°$ complex. Moreover, the analysis offers a simple account of why clitic climbing is impossible in modern French: neither the clitic nor the infinitival verb complex move far enough to put the clitic in a position where it would be governed and excorporated by the matrix verb. I hope to have shown that an analysis of clitic climbing based on obligatory clitic movement, ascribing the optionality of clitic climbing to nonmorphological factors, is superior to an account based on optional clitic movement.

Notes

*   A slightly different version of this paper was originally published as Rooryck (1994b). I would like to thank Judy Bernstein, Valentina Bianchi, Anna Cardinaletti, Andrea Ciccarelli, Denis Delfitto, Yves d'Hulst, Ximena del Río, Josep Fontana, Teresa Guasti, Teun Hoekstra, Richard Kayne, Francesca Parmeggiani, Pierre Pica, Mario Saltarelli, and Raffaella Zanuttini for comments, discussion, and/or judgments on the Italian and Spanish data. Needless to say, they do not necessarily agree with the analysis proposed.

1   In Chomsky's (1995) Minimalist framework, the difference between incorporation by adjunction and incorporation by substitution can be reformulated. Chomsky (1995) assumes that $V°-T°-AGR_S°$ complexes are taken from the lexicon fully inflected before being inserted in $V°$ position in the syntax. Roberts' (1991) incorporation by substitu-

tion then simply involves feature-checking of the $V°-T°-AGR_S°$ complex by movement to the relevant functional heads. Roberts' incorporation by adjunction could be viewed as truly syntactic incorporation: it is not likely that verbs are taken from the lexicon with clitics already attached to them. Note that clitics can carry inflectional gender and number morphemes (French *le/la/les*), which puts them on a par with lexical categories rather than with the morphologically simplex functional categories in Romance.

2 The severe limitations on split clitics could be explained in an excorporation analysis by an independent constraint on adjunction sites in heads. It could be assumed that Roberts' (1991) incorporation by adjunction only creates a single adjunction site. The adjunction of clitics to a head which already hosts a clitic then does not create a new adjunction site to the verbal complex, but incorporates the new clitic by creating an adjunction site on the previous clitic. This analysis probably could explain the fixed clitic ordering in most Romance languages, which is not expected in an analysis such as Roberts' where each clitic presumably has its own adjunction site. If this proposal is on the right track, excorporation could be argued to take place only along the lines of either the adjunction site involving the clitic cluster, or the substitution site involving the V–T–AGR complex. This would effectively prevent split clitics, while allowing them in the cases mentioned by Kayne (1991a) where the clitics separately adjoin to different functional projections, e.g. Infn° and T°.

3 Kayne (1989c, 1991a) convincingly shows that attachment to V is not a fundamental property of Romance clitics, in view of the fact that clitics can be separated by phrasal adverbs in a number of Romance languages:

i.   (*)Jean a promis de les bien faire   (= Kayne 1989c: (3))
     John has promised for/to them well do

Kayne (1991a) suggests that (i) constitutes a case of clitic climbing to T° rather than to $AGR_S°$. In Kayne's analysis, clitics can move to either the head Infn° which represents the infinitival morphology, or to T°.

4 It is unclear whether Spanish *qué* 'what' should also be analyzed as having a clitic allomorph. Spanish *qué* seems to behave like a *Wh*-NP. This could be a potential problem for the extension of the analysis presented here to (7b), since there would be no reason for the Spanish infinitive to move all the way to C° if *qué* 'what' can move independently to SpecCP. Nevertheless, there seems to be some limited evidence that the infinitive does move to C° in Spanish *qué*–infinitive clauses. *Wh*-infinitives with negation are only acceptable if negation is stressed. If the negation is associated with an adverb, which prevents stressing, the sentence is downgraded.

i.   Me pregunto qué NO decirle
     'I wonder what not to tell him'

ii. *? Me pregunto qué todavía no decirle
     'I wonder what not to tell him yet'

It might be that stressed negation can move along with the infinitive to C°, perhaps after reanalysis with the verb, an option unavailable for unstressed negation.

5 As argued by Rooryck (1992b, this volume ch.4), the provision (10iii) on c-command has to be weakened in X° complexes, since despite appearances, all X° elements in an X° complex are hierarchically on the same level. This also explains how the verb is capable of properly governing the trace of the clitic in the infinitival complex moving to $AGR_S°$.

6 Haverkort (1993) suggests that clitic climbing over a *Wh*-phrase is fairly marginal at best, since the acceptability of sentences such as (3) depends on various factors such as the choice of the clitic, the occurrence of negation in the matrix clause, and the choice

of the matrix verb (see Moore 1991 for Spanish). However, such examples cannot be dismissed as a strange quirk of Italian and Spanish. While verifying sentences such as (3) with Italian and Spanish native speakers, I noticed that the factors in both languages are not the same. For Italian speakers, there was a tendency to exclude sentences with a matrix tense other than the conditional. Some speakers had a contrast between the conditional and the imperfect tense:

i.   Non ti ?saprei/*sapevo che regalare
    Not to-you I-would-know/I-knew what to-give

In Spanish, on the other hand, Josep Fontana (p.c.) reports a strong tendency to exclude these structures with embedded verbs other than *decir* 'say.' Unlike Italian speakers, Spanish speakers more readily allow for various tenses to be used in the main clause:

ii.   No te sabía/sé qué decir/*?regalar
    Not to-you I-knew/I-know what to-say/give

Whatever the marginality of these sentences in both languages, the fact that they exist in both Italian and Spanish, but not in French, must receive a structural explanation.

7   Rosen (1990) bases her homonymy analysis for *volere* 'want' on three types of evidence: clitic climbing, long object preposing in the impersonal *si* construction, and auxiliary selection (cf. (18)).

i.   Questi libri si volevano/cominciavano a/dovevano proprio leggere
    These books self wanted/began/had to really read
    'We really wanted/began/had to read those books'

The fact that *volere* in the clitic climbing construction takes on the auxiliary of the embedded verb is taken as evidence that the embedded verb chooses the auxiliary in the clitic climbing construction. In the non-clitic climbing construction, the 'heavy' version of the verb selects the auxiliary itself. However, Kayne (1989c: 253; 1991a) shows that auxiliary selection can be dealt with by movement of the embedded $T°$ to the higher $T°$ in case of clitic climbing. As a consequence, auxiliary selection does not illustrate the necessity of two different argument structures for clitic climbing verbs. Long object preposing does show that the subject of *volere*, as well as that of aspectual and modal clitic climbing verbs, is thematically empty. If aspectual and modal verbs are analyzed as raising verbs, this is hardly surprising. However, Rosen (1990) does not offer any hard evidence for a second, fully thematic, structure of modal and aspectual verbs. She also fails to point out that not all clitic climbing verbs have long object raising:

ii.   L'ho cercato di/provato a/saputo riparare
    I it have tried/tried/been able to repair

iii.   Queste macchine si *cercavano di/*si provavano a/si sapevano riparare
    These cars self tried/tried/were-able to repair
    'We tried/were able to repair these cars'

This suggests that at least some clitic climbing verbs always have CP complementation, the SpecCP A'-position preventing the DS embedded object from moving to the higher SpecAGR$_S$-P A-position (cf. Chomsky 1986a: 74). Again, no double argument structure is necessary. The only troublesome case is *volere* 'want,' which cannot have CP complementation in view of long object preposing, and cannot be a raising verb since it does not take weather verb subjects. However, a single argument structure for *volere* 'want' can be maintained if the existence of control verbs with AGR$_S$-P (IP) complementation is accepted (Rochette 1988). Long object movement as in (i) can then be explained as a case of a 'double' impersonal *si* construction both on *volere* 'want' and on *leggere* 'read,' forcing the embedded object to move to the matrix subject position, which is thematically vacated as in any passive structure of a transitive verb. The matrix *si* 'self' then actually represents both the matrix and the embedded impersonal *si* 'self.' Notice that AGR$_S$-P complementation for *volere* 'want' is specific for Italian: in Spanish, *querer* 'want,' which has clitic climbing, does not have long object preposing for most speakers, suggesting the infinitive is a CP complement. Aspectual (raising) verbs do display long object preposing.

iv   Lo quiere hacer
       It s/he-wants to do
       'S/he wants to do it'

v.   Estos libros se *quisieron/empezaron a leer
       These books self wanted/began to-read
       'We really wanted/began to read these books'

Summarizing, Rosen's (1990) evidence only shows that clitic climbing verbs have either the argument structure of raising verbs or that of control verbs.

    The fact that long object movement and clitic climbing do not always occur together also raises a serious problem for 'unifying' analyses such as Sportiche (1995) and Bok-Bennema & Kampers-Manhe (1993) which crucially rely on the cooccurrence of both phenomena in all cases.

8   Alternatively, and more in line with the hypothesis of uniform CP complementation defended in chapter 1 of this volume, it could be proposed that the raising verbs allowing for clitic climbing feature CP complements in which AGR$_S$P has moved to SpecCP before raising of the embedded subject (and clitics) to their positions in the matrix clause. It is not clear whether uniform CP complementation can be maintained for non-raising verbs such as *cercare* 'try' which feature clitic climbing. I will leave this problem for future research.

9   I will have nothing to say here about the status of the elements *a* and *di* introducing the IP complements of aspectual raising verbs such as *cominciare* 'begin,' or *cercare* 'try.' It might be that these elements are case-markers (Rochette 1988), or clitics (Rizzi 1982). In any case, I assume that they do not prevent government of the embedded C° of *cercare* 'try' or the embedded AGR$_S$° of the matrix aspectual verb *cominciare* 'begin.'

10   Interestingly, Spanish *querer* 'want' does not show the temporal coindexation effects noted for Italian by Napoli (1981) and Rosen (1990). For most speakers, contradictory time adverbs are possible in the matrix and embedded clauses. There is a minimal contrast between (i) and (14b):

i.   En este momento lo quiero hacer mañana
       'Right this moment, I would like to do it tomorrow'

Spanish speakers do not seem to have the difference reported in (14) for Italian. In the framework adopted here, this means that there is no T° climbing. The absence of T° climbing can be related to the fact that Spanish *querer* 'want' does not have AGR$_S$-P complementation but CP complementation. This is confirmed by the fact that *querer* does not allow for long object preposing, as opposed to Italian *volere* 'want' (cf. note 7). If Spanish *querer* 'want' has CP complementation, clitic climbing as in (i) can be explained in the same way as in clitic climbing out of *Wh*-infinitives: the entire verb complex moves to C° in order to escape the effects of RM, and the clitic in the infinitival verb complex in C° is forced to excorporate into the matrix clause, being governed by the matrix V°–T°–AGR$_S$° complex. T° does not climb further than C° because there is no compelling reason for it to do so. Consequently, there are no temporal coindexation effects for Spanish *querer* 'want.'

11   This forces us into the inelegant but descriptively correct assumption that French X° *que* 'what' can move over negation (*ne pas*), whereas its Italian counterpart *che* 'what' cannot move over Italian negation (*non*) in infinitives. This may be due to the syntactic nature of negation in each language. Admittedly, the possibility of negation in French *que* infinitives is quite restricted, and cannot be generalized:

i.   *N'oubliez pas de rappeler aux enfants que ne pas manger avant d'aller dormir
      'Don't forget to remind the children what not to eat before going to bed'

ii.   (?) Je me suis demandé que ne pas prendre en vacances
      'I wondered what not to take with me on vacation'

It is not clear what factors influence this acceptability. Also note that in (13a), stressing negation makes the sentence more acceptable, whereas (13b) does not need such stress. Similarly, sentences with adverbs between *que* and the infinitive are excluded in all cases

iii. *Je ne sais pas que discrètement dire au président
      'I don't know what to discreetly tell the president'

However, in this case, the exclusion might be independently related to the fact that root questions with the adverbs in the same position are not very good either:

iv.   ?/?? Qu'aviez-vous discrètement dit au président?
      'What did you discreetly tell the president?'

I hope to come back to this observation elsewhere.

12   Richard Kayne (p.c.) informs me that this analysis does not extend plausibly to literary French *Il en faut parler* 'It of-it is necessary to talk,' since it would predict that long infinitive raising to AGR_S° and C° should be possible in this case. However, sentences such as *Il faut ne dire pas cela* 'It is necessary not to say that,' which would attest to raising to AGR_S°, do not occur in literary French (Kayne, p.c.). Despite the correctness of this observation, long infinitive raising does marginally occur in literary French (Zanuttini 1991: 24fn.22):

i.   On peut être très intelligent et n'aimer pas les vers (quoted by Grevisse 1986:
      §1487) 'One can be very intelligent and not like NEG poetry'

It seems, then, that long infinitive raising is optional in literary French, but with a tendency to disappear altogether. To the extent that literary French constitutes a coherent dialect (an admittedly questionable assumption), it can be proposed that its optional infinitive raising is intermediate between Old French (obligatory infinitive raising) and Modern French (no infinitive raising). In the literary *Il en faut parler* case, infinitive raising to AGR_S° or C° exceptionally applies and therefore triggers the archaic clitic climbing, even though this same infinitive raising does not occur in *Il faut ne dire pas cela*, which already obeys the system of Modern French.

6

NEGATIVE AND
FACTIVE ISLANDS

1 Introduction*

Several restrictions on successive-cyclic *Wh*-movement appear not to be exclusively linked to general principles of the grammar, but seem to be in some sense lexically determined. It has been pointed out repeatedly that *Wh*-movement of subjects and adjuncts out of complement CPs of factive verbs strongly contrasts with *Wh*-movement of internal arguments out of these CPs (Rouveret 1980; Kayne 1981a; Zubizarreta 1982; Adams 1985):

(1) a. *Who do you regret/understand/forget likes this book?

                               (=Adams 1985:(4b))

    b. *How did he deeply regret that his son had fixed the car?

    c. ? Which article did you regret/understand/forget that I had selected?

This type of restriction is not displayed by nonfactive verbs such as *believe*:

(2) a. Who do you believe likes this book?

                                 (=Adams 1985:(4a))

    b. How do you believe that I selected the article?

    c. Which article did you believe that I selected?

However, *Wh*-movement of the adjunct in (2b) is blocked by an intervening negation (Ross 1984; Travis 1984; Kayne 1986: fn.17; Rizzi 1990a: 15):

(3) a. (?) Who don't you believe would like this book?

    b. *How don't you believe that I selected the article?

    c. (?) Which article didn't you believe that I selected?

The negative islands in (3) present a case of adjunct vs. argument asymmetry and the factive islands in (1) present cases of a subject/adjunct vs. object asymmetry with respect to *Wh*-movement. In the framework of Chomsky (1986a), this type of asymmetry is usually linked to the ECP: traces of subjects and adjuncts must be antecedent-governed by intermediate traces, whereas traces of object arguments are properly governed by the selecting verb. At first sight, these data suggest that the intermediate trace in the Specifier of CP (hereafter SpecCP) in (1ab, 3b) is not antecedent-governed by the successive cyclically-moved *Wh*-phrase. Obviously, this type of solution will not suffice in light of the difference between the asymmetries in both types of islands.

With respect to negative islands in (3b), Rizzi (1990a) argues that the negation in the matrix clause is a potential antecedent governor for the trace in the embedded SpecCP. The *Wh*-phrase in the higher SpecCP will be unable to antecedent-govern its intermediate trace in the embedded SpecCP position, thus violating the ECP. The problem with this analysis is that there are a set of counterexamples where negation does not seem to intervene to create opacity effects. Melis (1988) observes that the asymmetry noted in (3) does not extend to identical constructions with volitional verbs in French such as *vouloir* 'want.'[1]

(4) a. Qui ne veux/désires-tu pas qui vienne encore chez nous?
'Who don't you want (that) still comes to see us?'

b. Voilà la façon de laquelle je ne veux/désire pas qu'il répare la voiture
'This is the way in which I don't want that he fixes the car'

c. Voilà les moments auxquels je ne veux/désire pas qu'on me dérange
'These are the times during which I don't want that anyone bothers me'

Other nonfactive verbs which behave like *want*-type verbs are verbs such as *prétendre* 'claim.' Admittedly, the negation in these sentences has to be stressed and the interrogative element has a universal reading. These sentences are clearly not echo questions, though, and they are not necessarily rhetorical questions.[2]

(5) a. Cet imposteur a prétendu que les personnes les plus diverses viendraient à la fête. Qui n'a-t-il PAS prétendu qui viendrait à la fête?
'That impostor claimed that lots of different persons would come to the party. Who did he NOT claim (that) would come to the party?'

b. Ce type a prétendu avoir réparé des voitures de toutes les façons imaginables. Mais comment n'a-t-il PAS prétendu qu'il avait réparé des voitures?
'That man claimed to have fixed cars in all possible ways. But how did he NOT claim that he had fixed cars?'

c. Si je me souviens bien, il a prétendu qu'il est resté à Chicago pendant quinze jours. Savez-vous pendant combien de temps il n'a PAS prétendu qu'il est resté à Chicago
'If I recall correctly, he claimed that he had stayed in Chicago for two weeks. For how long did he NOT claim that he stayed in Chicago?'

The sentences (4–5) display exactly the same configuration as the sentences in (3): in both cases, negation intervenes between the *Wh*-element in the matrix clause and its trace in the embedded SpecCP position. If Relativized Minimality were responsible for the acceptability status of the sentences in (3), the sentences (4–5) should have the same status. This is clearly not the case. Against the predictions of Relativized Minimality, the matrix negation does not seem to function as a potential governor for the trace in the embedded SpecCP in (4) and (5). Apparently, there seem to be verbs which allow *Wh*-subjects and adjuncts to be extracted over negation. Therefore, the exclusive appeal to Relativized Minimality and the ECP cannot account for negative islands. Instead, the solution could be sought in lexical properties of verbs of the *believe* type that are different from those of verbs of the *want* and the *claim* type.

A similar problem arises with existing accounts for the islandhood of factive complements. Preceding analyses (Rouveret 1980; Kayne 1981a; Zubizarreta 1982; Adams 1985; Rizzi 1990a) crucially rely on the special status of CPs selected by factives. Rouveret (1980), Kayne (1981a), and Adams (1985) exclude (1a) by the ECP. Rouveret's (1980) solution prohibits movement to the [+ N] Comp of the clausal complement of factive verbs. Kayne (1981a) stipulates that a factive verb cannot govern Comp: as a result, the *Wh*-trace would not be properly governed. Adams (1985) rightly criticizes Rouveret's (1980) and Kayne's (1981a) solutions for being too stipulative, and explains (1a) by the fact that a factive [+ N] Comp, like other nominal elements, cannot properly govern across IP into the subject position. Nonfactive verbs have [– N] complementizers which can properly govern the subject position. Adams (1985) nevertheless still accepts the stipulation that a verb can assign a nominal feature to the head of CP. Zubizarreta (1982) explains (1a) by a modification of the i-within-i condition which again crucially involves the nominal character of factive complementizers. Zubizarreta's and Adams' analyses rely crucially on the special status of the subject with respect to the nominal character of C, and hence do not allow for an explanation of the impossible extraction of adjuncts as in (1b). Rizzi (1990a: 112) acknowledges the adjunct extraction facts, and assumes that the sentential complements of factive verbs are inherent Barriers. He relates this Barrierhood to the analysis of factive verbs by Kiparsky & Kiparsky (1970), according to which the sentential complement is selected by an N node. I will try to show that there are no independent arguments for either the nominal property or the empty nominal projection of sentential complements selected by factive verbs. In any case, it will be clear that a solution for factive islandhood invoking either nominal properties or invisible nominal projections of sentential complements is less attractive than an analysis that can do without such stipulations.

I would like to argue that, despite appearances, the restrictions on *Wh*-movement out of negative and factive islands cannot and indeed should not be solely explained by the ECP, but that semantic properties assigned to the embedded C° by the matrix verbs also intervene. In the approach advocated here, the apparently unrelated restrictions on *Wh*-movement of adjuncts out of negative islands and both subjects and adjuncts out of factive islands will be explained by essentially the same means: successive-cyclic *Wh*-movement is restricted by the value attributed to the embedded C° by, respectively, the matrix V or the matrix negation. The analysis presented here crucially involves the value given to the head C° of CP by verbs of the *believe* type and factive verbs. I will argue that *Wh*-phrases passing through the Spec of the embedded CP pick up the value attributed to C° by Spec–Head agreement, and that this value interacts with independently motivated principles in the grammar to prohibit successive-cyclic movement of the *Wh*-phrases to the higher SpecCP. Extraction out of negative and factive islands involves the interaction between the ECP and semantic properties of intermediate C°s.

2 On inner islands, Neg-raising and negation-bound C°

The contrast between *believe*-type verbs in (2–3a) and *want*- or *claim*-type verbs in (4–5) suggests that its explanation involves a semantic property of these verbs which interacts with negation. I would like to claim that this property is what used to be known in generative grammar as Neg-raising (Lakoff 1970; see Horn 1978, 1989 for a detailed overview). The term Neg-raising covers the paraphrase relation which holds between sentences (6a) and (6b): the negation of the embedded clause seems to have scope over the matrix clause as well:

(6) a. I do not think that he will come

     b. I think that he will not come

Volitional verbs such as *wish, desire, hope, want* do not intrinsically involve Neg-raising: Lakoff (1970) notes that *want* is a Neg-raising verb in English, but not *desire* or *wish*: this observation can be explained by relating it to the fact that *want*, but not *desire* or *wish*, has an ECM construction:

(7)   I don't want him to come/I want him not to come

It is well known that French *vouloir* 'want' in (4) does not have the ECM construction, although ECM constructions of course do exist in French. It is important then to point out that the Neg-raising property of *want* is not linked to the semantic class of *want*-type verbs, since *wish* and *desire* do not have Neg-raising. Rather, Neg-raising of *want* is linked to the ECM construction: it seems that the matrix negation in ECM constructions necessarily has scope over the embedded IP. Outside of the ECM construction, volitional verbs do not have Neg-raising.

Horn (1978: 151) points out that verbs of volition only display Neg-raising with infinitival complements. In particular, he observes that (8a) and (8b) are equivalent, but not (9a) and (9b):

(8) a. I don't/never wish to see you again

(= Horn 1978: (54a))

b. I wish not/never to see you again

(= Horn 1978: (54a´))

(9) a. I don't/never wish that I will see you again

(= Horn 1978: (54b))

b. I wish that I will not/never see you again

(= Horn 1978: (54b´))

However, it is not possible to view volitional verbs as Neg-raising verbs with infinitival complements. Horn (1978: 192) quotes the examples from de Cornulier (1974: 50) where the first sentence certainly cannot serve as a paraphrase for the second:

(10) a. Je ne voudrais pas être Dieu
'I wouldn't want to be God'

b. Je voudrais ne pas être Dieu
'I would want not to be God'

With French *croire* 'believe,' which unlike English *believe* can be a control verb, the two sentences do have a paraphrase relation:

(11) a. Je ne crois pas être Dieu
'I do not believe to be God'

b. Je crois ne pas être Dieu
   'I believe not to be God'

The question remains, however, why in a lot of cases sentences with volitional verbs do have a paraphrase relation of the type exemplified in (7). Horn
(1978: 180) cites the following as almost synonymous:

(12) a. Je ne veux pas que vous sortiez
       'I don't want you to leave'

   b. Je veux que vous ne sortiez pas
       'I want you not to leave'

Comparing (10) and (12), the reason for this is easily found. The unmarked
interpretation of the embedded sentential complement of volitional verbs
typically refers to the future (Stowell 1982). When the presuppositions of
the embedded sentence comply with a future interpretation as in (12), both
sentences will be in a paraphrase relation. When the presuppositions of the
embedded sentence do not exclusively refer to the future, as in (10b), the
paraphrase relation with a sentence having only the future interpretation for
the embedded sentence is impossible. This can also be checked for a tensed
embedded sentence corresponding to (10):

(13) a. Je ne veux pas que mes poissons soient malades
       'I do not want that my fish be sick'

   b. Je veux que mes poissons ne soient pas malades
       'I want that my fish not be sick'

Sentence (13a) only has the interpretation that the fish aren't sick yet and
that I don't want it to happen. Sentence (13b) can have both this interpretation and the interpretation that they are indeed sick and that I would want
them not to be sick anymore. Again, sentences such as (13) cannot be
constructed for *croire* 'believe.' This of course shows that volitional verbs are
not Neg-raising verbs, but there is more. Informally stated, the fact that the
presuppositions of both sentences can be different means that they can have
independent truth values. *Believe*-type verbs do not seem to allow their
embedded sentences to have independent truth values: the matrix and
embedded sentences seem to constitute a single truth value domain.

Unlike the properties of volitional verbs with respect to Neg-raising, the
properties of *claim*-type verbs and factive verbs are immediately obvious:
(14a) is not in a paraphrase relation with (14b):

(14) a. I claim/regret that George hasn't thought of the long-term consequences

b. I don't claim/regret that George has thought of the long-term
consequences

It can be concluded that *believe*, *think*-type verbs are Neg-raising verbs,
whereas volitional verbs such as *want*, *wish*, *claim*-type verbs and factive verbs
are not.

How can the informal insight that *believe*-type verbs have a single truth
value domain for their matrix and embedded clause be implemented in an
updated generative grammar? More importantly, how can it be linked to an
explanation of negative islands? Obviously, it would be quite difficult, if not
impossible,[3] in present-day generative grammar to view the paraphrase relation between the sentences in (7) as the result of a rule raising the negation
of the embedded clause to the matrix clause. Instead, I would like to
formalize the observation that the matrix and embedded sentences of *believe*-
type verbs constitute a single truth value domain. If this observation is
correct, there must be a way in which the domain of the matrix sentence is
extended to the embedded clause in order to allow negation to have scope
into the embedded clause. Clearly, scope of negation cannot be a property of
matrix verbs themselves. More likely, certain properties of the embedded
clauses which are determined by matrix verbs can or cannot be targets for
the scope of negation. Matrix verbs govern the head C° of their embedded
CP, and determine the semantic properties of C° in the same way as they
determine selectional properties of NPs. For example, it has long been noted
that the temporal interpretation of infinitives is determined by the matrix
verb: for volitional verbs of the *want* type, the infinitive is interpreted as a
future event with respect to the tense of the matrix verb, but the interpretation of the infinitival complement of a verb such as *regret* involves a past
event. Stowell (1982) explains this temporal determination of the infinitival
complement by the matrix verb by postulating a temporal operator in the
infinitival Comp, the value of which is determined by the governing matrix
verb. It is likely that certain values of the head C° of an embedded CP can
function as variables for the negation of the matrix verb, whereas other values
cannot function in this way. I would like to propose that the precise value
attributed to the head C° of CP by *believe*-type verbs allows the truth value
of the matrix clause to be extended to the embedded clause. With respect to
the negation of the matrix clause, this means that the head C° of the
embedded CP of *believe*-type verbs is a variable for the negation of the matrix
clause. In this way, the negation of the matrix clause has scope over the
embedded clause. The matrix and the embedded clauses thus constitute one
single domain for negation. This operator–variable relation can be morphologically expressed in French. Embedded tensed clauses in French can be

either in the subjunctive or in the indicative mood, depending on the semantics of the matrix verb. *Believe*-type verbs have the peculiar property of changing modality restrictions from indicative to subjunctive if the matrix *believe* verb is negated:

(15) a. Je crois que Dorine est/*soit contente de son livre
'I believe Dorine is happy with her book'

b. Je ne crois pas que Dorine est/soit contente de son livre
'I do not believe Dorine is happy with her book'

In the framework developed here, this change of modality in the embedded clause can be viewed as a morphological expression in the embedded clause of the operator–variable relation between negation and C°: the negation-bound C° triggers the subjunctive mood in the embedded clause. Embedded C°s of volitional verbs, factive verbs, and *claim*-type verbs cannot be bound by the negation of the matrix verb. The semantic value which these verbs attribute to their embedded C° does not allow this C° to function as a variable for negation. In this way, the informal observation that the matrix and embedded clauses of these verbs have independent truth value domains can be formally represented.

The adjunct vs. argument asymmetries of negated *believe*-type verbs can now be explained straightforwardly. *Wh*-phrases moving successive-cyclically to the higher clause will pick up the negative value of the embedded C° by Spec–Head agreement while moving through the embedded SpecCP. This means that by passing through the SpecCP position, *Wh*-phrases become themselves variables of negation by Spec–Head agreement with the negation-variable C. The *Wh*-phrases moved to the SpecCP of the matrix verb then end up as elements with a negative feature, the value of a negation-bound variable. It is well known that general principles governing operator–variable relations at Logical form require that a variable must be in the scope of its operator at LF. The *Wh*-elements in the matrix clause which have moved through the lower SpecCP have become negative variables by doing so. These negation-bound *Wh*-elements are not in the scope of the negative operator at S-structure. Consequently, the resulting sentences will be excluded in LF.

Adjunct *Wh*-phrases extracted from the clausal complements of negated *believe* verbs can only move successive-cyclically, since their traces have to be antecedent-governed following the ECP (Chomsky 1986a). Consequently, these *Wh*-phrases necessarily pick up the negative value from C° via Spec–Head agreement. Upon arrival in the matrix SpecCP, the *Wh*-adjunct is outside of the scope of its negation.[4] Consequently, the sentence (3b) will be ruled out at LF. *Wh*-phrases originating in internal argument positions have another option, since their traces are properly governed by the verb selecting them. These *Wh*-phrases may move over the embedded CP Barrier, yielding sentences with at best a weak *Wh*-island violation as in (3c).[5] The ECP is thus only indirectly involved in the explanation of the adjunct vs. argument asymmetries under discussion: the ECP only ensures that adjunct *Wh*-phrases move through the embedded SpecCP, but it does not directly account for the unacceptability of the relevant sentences. This analysis is confirmed by the impossibility of Stylistic Inversion in these sentences. Kayne & Pollock (1978) convincingly show that *Wh*-phrases or their traces in SpecCP trigger Stylistic Inversion in French.

> (16)   L'homme que je crois qu'aime Euphrasie
> 'The man that I think Euphrasie loves'

The sentence (17) shows that Stylistic Inversion is not possible when the matrix *believe* verb is negated, and thus confirms that no *Wh*-phrase moved through the embedded SpecCP.

> (17)   *L'homme que je ne crois pas qu'aime Euphrasie
> 'The man that I do not believe that Euphrasie loves'

The account presented here can be extended to the other cases of inner island effects cited by Rizzi, who observes (1990a: 19) that inner island effects are not limited to sentential negation, but that negative-like 'affective' operators induce the same behavior:

> (18) a. It is by lethal injection that many people believe that John was
> executed
>
>> (Rizzi 1990a: (51a))
>
> b. *It is by lethal injection that few people believe that John was
> executed
>
>> (Rizzi 1990a: (51b))

'Affective' operators are operators licensing negative polarity items. It can be assumed that the negation-sensitive embedded C° of *believe* verbs can function as a variable of the 'affective' operator. The embedded C° of *believe* verbs then functions in the same way as a negative polarity item bound by its operator, assuming the syntactic approach to the licensing of negative polarity items by operators proposed by Progovac (1988, 1991). In (18b), then, the *Wh*-operator passing through the embedded SpecCP picks up the variable value of C° by Spec–Head agreement before moving successive-cyclically to the higher SpecCP. In the matrix SpecCP, however, the relative *Wh*-operator will be outside of the scope of the operator *few* which licenses its negative value picked up in the lower SpecCP, and the sentence will be ruled out.

How does this solution interact with the extraction of subjects? Subject extraction seems to have the same degree of acceptability as object extraction, as shown in (3a) (Rizzi 1990a). According to the Barriers framework (Chomsky 1986a), subjects are not theta-governed, so it is expected that *Wh*-elements originating in this position move through the SpecCP position before moving further up to the matrix SpecCP position. Under the analysis presented here, however, the sentence (3a) should be disallowed, since the *Wh*-element would have picked up the negative value of $C°$ while passing through the lower SpecCP. The proposed analysis then seems to make the wrong prediction for subjects extracted out of negative islands. However, the solution proposed here cannot be entirely wrong since the counterparts of (3a) in Standard[6] French are entirely unacceptable, as pointed out by Melis (1988):

(19) a. (?) Who don't you think can help us?

$\qquad$ (= Rizzi 1990a:83(23))

   b. *Voilà la personne que tu ne croyais pas qui pouvait nous aider
      'This is the person who you did not think could help us'

In some Southern Dutch dialects (e.g. West Flemish, Haegeman 1983) there is an optional rule which replaces the neutral complementizer *dat* with *die* when the subject has been extracted. Interestingly, sentences with the complementizer *dat* are acceptable in the context of a negative island, whereas the form of the complementizer agreeing with the subject *die* yields unacceptable sentences:

(20) a. Dit is de man die ik dacht die/dat zou komen
      'This is the man who I thought (who/that) would come'

   b. *Dit is de man die ik niet dacht die zou komen
      'This is the man who I did not think (who) would come'

   c. (?) Dit is de man die ik niet dacht dat zou komen
      'This is the man who I did not think (that) would come'

It seems, then, that languages which have a productive rule of $C°$ agreeing with both its Spec and its complement do not allow this agreement to take place in the context of a negative island. These data can be accounted for if Rizzi's (1990a) analysis of agreement in the domain of $C°$ is taken into account. In order to explain *that*-trace effects, Rizzi (1990a) suggests that empty embedded $C°$s are manifestations of an empty

AGR-C° morpheme which agrees with the *Wh*-element passing through the embedded SpecCP.

(21)   Who$_i$ did you think [$_{CP}$ t_i AGR-C° [$_{IP}$ t_i came]]

This empty AGR-C° is in complementary distribution with *that* in standard English, and head- governs the subject trace in [Spec, IP]. Rizzi (1990a: 83) shows that theta- government is insufficient to explain (19a) for two reasons: either a trace in SpecCP should be antecedent-governed by the intervening negation under Relativized Minimality, ruling out the sentence, or there would be no trace in SpecCP but then the trace in SpecIP is not licensed by a governing head. Surprisingly, Rizzi (1990a) does not come back to this example to explain why it has the status of a weak *Wh*-island violation. In Rizzi's framework, which will be adopted in the remainder of this section, the subject trace in (3a, 19a, 21a) is head-governed.

Rizzi (1990a: 99) then proposes that the object trace can be connected to its antecedent in (22a) by both Binding and antecedent government. In (22b), only Binding can establish the required relation over the embedded CP Barrier, yielding a weak *Wh*-island violation.

(22) a. Which book do you think [*t* [John gave *t* to Bill]]

(=Rizzi 1990a: (51a))

b. ?Which book do you wonder [why [John gave *t* to Bill]]

(= Rizzi 1990a: (51b))

Extending this analysis, there are two options for the subject trace to be connected to its antecedent in (3a, 19a). Recall that in the analysis of negative islands proposed here, the intermediate trace in the embedded SpecCP is not separated from its antecedent by the negative A′ binder as in Rizzi's (1990a) analysis. In the proposed analysis, however, the trace in the embedded SpecCP marks the position in which the *Wh*-element picks up the value of the negative variable in C°. The antecedent-government strategy then yields an unacceptable sentence, as outlined above. However, the relation between the trace in [Spec, IP] and the antecedent in the matrix SpecCP can also be reconstructed via Binding, since the trace in [Spec, IP] will be governed by AGR-C°. The trace in SpecCP through which the negative value was given to the *Wh*-element by Spec–Head agreement will then be disregarded. Since the antecedent-government chain is no longer taken into account, the *Wh*-element in the higher SpecCP does not have the value of the negative variable anymore either. Consequently, the sentence (3a, 19a) receives the status of a weak *Wh*-island violation in exactly the same way as (3c, 22b).

How can the unacceptable cases (19b, 20b) of French and Southern Dutch be explained? Rizzi (1990a) proposes that in these languages, agreement of C° is both with the SpecCP and with the complement, whereas agreement of AGR-C° in English is only with SpecCP. This explains the fact that *qui/die* can only appear when the subject is moved through SpecCP. Since agreement is both with SpecCP and with the complement in these cases, the trace in SpecCP and the trace in Spec IP are necessarily identical in every respect. Consequently, under this analysis, the trace in Spec IP will have to receive the value of the negation variable in C°. The sentences with *qui/die* will then be ruled out on the analysis presented here, because the *Wh*-element in the higher SpecCP necessarily has the value of the negation variable, but is out of the scope of its negation. In English, this problem will never arise, since the AGR-C° never agrees with its complement: in the sentences (3a, 19a), the negation-variable AGR-C° will head-govern the trace in Spec IP without being able to transmit its negative value to it by agreement. In Southern Dutch, still another option exists: the *Wh*-element originating in subject position does not have to move through the embedded SpecCP. In (20c), the subject does not pass through the SpecCP to agree with the complementizer and hence does not yield *die*. The complementizer *dat* remains in C°, and the sentence has the status of, at most, a weak *Wh*-island violation. The difference between French and Southern Dutch dialects is that in French the *Wh*-element must move through the embedded SpecCP position to license an AGR-C° head that may head-govern the subject. Hence, there never are sentences parallel to Southern Dutch in French, such as (23):

(23) *Voilà l'homme que je ne croyais pas qu'allait venir
      'This is the man who I did not think (who/that) would come'

Dutch being a verb-second language, it can safely be assumed that the *dat* C° is a sufficient head governor for the trace in subject position without having recourse to the AGR-C° licensed by a trace in SpecCP. The analysis of negative islands proposed here can thus be reconciled with Rizzi's analysis of agreement in the domain of C°.

The approach in terms of variable Binding does not extend to the other negative island constraints noted by Ross (1984) which concern the extraction of certain types of adverbials and amount quantifiers in root sentences. Ross has playfully pointed out a number of interesting cases of negative islands:

(24) a. What did no imitation pearls touch?

(= Ross 1984: (2a))

    b. *What did no imitation pearls cost?

(= Ross 1984: (2b))

The unacceptability of these sentences has been successfully dealt with by Kroch's semantic analysis of the restrictions on amount quantifier *Wh*-movement. Kroch (1989) explains the impossibility of (24b) in terms of the fact that this sentence does not have plausible presuppositions.

(25) a. *How much didn't it cost?

(= Kroch 1989: (32a))

b. *How much didn't you pay?

(= Kroch 1989: (32b))

Kroch convincingly points out that the sentence becomes markedly better when a definite amount is being introduced in a relative clause (26a), or in an ironic context (26b):

(26) a. How much didn't you pay that you were supposed to?

(= Kroch 1989: (38))

b. Oil prices change so rapidly that one might ask: how much didn't it cost?

(cf. Kroch 1989)

c. What didn't that repair job cost you that you thought it would have cost?

Notice that in both cases negation is stressed. A similar interpretation can be constructed for (24b). Kroch's analysis can be extended to the remaining cases of inner islands which involve adverbs.

(27) a. *It was with this stiletto that they (never) stabbed the lasagne.

(= Ross 1984: (10b))

b. (Mafioso to judge:) I can assure you, your Honor, it is precisely with this type of stiletto that we would never stab a lasagne

But finding a context which works for Ross's (1984) examples doesn't really solve the problem he pointed out. It remains puzzling why certain *Wh*-sentences require this very specific context and some don't. Ross (1984: 262) points out that locative, temporal (*when*), durational, conditional and comitative adverbs never show any inner island effects. Importantly, the examples cited by Ross (1984) involve adverbials that are not restricted by the thematic structure of the verb. Ross then cites a number of cases involving manner, benefactive, and instrument adverbials which show a minimal opposition between immediately acceptable and less acceptable cases:

(28) a. How did(*n't) you find a solution?

(= Ross 1984: (17a. i))

b. How did(n't) you fulfill the requirements?

(= Ross 1984: (17a. ii))

(29) a. It was with this spoon that they (*didn't) put the milk into the bottle

b. It is with this kind of glue that one should (never) repair shoes

(30) a. For whom did(*n't) you enter the race?

(= Ross 1984: (18))

b. *It was for my dog that I didn't change jobs

(= Ross 1984: (18))

Some other cases with locatives and directionals can be added:

(31) a. Along which road did(n't) you drive home every day?

b. Along which lines did(*n't) you develop the argument?

(32) a. It was near Paris that we didn't find/found gasoline

b. It was near the refrigerator that we (spotted/*didn't spot) the cockroach

Pace Kroch's (1989) solution, some additional factor must be at work here which prevents certain adverbials from being outside the scope of a nonstressed negation. It seems that the relevant factor involved has to do with the selection of adverbials. The adverbials cited in (28–32) are all restricted by the thematic structure of the matrix verb to a greater or a lesser extent. I would like to suggest that it is precisely the extent of semantic selection which determines the contrasts noted in (28–32). The inner island effects noted are limited to those cases where the adverb is closely restricted by the matrix verb. In (28a), *how* can only refer to a limited set of manner adverbials which determine the specific Theme of *find* (*She easily/*attractively found the solution* vs. *She easily/attractively decorated the room*). It cannot refer to the much larger set of attitude adverbials such as *courageously* which are only restricted by Agency, since *find* isn't agentive. *How* in (28b), however, only refers to this set of attitude adverbials which is not restricted by the specific Agent selected by *fulfill*, but by Agency in general (*Fulfill the requirements courageously/brilliantly/prudently etc.*). A similar argument can be made for the contrast in (29): the instruments with which milk can be put in a bottle are more restricted than those with which shoes can be repaired: milk cannot be put in a bottle with a round rock, but one can imagine a situation in which shoes can be repaired with a rock, for example when hammers are lacking, or even with a spoon. The same is true for stabbing in (27), an activity which clearly limits its instruments to sharp objects, preferably stilettos, but round rocks won't do. Benefactives in (30) arguably change the thematic structure of the verb. The Path adverbial in (31a) is clearly less restricted than the more abstract Manner/Path of (31b). The locative adverbial in (32) is restricted by a verb such as *spot* which presupposes a specific location, but not by a verb such as *find*.

Frequency adverbials do not exhibit inner island effects because they are not as restricted semantically as other adverbs. Frequency adverbials modify the whole thematic structure, not just parts of it, they are event-external.

(33) a. ?It was six times that he didn't talk to me

(= Ross 1984: (17d.i))

b. How many times did(n't) they show up?

(= Ross 1984: (17d.ii))

In fact, the idea that only adverbials which are narrowly linked to the thematic structure of the verbs cannot be outside the scope of unstressed negation fits in nicely with Kroch's (1989) account. Being selected by the thematic structure, the adverbials mentioned are like amount quantifiers in the sense that they are presupposed by the verb and hence the sentence. It seems then that there is a way of getting Ross's (1984) 'pretty tatterdemalion set of cases' under control. Adverbs which are restricted by the thematic structure of the verb must occupy structural positions within the domain of negation. These adverbs cannot be extracted beyond the domain of negation, presumably because negation acts as a Barrier for antecedent government.[7]

It thus appears that some inner island effects first observed by Ross (1984) are better explained in terms of Binding of the embedded C° by negation or negative polarity operators, and the general principle requiring that a variable be in the scope of its operator at S-structure. The C-variable Binding approach has allowed us to effectively explain the differences between *believe*-type verbs and volitional and *claim*-type verbs with respect to the interaction of negation and extraction. I will now try to explain the extraction asymmetries out of the complements of factive verbs in a way which is quite similar to the explanation of negative islands.

3 On factive islands and Wh-feature compatibility

Before going into the explanation of the restriction on extraction out of sentential complements of factive verbs, I would like to discuss the hypothesis that the CP complement of factive verbs is nominal, and take a closer look at the acceptability status of the extraction data given in (1). First of all, I would like to dispell the idea that the sentential complements of factive verbs have in some sense a nominal feature. As pointed out in the introduction to this chapter, this idea originates in Kiparsky & Kiparsky (1970), and has been implemented into more recent frameworks by attributing a nominal value to the head C° of the CP selected by factive verbs (Rouveret 1980; Zubizarreta 1982; Adams 1985), or by assuming that there is an empty nominal projection which would make the selected CP an adnominal complement and as such an island to extraction (Rizzi 1990a). The [NP [CP]] analysis of factive complements has also been rejected by Cinque (1991: 30) and Cardinaletti (1989). A first additional criticism of the analyses which assume the nominal character of factive CP complements has to do with the nature of C. Since C° is usually viewed as a temporal element (Stowell 1982; Radford 1988: 307 and references therein) which can in addition bear interrogative and declarative values, it remains unclear what it means for C° to bear a nominal value. It has already been pointed out that any solution to factive islandhood that can do without such a stipulation would be preferable to one that crucially relies on this assumption. Let us nevertheless focus for a moment on the arguments for the nominal character of these CP complements. Adams (1985) agrees that the contrasts pointed out by Kiparsky & Kiparsky (1970) between factive and nonfactive verbs concerning the selection of gerunds, complements, and the noun *fact* do not necessarily point to the nominal character of the CP of factive verbs.

(34) a. Sally regrets having come to the party/the fact that she came to the party

b. *Sally claims having come to the party/the fact that she came to the party

Adams (1985) offers some other arguments in favor of the nominal character of the CP of factive verbs. Following Kiparsky & Kiparsky (1970), she observes that only nonfactive complements can be pronominalized by the anaphor *so*:

(35) a. You believe that Tom is ill, and I believe so, too
(= Adams 1985: (7a))

b. *You regret that Tom is ill, and I regret so, too
(= Adams 1985: (7b))

Adams claims that this result is predicted by the nominal CP hypothesis, since *so* is an anaphor only for CP and VP, not for NP. Notice that the argument for the nominal character of these CPs is only negative: it does not positively show that these CPs have nominal features, but it derives this feature from properties factive CPs do not have. The argument in favor of the nominal character of factive CPs overlooks the reason why *so* is an anaphor for VP and CP. The reason for this certainly cannot be categorial: CP and VP have no categorial features in common. Therefore, it must be that VP and certain semantic types of CP have a feature in common which is not shared by the CPs of factive verbs, and which can be morphologically expressed by *so*. A good candidate for such a feature is the notion Eventuality. VPs do not have an independent Tense and are as such not linked to a precise reference point on a time axis. In this sense, they can be considered inherent Eventualities, a temporal value that can be expressed morphologically by the infinitive. This semantic analysis of VPs has been proposed by Carlson (1984). The CPs selected by nonfactive verbs can also be argued to have a feature not unlike Eventuality: the truth value of nonfactive sentential complements is never presupposed as a fact by the nonfactive matrix verb, they are possible events. Factive verbs however assign a 'factive' truth value to their CP complements: these complements are never presented as merely possible, but as presupposed events. This semantic difference in truth value of the sentential complements between factive and nonfactive verbs is mirrored in the selection of NPs such as *fact* (34). The difference between factive and nonfactive verbs with respect to *so* pronominalization is more likely to be linked to the semantic value of *so* than to the nominal character of the CPs *so* cannot replace.

Adams (1985) cites one more so-called nominal property of factive CPs that was noticed by Zubizarreta (1982). In Spanish, only the complements of factive verbs can be preceded by a determiner.

(36)   Lamento/*creo el que Pedro no haya pasado el exámen

                                                                (= Adams 1985: (8))

        'I regret/believe DET that Pedro did not pass the exam'

However, no arguments are given to show that *el* really is the determiner of CP. Rather, it seems to be the case that *el* introduces an empty nominal head (or that it is itself the head of DP). The construction in (36) then reduces to a noun–complement construction of the type *the fact that*. An argument for this analysis comes from extraction phenomena in Spanish. Zubizarreta (1982) observes that extraction of internal arguments out of the factive complement in Spanish is quite good. However, if the CP is preceded by *el*, the sentence receives the same acceptability status as extractions out of noun – complement structures where the noun does not L- mark the sentential complement. In a Barriers framework, both sentences are ruled out by Subjacency, since the Barrier of the adnominal complement is inherited by the nominal projection in (37bc) (Chomsky 1986a: 34).

(37) a. ?¿A quién lamentas que Juan haya llamado?

(=Zubizarreta 1982: (13))

'Whom do you regret (that) Juan has called?'

b. *¿A quién lamentas el que Juan haya llamado?
'Whom do you regret (Det that) Juan has called?'

c. *Whom did you cite the fact that John called?

The contrast between (37a) and (37b) also provides evidence against Rizzi's (1990a: 112) analysis of factive CP complements as having an additional NP projection. This projection prevents direct selection and L- marking by the matrix verb, and the CP complement can be viewed as an adnominal CP. Intermediate traces in SpecCP of this sentential complement cannot be antecedent-governed because of this intervening Barrier. The problem with Rizzi's (1990a) analysis is that the 'invisible' nominal projection in (1) and (37a) should inherit the Barrierhood of the CP complement in the same way as the explicit noun–complement constructions in (37bc). In short, for an ECP-type approach to extraction from factive islands to work, one needs a single inherent Barrier, the factive CP. Rizzi's additional nominal projection predicts that (37ab) are both ruled out by Subjacency, unless some additional stipulation is made for 'invisible' nominal projections. An approach which can do without such a stipulation seems more promising to us.

Despite the subject/adjunct vs. object asymmetry observed in (1), I would like to argue that sentential complements of factive verbs do not constitute inherent Barriers to government. This assumption not only amounts to a mere stipulation, it would also prevent an explanation of the obvious selectional properties factive verbs express on their complements. The fact that the ECP is not involved in an explanation of the restrictions on extraction from factive islands can also be derived from the acceptability status of the unacceptable sentences. It is necessary to reassess the judgments on sentences such as (1ab). It seems that extraction of adjuncts out of the clausal complements of factive verbs is marginally possible as long as it is clear that the adjunct cannot be construed with the matrix clause. This gives rise to echo question interpretations in the case of interrogatives, and marginal but not impossible relative clauses.

(38) ??HOW did he deeply regret that his son had fixed the car?

(39) a. ??In WHICH hotel did we regret that they would hold the meeting?

b. ??This is the hotel in which LSA members regretted that they would never hold a meeting

(40) a. ??HOW did John very well know that his son would have fixed the car?

b. ??This is the precise way in which John knew that his son would fix the car

(41) a. ??In WHAT year did we discover two months ago that Stendhal wrote some chapters of *Armance*?

b. ??This is the year in which we discovered two months ago that Stendhal wrote some chapters of *Armance*

It is important to point out that these sentences do not have the flavor of ECP violations which are typically much stronger. Compare the preceding sentences with the following:

(42) a. *How did John very well know who would have fixed the car?

b. *In what year did we discover two months ago who really wrote *Ficciones*?

Note that in these cases echo-question interpretations are excluded. In a Barriers account, (42) is excluded by the ECP because the VP-adjoined trace in the embedded clause is not antecedent-governed by an intermediate trace in SpecCP, this position being occupied by *who*. The intermediate matrix VP-adjoined trace of *Wh*-adjuncts in (42) cannot govern over the embedded CP inheritance Barrier (Chomsky 1986a: 11). In view of examples such as (38–41), I would like to propose that the judgments on (1) should be revised. It seems that sentences such as (1ab) are possible as echo questions in the same way as (38–41). Relative clauses are marginally possible if the selectional restrictions of the factive verb in the relative clause are different from those of the subject of the factive complement clause, so as to prevent interpretations where the relativized complement is interpreted as a complement of the factive verb:

(43) a. ??WHO did you regret did not help you for the party?

b. ??WHO did you understand would organize the colloquium?

(44) a. ??This is the person who I knew/regretted would organize the colloquium

b. ??This is the person who I understood would organize the colloquium

(45) a. 'It is a question that I am discovering that does not want to answer itself'

(NPR, Radio Reader, November 14, 1990)

b. 'This is a man who you know full well is on the right side of this issue'

(overheard on a television debate)

If this interpretation of the extraction facts out of factive clausal comple-ments is correct, the subject–object asymmetry remains, even if the accept-ability status of the sentences involved has been reevaluated and made more precise. Indeed, the extraction asymmetry involves an opposition between subjects and adjuncts on one hand and internal arguments on the other hand. In view of Chomsky's (1986a: §7) discussion of Island Violations, the fact that traces of internal arguments are theta-governed can be expected to play an important role in the relative acceptability of (1c). However, it is unlikely that the ECP is involved in the marginal acceptability of (38–41) and (43–45). If these sentences were to be excluded by the ECP as (42) is, even the echo-interpretation should be impossible as this is the case in (42). Moreover, to exclude these sentences by the ECP, there should be a Barrier preventing antecedent government in (38–41). This does not seem to be the case, since SpecCP is in principle available for successive-cyclic movement and the matrix verb L-marks its complement. The question then remains why these sentences are marginal. This problem will be addressed shortly.

In order to stress even more clearly the fact that the ECP is not what is involved in the subject/adjunct vs. internal argument asymmetry under discussion, let us briefly consider some more data with untensed CPs. A specific subset of factive verbs such as French *discuter* 'discuss,' *parler* 'talk' selecting infinitival constructions differ crucially from the other factive verbs in that they have arbitrary control properties. These verbs are minimally different from obligatory subject control verbs such as *se plaindre* 'complain,' which are also factive:

(46) a. Nous$_i$ avons discuté de PRO$_{arb/i}$ se$_{arb}$/nous$_i$ raser au rasoir traditionnel
'We discussed shaving oneself/ourselves with a traditional razor'

b. Nous$_i$ sommes contents de PRO $_{*arb/i}$ *se$_{arb}$/nous$_i$ raser au rasoir traditionnel
'We were glad to shave oneself/ourselves with a traditional razor'

Whatever the correct explanation for control in general, the minimal hypothesis would certainly be to explain cases of obligatory control by config-urational principles of government that exist independently in the grammar.

This line of reasoning has been pursued by various researchers (Williams 1980; Bouchard 1985; Manzini 1983; Koster 1984; Borer 1989) which will not be reviewed here. Most recently, Kayne (1991a) has proposed that all controlled PRO be governed at some level of representation. Since in (46), arbitrary PRO cannot be argued to be controlled by an implicit argument of the matrix clause, it could be proposed that these cases of arbitrary PRO be linked to the fact that PRO is either not governed or cannot be bound by an antecedent in its governing category, the matrix clause. Let us assume PRO cannot be bound by an antecedent in its governing category in (46a) because the embedded CP is an inherent Barrier in (46a) but not in (46b). I would like to suggest that the Barrier involved in (46a) is a result of *discuss*-type verbs not L-marking their complement. The reason for this might be that these verbs do not seem to impose selectional restrictions on their complement.[8] For the analysis of extraction phenomena which concern us here, it is important to point out that extraction out of the complement of *discuss*-type verbs confirms the presence of a Barrier. Contrary to other factive verbs, the marginal extraction of adjuncts is completely disallowed in this case.[9]

(47) a. ??De QUELLE façon ont-ils été contents de se raser pendant les vacances?
'In which way were they glad to shave themselves during the holidays?'

b. *De QUELLE façon ont-ils vivement discuté de se raser pendant les vacances?
'In which way did they vividly discuss shaving themselves during the holidays?'

(48) a. ??Pour QUELLE occasion se sont-ils souvent plaints de devoir se raser?
'For WHAT event did they often complain of having to shave?'

b. *Pour QUELLE occasion ont-ils souvent discuté de devoir se raser?
'For WHAT event did they often discuss having to shave?'

(49) a. ??Voilà le livre que nous avons discuté de lire ensemble

b. ?'This is the book we discussed reading together'

(50) a. ??Voilà la personne à qui nous avions discuté de donner les livres

b. ?This is the person to whom we discussed giving the books

If the embedded CP of *discuss*-type verbs is an inherent Barrier, the sentences in (47b, 48b) are ruled out by the ECP: the traces of adjuncts and subjects have to be antecedent-governed, and an intervening Barrier will prevent the trace in the embedded SpecCP from being governed by the VP-adjoined trace in the matrix clause. Extraction of internal arguments out of the complement clauses of *discuss*-type verbs is possible and the resulting sentences (49–50) receive the status of weak *Wh*-island violations: these internal arguments only cross one Barrier and their trace is properly governed. At the same time, these data show that the marginal, but nevertheless possible extraction out of the complements of other factive verbs such as *être content* (47a) and *se plaindre* (48a) cannot be an ECP violation.

After assessing the acceptability status of the subject and adjunct extractions out of factive islands, an explanation is still needed for the subject/adjunct vs. object asymmetry. As in the case of negative islands, I would like to link the impossibility of extraction out of factive complements to an independent and less well known lexical characteristic of these verbs. Under this view, this lexical characteristic involves the licensing of embedded *Wh*-sentences. Lahiri notes that Berman's (1989) view on the quantificational variability of indirect questions entails that all factive predicates must be able to take embedded questions. Lahiri points out that this is not the case, and that apparent *Wh*-sentences selected by factive verbs actually are free relatives:

(51) a. *I regret whether John came to the party

(= Lahiri 1990: 168)

b. I regret what John saw

(= Lahiri 1990: 171)

It is, however, important to point out that factive verbs do take *Wh*-complements that are not free relatives. Factive verbs such as *like* and *hate* select complement clauses introduced by an adjunct *Wh*-element in both French and English.[10] It is important to point out that these embedded clauses are not free relatives in adjunct positions, but complement clauses.[11]

(52) a. J'aime/déteste quand/comment tu chantes cette chanson

b. I love/hate when/how you sing that song

c. Je regrette combien d'efforts cette investigation vous a coutés

d. I regret how much effort this investigation has cost you

This is obviously not the case for nonfactive verbs:

(53) a. *Je veux/prétends/crois quand/comment tu chantes cette chanson

b. *I want/claim/believe when/how you sing that song

These observations prompt us to formulate a few remarks on the classical interpretation of *Wh*-sentences as involving questions and answers (Baker 1970; Bresnan 1972), on the licensing conditions for embedded *Wh*-sentences which should be specified in the grammar, and on the obligatoriness of *Wh*-movement in embedded clauses. First of all, it is important to realize that the value of $C°$ which determines *Wh*-movement does not coincide with the interpretation of *Wh*-constructions as questions or answers. This should not come as a surprise; after all relative clauses involve *Wh*-movement without a question/answer interpretation. There is no *a priori* reason in the grammar why *Wh*-movement should be tied to question/answer interpretation. Once this link is untied, however, the question remains as to exactly what determines *Wh*-movement. It is not my purpose to investigate this question here. It is sufficient to state that *Wh*-elements in SpecCP have to be licensed, in accordance with Rizzi's (1990b) interpretation of the Principle of Full Interpretation (Chomsky 1991). Following May (1985), Rizzi (1990b: 378) assumes that the occurrence and position of *Wh*-elements at LF is determined by principle (54), the *Wh*-criterion (=Rizzi 1990b: (9)):

(54) i. Each [+ *Wh*-] $X°$ must be in a Spec–Head relation with a *Wh*-phrase.

ii. Each *Wh*-phrase must be in a Spec–Head relation with a [+ *Wh*] $X°$.

Obviously, in the case of embedded *Wh*-complements, the [+ *Wh*-] value of $C°$ is determined by the matrix verbs, following Bresnan (1972). More specific and largely unknown restrictions of the matrix verb determine the modalities of the restrictions on a [+ *Wh*-] $C°$. It is well known that verbs of the *wonder* type always require a [+ *Wh*-] feature to be spelled out. Other verbs such as *know* can trigger a [+ *Wh*-] embedded $C°$ depending on [+ *Wh*-] conditions in the main clause. The contrast between (56a) and (56bc) illustrates that the embedded $C°$ of verbs such as *know* and *ask* can be [+ *Wh*-] or [– *Wh*-].

(55) a. I wonder whether/*that George had this in mind long before the deadline

b. I wonder (when)/what George had (this) in mind

(56) a. I know that George had this in mind long before the deadline

   b. Do you know whether George had this in mind long before the deadline?

   c. I know (when)/what George had (this) in mind

It thus appears that the obligatory or optional appearance of a $[+ Wh-] C°$ is somehow determined by lexical features. It seems that factive verbs, like verbs such as *know* and *ask*, select a $[\pm Wh-] C°$. The $C°$ selected by factive verbs is only special in the sense that $[+ Wh-]$ feature cannot be realized on this complementizer.

Obviously, the meaning of the verb determines the interrogative or declarative interpretation of the embedded *Wh*-clause. However, the existence of sentences such as (52) shows that providing the *Wh*-clause with such an interpretation is not a requirement for the matrix verb. Once the question/answer interpretation is removed from the $C° \text{ }Wh$-feature, the question as to whether (51b) is a free relative or not becomes important: it has to be determined whether *Wh*-movement in the complements of factive verbs is restricted to adjuncts or not. Some factive verbs such as *know* and *realize* obviously select *Wh*-complements with both arguments and adjuncts of the complement sentence in SpecCP, the traditional indirect questions/answers. It is unclear whether this property can be generalized to all factive verbs. One well-known difference between free relatives and indirect interrogatives is the Matching phenomenon: unlike indirect interrogatives, free relatives require that the phrase introducing the relative clause conform in category (and in some languages, case) to the selectional restrictions and subcategorization requirements of the governing verb. This can be illustrated by the contrast between (57) and (58):

(57) a. I visited who you want

   b. J'ai rencontré qui tu voulais que je rencontre
                                        (=Hirschbühler 1976: (1a))
     'I met whom you told me to meet'

   c. He will go where no man has gone before

   d. I will visit the town with whom/how/when I want

(58) a. *I visited with whom you talked
                                          (=Harbert 1983: (1a))

   b. *J'ai rencontré à qui tu m'as dit de parler
                                        (Hirschbühler 1978)
     'I met with whom you told me to talk'

   c. I play what/*whom I found

If *Wh*-complements of some factive verbs do not have the properties of a *Wh*-element in SpecCP whose selectional restrictions do not correspond to those of the matrix verb, it can be concluded that the factive verb selects free relatives and not indirect questions. Factive *regret* does not easily select animate objects, and does not allow animate *Wh*-elements in the Spec position of the CP it selects.

(59)   *I regret who John saw   (=Lahiri 1990: (24))

Another difference between free relatives and indirect interrogatives is that only indirect interrogatives allow for adjectival *Wh*-phrases contained in NPs in French (60ab).[12] The sentence (60c) shows that *regretter* 'regret' patterns with free relatives in this respect:

(60) a. Je me demande quelle décision Jean a prise
         'I wonder which decision John made'

     b. *J'accepterai quelle décision Jean a prise
         'I will accept which decision John made'

     c. *Je regrette quelle décision Jean a prise
         'I regret which decision John made'

It can be concluded that factive verbs do assign a [+ Wh-] feature which is not spelled out by the C° of the CP they select. This *Wh*-movement in the complements of factive verbs such as *love, hate, regret* seems to be restricted to adjuncts.[13]

This restriction is of course lexically determined by the restrictions of the matrix factive verb on C°, but it is important to find out why there is such a restriction in the first place. What is the property of C° restricting *Wh*-movement in factive complements to adjuncts? It seems that a close look at the interpretation of (52) may answer this question. In (61a), the embedded *when* can be replaced by *whenever*, showing that the embedded sentence has a universal operator in C°, following standard formal semantic analyses of *when*-clauses (Kamp 1981; Heim 1982). This *whenever* interpretation is obligatory in (61a). Interestingly, it is excluded for verbs selecting indirect interrogatives:

(61) a. I love when(ever) you sing that song

     b. I asked you when(*ever) you sing that song

In French, there is another test to establish this difference. Nongeneric interrogative *when*-clauses can take what can be analyzed as the complex C°

morpheme *est-ce que/c'est que* 'is it that' (62a), but it cannot appear in free relatives (62b).

(62) a. Quand est-ce/c'est que tu chantes cette chanson?
    'When [is it that] do you sing that song?'

b. Quand (*c'est/est-ce que) tu chantes cette chanson, tout le monde pleure
    'When [is it that] you sing that song, everybody weeps'

In embedded clauses, indirect interrogatives allow for *est-ce que/c'est que* 'is it that,' but this complex complementizer cannot appear in factive complements:

(63) a. Je me demande quand/comment (est-ce que/c'est que) Jean a fait ça
    'I wonder when/how [it is that] he did that'

b. J'aime/déteste quand/comment (*est-ce que/c'est que) Jean a fait ça
    'I wonder when/how [it is that] he did that'

I would like to claim that the universal operator in C°, which is determined by the factive verb, is incompatible with the presumably existential value of *est-ce que/c'est que* 'is it that.'[14] This universal operator in C° also explains the restriction of *Wh*-movement in factive complements to adjuncts. With the exception of free relatives, clauses involving *Wh*-movement of an argument, both interrogative and relative, always presuppose the existence of the *Wh*-moved element, either by the truth-functional properties of interrogation or by the predication involved in relative clauses. This referential property of certain *Wh*-elements has been emphasized recently by Rizzi (1990a) and Cinque (1991) with respect to their possibilities for extraction. This characteristic can be represented as an existential property of C°.[15] It is likely, then, that the universal operator in the C° of factive complements in (52) conflicts with the existential value required by *Wh*-elements originating in argument positions. Only nonreferential or adjunct *Wh*-elements can move to the embedded SpecCP position, since only these elements are compatible with a universal operator in C°. It can be concluded that the embedded C° of factive verbs such as *love*, *hate* and *regret* receives from these verbs both a [+ Wh-] feature and the value of an universal operator.

How can this analysis of lexical restrictions on C° explain the problem of the restriction on subject/adjunct extraction out of factive complements? I would like to suggest that these restrictions are related to the compatibility of the [+ *Wh*-] feature of the embedded C° with the [+ *Wh*-] feature of the higher C. A *Wh*-element which moves successive-cyclically to the higher clause picks up the lexically determined [+ *Wh*-] feature of the embedded C° by Spec–Head agreement when passing through the embedded SpecCP position. It is not unreasonable to assume that the [+ *Wh*-] value the *Wh*-element picks up in this embedded CP through Spec–Head agreement will be incompatible with the [+ *Wh*-] feature of C° in the matrix clause. [+ *Wh*-] values of the lower and the higher C° are communicated to the *Wh*-phrase by successive-cyclic Spec–Head agreement (cf. principle (54)). As a consequence of the incompatibility of both [+ *Wh*-] values, the sentences receive a marginal interpretation. This is what accounts for (1ab) with their values reassessed as in the sentences of (38–41) and (43–45). Adjunct *Wh*-traces have to be antecedent-governed. In other words, adjunct *Wh*-phrases have to move through the embedded SpecCP position in order to be properly (antecedent-)governed. However, by doing so these *Wh*-elements will pick up the [+ *Wh*-] value of the embedded C°, and cause a *Wh*-feature incompatibility in the higher SpecCP. One might ask at this point why *Wh*-elements originating in subject position behave in the same way as adjunct *Wh*-elements: in the section on negative islands, it was observed that subject traces can be head-governed and hence properly governed by an AGR-C°. However, this option is not available in the domain of a factive C°: Rizzi (1990a: 57) explicitly limits the AGR-C° expansion to [– *Wh*-] C°s. As a consequence, the *Wh*-trace of the subject in the embedded clause of factive verbs cannot be head-governed, since factive verbs select an embedded C° that is [+ *Wh*-]. Hence, the subject trace must be antecedent-governed, forcing the *Wh*-element to move through the embedded SpecCP in the same way as *Wh*-elements originating in adjunct positions. It can be concluded that subject and adjunct *Wh*-phrases do not have the option of moving out of the factive island without passing through SpecCP. By moving out of the factive island through this embedded SpecCP position, they always cause rather unacceptable *Wh*-feature compatibility conflicts upon arrival in the higher SpecCP. The observation that subject extraction out of factive islands is on a par with adjunct extraction can thus be explained by the fact that the embedded C° cannot govern the trace in subject position, a fact which is in turn related to my claim that this embedded C° has a [+ *Wh*-] feature.

It might even be argued that the echo interpretation in the interrogative sentences of (38–41) and (43–45) is the result of the impossibility of Spec–Head agreement in the matrix clause. Nonfactive verbs such as those of the *believe* type do not assign a [+ *Wh*-] feature to their embedded C°. *Wh*-phrases moving successive-cyclically to the higher clause do not pick up any [+ *Wh*-] feature through Spec–Head agreement when passing through the embedded SpecCP. No incompatibility arises, and the sentences are acceptable. This accounts for the sentences in (2). The *Wh*-compatibility requirement can be easily integrated into Rizzi's principle (54ii) by including the exclusiveness in its formulation: each *Wh*-phrase must be in a Spec–Head relation with one and only one [+ *Wh*-] X°.

This explanation does not immediately account for the relative acceptability of (1c) and (37a). Recall however that the *Wh*-traces of internal arguments are theta- governed and hence properly governed, so that *Wh*-phrases originating in internal argument positions do not have to move through the embedded SpecCP. In this way, *Wh*-phrases originating in internal argument positions do not pick up the [+ *Wh*-] feature of the embedded C°. The *Wh*-phrases only cross CP which is a Barrier by inheritance from IP, and move to the matrix SpecCP. This results in a weak *Wh*-island violation which is reflected in the judgments of (1c) and (37a). The analysis presented here then explains Adams' (1985: fn.1) observation that 'Factive verbs do not as a rule make good bridge verbs. Some speakers therefore find awkward any extraction out of factive complements. Even for these speakers, however, the relative subject–object asymmetry seems to hold.'

This analysis of the extraction of internal arguments out of the clausal complements of factive verbs offers an immediate explanation of the fact that Stylistic Inversion in French is only possible in clausal complements of nonfactive verbs, as observed by Kayne (1981a) and Adams (1985).

(64) a. Le livre que Jean croit que Marie aime

(=Adams 1985: (1a))

'The book that Jean believes that Marie likes'

b. Le livre que Jean croit qu'aime Marie

(=Adams 1985: (1b))

(65) a. Le livre que Jean regrette que Marie aime

(=Adams 1985: (2a))

'The book that Jean regrets that Marie likes'

b. *Le livre que Jean regrette qu'aime Marie

(=Adams 1985: (2b))

According to the analysis presented here, Stylistic Inversion in (65b) is impossible for the simple reason that there is no *Wh*-trace in the embedded SpecCP of (65b). Notice that in this analysis, the absence of Stylistic Inversion in the clausal complements of factive verbs is exclusively linked to the presence of *Wh*-elements or their traces in SpecCP as predicted by the analysis of Kayne & Pollock (1978).

4 Conclusion

With respect to negative islands, I have shown that the examples in (4–5) offer conclusive evidence against an account in terms of Relativized Minimality as proposed by Rizzi (1990a). Negation does not function as a potential governor for *Wh*-traces. I have argued that *believe*-type verbs allow negation to bind the head $C°$ of their embedded CP, thus effectively extending the scope of negation to the embedded CP. Neg-raising can then be viewed as an instance of an operator–variable relation from the matrix clause into the embedded clause. This option is disallowed for other verbs. *Wh*-elements moving to the higher SpecCP through the embedded SpecCP will pick up the negative value of $C°$. This then results in a structure where the *Wh*-element with the negative value in the higher SpecCP is outside of the scope of its negative operator at S- structure. This structure is ruled out given standard assumptions about operator–variable relations.

A similar explanation involving the value of the embedded $C°$ has been extended to extraction phenomena out of factive complements. In the case of extraction out of factives, the head $C°$ of the CP selected by factive verbs has a [+ *Wh*-] feature which is picked up by *Wh*-elements moving successive-cyclically to the higher SpecCP, and is incompatible with the [+ *Wh*-] feature of the higher $C°$, resulting in an unacceptable sentence. Importantly, the possibility of an embedded AGR-$C°$ in the case of negative islands and the conspicuous absence of this possibility in the case of factive islands has allowed us to explain the fact that negative islands display argument vs. adjunct asymmetries whereas factive islands involve subject/adjunct vs. object asymmetries. Factive islands are reduced to *Wh*-islands.

In the approach presented here, the restrictions on extraction of subject and adjunct *Wh*-phrases out of the sentential complements of both factive verbs and negated *believe*-type verbs can be derived by the lexically determined value of the embedded $C°$, a [+ *Wh*-] feature and a negation-variable feature, respectively. Lexical semantic properties expressed on $C°$ under government by the matrix verb interact with general principles of operator–variable relations, Spec–Head agreement, and feature compatibility to yield the desired array of data. The ECP is only indirectly involved in the explanation of the subject/adjunct vs. object asymmetries discussed here by ensuring that subject and adjunct *Wh*-phrases move successive-cyclically. With the exception of extraposition islands, all so-called 'weak' islands (Cinque 1991) can be reduced to cases of operator (*Wh*-) islands or ($C°$) variable islands.

Notes

*   This chapter was first published as Rooryck (1992a). I would like to thank Andrew Barss, Judy Bernstein, Guglielmo Cinque, Yves d'Hulst, Richard Larson, Ludo Melis, Ljiljana

Progovac, Mel Scullen, Raffaella Zanuttini, Nigel Vincent, Laurie Zaring, and two anonymous *Journal of Linguistics* referees for useful suggestions and discussions. Thanks also to audiences at *The 27th Meeting of the Chicago Linguistics Society* and the KULeuven, where preliminary versions of this paper were presented.

1   Recall that *want*-type verbs are not ECM verbs in French as they are in English. As observed by Lakoff (1970), *want* in English is a Neg-raising verb, but not *desire* or *wish*. This is due to the fact that the Exceptional Case Marking construction of *want* has Neg-raising:

i.   I don't want him to come/I want him not to come

The French counterpart of *want*, *vouloir*, does not display the ECM construction, and consequently it does not have Neg-raising. In English, then, the ECM construction of *want* obscures the fundamental difference with respect to Neg-raising between volitional verbs on one hand and verbs such as *think* on the other (cf. *infra*).

2   This very specific reading is probably due to the fact that the matrix negation of verbs such as *prétendre* 'claim' may not have scope over *Wh*-elements originating in the embedded clause, unlike the negation of volitional verbs. I will make abstraction of this difference between verbs such as *prétendre* 'claim' and volitional verbs, since it is linked to independent factors regarding scope of negation (cf. *infra*). It is pointed out to me by an anonymous reviewer that negation in these cases involves constituent negation. The negation not being clausal, it does not intervene in the operator–trace relation. Since this problem does not crucially affect the arguments to be developed, I will leave it for future research.

3   One anonymous reviewer suggests that it would be possible to view the paraphrase relation in Neg-raising as resulting from head-to-head movement of the embedded negation to the higher clause, combined with reconstruction for the scope of negation. This ability to reconstruct the scope of negation would depend on properties of the matrix verb. It seems to us that this solution would raise more problems than it solves. In view of Kayne's (1989c) work on clitic climbing as head movement of the clitic to the matrix clause, one may wonder why only negation would be allowed to move to the matrix clause in the case of *believe*-type verbs. Also, if reconstruction of negation into the embedded clause depends on lexical properties of the matrix verb, one would like to know exactly which properties are involved. One does not want to stipulate a feature [± reconstruction of negation]. The analysis developed here does not face these problems: the semantic feature of the matrix verb which derives Neg-raising involves selectional properties expressed on the embedded C°. These selectional properties give a value to C° which enables it to function as a variable for the matrix negation.

4   An anonymous referee points out that the following example, from Cinque (1991: 85), might pose a problem for the analysis presented here:

i.   In un modo diverso, non credo che si comporterà
     'In another manner, I don't think that he will behave'

At first sight, the adjunct moves through the lower SpecCP and ends up outside the scope of negation. However, Cinque extensively argues that cases of clitic left dislocation involve no *Wh*-movement. Moreover, dislocated elements must be in the scope of negation (1991: 84). This sentence then confirms the analysis presented here: as long as (dislocated or *Wh*-moved) elements are in the scope of negation, sentences should be fine under the analysis.

5   The analysis presented here should be slightly modified in view of some additional data. For ease of exposition, I have hitherto assumed that Neg-raising with *believe*-type verbs is obligatory: the matrix negation binds the embedded C°. Data from French suggest

that this binding of C° by the matrix negation may be optional. In the discussion of (15), I have assumed that negative binding of C° triggers a change of mood in the embedded clause to the subjunctive. Interestingly, for several French speakers, extraction out of the embedded clause in believe sentences becomes much better if the embedded clause is in the indicative:

i.   C'est une procédure par laquelle je ne crois pas que nous ? avons/*ayons déjà sélectionné un article
      'This is a procedure by which I don't think we have already selected an article'

Slightly modifying the analysis, it can be assumed that the matrix negation optionally binds the embedded C°. When C° is bound by negation, the analysis developed in the text for *believe* verbs applies. When C° is not bound by the negation of the matrix clause, there is no negative value to be picked up in the embedded SpecCP and the sentences will be acceptable. With the indicative mood in the embedded clause, *believe*-type verbs then behave exactly like *want*- or *claim*-type verbs: there are no negative islands. The optionality of negative binding of C° (and hence Neg-raising) then can be checked in French by the switch in indicative or subjunctive mood.

This also explains an objection raised by an anonymous referee with respect to the predictions of this analysis regarding the relation between extraction over a *Wh*-island and over a negative C°. At first sight, this analysis predicts that (ii) and (iii) should be equally bad.

ii.   (?) Who don't you think John wants to visit?

iii. ?? Who do you wonder whether John wants to visit?

The reviewer correctly points out that (iii) is worse than (ii). I would like to suggest that the acceptable reading of (ii) corresponds to the reading without Neg-raising, hence without binding of C° by the matrix negation.

6   I am informed that sentences without *qui* 'who' in Québec French are entirely acceptable. Québec French then functions in the same way as English.

7   I owe this idea to an anonymous reviewer.

8   These verbs take any type of nominal complement [+/– animate], [+/– abstract] etc. In itself, this is not an argument for the absence of selectional restrictions, since this type of selection is not an exclusive property of *discuss*-type verbs; verbs such as *love* and *hate* can also take any type of complement. However, *discuss*-type verbs allow for a 'conceptual' interpretation of their complements, which is absent in other verbs taking any type of complement. *Love*-type verbs assign a concrete interpretation to [+ abstract] nouns they select: a sentence such as *Jeff loves courage/interpretation* does not normally mean that Jeff loves the concept courage or the concept of interpretation, but specific instances of it, or all of these instances together. *Jeff discussed courage/interpretation* freely allows for the concept interpretation, showing that no restrictions are imposed on the complement by the matrix verb. If it is accepted that such interpretive notions are part of selectional restrictions, it can be argued that *discuss*-type verbs do not impose selectional restrictions on the complement, thus allowing for 'conceptual' readings of their complements. The syntactic counterpart of this 'conceptual' interpretation then arguably is a Barrier. This is also true for *compare*-type verbs, which also have arbitrary control readings as in *John compared shaving oneself to daily torture.*

9   Notice also that subject extraction out of the clausal complements or *discuss*-type verbs cannot be checked in English and in French. This is because in English subject extraction out of the clausal complements of verbs which have obligatory complementizers (*like*, *discuss*) would give rise to *that*-trace configurations which are excluded independently. In French, extraction out of a tensed clausal complement introduced by a preposition is

always impossible. Compare the following.

i. Voilà le livre que je me suis félicité d'avoir lu
    'This is the book I am glad to have read'

ii. *Voilà le livre que je me suis félicité de ce que Jean a lu
    'This is the book I am glad (of it that) John read'

Verbs such as *discuter* 'discuss' also select a *de ce que* tensed complement. Consequently, extraction of this complement may be excluded for independent reasons linked to the syntactic nature of *de ce que*.

10 Some caution is in order here. Weerman (1989) points out that embedded *Wh*-clauses with *Wh*-phrases originating in argument positions are possible for factive verbs when the embedded clause has an exclamative value:

i   Henk regrets what a mess he has made

(= Weerman 1989: (127b))

However, in this case the *Wh*-trigger clearly is related to the interpretive exclamative value of the embedded C in the same way root *Wh*-sentences can have an exclamatory value (What a mess you have made!). In short, the *Wh*-movement in (i) is not imposed by the selectional [+ *Wh*-] properties of the matrix verb, but, importantly, it is not in contradiction with these 'adjunct *Wh*-' properties of factive verbs either.

For *when*-clauses in English, these sentences are also impossible when the expletive *it* precedes the *Wh*-clause. Nigel Vincent informs me that it is obligatory for him with when-clauses selected by factive verbs. For one anonymous reviewer, a verb such as *regret*, but not *hate* and *love*, require it. I will not give an explanation for this variation. From a formal point of view, it can be argued that the expletive *it* is coindexed with the extraposed (possibly VP-adjoined) *Wh*-clause. They are clearly not base-generated as adjuncts.

ii. I love it$_i$ [when you sing that song]$_i$

iii. * [When you sing that song]$_i$, I love it$_i$

Notice that the *Wh*-contructions with factive verbs are limited to tensed clauses:

iv. * J'aime/déteste quand/comment chanter cette chanson
    * I love/hate when/how to sing that song

The reason for this is that untensed *Wh*-CPs have a deontic meaning (cf. Rooryck, this volume Ch.4): *I asked him what to do* does not mean 'I asked him what I will do,' but 'I asked him what I should/can do.' This deontic, and hence unrealized truth value internal to the [+ *Wh*-] infinitive is incompatible with the universal truth value restriction imposed by the matrix factive verb on the sentential complement which is presupposed as a fact. In syntactic terms, two identical operators, one selected by the matrix verb and one by the deontic modal value of the infinitive, would compete for C°.

11 This can be shown by the scope of certain adverbs such as *really*. In (i) *really* has scope over the embedded sentence, whereas it only has scope over the object in (ii), but not over the free relative:

i. I really love when you sing that song

ii. I really love all mankind when you sing that song

12 French *quel(le)(s)* 'which' cannot have the 'whichever' interpretation available in English.

13 At first sight, it seems that factive verbs expressing cognition such as *know*, *realize*, and

admit allow for the classical indirect questions with both arguments and adjuncts of the embedded sentence in SpecCP. Factive verbs expressing emotion (*love*, *hate*, *regret*) only seem to allow for *Wh*-adjuncts in the embedded SpecCP.

14   This analysis may also explain why embedded interrogatives can be truncated, but not the embedded *Wh*-complements of factive verbs:

    i.   I wonder when/how
           *I love/hate when/how

It seems that sentences with a universal operator in C° cannot be truncated.

15   Perhaps the *Wh*-criterion can be made more explicit with respect to the expression [+ *Wh*-] feature. It is not clear what a *Wh*-feature is supposed to represent: as stated in Rizzi's *Wh*-criterion, the [+ *Wh*-] feature is just an indexical device which does not reveal anything about the semantics of *Wh*-movement. I would like to tentatively propose that the [+ *Wh*-] feature Rizzi has in mind really is an existential or universal operator. The existential operator is present in relative clauses predicated of a noun, and in embedded and root questions. The universal operator is present in free relatives, and optionally in the complement clauses of factive verbs. This analysis fits in nicely with Rooryck's (1994a) analysis of free relatives in which it is argued that free relatives are not headed by an empty noun, but are in fact bare CPs: if predication is related to the presence of an existential operator in relative clauses, there can be no predication in the case of free relatives since they involve a universal operator.

7

ON TWO TYPES OF
UNDERSPECIFICATION

Evidence from agreement in relative clauses

1 Syntactic underspecification[*]

Recently there have been some interesting attempts to extend the phonolog-ical notion of feature underspecification (e.g. Archangeli 1984) to features of syntactic agreement. Burzio (1992) has made use of the notion of underspec-ification to describe the parameterization of anaphors across languages, and Van Gelderen (1992) argues that Dutch *het* 'it' and Middle English *it* are unspecified for number. Kayne (1989b) has argued in favor of an underspec-ified analysis of English so-called 'third person' *-s* (*Rain falls*), suggesting that this morpheme does not mark [3rd person] but [+ sg] in English. Kayne argues that first and second person are unmarked for number. Vanden Wyngaerd (1994) discusses Kayne's proposal, and convincingly argues that unmarkedness of features has to be represented by zero-marked features, which can be taken to be [0number, 1st person] in the case of *I*. Similarly, third person *-s* should be [+ sg, 0person, 0gender]. Vanden Wyngaerd (1994: 164) shows that unmarkedness cannot correspond to the mere absence of fea-tures, since the mere absence of features cannot give rise to a feature clash. He argues that in *you sing* the [2nd person, +pl] *you* cooccurs with the bare form of the verb which is unmarked for features. Since in this case the absence of common features does not give rise to a feature clash, there should not be a feature clash either in the cooccurrence of [1st person] *I* and [+ sg] *-s* in * *I sings*. Vanden Wyngaerd therefore concludes that the absence of number in the feature specification of *I* should be marked by a zero number feature that would clash with [+ sg] *-s*, on the plausible assumption that agreement requires strict identity of features. A feature [0number] (= Vanden Wyngaerd's (1994) [0 sg]) would certainly clash with [+ sg] *-s*.

The idea of extending phonological feature theory to syntactic feature theory dates back to the very beginnings of generative grammar. An inter-esting question is to what extent this conceptual similarity between under-specification in the syntax and underspecification in phonology reflects intrinsic properties of the representation of features in the language faculty. If phonology and syntax both make use of underspecified features, then the notion of underspecification itself, and, more generally, feature theory itself, might reflect a fairly deep property of the language faculty shared by representations in phonology and syntax. More specifically, the question arises as to whether the representation of features as being specified or underspecified is an intrinsic modular element of the faculty of language which is shared by planes of representation in phonology and syntax. There is no logical necessity that the answer to this question be positive: it might just as well be the case that the correspondence between (under)specification in the syntax and (under)specification in phonology is a fairly superficial one, and that there are two entirely different mechanisms which only share some surface similarity in that, for instance, positive and negative values of features are present. Before any strong conclusions are warranted about feature theory as a plane of representation of both phonology and syntax, it remains to be shown that underspecification in the syntax and in phonology are sufficiently alike.

It is the purpose of this chapter to show that syntactic and phonological underspecification are indeed sufficiently similar to allow for a positive answer to the question raised. I would first like to show that two types of underspecified features should be distinguished in syntax and phonology. More particularly, it will be argued that there is a difference between *variable* underspecified features (α-features) and *nonvariable* underspecified features (0-features). 'Nonvariable' or 0-features should be thought of as 'neutral' features: they have no positive or negative value for a given feature, they simply mark the absence of a specific feature *value*. In terms of an Attribute-Value feature system, this means that a given feature has an Attribute specification without a Value. More specifically, a 0-feature for [person] can be represented with the Attribute [person :   ], while a positively specified feature for person can be represented with both an Attribute and a Value: [person : 1st]. The second type of syntactically underspecified φ-features, which I introduced as *variable* underspecified features, should be thought of as 'chameleonlike' features, or α-valued φ-features: these features have [αperson, αgender, αnumber] values, that is they are sensitive to *any* value of person, gender, number. 'Variable' or α-features do not have a value of their own: their value needs to be 'filled in' by the features of the elements surrounding them. At first sight, underspecified α-valued features simply appear to be *un*specified features, but I argue that their complete absence of specification plays a role in the grammar: 'variable' or α-features have no 'fixed' value, but can 'pass on' the features of the elements surrounding them. This can be represented in terms of an Attribute-Value system by the complete absence of an Attribute-Value set: an α-valued feature for [person] would be specified as [:   ]. Again, this *under*specification does not merely mean that the Attribute-Value set is simply *un*specified: if the Attribute-Value set were unspecified, it would mean that it plays no grammatical role whatsoever. In other words, 0-features are inherently neutral features, α-features are inherently flexible and 'open' or 'transparent' for the features surrounding them. This yields the following three-valued system:

(1)	underspecified	specified
variable	α	
nonvariable	0	+(−)

To the extent that the distinction between 0-and α-features is justified in both syntax and phonology, there is evidence that the notion of underspecification is neither phonology- nor syntax-specific, and that it should be viewed as an independent module of feature representation in the language faculty which is accessible to both syntax and phonology. The system of 0-, α-, and +/− features then can be viewed as independent of its phonological or syntactic content.

I will show that both types of underspecification are syntactically necessary and operative in the domain of agreement in $C°$, that is, the familiar locus of *that*-trace effects in English and French *que* —> *qui* alternations (Kayne 1976; Rizzi 1990a). The $0/α$ distinction eliminates some stipulations entailed by Rizzi's (1990a) analysis of agreement in $C°$, and conforms to Chomsky's (1995) Minimalist Program where all variation is reduced to morphological differences.

The first section of this chapter will focus on the syntactic motivation for a distinction between 0- and α-features. Evidence for this distinction will be drawn from $C°$ agreement in French (*que* —> *qui*), and from a curious *that*-trace effect in French matrix interrogatives. In both cases, it will be shown that Rizzi's (1990a) solution, while essentially correct, is not morphologically refined enough to capture the relevant facts. Finally, I will briefly illustrate that the distinction between 0- and α-features is also present in cases of phonological vowel harmony, although in a very different guise. This last section will be devoted to an attempt to represent the phonological and syntactic $0/α$ distinction in the same way.

2 On 0- and α-features in the domain of $C°$

2.1 Qui —> qui *agreement*

Rizzi (1990a) claims that the *that*-trace effect is a case of agreement between $I°$ and $C°$. A zero $C°$ with AGR features appropriately head-governs a subject trace in SpecIP (2). By contrast, the C° *that* is inert for government, hence the subject trace is not appropriately head-governed, violating the ECP. Rizzi (1990a) claims that the *that*-trace effect thus merely is a special instance of agreement in Comp, a process present in a variety of languages from Kinande to Modern Irish.

(2)   Who$_i$ did you think
      [$_{CP}$ t'_i *that/Ø-AGR$_C^\circ$ [$_{AGR-S-P}$ t_i AGR$_S^\circ$ left]]

(3)   The thing
      [$_{CP}$ O$_i$ that/*Ø-AGR$_C^\circ$ [$_{AGR-S-P}$ t_i AGR$_S^\circ$ happened]]
      is terrible

Under these assumptions, the sentence (3) raises a problem. Why is it the case that the C° *that* can properly head-govern the adjacent subject trace in the relative clause of (3), while the very same *that* is excluded in the case of an embedded declarative as in (2)? Rizzi (1990a) claims that this is due to the fact that the complementizer *that* in (3) is in a predicative relation with the NP *the thing* which is the 'subject' of predication. Rizzi (1990a: 70) reasonably assumes that predication involves agreement, and suggests that there is an abstract agreement relation between the head of the relative and the C° *that*, which he calls A-agreement. Rizzi (1990a: 67) suggests that besides the feature [±*Wh*-], complementizers have a feature [± pred]. Relative *that* in (3) is [+ pred] while the declarative *that* in (2) is [− pred]. Agreement in a relative clause as in (3) then is a result of a [+ pred] C° being subject to A-agreement. In (3), the C° *that* heading the relative clause has the additional feature [+ pred], and is as such an appropriate head-governor. Zero (Ø-)AGR$_C^\circ$ is [− pred] and is thus excluded in (3).

Rizzi (1990a:56) then suggests that the same analysis applies to the conversion of the French complementizer *que* 'that' to *qui* in *Wh*- constructions (cf. Kayne 1976). French *qui* also marks agreement of AGR$_S^\circ$ and AGR$_C^\circ$. Since *qui* appears in both relative (4c) and embedded (4a) contexts, Rizzi (1990a) claims *qui* does not encode the difference between the features [+ pred] and [− pred].

(4)   a.   L'homme$_i$ que je crois [$t_{i'}$ qui [t_i viendra]]
           'The man who I think that will come'

      b.   L'homme$_i$ que je crois [$t_{i'}$ que/*qui [Jean connaît t_i]]
           'The man that I think that Jean knows'

      c.   L'homme$_i$ [O$_i$ qui t_i est venu]
           'The man who came'

In this case, Rizzi (1990a) proposes that *que* to *qui* conversion simply is a restricted form of Spec–Head agreement of the C° *que*: *que* only becomes *qui* when a subject adjacent to C° is extracted. For Rizzi, *qui* is a C° that agrees both with its specifier and with its complement, and agreement with the complement can only arise when the subject adjacent to *que* moves through SpecCP. Since complementizer *qui* cannot appear in interrogative clauses, Rizzi (1990a) suggests it is a *–Wh-* C°.

Rizzi's (1990a) [±pred] is inadequate both theoretically and empirically. On the theoretical side, it is not plausible to represent a relational syntactic notion such as predication as a morphosyntactic feature. This equals viewing predication as a syntactic primitive rather than as a structurally derived notion. As features go, φ-features clearly have morphosyntactic import, and the *Wh*-feature can be related to quantificational properties, but it is less likely that predication should be expressed as a feature on heads, since it is essentially a relational notion like subject and object, not a semantic or a morphosyntactic one. Moreover, while the feature [± pred] does the job of distinguishing both types of complementizers, it amounts to little more than a diacritic stating that a C° of a (relative) CP that is predicated is somehow different from a (complement) CP whose C° is governed by V°. The real question remains: what is the nature of the feature [± pred]?

Empirically, Rizzi (1990a) glosses over the fact that $AGR_C°$ *qui* transmits φ-features of the NP to the AGR_S-P of the relative clause.[1] This feature transmission comes about via Spec–Head agreement with the operator in SpecCP and the coindexation of this operator with its trace in SpecIP.

(5) a. $Vous_{2PL}$ qui $êtes_{2PL}$ venus
'You who have come'

b. $Nous_{1PL}$ qui $sommes_{1PL}$ là
'We who are there'

However, there are varieties of French where *qui* does not fully transmit all φ-features.[2] In one variety, the value for person is not transmitted as in (6). This is most obvious in (6c) where the adjective bears gender and number agreement, but the verb form is third person, which is unexpected from the point of view of the Standard variety of French.

(6) a. C'est moi_{1SG} qui est_{3SG} venu
'It is me who has come'

b. C'est $nous_{1PL}$ qui $sont_{3PL}$ venus
'It is us who have come'

c. '(. . .) c'est *moi qui sera* infiniment reconnaissante envers vous'
'it is I who will be$_{3SG}$ extremely grateful$_{SG.FEM}$ to you'
(quoted by Frei 1929: 163)

In another variety of French, no features seem to be transmitted into the relative clause at all. The verb form in the relative invariably is third person, the 'default' form of agreement in French:

(7) a. Il n'y a que *vous qui peut* le faire; C'est pas *nous qui peu(t)* y aller
'There is only you who can$_{3SG}$ do it; It is not us who can$_{3SG}$ go there'

(Frei 1929: 163)

b. Au lieu que c'est *nos hommes qui boit*, c'est *nous qui s'soûle*, à çt'heure
'Instead of it being our men who drink$_{3SG}$, it is us who get$_{3SG}$ drunk at this hour'

(quoted by Frei 1929: 163)

Importantly, Rizzi's (1990a) notion of [±pred] cannot explain this type of variation: the presence of the feature [±pred] either allows for or prevents full person, number, and gender agreement, but it cannot be used to explain the partial agreement present in (6–7). In Rizzi's system, some additional stipulation is necessary besides [+ pred] to exclude person agreement in relative clauses of these varieties of French. From a descriptive point of view, complementizer *qui* itself seems to be either partly or entirely 'flexible' in features, and 'passes on' the features of the NP of which the relative CP is predicated. How should this 'feature transfer' property be conceived of? I would like to claim that *qui* in (5) simply has α-valued φ-features, [αperson, αgender, αnumber], which can pick up any value from the NP the relative CP is adjoined to, and transmit it to the AGR$_S$ of the relative clause. The variety of French in (6) has a *qui* which is [0person, αgender, αnumber]: number and gender features are transmitted to the AGR$_S$ of the relative clause, but person features are 'neutralized,' showing up as a 'default' third person agreement on the AGR$_S$ of the relative clause. The variety in (7) has a *qui* which is [0person, 0number] (and presumably [0gender]), which again shows up in default third person agreement on the AGR$_S$ of the relative clause. I have chosen the features [0person, 0number] here rather than the 'positive' features [3rd person, +sg] to account for the fact that morphosyntactically, relative *qui* behaves in a way very similar to impersonal *il* which also triggers 'default' third person singular agreement. It seems a plausible assumption that a nonreferential element such as impersonal *il* has no positively specified features at all: what could be the arguments to endow *il* 'it/he' in *il pleut* 'it rains' with a positive specification [singular, masculine, 3rd person]? In the absence of such arguments, I will assume *il* 'it/he' is [0number, 0gender, 0person].[3] Also note that *qui* and *il* share the morpheme /i/, which is a further argument for their nondistinctness featurewise. The evidence for 0-features in the domain of $C°$ will be further corroborated in section 2.2. In any case, the notion of α-valued features is empirically superior to [±pred].

Returning now to the problem of *that*- trace effects in English, I still have to say something about the theoretical problems Rizzi's (1990a) analysis faces with respect to the nature of agreement in $C°$. Recall that Rizzi stipulates a [±pred] feature to distinguish between [– pred] declarative and [+ pred] relative agreeing $C°$ in English, and that he introduces a corresponding difference between A- and A´-agreement (respectively predication agreement and Spec–Head agreement).

It is now possible to do away with the [±pred] feature, while capitalizing on Rizzi's distinction between predication (A-) agreement and Spec–Head (A´) agreement.

By their very nature α-features are 'transmitters' of features. Transmission of features in declarative $C°$ straightforwardly obtains via Spec–Head agreement. In relative CPs, the possibility of Spec–Head agreement to transmit features from outside of the clause is of course not available. Now, α-features have no fixed value of their own, but 'await' features which they can transmit into the clause. As a result, any feature index of the projection of $N°$ to which a relative CP is adjoined will automatically percolate to the α-featured $C°$ head of the relative clause. An $AGR_C°$ with α- features is sensitive to whatever nominal features are near.[4]

In the analysis presented here, both declarative and relative $AGR_C°$ have α- features. Declarative AGR_Cs have α- features because subject NPs with any features can be extracted from an embedded clause, without triggering morphological differences on the $AGR_C°$ *qui* of the embedded clause. Featurewise, declarative and relative $AGR_C°$ are identical, contrary to Rizzi's [±pred] distinction. This analysis immediately eliminates Rizzi's stipulation that French *qui* is the agreeing form of the complementizer, which is both insensitive to the [±pred] distinction and to the A/A´-agreement distinction. In the analysis advocated here, the identity of French relative and declarative *qui* follows straightforwardly from their identity in features: *qui* is an element expressing $I°$–$C°$ agreement with α-valued φ-features.

I have not yet quite shown however that [±pred] can be done away with altogether: recall Rizzi (1990a) uses [±pred] as a descriptive device to distinguish between [+ pred] relative $C°$ which must appear as *that* in a configuration where an empty operator is moved to SpecCP from subject position in a relative clause, and [– pred] declarative $C°$ which cannot appear as *that* when an empty operator, or any other *Wh*-NP has moved through SpecCP from subject position. In all other cases when an empty operator is moved to SpecCP (from object position), *that* is optional. The relevant sentences are repeated here for convenience:

(8) a. Who$_i$ did you think
 $[_{CP}$ t'_i *that/Ø-AGR$_C°$ $[_{AGR-S-P}$ t_i AGR$_S°$ left]]
 {– pred}

 b. The thing
 $[_{CP}$ O$_i$ that/*Ø-AGR$_C°$ $[_{AGR-S-P}$ t_i AGR$_S°$ happened]]
 {+pred}
 is terrible

 c. Who$_i$ did you think $[_{CP}$ t'_i (that) Sue saw t_i]

 d. The thing $[_{CP}$ O$_i$ (that) Sue saw t_i]

Recall also that in Rizzi's system, movement of an element from subject position to SpecCP triggers I°–C° agreement by transitivity of Spec–Head agreement (first in the domain of IP, and then in CP). With an empty element (operator/trace) in SpecCP, the complementary distribution of English C° then is as follows in Rizzi's system:

(9) C° ⟶ that — / I°–C° agreement, C° {+ pred}
 ⟶ Ø — / I°–C° agreement, C° {– pred}
 ⟶ (that) — / no I°–C° agreement {± pred}

Under this analysis, it remains quite odd that the complementizer *that* can at the same time express a [± pred] C° if there is no I°–C° agreement, while it is only capable of expressing a [+ pred] C° if there is I°–C° agreement. Why should this be so?

I would like to say that there is no such causal relation between I°–C° agreement and the feature [±pred] because there is no feature [±pred]. The distribution of *that* is not as in (9), but it rather depends on the directionality of agreement in the domain of C°. Obligatory *that* expresses *bidirectional* Spec–Head agreement in C°: the subject of the relative clause moves to SpecCP and triggers agreement of C° with I°, and the relative C°, whose α-features have 'absorbed' the features of the N° heading the relative clause, in turn checks the [person, number, gender] features of the element in SpecCP. Obligatory *that* in a sense 'exchanges' agreement with the element in SpecCP. The idea here is that a bidirectional Spec–Head agreement is 'strong' agreement and needs to be spelled out overtly. The obligatory absence of *that* is related to *unidirectional* Spec–Head agreement by the element in SpecCP: a declarative C° has no [person, number, gender] features to check: rather, it only 'receives' both I°–C° agreement and [person, number, gender] features from the element passing through SpecCP (Spec-to-Head agreement).[5] Optional *that* then simply marks the absence of I°–C° agreement.[6] French *qui*, marking I°–C° agreement, then is not sensitive to the directionality of agreement in C°, while English C° expresses

I°–C° agreement by the obligatory presence or absence of *that*, depending on the directionality of the additional [person, number, gender] features.

It can be concluded that the notion of α-valued feature advantageously subsumes the feature [± pred] which has been shown to give rise to a fair number of stipulations.

2.2 That-*trace effects in French matrix interrogatives*

The evidence in favor of the existence of 0-valued φ-features in C° comes from a restricted *that*-trace effect in French matrix interrogatives.

French has a complex interrogative complementizer *est-ce que* which is restricted to matrix interrogatives in Standard French. This complementizer can also appear in embedded interrogatives in colloquial varieties of French.

(10) a. Est-ce que Euphrasie est arrivée?
'Is-it-that Euphrasie has arrived?'

b. Je me suis demandé quand ((*) est-ce que) Euphrasie est arrivée
'I wondered when is-it-that Euphrasie has arrived'

c. Quand est-ce que Euphrasie est arrivée?
'When is-it-that Euphrasie has arrived?'

As a complex complementizer, *est-ce que*, which I will gloss as 'that₂,' should not be analyzed as an intervening sentence containing an inflected form of *être* 'be.' This analysis is of course possible, but the formal properties of *est-ce que* as a complex C° and *est-ce que* as an intervening sentence are quite different. As an intervening sentence, with *est* a verb, *est-ce que* bears a descending intonation, and the sentence is interpreted as 'Does this mean that Euphrasie has arrived?'. The correct answer to the question would be: *Oui, c'est qu'elle est venue* 'Yes, this means that she came.' In this case, *être* 'be' can be used in the past tense. As a complex complementizer, *est-ce que* does not bear any intonation, and means 'Is it true that Euphrasie has arrived?,' with a corresponding answer 'Yes, she has arrived.' In this use of *est-ce que*, *être* cannot be put in the past tense without triggering falling intonation and a corresponding change in interpretation. This much should make it clear that *est-ce que* functions as a single complex interrogative C°.

The C° *est-ce que* also undergoes *que/qui* conversion if an adjacent subject is moved to the domain of C°. It appears, however, that movement to the domain of C° and subsequent conversion to *est-ce qui* is limited to the interrogative animate *Wh*-pronoun *qui* 'who' and the inanimate *Wh*-pronoun *que* 'what.'[7] No other *Wh*-NPs, including simplex *Wh*-pronouns such as *combien* 'how many,' can similarly trigger *est-ce qui* conversion if they originate in SpecIP. When *est-ce que* is not expressed in C°, the sentences are fine.

(11) a. Qui/Qu'est-ce qui est arrivé?
'Who/what that$_?$ has arrived?'

b. Quels enfants (*est-ce qui) [*t* sont arrivés?]
'Which children (that$_?$) have arrived?'

c. Quel paquet (*est-ce qui) [*t* est arrivé?]
'Which package (that$_?$) has arrived?'

d. Combien (*est-ce qui) [*t* en sont arrivés?]
'How many (that$_?$) of-it have arrived?'

To the best of my knowledge, this fact has gone unobserved in the generative literature. Importantly, *est-ce que* is possible if the *Wh*-NP does not transit through SpecIP, or, for that matter, if any 'non-subject' *Wh*-element moves to SpecCP:

(12) a. Quels enfants est-ce que [tu as vus *t*]
'Which children is-it-that you have seen?'

b Combien est-ce que [tu en a vus *t*]
'How many is-it-that you of-it have seen?'

c. Quand/comment/avec quels arguments est-ce que tu as convaincu Nestor?
'When/how/with which arguments is-it-that you have convinced Nestor?'

Clearly, then, the sentences (11bcd) testify to an unadulterated *that-* trace effect in French matrix interrogative clauses. The question now is: why is *est-ce qui* possible with interrogative *qui* 'who' and *que* 'what' in SpecCP and C° respectively? Clearly, Rizzi's (1990a) [± pred] is of no avail here.

The question raised by the examples in (8) is why interrogative *qui* and *que* can agree with the C° *est-ce qui*, while full *Wh*-NPs and quantifying pronouns cannot. I would like to suggest that *est-ce qui* represents an AGR$_C$° with φ-features that are specified as [0person, 0gender, 0number]. When in SpecCP, only interrogative *qui* and *que* can agree with this 0-specified *est-ce qui*, since they also have 0-specified φ-features. Full *Wh*-NPs and pronouns such as *combien* 'how many' have positively specified features, at least for number. As a result, they cannot agree with 0-specified AGR$_C$° *est-ce qui*. The fact that *est-ce que* is also prevented from appearing in these contexts is due to the fact that the AGR$_C$° agreeing with full *Wh*-NPs and pronouns originating in SpecIP is a null morpheme.

At this point, one might ask why 0-features are introduced rather than the minus value of the widely adopted binary [±] system for features.[8] For one thing, it is not very clear what would be the import of features of the type [– person, – gender, – number]. As far as I know, these never trigger any syntactic processes of agreement. Moreover, a growing body of work in phonology (e.g. Ewen & van der Hulst 1985; Rennison 1986; Anderson & Ewen 1987) argues in favor of a unary system of features, and the question arises as to whether the same move should not be made in the morphosyntactic feature system. In what follows, the reasons for my choice of the 0 value will become clearer.

There is independent evidence that interrogative *qui* and *que* have indeed 0-specified features. If it is assumed that agreement involves identity of features, this evidence will indirectly testify to the 0-specified nature of *est-ce qui*. A first argument for the 0-specified nature of *qui* 'who' comes from Binding theory. Interrogative *qui* 'who' can agree with the anaphor *soi* 'self':

(13)   Qui ne pense jamais à soi?
        'Who doesn't ever think of self?'

Burzio (1992) claims that the anaphor *soi(-même)* has no φ-features, and marks it with [0person, 0gender, 0number] features, undetermined for person, gender, and number. The anaphor *soi(-même)* indeed only takes for antecedents a restricted set of quantifiers such as *chacun* 'everyone,' *quiconque* 'whoever,' *tout le monde* 'everyone,' *personne* 'nobody' (Grevisse 1980: §1083–1084). Importantly, it also binds an empty *pro* object as in (14).

(14) a. Chacun/tout le monde pense toujours à soi
         'Everybody always thinks about self'

     b. La bonne musique réconcilie __ avec soi-même

     c. '*Good music reconciles __ with oneself'

Rooryck (1992d) has suggested that object *pro* is [0person, 0number, 0gender] to explain the different restrictions on Binding of *pro* by anaphors in French, Dutch, and English. Note that it would not make much sense to attribute [– person, – gender, – number] features to *pro*, and correspondingly to *soi-même* 'oneself.' Rooryck (1992d) argues that English *one*, and hence *oneself*, is [+ sg] since it agrees with third person *-s*. Similarly, Dutch *zichzelf* arguably has [+ 3rd person, 0number, 0gender] features. As a result, these anaphors clash with the 0-featured antecedent *pro*. For French, Rooryck assumes Burzio's (1992) claim that *soi-même* is entirely underspecified for features. Since both *pro* and *soi-même* are [0person, 0gender, 0number], the anaphor *soi-même* can be bound by *pro*. Since interrogative *qui* 'who' also agrees with *soi* 'self,' the requirement of identity of features implicit in Binding suggests that interrogative *qui* 'who' is also endowed with 0-specified features.

A second argument in favor of the idea that interrogative *qui* and *que* have 0-specified features comes from its interaction with the floating quantifier *tous* 'all' (cf. Doetjes (1992) for a recent analysis). *Tous* 'all' can modify a *Wh*-NP, but not interrogative *qui* 'who' or *que* 'what.'

> (15)   Quels enfants/*qui/*qu'est-ce que tu as tous vus?
>   'Which children/who/what is-it-that you have all seen?'

It might of course be argued that interrogative *qui* and *que* are [+ sg], and therefore cannot cooccur with [+ pl] *tous* 'all.' At first sight, this objection seems to be corroborated by the fact that interrogative *qui* and *que* can cooccur with [+ sg] floating *tout* in the standard variety of French spoken in Belgium:

> (16) a.   Qui est-ce que tu as (tout) vu à la fête?
>   'Who is-it-that you have all seen at the party?'
>
>   b.   Qu'est-ce que tu as (tout) fait pendant les vacances?'
>   'What is-it-that you have all done during the holidays?'

In this case, floating *tout* adds a specification to the possible answer to the question. Without *tout*, the answer to (16a) might include a single person, several people, or even a group. With *tout*, (16a) can only have a (plural) list answer, never a group. This suggests that the addition of *tout* pares down the interpretive possibilities of interrogative *qui*. *Mutatis mutandis*, the same is true for *que* 'what.'

If one is to claim that *qui/que* are [+ sg] syntactically, it will have to be argued that at least semantically *qui/que* can be both plural and singular. However, if *qui* is syntactically singular, it remains distinctly odd that no other singular *Wh*-NP can cooccur with *tout* in this way. Floating *tout* with a list reading is possible with a plural *Wh*-NP, but list-reading *tout* cannot cooccur with any singular NP. [9]

> (17) a.   Quels tableaux est-ce que tu as (tout) vendus cet été?
>   'Which paintings is-it-that you have (all) sold this summer?'
>
>   b.   Quel livre est-ce que tu as (*tout) lu
>   'Which book is-it-that you have (all) read?'

This of course could again be attributed to the fact that interrogative *qui* and *que* are the only elements to combine syntactic [+ sg] features with semantic [0number] features. But this answer of course begs the question as to how the syntactic [+ sg] features can be distinguished from the interpretive [0number] features on theoretical grounds. The conceptually simpler analysis is to say that interrogative *qui* and *que* are 0-specified for all φ-features. As such, they are semantically compatible with both singular and plural answers. List-reading *tout* functions as a distributive adverb that does not agree with its antecedent.

The behavior of *tout* in (16) can be interpreted as an argument in favor of the 0-specified status of interrogative *qui* and *que*. First, *que* and *qui* cannot be [+ pl], since they trigger [+ sg] agreement. Secondly, it is clear that *que* and *qui* cannot be simply [+ sg] either, since [+ sg] NPs cannot cooccur with list-reading *tout*. If it is argued that interrogative *qui* and *que* have no specific feature associated with number, and in fact have [0number] features, both observations can be reconciled: [0 number] implies that the number feature can be semantically interpreted either as singular or as plural. List-reading *tout* then selects the semantically plural reading. Morphosyntactically, the fact that interrogative *qui* 'who' and *que* 'what' originating in SpecIP position trigger *third* person agreement should be viewed as default agreement. The third person inflection on the verb with interrogative *qui* and *que* subjects then is similar to that with impersonal or weather subject *il* 'it.' Impersonal *il* 'it' and interrogative *qui* and *que* are identical in φ-features, they only differ in that interrogative *qui* and *que* also carry semantic [± animate] features.[10]

To conclude, it appears that French has an $AGR_C{^\circ}$ *est-ce qui* with 0-valued φ-features that can only agree with other 0-valued *Wh*-elements, *in casu* interrogative *qui* 'who' and *que* 'what' originating in SpecIP position. The result of the analysis is that the interrogative animate *Wh*-NP *qui* as well as the $C{^\circ}$ *est-ce qui* have totally 0-specified features, whereas $C{^\circ}$ *qui* can have [αperson, αgender, αnumber] features in Standard French and either [0person, αgender, αnumber] or [0person, 0gender, 0number] features in the varieties of French described by Frei (1929).[11] Note that all variation is reduced to morphological differences, in conformity with Chomsky's (1995) Minimalist Program.

3 α- and 0-features in syntax and phonology

Finally, the theoretical relevance of both types of syntactic underspecification should be discussed in the light of underspecification theory in phonology. In the history of generative grammar, syntactic feature theory has always been inspired by phonological feature theory. As has already been mentioned in the introduction to this chapter, the question arises whether this influence is accidental or not. If the feature systems of syntax and phonology are organized quite differently, the syntactic distinction between 0- and α-features is not expected to turn up in phonology. If, on the contrary, the syntactic 0/α distinction does have a counterpart in phonology, it might reflect an organization of feature theory that would be shared by both syntax and phonology.

I will discuss some indications from vowel harmony (the phonological counterpart of α-agreement) that the latter conclusion is warranted. Tangale, a member of the Chado-Hamitic language group spoken in Nigeria, has nine vowel phonemes which can be represented in the following chart from Jungraithmayer (1971), as quoted by Hulst & van de Weijer (1995).

(18)	front		back		
high	i			u	close/ATR
		ɪ			open/RTR
mid	e			o	close/ATR
		ɛ		ɔ	open/RTR
low			a		open/RTR

(= Hulst & van de Weijer (1995): (1))

Jungraithmayer subdivides Tangale vowels into two subsets, the open set / ɪ ʊ ɛ ɔ a / and the closed set / i u e o /, which are called harmonic sets. The open/closed distinction was later argued to involve the feature [ATR] (advanced tongue root) (Hulst & van de Weijer 1995). Vowel harmony in Tangale is stem-controlled: a stem with a closed vowel triggers the ATR variant of the vowel on all affixes, and a stem with an open vowel triggers the RTR (retracted tongue root) variants of the vowel on the same affixes. Vowels on stems are fixed, vowels on affixes act like chameleons (Hulst & van de Weijer 1995).

(19)	ŋʊldɛdɛ	'dog'
	seb-u	'look-IMP'
	kɛn-ʊ	'enter-IMP'
	tug-o	'pounding'
	wʊd-ɔ	'farming'

(= Hulst & van de Weijer (1995): (2))

Importantly, the low vowel / a / does not show a distinction between an RTR and an ATR vowel: there is no harmonic counterpart. The potential distinction is neutralized (Hulst & van de Weijer 1995). The neutral vowel is nevertheless classified as RTR since it selects suffixes with vowels from the open set:

(20)	ʔn kas-kɔ	'I have cut'
	ʔa-nɔ	'my belly'
	war-ʊ	'go-IMP'

(= Hulst & van de Weijer (1995): (3))

210

When the neutral vowel / a / appears in affixes, it simply remains / a /, without an ATR or RTR variant, irrespectively of whether the stem has an ATR or an RTR vowel.

(21)	top-a	'start-NOM	peer-na	'compelled'
	tɔp-a	'answer-NOM'	pɛd-na	'untied'

(= Hulst & van de Weijer (1995): (4))

Importantly, when a suffix is added to a suffix with /a/, the added suffix does not agree with the stem vowel, but with the /a/ immediately preceding that suffix:

(22)	ped-na-n-gɔ	'untied me'
	peer-na-n-gɔ	'compelled me'
	dob-na-g-gʊ	'called you-PL'
	dib-na-m-gʊ	'cooked for us'

(= Hulst & van de Weijer (1995): (6a))

The neutral vowel / a / thus blocks the vowel harmony, and is correspondingly called an opaque vowel (Hulst & van de Weijer 1995).

Hulst & van de Weijer point out that not all neutral vowels are opaque: in the Finnish vowel harmony system, there are neutral vowels that are transparent. These vowels are like consonants in that they do not block the 'transmission' of the vowel harmony to the vowels of the affixes lower down the line. Finnish has the following vowel system:

(23)	*front*		*back*		
non-round	*round*		*non-round*	*round*	
i	ü			u	high
e	ö			o	mid
ä			a		low

(= Hulst & van de Weijer (1995): (7))

Hulst & van de Weijer define Finnish vowel harmony as an example of a palatal harmony system: vowels in a word are all front or all back.

(24) tyhmä – stä   'stupid-ILL'   tuhma – sta   'naughty-ILL'

(= Hulst & van de Weijer (1995): (9))

The vowels /i/ and /e/ have no back counterparts and are traditionally called neutral vowels. Importantly, the [front] feature of the neutral vowels /i/ and /e/ has no influence on vowel harmony:

(25) a. värttinä   'spinning wheel'
       värttinä – llä – ni – hän   'with spinning wheel, as you know'

    b. tuoli – lla   'on the chair'
       palttina   'linen cloth'
       palttina – lla – ni – han   'with linen cloth, as you know'
                            (= Hulst & van de Weijer (1995): (10–12))

Neutral vowels are therefore called transparent vowels (Hulst & van de Weijer 1995).

In essence, then, there are two types of neutral vowels intervening in a vowel harmony chain: some block the harmony (Tangale), others transmit the harmony (Finnish).

(26) For X a feature participating in vowel harmony, and Y a neutral vowel:

    a.   C   V   C   V   C   V   C   V   (Finnish)
              X X Y X
                        'transparent'

    b.   C   V   C   V   C   V   C   V   (Tangale)
              X X Y Z
                        'opaque'

Now, abstracting away from the CV structure in (26), a similar pattern shows up in relative clauses in French. Recall that there is variation in French regarding the exact morphosyntactic features that can be transmitted to the embedded AGR_S:

(27) a. C'est moi$_{1SG}$ qui suis$_{1SG}$ venu
       'It is I who have come'

    b. Nous$_{1PL}$ qui sommes$_{1PL}$ là
       'We who are there'

(28) a. C'est moi$_{1SG}$ qui est$_{3SG}$ venu
       'It is me who has come'

    b. C'est nous$_{1PL}$ qui sont$_{3PL}$ venus
       'It is us who have come'

In (27), all [person, number, gender] features of the N heading the relative clause are transmitted to the relative clause, since $AGR_C°$ *qui* has α-valued ϕ-features or is 'transparent'; in (28) only [gender, number] features are transmitted since the feature for person has a 0-value, or is 'opaque.' This can be represented abstractly as follows:

(29) a. N (. . .) $AGR_C°$ (. . .) $AGR_S°$ (Standard French)
       Xperson Yperson   Xperson
               (α-person)
               'transparent'

   b. N (. . .) $AGR_C°$ (. . .) $AGR_S°$ (Nonstandard French)
       Xperson Yperson   Zperson
               (0person)   ('default' 3rd person)
               'opaque'

Both vowel harmony in (26) and the agreement in (29) have several properties in common: both are instances of a nonlocal feature dependency; in both cases the intervening element does not change itself, despite blocking/transmitting the agreement. If it is granted that the phonological and syntactic feature systems are sufficiently alike in this respect, the question arises as to how to adequately represent them. In phonology, there has been a move away from the purely binary feature systems of the 1960s towards binary feature systems making use of underspecification (Archangeli 1984) or even more restrictive unary feature systems (Rennison 1986; Anderson & Ewen 1987; Ewen & van der Hulst 1985). In GB syntax, there has not been a comparable move to question the representation of feature values, except for the references noted in the introduction. A lot of recent work has gone into the multiplication of functional heads for feature *attributes* such as person, gender, and number (Bernstein 1991; Ritter 1991; Picallo 1991), but to my knowledge there has been much less work on the representation of the values corresponding to those attributes, namely values such as +, −0, or α. Ideally, in a restrictive unary system, the feature values +, 0, and α would follow from a representation rather than be stipulated within the system as feature values *per se*.

Let us represent agreement features as hierarchically structured pairs of attributes and values, where a value for a given attribute can in turn become the attribute for a further value. These terms are taken from Scobbie's (1991) work on Attribute-Value Phonology. In this way, the node representing the attribute ϕ-features contains the nodes [png] and case as its values. The case node will not be represented here. The node [png] is in turn the attribute for the three values person, number and gender. Person, number and gender then are the attributes for respectively [1st/2nd/3rd person], [sg./pl.], [fem/masc] (see the Appendix to this chapter for a more precise unary rendering of terminal feature values). In this way, Attribute-Value sets (AV sets) are obtained which are always partly embedded in each other. A sentence such as (30a) then has a feature representation as in (30b), where I assume for ease of exposition that *nous* 'we' has [masc] features.[12] The brackets in the structure (30b) are meant to give a representation of the embedding of the various Attribute-Value sets, levels are given for mnemonic purposes only.

In this structure, I assume that $AGR_C°$ does have an attribute [person, number, gender], but that this attribute does not have a further Attribute-Value structure. As a result, it is transparent with respect to feature transmission: $AGR_C°$ then is completely 'neutral' or 'transparent' with respect to the transmission of agreement into the relative clause. The absence of a complete [attribute : value] set corresponds to the value α.

In the relative clauses of Nonstandard French, relative *qui* does have an attribute for person, but no specific value associated with it. The presence of the attribute [person], or rather of the AV set [[png] : pers], now blocks transmission of the corresponding value of the head noun, triggering 'default' third person agreement on $V°–T°–AGR_S°$ complex of the relative clause. This suggests that the relative $AGR_S°$ takes over the unspecified person attribute of *qui*. The 0-value of a feature then corresponds to an attribute without a feature specification: [attribute:].

(30) a. C'est nous₁PL qui sommes₁PL venus   (Standard French)
       'It is we who have come'

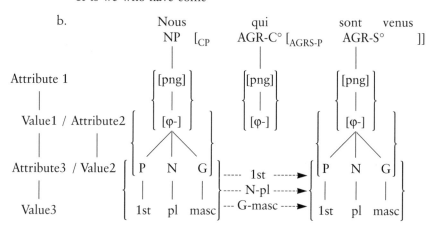

(31) a. C'est nous$_{1SG}$ qui sont$_{3SG}$ venus   (Nonstandard French)
    'It is us who have come'

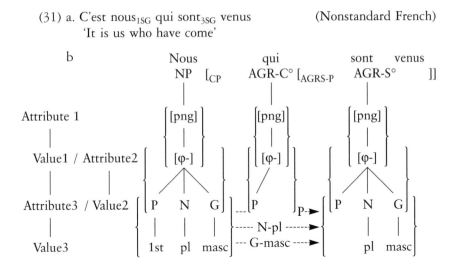

Since no AV sets for number and gender are present on the [png] attribute in this dialect of French, the AV sets for number and gender of *nous* 'us' are transmitted down to AGR$_S$ without encountering anything to block them.

Interrogative *qui* 'who' and *que* 'what,' with so-called 0-features, can then be described as elements of which the [person], [number], and [gender] attributes are projected, but without being specified, i.e. without receiving a specific value. The feature specification of *nous* 'we' then compares to that of interrogative *qui* 'who' and *que* 'what' in the following way:

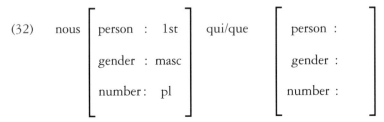

Note that the feature values of interrogative *qui* 'who' and *que* 'what' now help explain their morphological similarity to the complementizers *qui* and *que*: both elements are definable in terms of 0- and α-valued features. Interrogative *qui* 'who' and *que* 'what' always have person, number, and gender attributes without values (are always 0-specified), complementizer *qui* and *que* have either no Attribute-Value sets at all for person, number, gender features (Standard French (5)), or they have certain attributes (in the same way as interrogative *qui* and *que*) without values (Nonstandard varieties of French (6–7)).

215

The 'opaque' aspect of vowel harmony in Tangale can be represented in a perfectly similar way. In (33), only the feature set relevant to the harmony is represented:

(33)

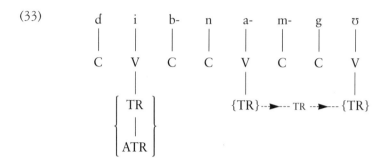

The reason why /a/ is represented without a feature-value RTR for the attribute TR is the economy of a unary feature system: no reference to RTR(-ATR) is to be made if it is not necessary. Hulst & van de Weijer (1995) point out that vowel harmony systems such as Tangale have usually been described in terms of ATR spreading. It therefore stands to reason that only this feature-value would be used, while the feature-value RTR is left underspecified, only to be 'filled in' phonetically as a 'neutral' or 'default' tongue root position RTR. RTR is a phonetic, not a phonological property. 'Default' third person agreement in AGR$_S$° arises in the same way in the syntax. The valueless [TR :] also participates in the vowel harmony: this stems from the idea that the harmony/agreement system has no access to what is inside the Attribute-Value box: the harmony only sees the label TR on the box that is to be transmitted. Nothing essential hinges on this idea, however. The segment structure condition that has traditionally been related to the neutralization, namely that the combination of the features [low] and [ATR] is impossible (Hulst & van de Weijer 1995), can here be restated by saying that the Attribute-Value set [height : low] prevents the attribute [TR] from projecting the feature [ATR].

Finally, 'transparent' Finnish vowel harmony can be represented in the same way as its syntactic counterpart AGR$_C$° *qui* in Standard French. Following Hulst & Smith (1986), I will assume that the feature [front] spreads in Finnish. The feature [back] (34b) is not represented as a feature-value. The underspecified value of the attribute [TB] (tongue body) will be 'filled in' as [back] as a phonetic 'default' procedure. For the vowels / i / and / e /, this implies that the absence of the entire [TB] Attribute-Value set results in their being spelled out as 'default' [front] vowels. The feature geometry of the vowels in (34) is of course not complete: only the features relevant to vowel harmony have been represented. The other elements determining the feature geometry of / i / and

/ e /(non-round, high /mid), which are not represented in (34), must be thought of as constraining the surface phonetic manifestation of vowels without a phonological [TB] attribute in such a way that / i / and / e / are 'filled in' as the result of a phonetic process.

(34) a.

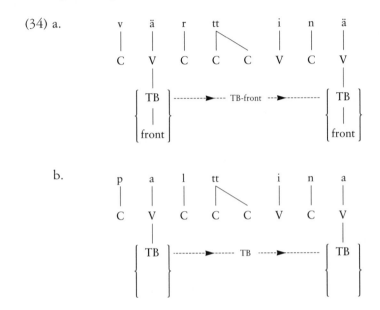

In Finnish, then, there are two ways in which [front] can be realized: either as a 'hardwired' phonological feature that spreads via vowel harmony, yielding / ü /, / ö /, / ä / , or as a phonetic feature that shows up as a 'default' value for vowels that miss a [TB : front] dimension altogether, yielding / i / and / e /. The phonetic [back] feature is realized as a 'default' value for vowels that have a [TB] attribute without an associated value: [TB :].

If this line of reasoning is correct, there is evidence of a system of feature organization that might be common to the morphosyntax and the phonology. In this chapter, I have tried to show that a descriptive difference between +, 0- and α-values of features is necessary in morphosyntax, and that a similar distinction has long been made for phonological harmony systems. An attempt was made to argue that both the phonological and morphosyntactic harmony systems can be represented in the same way. Therefore, there seem to be good reasons to assume that the basic elements of feature theory are common to syntax and phonology. Such a common ground for the organization of features constitutes strong evidence for a separate module of feature theory in the language faculty, based on something like Scobbie's (1991) Attribute-Value model, that would be accessible to both syntax and phonology.

4 Appendix: the specification of features

One reviewer makes the interesting observation that despite the system proposed here, there are differences in the organization of features in phonology and morphosyntax. He argues that phonological features are either maximally binary or, as assumed here, unary, while syntactic features are not binary but can have more than two specifications, as is the case for the [person] feature. The observation made is an important one, and needs some qualification. First of all, it should be specified that classical (say SPE) phonology assigns binary features, but that it has been argued in the literature that a phonological feature such as [height] needs to have three feature-values. Secondly, the Attribute-Value system used here does not take position with respect to the binary or multiple specification of features: note that one Attribute-Value set always is the Value of another Attribute-Value set: this creates nesting AV sets. In the system proposed here, the nesting of AV sets is assumed to be multiple for ease of exposition, as for the [person, number, gender] features in (30b), where [png] ends up having three branches. Nothing hinges on this, however. In a more complete representation, there are even a number of arguments to split [png] in a binary way, distinguishing person on the one hand, and [gender, number] on the other. The separate branch [gender, number] then divides up further into gender and number. The reason for this would be that in a number of languages, if agreement has gender, it also involves number, but not necessarily person (cf. past participle agreement in Romance). The maximal branching of nesting Attribute-Value sets therefore can, and maybe should, be argued to be binary.

A further issue, and a more crucial one for the binary nature of features, concerns the value of the terminal nodes in the Attribute-Value system advocated here. Only the terminal nodes are required to have a unary value. Once more, the representations in the main text are reductionist and non-unary for purposes of exposition. However, in a more constrained system, a feature like number only has two representations as an AV set: plural is represented as [number : plural], and singular, the 'default' value, can always be represented as a 0-feature [number :   ]. Similarly, feminine gender, being marked, should be represented as [gender : feminine], and masculine, the default value, should be represented as a zero-valued Attribute [gender :   ]. This last representation for masculine does not show up in the representations in (30–32) in order to make the case for 'transmission' of features as clearly as possible. As for person features, it seems at first sight that they involve multiple specification: first, second, third. However, it has been argued that third person functions as 'nonperson' in various languages (Benveniste 1966). In Yorùbá, third person is less marked morphologically (Déchaine 1992). Hale (1973) argues that while first person in Walbiri should be described with the features set [+ I, –II] and second person with [– I, +II], third person is [– I, –II], another way of representing 'nonperson.' Similarly, in Romance, third person functions as 'default' person for agreement with impersonal (= nonreferential) subjects.

These observations clearly make a case for distinguishing third person as a 0-valued AV set [person :], while first and second persons could be viewed as constituting their own AV sets binarily branching off the person Attribute. In order to clarify this point, I represent the second person pronouns *tu* 'you$_{SG}$' and *vous* 'you$_{PL / HON. SG,}$' as well as third person *il* 'it / he' in French as follows:[13]

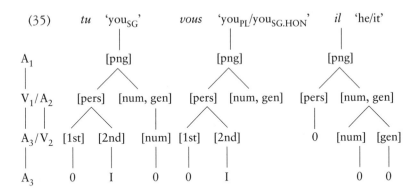

The numbering of AV sets in (35) is again for mnemonic purposes only. In the representations for *tu* 'you$_{SG}$,' the complete absence of the AV set for gender translates the idea that gender for second person *tu* 'you' must have a 'transparent' α-value, since it can be both masculine and feminine, depending on the referent, triggering the corresponding agreement where necessary (*tu es content(e)* 'you are happy'). The representation for second person *vous* 'you' captures its interpretation as either an honorific second person singular, or a second person plural: the 'transparent' α-value for gender and number leaves these features open. The 0-marking of features for *il* 'it/he' represents its 'default' value (cf. note 10). With this in mind, it is useful to again recall the representations for *qui* in Standard and Nonstandard French respectively (cf. 30–31). Both Standard and Nonstandard French *qui* are 'transparent' only for those features whose AVC set is left unspecified. While Standard French *qui* is entirely 'transparent,' Nonstandard French *qui* blocks person agreement since it is 0-specified for it.

(36)   'transparent' *qui* in   'person-blocking'*qui* in
          Standard French (= 30)   Nonstandard French (= 31)

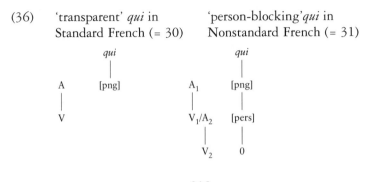

It may be that the feature representation I have adopted here is too rich. It should nevertheless be viewed as an attempt to provide an explicit formalization of feature blocking and transmission in both phonology and morphosyntax.

Notes

*   This chapter was first published as Rooryck (1994a). I would like to thank Rose-Marie Déchaine, Yves d'Hulst, Teun Hoekstra, the audiences at *Going Romance 1993*, University of Utrecht, December 11–12, 1993, and the *Morphology – Syntax Connection*, MIT January 4–5, 1994, as well as two anonymous and very helpful reviewers of *Probus* for useful discussions and comments. Special thanks to Harry van der Hulst for his invaluable help in formalizing the comparison of morphosyntactic and phonological features in terms of Scobbie's (1991) Attribute-Value feature system. The usual disclaimers apply.

1   As pointed out to me by Teun Hoekstra, in Dutch this transfer of φ-features is case-sensitive:

    i.   Ik denk aan jou die zo knap is/*bent
          I think of you who so smart is_{3SG}/are_{2SG}

    ii.   Jij die zo knap *is/bent . . .
          You who so smart is_{3SG}/are_{2SG}

    iii. Wij die zo knap zijn /   Aan ons die zo knap zijn /   Aan mij die zo knap is
          We who so smart are_{PL} /To us who so smart are_{PL} /   To me who so smart is_{3SG}

    Jij is the Nominative form of *you*, *jou* is the Oblique form. If the case of the NP *jij* 'you' governing the relative CP coincides with the case of the trace of the *Wh*-operator in SpecCP, the embedded verb form agrees in person and number. If the case of the NP does not coincide with that of the trace of the *Wh*-operator in SpecCP, agreement is only in number, while agreement in person reduces to a 'default' third person verb form (*is* 'is' /*zijn* 'are').

2   Thanks to Rose-Marie Déchaine for pointing this out to me.

3   In its 'personal' use, the pronoun *il* 'it/he' marks third person masculine nouns, both animate and inanimate (*Le train/Jean, il est arrivé* 'the train/Jean, it/he arrived'). I would like to suggest that this is not an inherent property of *il* 'it/he,' but one that is contributed by the selectional restrictions on the subject of particular verbs. *Il* 'it/he' then always has the feature specification [0person, 0gender, 0number]; the fact that it seems to mark masculine simply follows from the fact that masculine is the 'default' gender in French, as is evident from agreement (*Jean et Marie sont heureuxMASC* 'John and Mary are happy'), and the 'default' masculine gender exocentric compounds receive (*unMASC lave-vaisselle* 'a dishwasher').

4   The existence of α-features not only makes reference to a feature [± pred] unnecessary, but it also provides a straightforward explanation of how the features of the head of the relative CP end up inside that CP. One might even formulate this a little more strongly: it might be that all predication of adjuncts simply involves agreement with α-features, e.g. *John drank his tea fully dressed*, where an AGR projection can be assumed to 'cap off' the AP headed by *dressed*. If subject depictives are adjoined to AGR_S-P, as convincingly argued by Déchaine (1994), the α-features of the AGR_S-P subject depictive can be assumed to simply absorb the features of AGR_S, which correspond to those of the subject.

5   It has come to my attention that the distinction drawn here between *bidirectional* and *unidirectional* agreement in the domain of C° has been independently proposed by Rizzi (1991). Rizzi's *static agreement* involves matching of features instantiated on a head against the features of the specifier (bidirectional agreement), and his *dynamic agreement* occurs when a specifier provides the head with its features (unidirectional agreement). Rizzi introduces these notions to account for French *Qui as-tu vu?* 'Who have you seen,' where *qui* 'who' endows C° with a *Wh*-feature, thus satisfying his *Wh*-criterion. The distinction between bidirectional/static agreement and unidirectional/dynamic agreement therefore seems to be justified independently of the distribution of relative and declarative C°. As a result, the introduction of the notion of bidirectional agreement is not merely dependent on the presence of a predicative relation between C° and the nominal head. In other words, bidirectional agreement is justified independently in the domain of C°, while Rizzi's (1990a) [± pred] is not.

6   A reviewer notes that the solution proposed here for 'optional' *that* does not address the 'ineliminable ambiguity of *that*.' Why should *that* optionally surface to mark absence of agreement? I think this objection presupposes a reductionist view of morphological marking: only the presence and absence of morphemes 'count' as *bona fide* morphological manifestations of a syntactic relation. It is my contention that the optionality of *that* should be viewed as a morphological property in and by itself: in this way, obligatory *that* and optional *that* are two elements that are formally and morphosyntactically different.

7   The careful reader will have noted that I use the term 'movement to the domain of C°' for interrogative *qui* 'who' and *que* 'what' rather than 'movement to SpecCP.' The reason for this is that only interrogative *qui* is a *Wh*-NP, which moves to SpecCP. As shown by Bouchard & Hirschbühler (1986), interrogative *que* 'what' is a [+ Wh-] clitic in French which forces movement of the *que* + V°–T°–AGR$_S$° complex to C° so that interrogative *que* 'what' can check its [+ Wh-] properties in C°.

i.   Que fait Marie?
     What does Marie?

ii. *Que Marie fait
     What Marie does

As such, *que* 'what' is the counterpart of clitic *le* 'it.' Interrogative *que* 'what' can also move out of the V°–T°–AGR$_S$° complex to C° if the complex complementizer *est-ce que* is present in C°:

iii. Qu'est-ce que tu fais?
     What that₂ you do?

iv. Qu'est-ce qui est arrivé?
     What that₂ happened?

This excorporation out of the V°–T°–AGR$_S$° complex into C° *est-ce que* is not surprising: Kayne (1991a) has demonstrated that attachment to V° is not an intrinsic property of clitics, but that clitics are adjoined to functional projections.

8   For a carefully worked out binary [±] system of syntactic features, see Kerstens (1993).

9   At first sight, floating *tout* with interrogative *qui* and *que* resembles Dutch *zoal* 'among others' or *allemaal* 'all,' which also trigger a list reading with interrogative *wie* 'who':

i.   Wie heb je allemaal/zoal gezien?
     'Who have you all/among others seen?'

Since the appearance of *qui/que . . . tout* seems to be limited to Belgian French, it is tempting to see influence from Southern Dutch dialects here. Nevertheless, Dutch *alle-*

maal is not adequately translated as *tout/tous*. Unlike French *tout/tous* 'all,' the Dutch quantifiers *allemaal/zoal* can also cooccur with a plural *Wh*-NP, and always yield a list reading:

ii. Welke boeken heb je allemaal/zoal gelezen?
'Which books have you all/among others read?'

Agreeing *tous* 'all' in (15) does not impose a list reading, while *tout* in (16) requires a list reading. If Belgian French *qui/que . . . tout* were due to Dutch influence, it is not immediately obvious why the quantifier *tout/tous* was picked since it does not require a list reading in Standard French.

10   In fact, it should be stated more radically that the third person morpheme *il* 'he/it' is always underspecified as [0person, 0gender, 0number]. The fact that *il* 'he/it' functions both as so-called impersonal or weather *il*, and as the third person masculine singular nominative pronoun is not just a result of homonymy: *il* 'he/it' is always underspecified, and the selectional properties associated with the argument of the verb ending up in SpecIP position determine the personal [±animate] or impersonal status of *il*. Notice that an underspecified analysis of *il* 'he/it' explains why the morpheme /i/ also shows up on the complementizer *qui*: *i(l)* 'he/it' is the only morpheme in the subject clitic paradigm that is fully underspecified. As such, it is the only morpheme compatible with an underspecified complementizer. Under the view that subject clitics are heads in or related to AGR_S (e.g. Roberge 1986), Kayne's (1976) and Rizzi's (1990a) analysis of complementizer *qui* marking $AGR_S°$–$AGR_C°$ agreement could be viewed as head movement of *i(l)* 'he/it' to $C°$. *I(l)* 'he/it' then is the only subject clitic so to move since its underspecified nature make it uniquely compatible with α-specified $AGR_C°$. Notice that this analysis would still require a change in the type of feature underspecification of subject clitic *il* from [0person, 0gender, 0number] to [0person, 0gender, 0number] of *i(l)* 'he/it' in complementizer *qui*. This same problem arises with respect to the similarity of interrogative *qui* 'who' [0person, 0gender, 0number], and complementizer *qui* which is either [αperson, αgender, αnumber] (Standard French), or a combination of 0- and α-valued features in Nonstandard French. I will leave this problem for further research, noting that the analysis presented here at least allows for a descriptive explication of the similarities involved.

11   0-specified features are presumably excluded from occurring in a declarative $C°$, since otherwise extraction out of an embedded sentence would be extremely limited: only interrogative *qui* and *que* would be able to move through the domain of $C°$ on their way to the matrix clause. As a result, 0-featured $AGRC°$ *est-ce qui* in French will only show up where *Wh*-movement is local: in matrix and embedded interrogatives.

12   The gender feature of *nous* 'we' is represented here as [gender : masc] for ease of exposition. In fact, *nous* 'we' is always α-specified for gender. This α-specification can be defended in view of the fact that gender agreement with *nous* 'we' depends on extralinguistic context: referring to an all-female group, *Nous sommes contentes* 'We are happy$_{FEM.PL}$' shows feminine agreement, while a mixed group would trigger masculine (default) agreement (*Nous sommes contents* 'We are happy$_{MASC.PL}$'). Only α-specification of the gender feature on *nous* 'we' can explain this 'referential' agreement; 0-specification would trigger 'default' or so-called masculine agreement in all cases.

13   The indexing of AV sets is intended to show more clearly the 'nesting' of AV sets: an Attribute with index *n* contains as its value *n* an Attribute-Value set with index *n+1*.

8

A UNIFIED ANALYSIS
OF FRENCH
INTERROGATIVE AND
COMPLEMENTIZER *QUI/QUE*

1 Introduction*

The French interrogative DPs *qui?* 'who' and *que?* 'what,' and the complementizers *qui* 'that' and *que* 'that,' have often been argued to involve different lexical items in view of the differences in their syntactic distribution and interpretation. The unfortunate result is that interrogative *qui* and complementizer *qui*, as well as interrogative *que* and complementizer *que*, are thus treated as accidental homonyms, despite their obvious formal identity. In this chapter, I would like to show that the identical form of interrogative and complementizer *qui* and *que* reflects identical underlying syntactic structures. Moreover, it will be argued that interrogative and complementizer *qui* and *que* do not exist as independent entries in the lexicon. Rather, interrogative *qui* 'who' and *que* 'what,' and complementizer *qui* 'that' are to be viewed as morphologically complex items, a combination of the C° *que* on the one hand and the pronouns *i(l)* 'he/it' and *le* 'him/it' on the other. The puzzling syntactic differences between interrogative *qui?/que?* and complementizer *qui/que* are derived from the interaction of morphological composition, X′ projection, and 'default' interpretation.

2 Differences between interrogative
and complementizer *qui* and *que*

French interrogative DPs (*qui?* 'who,' *que?* 'what') and complementizers (*qui* 'that,' *que* 'that') appear as formally identical elements. Despite their morphological similarity, there are a number of syntactic and semantic differences between interrogative and complementizer *qui* and *que*. First, interrogative *qui?* and *que?* function as DPs in that they can occur as *Wh*-subjects and objects, with the exception that *que* cannot be a subject:

(1) a. Qui$_i$ t_i est arrivé?   b. Qui$_i$ as-tu vu t_i?
      'Who arrived?'   'Who did you see?'

c. *Qu'est arrivé?   d. Qu'as-tu vu?
   'What arrived?'   'What did you see?'

Complementizer *qui* only occurs in the context of *Wh*-moved subjects, as shown in (2):

(2)   a.   [Le paquet]$_i$ que/*qui j'ai vu t_i
        'The package that I have seen'

      b.   [Le paquet]$_i$ qui/*qu' t_i est venu
        'The package that came'

This restriction has led to an analysis of complementizer *qui* as a subject-agreeing form of complementizer *que* (Moreau 1971; Kayne 1976; Pesetsky 1982b). The most recent implementation of this idea is by Rizzi (1990a): if complementizer *que* head-governs a subject trace in SpecIP, it agrees with the lower AGR$_S$, and the agreement is spelled out morphologically through a change from *que* to *qui*. Complementizer *que* is used in all other cases of (noninterrogative) complementation.

Note that this classical analysis does not explain why the agreement morpheme *-i* on complementizer *qui* is identical to the morpheme *-i* in interrogative *qui?* or to the *-i* in the third person clitic pronoun *il* 'he/it.' Within the *que* —> *qui* analysis, the formal identity of these morphemes is merely accidental. However, other languages show similar alternations: West Flemish features C° *dat* —> *die* alternations in the same context as French (Bennis & Haegeman 1984). Importantly, the *-ie* morpheme also shows up in Dutch and West Flemish demonstrative D° *die*, interrogative *wie?* 'who,' and the third person unstressed pronoun *ie* 'he.' This suggests that the agreement morphemes *-i* in French *qui* and *-ie* in West Flemish *die/wie* must be viewed as bound morphemes that occur in various contexts, interrogative, pronominal, and/or demonstrative. This property of *qui* should be accounted for in a proper analysis of interrogative and complementizer *qui*.

A second major difference between interrogative and C° *qui/que* concerns their interpretation. Interrogative *qui?* and *que?* have 'fixed' φ-features. Interrogative *qui* has the feature set [+ animate, 3p.sg.masc], while interrogative *que* 'what' has the feature set [– animate, 3p.sg.masc]. This can be illustrated by both the agreement facts and the interpretive differences illustrated in (3):

(3)   a.   Qui est venu?/*Qui sont venus? *Réponse:* Jean/Marie/*le
                                          paquet
        'Who has/have come?'   *Answer:* 'John/Mary/the
                                          package'

   b. Qu'as-tu vu(*e)?   *Réponse:* le paquet/*Marie/*Jean
      'What have you seen(FEM)' *Answer:* 'the package/Marie/*Jean'

If the idea that *qui* is a subject agreement marker in C° is taken seriously, complementizer *qui* must be assumed to have 'variable' φ-features, since it is able to agree with any person, number, or gender feature from the head of the relative clause. This is illustrated in (4):

(4) a. Les carottes qui sont cuites
       The carrots$_{3.FEM.PL}$ which are$_{3.PL}$ boiled$_{3.FEM.PL}$

    b. C'est moi qui suis venu
       'It is I who have$_{1SG}$ come'

    c. C'est vous qui avez tort
       'It is you who are$_{2PL}$ wrong'

As far as Case features are concerned, complementizer *qui* should be taken to be nominative, since it expresses agreement between C° and I° under Rizzi's (1990a) analysis of the *que* —> *qui* alternation.

Complementizer *que* is insensitive to agreement. Agreement on the participle in (5) is triggered by overt movement of the *Wh*-operator through the Specifier of AGR_OP (Kayne 1985a, 1989a; Chomsky 1991).

(5)   Les carottes que Théophile a cuites
        'The carrots$_{3.FEM.PL}$ which Théophile has boiled$_{3.FEM.PL}$'

On the basis of these facts, the standard analysis of *qui* and *que* distinguishes two lexical entries for interrogative and complementizer *qui* and *que*: interrogative *qui?* is an NP, complementizer *qui* an AGR_C°. Likewise, complementizer *que* is a C°. Interrogative *que* is not entirely parallel to interrogative *qui*, however. Bouchard & Hirschbühler (1986) argue convincingly that interrogative *que?* is an accusative N° clitic with the same distribution as the object clitic *le* 'it/him.' They analyze interrogative *que* as an allomorph of the *Wh*-NP *quoi* 'what' (see also Hirschbühler 1980; Friedemann 1989). The accusative nature of interrogative *que* immediately accounts for its inability to function as a subject, illustrated in (1c). The clitic nature of interrogative *que* explains the fact that it can never be separated from the verb except by other clitics, as illustrated in (6):

(6) a. *Tu as dit que/le?
       'You have said what/it?'
    b. Que/le (lui) as-tu dit?
       'What/it (to-him) did you say?'

c. *Que/le tu (lui) as dit?
'What/it you (to-him) did say?'

(7) a. Tu as dit quoi?
'You have said what?'

b. *Quoi (lui) as-tu dit?
'What (to-him) did you say?'

c. *Quoi tu (lui) as dit?
'What you (to-him) did say?'

The analysis of interrogative *que?* as an accusative N° clitic is not entirely correct, however. Interrogative *que?* also functions as a *Wh*-element for predicates, which do not receive accusative case. This is illustrated in (8):

(8) a. Qu'est ceci?
'What is this?'

b. Qu'est-il devenu?
'What did he become?'

In other words, interrogative *que?* can be accusative, but it need not be. The various properties of interrogative and complementizer *qui/que* are represented in the following table:

(9)	QUI		QUE	
	interrogative	comp	interrogative	comp
category	N	C	N	C
X′ status	XP	X°	X°	X°
pers/num/gn	3p.sg.masc	variable	3p.sg.masc	insensitive
animacy	+ animate	± animate	− animate	n.a.
case	any case	nominative	(accusative)	n.a.

However descriptively correct, the analysis outlined above fails to account for the morphological similarity of interrogatives and complementizers in French. Within generative grammar, it has been a long-standing challenge to develop an account of these differences without postulating two homonymous *qui* and *que*, an interrogative and a complementizer (see, e.g. Obenauer 1976, 1977; Huot 1979). Most of these analyses are heavily theory-dependent, and cannot be translated into more recent frameworks without a large number of stipulations. In the remainder of this chapter, an analysis will be developed that preserves the insights of the traditional generative analysis of interrogative and relative clauses, while at the same time accounting for the morphological similarities of the elements involved.

3 A unifying analysis of *qui* / *que*

3.1 Deriving qui

I would like to argue that *qui* does not exist as an independent entry in the lexicon. Morphologically, *qui* is to be analyzed as a combination of the $C°$ *que* and $D°$ *i(l)* 'he/it', the third person pronoun.[1] As a third person clitic pronoun, I assume that $D°$ *i(l)* projects up to DP in the syntax in Standard French and cliticizes only at PF, essentially following Kayne (1975).[2] However, when $D°$ *i(l)* forms a morphological compound with $C°$ in the complex $[[_{C°}$ qu $]$ $[_{D°}$ i $]]$, either $C°$ or $D°$ can project to the XP level, in accordance with Chomsky's (1995) suggestions on X' projections. If $D°$ projects, thus determining the XP level, an (interrogative) DP *qui* will ensue as in (10a). If $C°$ determines the projection, projecting a CP, the $C°$–$D°$ complex will remain a $C°$, as in (10b). The $C°$–$D°$ combination can be viewed as a 'functional compound,' to distinguish it from compounds based on lexical categories.

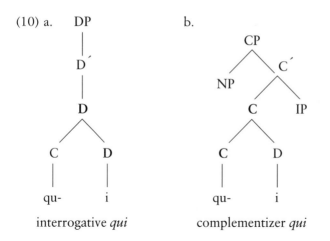

(10) a.   interrogative *qui*   b.   complementizer *qui*

The representations in (10) also make clear why it is important to theoretically distinguish 'functional' from 'lexical' compounds: functional compounds do not obey a generalization such as the Right-Hand Head Rule (Williams 1981; di Sciullo & Williams 1987) developed for lexical compounds. I will not go into the theoretical consequences that this difference may entail. Instead, I would like to show how the projection differences in (10) allow for a reduction of interrogative and complementizer *qui* to the same basic configuration.

Chomsky (1995) argues that elements such as proper names are at the same time $X°$ and XP. Projection as an $X°$ or an XP does not appear to make any interpretive or syntactic difference in the case of proper names. I would like to argue that projection of *qui* as an X° (C°) or as an XP (*Wh*-NP) does involve interpretive and syntactic differences. Syntactically, the analysis in (10) predicts that the X′ properties of the projecting element determine the properties of the complex. Kayne (1975) has argued that subject clitics such as *i(l)* 'he/it' are XPs which cliticize at PF in Standard French, unlike X° oblique clitics which cliticize in the syntax. The syntactic XP status of interrogative *qui* can thus be attributed to the property of D° *i(l)* which, as a pronoun, projects to DP. The X° status of complementizer *qui* is due to the X° status of the complementizer *que*.

The table in (9) shows that the interpretive differences between projecting *qui* as an X° or as an XP involve its D° features, both morphological (person, number, gender) and semantic (±animate). I would like to argue that this variation is due to the different relations between the projecting and the nonprojecting items.

If *qui* projects as a C°, the D° properties of *i(l)* 'he/it' modify the complementizer, yielding the (relative) C° *qui*. If it is the D° *i(l)* which projects within the *qui* complex, the projection will result in a *Wh*-NP. In the latter case, the complementizer is in a modification relation to *i(l)* within the *qui* complex: *que* contributes *Wh*-properties to the interrogative pronoun, effectively turning *i(l)* into a variable (for which x = *i(l)*). The interpretation of the D° features of interrogative *qui* are entirely determined by those of *i(l)*. The pronoun *i(l)* arguably has [3p.sg.masc] features. These [3p.sg.masc] features also show up on *qui*, as shown in (3).

The determination of the features of *qui* by *i(l)* 'he/it' is not limited to French. In Dutch, the *Wh*-interrogative NP *wie* 'who' can be characterized as [αnumber], agreeing with both singular and plural verbs as in (11a). This property is shared by the demonstrative *die* 'that/those,' as shown in (11b).

(11) a. Wie hebben/heeft er een appel gegeten?
Who have/has there an apple eaten?
'Who has eaten an apple?'

b. Die hebben/heeft een appel gegeten
'Those guys have/That guy has eaten an apple'

I will assume that, similar to French *qui*, Dutch *wie* 'who' is a complex made up of the *Wh*-morpheme *w-* and the N°/D° element *-ie*, which also occurs in *die* 'those/that' and the unstressed pronoun *-ie* 'he.' In fact, *-ie* corresponds to *die* 'that' minus the D° marker of definiteness *d-* which also shows up in *de* 'the' and *dat* 'that.' To explain the facts in (11), it is sufficient to assume that *-ie* is underspecified for number, allowing both singular and plural agreement on the verb. Thus, both *wie* 'who$_{SG/PL}$' and *die* 'those/that' carry the feature [αnumber]. The complementary distribution of the *d-*morpheme and the *Wh*-morpheme *w-* is not surprising: the *d-* morpheme is

a definiteness marker, and the *Wh*-morpheme *w*- carries the indefinite interpretation of *Wh*-morphemes.

The comparison with Dutch also allows for an explanation as to why the *-l*
morpheme of *i(l)* 'he/it' never occurs in interrogative *qui*. The element *-l* in
i(l) plays the same role of marking definiteness as *d-* in Dutch: notice that *l*
also occurs in the D° and accusative clitic *le* 'him/it' and in dative *lui* 'to
him/her.' The indefinite *qu-* and definite *-l* morphemes thus appear to be in
complementary distribution with respect to the third person *-i* morpheme.[3]
It can therefore be concluded that *i(l)* 'he/it,' *l-e* 'him/it,' and *l-ui* 'to him/her'
are themselves bimorphemic.[4]

Let us now investigate more closely the different projections of *qui*, as a
Wh-NP and as a C°, and see how projection and interpretation are related.
At first sight, a problem arises with respect to [person, number, gender]
features. Under the analysis proposed, the [3p.sg.masc] features of *i(l)* 'he/it'
determine the properties of the interrogative pronoun *qui*. Those same
[3p.sg.masc] features of *i(l)* must be present in C° *qui*. At this point, the
problem arises. Under the assumption that the *-i* morpheme in C° *qui* is
identical to the pronoun *i(l)* C° *qui* should also display [3p.sg.masc] features.
This is not the case: C° *qui* is inherently 'variable' in its features, since it is
compatible with the features of any NP heading the relative clause, as illustrated in (4). The feature variability of C° *qui* was taken to mean that the
feature specification of C° *qui* is [αperson, αnumber, αgender]. As a result,
the claim that all N properties of interrogative and complementizer *qui*
derive from the pronoun *i(l)* requires qualification.

I have assumed that the nonprojecting element of the C°–D° *qui* complex
is in a modification relation to the projecting category. In complementizer
qui, the D° *i(l)* 'he/it' modifies C°. It thus appears that the N-features of *i(l)*
function as mere agreement markers within complementizer *qui*, while they
seem to be 'fixed' to [3p.sg.masc] in interrogative *qui*. This observation calls
for a principled explanation.

The differences in feature interpretation between *i(l)* 'he/it' within interrogative *qui* and within complementizer *qui* can be derived from the different
configurations they involve. I will assume that the lexical feature specification of *i(l)* is entirely underspecified. More particularly, the morpheme *i(l)*
involves [αperson, αnumber, αgender] features. I refer the reader to Kayne
(1989b), Vanden Wyngaerd (1994), and Rooryck (1994b, this volume ch.5)
for various syntactic applications of feature underspecification. In principle,
the underspecification of *i(l)* enables it to express any person, gender, or
number. This possibility is, however, severely constrained by the configuration into which *i(l)* is inserted. When *i(l)* modifies C° *que*, as in complementizer *qui*, it is in a Spec–Head relation with an NP which will provide
it with [person, number, gender] features. However, when *i(l)* occurs as a
pronoun, or when it is modified by C° *que* and projects as an interrogative

pronoun *qui*, *i(l)* is not in a Spec–Head relation providing it with [person, number, gender] features. Rather, such pronouns are inserted in argument positions. The lack of a Spec–Head relation determining the features of *i(l)* forces a 'default' interpretation on the underspecified (α-) features of *i(l)*. In French, the 'unmarked' or 'default' specification of person, number, and gender features corresponds to the set of features [3p.sg.masc]. This is the interpretation that *i(l)* and interrogative *qui?* end up with. The situation can be schematically represented as follows:

(12)

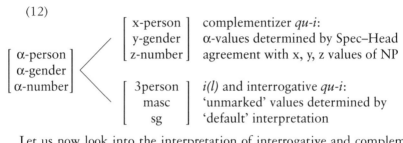

Let us now look into the interpretation of interrogative and complementizer *qui* as [± animate]. In this case as well, the interpretive properties of *i(l)* 'he/it' are expected to carry over to *qui*. The semantic interpretation of *i(l)* as [± animate] is dependent on the syntactic context. The pronoun *i(l)* can function as an impersonal subject and a 'weather' *it*, and refers to both + and – animate antecedents.

(13) a. Il pleut
'It rains'

    b. Il arrive des paquets
'There are arriving packages'

    c. Tu as vu les paquets$_i$/les linguistes$_j$? Ils$_{i/j}$ arrivent demain
'Did you see the packages/linguists? They are arriving tomorrow'

'Out of the blue' contexts, i.e. contexts in which the antecedent of *i(l)* 'he/it' is not present, yield a 'default' animate interpretation for *i(l)*. This is illustrated in (14): with a verb such as *arriver* 'arrive,' which can be construed indifferently with + or – animate subjects, questions elucidating the reference of *i(l)* always involve *who*, never *what*.

(14)   Speaker A: Il arrive demain.
                'He/*it arrives tomorrow'

    Speaker B: Qui?/*Quoi?
                'Who/*what does?'

The 'default' interpretation of *i(l)* as [+ animate] in contexts without an antecedent transfers easily to interrogative *qui*. By definition, *Wh*-sentences do not occur in contexts in which the referent of the *Wh*-element is given in the preceding context. As a result, the *i(l)* 'he/it' ensconced in interrogative *qui* will receive a [+ animate] interpretation in exactly the same way as *i(l)* 'he' in (14). As a result, the N properties of *i(l)* 'he/it' entirely determine the 'default' [animate, 3p.sg.masc] interpretation of the *Wh*-pronoun *qui*.

When *qui* projects as a C°, the D° properties contributed by *i(l)* 'he/it' modify the complementizer, yielding the (relative) C° *qui*. Again, the N properties of C° *qui* must be derivable from the interpretive properties of *i(l)*. The [±animate] interpretation of complementizer *qui* can be attributed to the fact that in relative clauses, the antecedent precedes the complementizer. The sentences in (13) illustrate that the pronoun *i(l)* can be [±animate] if the appropriate antecedent precedes. The same reasoning applies to *i(l)* within the complex C° *qui*: the [±animate] properties of the head of the relative clause determine the properties of C° *qui*.

As a result, the interpretation of both interrogative and complementizer *qui* in terms of animacy can be reduced to the properties *i(l)* 'he/it' displays with respect to animacy. Although these observations are descriptively correct, they raise a number of problems. Why is it specifically [+ animate] that arises as a 'default' interpretation for *i(l)*? Such an interpretation is by no means a necessary one. For instance, the accusative clitic pronoun *le* 'he/it' usually elicits a 'default' [– animate] interpretation.[5] This is illustrated in (15): with verbs such as *laver* 'wash,' which can be construed indifferently with + or - animate objects, questions elucidating the reference of *le* preferably involve *what*, and less felicitously *who*. Admittedly, judgments are less clear here than for *i(l)* 'he/it.'

(15) a. Speaker A: Sophie l'a déjà lavé
                'Sophie already washed it/ ?? him'
      Speaker B: Quoi?/ ?? Qui?
                'What?/ ?? who?'

    b. Speaker A: Paul l'a envoyé au doyen
                'Paul sent it/ ?? him to the dean'
      Speaker B: Quoi?/ ?? Qui?
                'What?/ ?? who?'

Another, more theoretical, problem is raised by reference to the notion [± animate] itself. Although [± animate] is not a φ-feature, it does seem to play a more prominent role in pronominal systems than other purely semantic features such as, say, [± concrete]. Hoekstra (p.c.) has suggested that [± animate] reduces to the phi-feature [person]. This suggestion should be viewed in the context of Benveniste's (1966) views on personhood.

Following the medieval Arabic grammatical tradition, Benveniste argues that third person corresponds to the absence of person, or 0person (cf. also Kayne 1989b). This entails that the feature [person] can only be specified with two values, i.e. first and second. First and second person, being related to speaker and addressee, directly entail animacy. As a result, animacy features can be derived from the feature [person], and need not be stipulated independently. Since third person may be both animate and inanimate, an account is still needed as to how animacy for third person comes about. I would like to link third person animacy to the notion of 0person. The 0 value for person should be viewed as a 'neutral' value: it is neither first nor second person, but still person, and hence animate. This interpretation of third person immediately raises a question as to the feature specification for inanimate nouns. Traditionally, inanimate nouns have been specified as third person. In the analysis suggested here, such a view becomes untenable, since third person or 0person entails animacy. I would like to propose that inanimate nouns are not specified for a person feature at all. Note that this is different from saying that inanimate nouns have a 0 value for person. While 0person is a 'neutral' value for person, hence animate, the absence of a person feature results in the impossibility of being interpreted as animate. I therefore suggest that if a noun is only specified for number and gender, it is inanimate.

This idea can shed some light on the discussion of the 'default' [+ animate] interpretation for *i(l)* 'he/it.' Let us assume the following principles for the interpretation of Ns with underspecified features:

(16) *Principle for the interpretation of underspecified features (PIOUF)*

    i.   A 'default' interpretation only affects N (or D) if its set of [person, number, gender] features is entirely underspecified (i.e. not Ns (Ds) containing both specified and unspecified (= α-) features).

    ii. If N (D) contains both specified and unspecified (= α-) [person, number, gender] features, these unspecified (= α-) features are eliminated at LF. (i.e. they do not receive an interpretation).

Recall now that the feature specification of *i(l)* 'he/it' was defined as [αperson, αnumber, αgender]. If no antecedent is available to determine at least some of the features of *i(l)*, the (i) clause of (16) applies. As a result, the underspecified features of *i(l)* get a 'default' interpretation with the 'unmarked' value for each feature: [3p.sg.masc]. In view of the discussion above, third person should be viewed as 'neuter' or 0person, that is neither first nor second person. Since the α-person feature within the underpecified *i(l)* defaults to 0person, *i(l)* must be interpreted as animate. The same reasoning applies to [+ animate] interrogative *qui*, in which *i(l)* likewise undergoes the 'default' interpretation to 0person.

Besides the interpretation of the inherently underspecified features of *i(l)* 'he/it' as the result of Spec–Head agreement in complementizer *qui*, and their 'default' interpretation in interrogative *qui*, the pronoun *i(l)* can also pick up its reference from the preceding context, as illustrated in (13c). In this case, *i(l)* can be + or - animate. In the feature system developed here, no reference is made to [± animate] as an independent feature. Rather, animacy is derived from the feature [person]. The question thus arises as to how *i(l)* can receive both + and - animate interpretations, since it was lexically specified as [αperson, αnumber, α-gender].[6]

The [± animate] interpretation of *i(l)* 'he/it' when an antecedent is present can be derived as follows. The presence of an antecedent provides the under-specified α- features of *i(l)* with the features of that antecedent. In case the antecedent is [+ animate], the underspecified person feature will be deter-mined by that antecedent, and *i(l)* will receive a third person interpretation. In case the antecedent is [– animate], this antecedent only possesses gender and number features. Recall it was assumed that inanimate nouns are char-acterized by the absence of the feature [person]. Since the number and gender features *i(l)* are determined by the antecedent, the still underspecified person feature of *i(l)* does not receive an interpretation and will delete at LF, in keeping with (16ii). Deletion of features can affect person, number, and gender features at the same time: this occurs in cases involving 'impersonal' *i(l)*, where the only 'active' feature of *i(l)* seems to be its (nominative) Case feature, but where person, number, and gender seem to be irrelevant. In this way, 'animate,' 'inanimate,' and 'impersonal' uses of *i(l)* can be derived from the interaction of the (under)specification of features and the syntactic context.

The interpretation of *i(l)* 'he/it' in the context of an antecedent raises another interpretive issue. It was observed in (4) that *i(l)* present in comple-mentizer *qui* can agree with NPs that have first, second, and third person features, both singular and plural, and that the underspecified features of *i(l)* transmit these features into the relative clause. The question now arises as to why *i(l)* cannot pick up the first and second person features of an antecedent as well. After all, in the analysis presented here, the feature composition of *i(l)* in pronoun *i(l)* 'he/it' and within complementizer *qui* is exactly the same, because they are assumed to be the same element. In other words, why can't *i(l)* pick up first and second person antecedents? The answer to this question lies in the way in which *i(l)* interacts with the elements of its paradigmatic class.[7] Traditional and structural gram-mars never fail to point out that *i(l)* is part of a paradigmatic closed class of (nominative) clitic pronouns containing *je* 'I,' *tu* 'you$_{SG}$,' *nous* 'we,' *vous* 'you$_{PL}$,' *on* 'one,' *elle* 'she/it.' I would like to argue that the apparent meaning of $i(l)$ as [3p.sg.masc] is the result of morphological Blocking within the paradigmatic class of clitic pronouns: the existence of clitic pronouns with first and second person specifications within the paradigmatic class of $i(l)$ prevents this pronoun from picking up first and second person antecedents. This paradigmatic opposition and Blocking does not apply to $i(l)$ when it is part of C° *qui*: since there is no paradigmatic class of agreeing complementizers that specifies all persons, *qui* will be able to agree with any person specification of its antecedent NP.[8]

A final issue in this discussion of the differences between interrogative and complementizer *qui* concerns Case. Interrogative XP *qui* is compatible with any Case position, while complementizer *qui* and $i(l)$ 'he/it' are restricted to nominative contexts. Recall complementizer *qui* is a marker of subject agreement on C° (Kayne 1976; Rizzi 1990a), and $i(l)$ is a nominative subject clitic. Once again, I would like to derive this difference from the interaction of feature specification and configurational context. Let us therefore assume that $i(l)$ is not only underspecified for person, number, and gender features, but also for Case (α-Case). If $i(l)$ within interrogative *qui* is [α-Case], the compatibility of interrogative *qui* with any Case position follows immediately. The nominative nature of $i(l)$ within complementizer *qui* can be made to follow from the fact that the agreeing, φ-feature-bearing, complementizer *qui* only occurs in cases of C°–AGR$_S$ agreement, that is, when C° agrees with a *Wh*-subject originating in SpecAGR$_S$P (Rizzi 1990a). The [α-Case] property of $i(l)$ in complementizer *qui* thus will be nominative through Spec–Head agreement with the nominative subject in SpecCP.

Deriving the nominative character of $i(l)$ 'he/it' as a subject clitic requires some more work. I would like to propose that the nominative property of $i(l)$ can be derived from its interaction with the allomorphs with which it is in complementary distribution: nominative $i(l)$ 'he/it,' accusative *le* 'it/him,' and dative *lui* 'to-him/her.' Let us restrict our attention to $i(l)$ and *le* for now, coming back to *lui* later. Recall that the feature composition of $i(l)$ is [αperson, αnumber, αgender, αCase]. The feature composition of clitic *le* must be minimally different. With respect to person, number, and gender features, the logic of the analysis pursued here forces us to endow *le* with the features [αgender, αnumber] only.[9] The underspecification of *le* allows it to pick up the reference of [masc. sg] antecedents, and the 'default' interpretation of underspecified number and gender features likewise involves [masc. sg]. It was observed in (15) that *le* has a 'default' interpretation as [– animate]. The analysis developed here derives features of animacy from the feature [person]: animate nouns have a 0person feature, and inanimate nouns are radically unmarked for a person feature. Within such an approach, the [– animate] 'default' interpretation of *le* can only be derived from its lack of a person feature. What are the case properties of *le*? Contrary to appearances, *le* cannot be analyzed as accusative. It is well known that *le* can also function as a placeholder for a predicate with verbs that have no accusative features:[10]

(17) a. Sophie est malade, et Pierre l'est aussi
'Sophie is sick and Pierre is (-it) too'

    b. Speaker A: Pierre est-il malade?   Speaker B: Il le semble
           'Pierre is (he) sick?'   'It (it-)seems so'

This means that, as far as the representation of its Case features go, *le* 'it/him' must be made compatible with, but not exclusively restricted to, accusative case. The simplest way of achieving this is to label *le* [αCase]. The result of this discussion is that *i(l)* is [αperson, αgender, αnumber, αCase], while *le* is [αgender, αnumber, αCase]. Both clitics are entirely underspecified for φ-features, and differ only in the presence or absence of the underspecified feature [αperson].

At this point, the question not only arises why *i(l)* 'he/it' is always nominative, being inherently [αCase], but also why [αCase] *le* 'it/him' can never appear in subject position. The answer to this question is fairly straightforward, and lies in the features of the AGR projections in which the third person clitics *i(l)* and *le* can check their features. Apart from differences with respect to Case properties, French AGR_S agrees in person and number features with the subject, while AGR_O only agrees in gender and number. Let us illustrate this with the pronoun *nous* 'we,' which is compatible with both masculine and feminine interpretations. In a form such as *nous mangeons* 'we eat$_{1PL}$,' the morpheme *-ons* on the verb expresses first person plural agreement with the subject *nous* 'we.' However, object agreement in AGR_O only manifests gender and number: in *Elle nous a conduites à la gare* 'She us-has driven$_{FEM.PL}$ to the station,' the participle shows feminine plural agreement with the direct object clitic *nous* (cf. Kayne 1985a, 1989a). Importantly, AGR_O never manifests person agreement. The fact that *i(l)* 'he/it' is always nominative and *le* 'it/him' non-nominative, can now be related to the fact that *i(l)* is specified as [αperson], and hence is inserted in the specifier of AGR_S which can check [person], while the features of *le*, which lack [person], will be checked by an AGR lacking [person]. In other words, the allomorph whose features correspond most closely to the features of the AGR head will check the features of that position. I submit that this distribution is an effect of Economy principles as applied to feature checking: specific allomorphs are distributed in such a way as to maximally identify, or check, the features of those allomorphs. As a result, the nominative character of *i(l)* is not due to an inherent nominative feature, but to its specification for [person].

The various aspects of the interpretive derivation of the feature values of interrogative and complementizer *qui* as well as *i(l)* 'he/it' can be represented in the following figure:

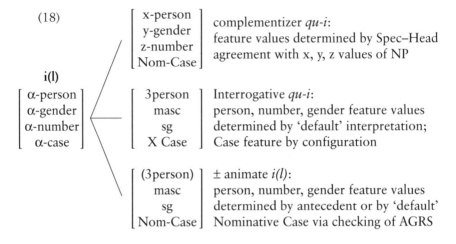

(18)

		complementizer *qu-i*:
x-person		feature values determined by Spec–Head
y-gender		agreement with x, y, z values of NP
z-number		
Nom-Case		

i(l)

α-person		3person	Interrogative *qu-i*:
α-gender		masc	person, number, gender feature values
α-number		sg	determined by 'default' interpretation;
α-case		X Case	Case feature by configuration

(3person)	± animate *i(l)*:
masc	person, number, gender feature values
sg	determined by antecedent or by 'default'
Nom-Case	Nominative Case via checking of AGRS

This figure accounts for the differences between complementizer and interrogative *qui* with respect to their interpretation and agreement properties, listed in (9) above. The differences in case properties between interrogative and complementizer *qui* will be discussed in conjunction with those of interrogative and complementizer *que* in section 3.2.

3.2 Deriving *que*

Turning our attention to interrogative and complementizer *que*, I would like to propose an analysis similar to that developed for interrogative and complementizer *qui*. In the same way as interrogative and complementizer *qui* involve different syntactic projections of a morphological complex consisting of the C° *que* and the pronoun *i(l)* 'he/it,' I propose that interrogative *que* involves the syntactic projection of a complex involving the C° *que* and the clitic (D°) pronoun *le* 'him/it.' As illustrated in (19), the projection of the clitic *le* in the complex will create a pronoun modified by the complementizer *que* which contributes *Wh*-properties to the *que* complex.

(19)

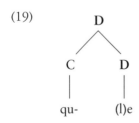

At this point, the attentive reader will ask why there is no C°–D° complex in which C° projects rather than D°. In the case of *qui*, the interrogative or complementizer interpretation of the C°–D° complex corresponded to the projection of D° or C°, respectively. Why, then, would there not be a 'relative' *que*, i.e. a complex complementizer identical to (19) in which *que* is modified by the clitic *le* which would confer object agreement properties to the C°–D° complex? The answer to this question is rather straightforward: there are no cases of object agreement in C°, hence a C°–D° complex of the type just sketched cannot be licensed in the C° domain. As a result, it is ruled out.

Let us now come back to interrogative *que*. Note that the *l-* morpheme of D° *le* drops in its combination with C° *que*. It has already been observed that the same morphological process applies to interrogative and complementizer *qui* where the *l-* morpheme of *il* is absent. In that case, it was observed that *i(l)* 'he/it' and *l-e* 'him/it' are bimorphemic, and that the C° morpheme *qu-* can take the place of the definiteness marker *-l*. However, while interrogative and complementizer *qui* exhibit morphological similarity with the D° *i(l)* they form a complex with, it is plain that the morphological complexity of interrogative *que* is much harder to observe. Interrogative *que* is entirely homophonous with the simplex subordinating complementizer *que* which introduces tensed complement clauses as in (20):

(20)   Je crois que Pierre est malade
        'I think that Pierre is sick'

This means that the evidence in favor of the morphologically complex nature of interrogative *que* is harder to come by. This has led some researchers to argue that interrogative *que* is simply an instance of the subordinating C° *que* (Obenauer 1977).

Nevertheless, there are a number of arguments that militate in favor of the analysis proposed in (19). The analysis predicts that the projecting head, *in casu le* 'it/him,' will determine both the syntactic and the semantic properties of the complex. Syntactically, this means that the clitic, hence X°, nature of *le* should carry over to the C°–D° complex in (19). Bouchard & Hirschbühler (1986) have observed that interrogative *que* does indeed behave as an accusative clitic, as illustrated in (6–7) above, repeated here:

(6) a. *Tu as dit que/le?   (7) a. Tu as dit quoi?
         'You have said what/it?'   'You have said what?'
     b. Que/le (lui) as-tu dit?   b. *Quoi (lui) as-tu dit?
         'What/it (to-him) did you say?'   'What (to-him) did you say?'
     c. *Que/le tu (lui) as dit?   c. *Quoi tu (lui) as dit?
         'What/it you (to-him) did say?'   'What you (to-him) did say?'

In the analysis presented here, the clitic (X°) nature of interrogative *que* is not just an idiosyncratic property of this *Wh*-element, but it must be viewed as a property inherited from the D° element *(l)e*, which determines the projection of the D°–C° complex *que*. Recall that the XP nature of interrogative *qui* was similarly related to the fact that the pronoun *i(l)* 'he/it' is at least syntactically an XP in Standard French, following Kayne (1975).

The function-sensitivity of interrogative *que* can be likewise derived from the fact that *que* involves a D°–C° complex containing *(l)e*. The examples in (6–7), as well as (8), repeated here, illustrate that interrogative *que* can be either an accusative or a predicative *Wh*-clitic.

    (8)   a. Qu'est ceci?
              'What is this?'

        b. Qu'est-il devenu?
             'What did he become?'

Interrogative *que* shares this property with the clitic *le* 'it/him.' The examples in (15) and (17) above show that *le* can function not only as an accusative clitic, but also as a placeholder for predicative complements. The fact that interrogative *que* and *le* share this property could of course be treated as a remarkable coincidence. However, it seems more reasonable to trace it back to the property of a single morpheme, *(l)e*, which appears both in the clitic *le* and in the interrogative C°–D° complex *que*.

Semantically, the structure in (19) predicts that the 'default' interpretive properties of *le* transfer to the interrogative C°–D° complex *que* as well, in the same way as the 'default' properties of *i(l)* 'he/it' were shown to transfer to interrogative *qui*. In table (9), it was noted that interrogative *que* has an interpretation as [– animate], and a feature specification [3p.masc.sg]. Similarly, it was observed in (15) that *le* has a [– animate] 'default' interpretation in contexts which do not identify an antecedent for it. Featurewise, it was assumed that clitic *le* has [αnumber, αgender], and lacks person. The 'default' interpretation of underspecified number and gender features is [sg.masc]. The fact that *le* lacks a feature [person] derives its 'default' interpretation as [– animate]. The only difference between *le* and *que* is that *le* can refer to animate antecedents in context (*Et Jean? Pierre l'a vu au café* 'And Jean? Pierre saw him at the café'), while *que* cannot. As in the case of interrogative and complementizer *qui*, I would like to relate this difference to the fact that *le* can pick up animacy from an antecedent, while *que* cannot do so, due to the antecedentless nature of interrogative contexts.

All these properties of *le* transfer to the interrogative C°-D° complex *que* containing D° *le*. Interrogative *que* likewise involves the features [sg.masc], and has a [– animate] interpretation. As in the case of interrogative *qui*, I argue that it is the very property of *Wh*-elements that their referent is not identified. This situation is identical to those cases in which *le* occurs in a context which does not identify an antecedent for it. As a result, the [sg.masc] features of the clitic *(l)e* ensconced in the interrogative C°–D° complex *que* will receive a 'default' interpretation as [– animate]. Finally, the presence of clitic *(l)e* within interrogative *que* also accounts for the fact that interrogative *que* can never occur in subject position: in the same way as *(l)e* , it is restricted to accusative and predicative contexts (cf. 6,7,8).

The analysis proposed above allows us to eliminate interrogative *que* from the lexicon altogether. Apart from the *Wh*-property, all syntactic and interpretive properties of interrogative *que* are identical to those of the clitic *le*. Interrogative *que* is more insightfully analyzed as a morphological C°–D° complex involving C° *que* and clitic *(l)e*.

3.3 Further issues: lui as X° and XP

At this point, the question arises whether there are other functional complexes displaying the 'double projection' behavior that was observed for *qui*. In French, a good candidate for such an analysis would be the pronoun *lui*, which can be both a dative clitic as in (21) and an XP pronoun compatible with any Case position,[11] as shown in (22).

(21)   Paul lui a donné un livre   (lui = à Marie/à Max)
         Paul to-him/her has given a book
         'Paul gave him/her a book'

(22) a. Paul pense à lui
         'Paul thinks of him'

     b. LUI a dit ça
         'HE said that'

     c. Paul a vu LUI (, pas Max)
         'Paul saw HIM (, not Max)'

The analysis proposed for both manifestations of *lui* is that of a D°–N° complex $[[_{D°}$ l-] $[_{N°}$ ui]]. Within this D°–N° complex, either D° or N° can project. If D° projects, as in (23a), the result will be D° clitic *lui*, which needs to move out of its DP to become licensed as a clitic. The structure (23a) is that of the clitic in (21) before the clitic has cliticized onto the verb. If N° projects, as in (23b), *lui* will end up as an N°. This N° further projects to the NP level, and N° moves to the D° position of the DP selecting it, following the analysis of Longobardi (1995) for proper names. The structure (23b), without N° to D° movement, is that of the XP pronoun in (22).

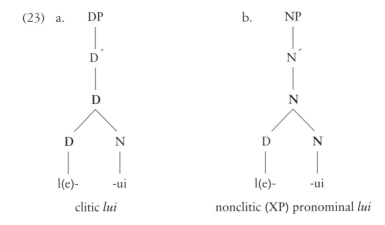

(23) a. clitic *lui*

b. nonclitic (XP) pronominal *lui*

The analysis proposed is reinforced by the fact that the *-ui* morpheme within *lui* can also attach to one other element to form nouns. In the rather old-fashioned noun *autrui* 'the other,' the adjective *autre* 'other' combines with *-ui* to form a noun that functions as an XP only:[12]

(24) a. Il faut aimer autrui
'One must love the others'

b. Autrui a facilement tort
'The other is often wrong'

c. Faire quelque chose pour autrui
'To do something for the other'

Let us briefly describe the properties of both projections of the D°–N° complex *lui*. Interpretively, clitic *lui* is underspecified for gender, since it can refer to both masculine and feminine antecedents (cf. note 9). Those antecedents can be both animate and inanimate, as (25a) shows,[13] but 'default' interpretations in 'out of the blue' contexts always involve animacy (cf. (25b)).

(25) a. (Ce livre/cette personne,) Max lui a accordé beaucoup d'attention
(That book/that person,) Max to-him/it has given a lot of attention

b. Speaker A: Max lui a accordé beaucoup d'attention

Speaker B: A qui?/*A quoi?
A: Max to-him/it gave a lot of attention.
B: To whom?/to what?

240

This suggests that in the feature notation used here, clitic *lui* is [αgender, αperson], with [αperson] deriving the 'default' animacy effects in the same way as for *il* 'he/it.' In the presence of an animate antecedent, the under-specified feature [αperson] is set to 0person, taking over the specification from the antecedent. In the context of an inanimate antecedent, [αperson] is not filled in by the antecedent, which means that [αperson] will be elim-inated at LF. In contexts where no antecedent is available, the 'default' interpretation of [αperson] will kick in, setting [αperson] to 0person, hence animate.

The examples with *autrui* in (24) show that the person feature of the D°–N° complex *lui*, made up of *le* and *–ui*, is in fact contributed by the morpheme *–ui*.[14] As an adjective, *autre* 'other' does not have an independent person feature, so *-ui* must be responsible for the animate, i.e. 0person, inter-pretation of *autrui*. This allows us to conclude that the same must be true for *lui*: D° *l(e)* contributes its [αgender, αnumber] properties to the D°–N° complex *lui*, while *-ui* contributes the [αperson] feature. As a result, *lui* must be viewed as a form of *le* modified by the N° *-ui*.

Turning to XP *lui*, it appears to have the feature [masc], and is always interpreted as animate. The value [masc] for the inherently underspecified [αgender] property of *lui* is easily explained away: as an XP, *lui* falls into a paradigmatic class with the XP pronoun *elle* 'she' which has the feature spec-ification [αperson.sg.fem]. The paradigmatic opposition between XP *lui* and *elle* and the ensuing Blocking effect ensures that the [αgender] property of *lui* is interpreted as [masc] only. Similarly, it can be assumed that both clitic and XP *lui* are not inherently singular, but rather [αnumber]. Its interpre-tation as singular arises from the paradigmatic opposition with the plural clitic *leur* and the XP *eux* 'them,' respectively.

The animate interpretation of XP *lui* raises another question: why is it that XP *lui* is always interpreted as animate? Recall *i(l)* 'he/it' and clitic *lui* receive a 'default' animate interpretation in the absence of an antecedent, but that these clitics can be animate or inanimate in the context of an appropriate antecedent. Not so for XP *lui*, which is always interpreted as animate, irre-spective of the context:

(26) Max a vu un gars$_i$/un livre$_j$ étrange; il pense encore souvent à lui$_{i/*j}$.
'Max saw an strange guy/book; he still thinks a lot about him/it'

I will set this problem aside, noting that what I have called 'default' interpretations for underspecified pronouns appear not to be limited to contexts lacking an antecedent for that pronoun.

Finally, the differences between the case properties of dative clitic *lui* as opposed to those of XP *lui* need to be addressed. If it is assumed that *lui* is inherently [αCase], the question arises why clitic *lui* is interpreted with dative case. Moreover, the analysis of clitic *i(l)* 'he/it,' *le* 'it/he,' and *lui* 'to him/it' seems to arrive at a paradox, since it predicts that *lui* has exactly the same feature content as *i(l)*. More specifically, both clitic *i(l)* and clitic *lui* carry the feature set [αperson, αgender, αnumber, αcase]. Clitic *i(l)* and *lui* only differ from *le* in that they have [αperson], which *le* lacks. This can be represented schematically as follows:

(27) i(l) 'he/it' {αperson, αgender, αnumber, αcase}
      le 'it/him' {αgender, αnumber, αcase}
      lui 'to-him/her/it' {αperson, αgender, αnumber, αcase}

The question thus arises why clitic *i(l)* does not occur in positions where clitic *lui* occurs, and vice versa. The answer to this question can be related to the different configuration of features within *i(l)* and *lui*. Recall *lui* was analyzed as a D°–N° complex consisting of D° *l(e)*- and -*ui*, with D° determining the projection of the complex. As a result, *lui* is a form of *le* modified by the N° -*ui*: D° *l(e)* contributes [αgender, αnumber] properties to the D°–N° complex, while -*ui* adds the [αperson] feature. The analysis of *i(l)* reveals no configurationally determined distribution: the -*i* morpheme carries the entire feature set.

Recall that the distribution of *i(l)* 'he/it' and *le* 'it/him' in SpecAGR$_S$P and SpecAGR$_O$P, respectively, was explained by the maximal compatibility of their features with AGR$_S$ and AGR$_O$. The [αperson] feature of *i(l)* is more compatible with AGR$_S$, which can display person agreement; the absence of person features is more compatible with AGR$_O$, which cannot display person agreement (cf. *supra*). Let us now assume that this maximal compatibility extends to the configuration in which features appear. The complex D°–N° *lui* displays a configurational distribution of its features, while the distribution of features within AGR$_S$ and within *i(l)* is not so determined. Within the paradigmatic set consisting of *il*, *le*, and *lui*, the pronoun *il* thus has the feature set corresponding most closely in all respects, including the absence of configurational structure, to that of AGR$_S$. As a result, the configurational distribution of features within the complex D°–N° *lui* excludes it from appearing in SpecAGR$_S$P.

This account raises another question: if *lui* must be viewed as a form of *le*, why does *lui* not simply function as an accusative [αperson] variant of clitic *le*? A partial answer is that it does. In many dialects of French (e.g. Franco-Albertan French, some varieties of Quebec French), clitic *lui* not only functions as a dative clitic as in (21) or as a pronominal XP as in (22), but it can also appear as an animate accusative clitic, in paradigmatic opposition with an accusative *le* which is restricted to an inanimate interpretation.[15]

(29) a. Je lui ai vu ce matin
'I saw him/her this morning'

    b. Je l'ai vu ce matin
'I saw it this morning'   (Franco-Albertan)

However, this answer partly skirts the question, because it still leaves unclear why *lui* can function as a dative clitic at all. The answer I would like to suggest is along the lines of the account which was offered earlier for the distribution of *i(l)* 'he/it' and *le* 'it/him,' and of *i(l)* and *lui,* in terms of the interaction of the notion of paradigmatic opposition and the requirement of maximal compatibility of clitics with the features of AGR_S and AGR_O. The feature composition of *le* is more compatible with the features of AGR_O than that of *lui*, which, as a $D°–N°$ complex, also carries the feature [αperson]. Within the paradigmatic set consisting of *il*, *le*, and *lui*, the interpretation of clitic *lui* with dative case then arises as a 'last resort': since *il* and *le* check the structural cases in the context of AGR_S and AGR_O, the only interpretation left for the [αcase] feature of clitic *lui* is dative case.

The question remains how *lui* can end up in some dialects as an accusative clitic with animate interpretation. I submit that in these dialects, the under-specified features of clitic *lui* receive a 'default' interpretation similar to that of XP *lui* in that [αperson, αgender, αnumber] default to [0person, sg], but different from XP *lui* in that the [αcase] feature defaults to [oblique]. The feature [oblique] then allows *lui* to function as an accusative clitic. I have no explanation as to why clitic *lui* receives a 'default' interpretation in these cases.

4 Conclusion

Recapitulating the results of the analysis presented here, interrogative and complementizer *qui* and *que* have been argued not to exist as separate entries in the lexicon. Rather, these elements are more productively analyzed as morphological complexes, or functional compounds, built up from the combination of $C°$ *que* and the clitic pronouns *i(l)* 'he/it' and *(l)e* 'it/him.' The various syntactic and semantic differences between interrogative and complementizer *qui* and *que* can be reduced to independent properties of $C°$ *que*, and the clitics *i(l)* and *(l)e*. The interaction of morphological composition, X' projection, and 'default' interpretation suffices to account for all properties observed.

In addition, the notions 'underspecification' and 'nonspecification' were exploited to derive the interpretive feature [± animate] from a proper interpretation of the more fundamental feature [person]. As a result, a conceptually simpler, yet more powerful, feature apparatus emerges.

A number of questions remain. For instance, it might be asked why there are not more languages that avail themselves of this compositional strategy to build *Wh*-elements. More particularly, why don't Italian or Spanish exploit this strategy? In this respect, it is worthwhile to note that Italian and Spanish do not have an X°/XP alternation for the counterparts of *lui* 'to-him/her/it' either. I will leave such questions for further research.

Notes

* I would like to thank Ana Arregui, João Costa, Yves d'Hulst, Aafke Hulk, Teun Hoekstra, Pierre Pica, Petra Sleeman, Rint Sybesma, Guido Vanden Wyngaerd, and the audience at LSRL 26, University of California, Irvine, on 20–22 February 1997, for comments and discussions. Thanks to Rose-Marie Déchaine for the data from Franco-Albertan French. The usual disclaimers apply.

1 I represent the clitic *il* 'he/it' as *i(l)* 'he/it,' because the final consonant of the pronoun *il* 'he/it' often drops in colloquial varieties of French, a variation that is attested since the twelfth century (Pope 1966: 324; Bourciez 1958: 187; Frei 1929: 126; Ashby 1984). I represent the category of *i(l)* as D°, in view of the *l-* morpheme and Longobardi's (1995) analysis of pronouns as DPs. More conservatively, *i(l)* might also be viewed as an N°. As far as I can see, the labeling of *i(l)* as N° or D° does not affect the argument made here.

   In dialects of French dropping the final *-l* of *il*, the disappearance of this final consonant, the subject status of *il*, and schwa deletion of complementizer *que*, lead to identical surface manifestations of *qu'i(l)* 'that he/it' and complementizer *qui* . This has sometimes been taken as an argument to the effect that complementizer *qui* is the result of phonological cliticization of the resumptive pronoun *il* 'he/it' onto the complementizer. Labelle (1990) makes this argument on the basis of facts in child language:

   i.   le garçon qu'il a le chien (J 4;02)   (Labelle (1990: 12(29a))
        'The boy that he has the dog'

   ii. le ceu (= celui) que i lance une boule de neige (M 4;09) (Labelle 1990: 11(28c))
        'The-one that he throws a snowball'

There clearly are social and developmental variants of French in which a resumptive pronoun strategy is used in relative clauses involving third person antecedents (see also Frei 1929). However, I do not think that the development of *qui* can be entirely attributed to this strategy. For one thing, the data involving resumptive pronouns only involve cases in which both *-i* and *il* are found (cf. the contrast in (i–ii)). There seem to be no examples involving the resumptive pronoun *il* (including *-l*) with a first or second person antecedent:

iii. *Nous/vous/moi qu'il vient
     'We/you/I that he comes'

By contrast, there are variants in which, contrary to Standard French, *qui* (without *-l*) does not enable the verb to agree with the antecedent (cf. Rooryck 1994b):

iv   'Il n'y a que *vous qui peut* le faire; C'est *pas nous qui peu(t)* y aller' (Frei 1929: 163)
     'There is only you who can $_{3SG}$ do it; It is not us who can $_{3SG}$ go there'

v.   . . . c'est *nous qui s'soûle*, à çt'heure   (Bauche 1920: 27)
     '. . . it is us who get$_{3\ SG}$ drunk at this hour'

In the analysis developed here, (iv–v) can be accounted for by assuming that these dialects do not feature a [αperson, αnumber, αgender] *qui* as Standard French, but that complementizer *qui* has received a 'default' [3p.sg.masc] interpretation similar to that of interrogative *qui*. The resumptive pronoun analysis of *qui* leaves unclear how in Standard French [3p.sg.masc] subject clitic *il* switches its feature value to [αperson, αnumber, αgender] after phonological cliticization to $C°$ *que*, thus enabling agreement on the verb in the relative clause (cf. (4)). The analysis presented here is not affected by this problem

Moreover, under a resumptive pronoun analysis for *qui* it remains mysterious why only the subject clitic *il* should be singled out for phonological cliticization to $C°$. In languages that feature subject clitics in $C°$, such as West Flemish, the entire range of person clitics can appear in $C°$, not just third person (Bennis & Haegeman 1984; Haegeman 1983).

2 *Pace* Roberge (1986), Miller (1991), Auger (1993), Zribi-Hertz (1994) who argue that subject clitics are inflectional affixes, hence $X°$ elements at some point of the derivation.

3 Of course this does not mean that the *l-* morpheme is in complementary distribution with respect to *Wh*-morphemes generally. In definite *Wh*-NPs such as *lequel* 'which,' the *Wh*-adjective *quel* 'which' is preceded by $D°$ *le* 'the.'

4 It is probably no accident that in those colloquial French dialects in which *il* is in free variation with an *l*-less variant/i/, it can occur with an indefinite antecedent such as *personne* 'nobody' (cf. Zribi-Hertz 1994).

i. Personne il a vu ça
    Nobody he saw that

5 For ease of exposition, I will abstract away here from the proposal by Corver & Delfitto (1993) who analyze the clitic *le* as the result of $D°$ movement out of a DP containing an empty NP (*pro*) in its complement. Whatever features and properties I attribute to *le* in the remainder of this discussion can be translated as those of *pro* in object position.

6 I would like to suggest a similar analysis for West Flemish *dat* —> *die* alternations in $C°$. I take the morpheme *d-* in both *dat* and *die* as being of category $C°/D°$, expressing specificity/definiteness, while *-ie* might be considered an $N°$ carrying the features [αgender, αperson]. In both Dutch and West Flemish, the [αperson] property of *-ie* appears in 'default' interpretations of *die* as a pronoun (DP) in contexts without an antecedent: *die is gevallen* 'that one has fallen' has an animate interpretation for *die*. The same is true for animate *wie* 'who,' which consists of the *Wh*-morpheme *w-* and *-ie*. The presence of [αperson] in the feature specification of *die* explains why specifically this element is taken as a complementizer agreeing with AGRS: since AGRS has person features to check, agreement in $C°$ will also have to display this feature. I have no insights as to why *die* is only a $D°$ in Dutch while it functions both as $D°$ and $C°$ in West Flemish. Bennis & Haegeman (1984) relate the function of *die* as an agreeing $C°$ to the fact that West Flemish displays agreement between AGR$_S$ and AGR$_C$ in nonrelative complement clauses as well.

7 The notion of paradigmatic opposition and its theoretical status have been given scant attention within generative grammar, a remarkable fact in view of the impressive amount of work done on functional categories in the last decade.

8 Menuzzi (1995) similarly exploits the notion of opposition of available elements within a paradigmatic class in the context of an optimality-like system, which is successfully applied to a number of surprising Binding data in Brazilian Portuguese.

9 I assume that the occurrence of *le* in a paradigm with *la* prevents the underspecified features of *le* from taking on a [fem] value. A similar assumption was made for *il* with respect to clitics expressing first/second person, as well as third (0-)person feminine *elle*. In the case of the [αgender] clitic *lui*, there is no element blocking interpretation of *lui* as either [fem] or [masc].

10 When *le* functions as a placeholder for a predicate, it is opaque to gender or number features of the predicate, as shown in (i–ii):

i.   Marie devient directrice et Louise le/*la devient aussi
      Marie gets to be a director$_{FEM}$, and Louise gets to be it$_{MASC/*FEM}$ also

ii   Paul est malade et irritable, et Louis l'est/*les est aussi
      Paul is sick and irritable, and Louis is it/*them also

In such cases, we take it that the [αgender, αnumber, αCase] properties of *le* are all deleted at LF, in keeping with clause (ii) of the PIOUF in (16).

11   The occurrence of XP *lui* in Case positions other than the complement of P is subject to poorly understood Focus restrictions. I will not go into these here, and assume that these restrictions do not preclude assignment of Case to XP *lui* in these positions. For an interesting analysis of the interaction between Case and Focus in terms of Optimality Theory, see Costa (1998).

12   The translation 'the other' for *autrui* is not entirely felicitous: *autrui* should be interpreted generically as 'any person different from oneself.' This generic interpretation is absent in the translation 'the other' as a result of the well-known fact that the English definite article cannot be interpreted generically in the same way as in French (cf. *Le poisson est bon pour la santé/(*The) fish is good for one's health*).

13   The observation that antecedents for *lui* can be both animate and inanimate is often obscured by the fact that verbs selecting an argument with dative case, such as *dire* 'tell' or *donner* 'give,' impose selection restrictions for animacy on that argument.

14   This leads us to assume that *-ui*, which originated as a dative marker (Lat. *alteri* > Fr. *autrui*, Lat. *illui* > Fr. *lui*) was reanalysed diachronically as bearing a person feature.

15   Similar alternations are well known in Spanish dialects for the clitics *le(s)* and *lo(s)* *(leísmo / loísmo)*, and in the interlanguage of second language learners of Standard French, who often consistently use *Ce garçon, je lui aime* rather than the Standard French *je l'aime*. Interestingly, Franco-Albertan French also allows for an accusative and animate (0person) reading of plural *leur* '(to)-them,' an exclusively dative and ±animate ([αperson]) clitic in Standard French. In the terms of the analysis proposed here, the animate interpretation of *lui* arises via the 'default' interpretation of its [αperson] feature as [0person].

BIBLIOGRAPHY

Abraham, W. (1982) 'Zur Kontroll im Deutschen', Groningen Arbeiten zum germanistischen Linguistik, 1: 112–67.

—— (1983) 'The control relation in German', in W. Abraham (ed.), *On the formal syntax of the Westgermania*, New York: John Benjamins, 217–42.

Adams, M. (1985) 'Government of empty subjects in factive clausal complements', *Linguistic Inquiry* 16: 305–13.

Albertini, J. (1972) *Précis de grammaire corse*, Corté: Editions du CERC.

Anderson, J., and Ewen, C. (1987) *Principles of dependency phonology*, Cambridge: Cambridge University Press.

Archangeli, D. (1984) *Underspecification in Yawelmani phonology and morphology*, PhD dissertation, Cambridge, MA: MIT.

Ashby, W. (1984) 'The elision of /l/ in French clitic pronouns and articles', in E. Pulgram (ed.), *Romanitas: Studies in Romance linguistics*, Michigan Romance Studies, Ann Arbor: University of Michigan, 1–17.

Auger, J. (1993) 'More evidence for verbal agreement-marking in Colloquial French', in W. Ashby et al. (eds), *Linguistic perspectives on the Romance languages: Selected papers from the XXI Linguistic Symposium on Romance languages*, Amsterdam: John Benjamins, 177–98.

Authier, J.-M. (1989) 'Arbitrary null objects and unselective binding', in O. Jaeggli and K. Safir (eds), *The null subject parameter*, Dordrecht: Kluwer, 45–67.

Bach, E. (1982) 'Purpose clauses and control', in P. Jacobson and G. Pullum, *The nature of syntactic representation*, Dordrecht: Reidel, 35–57.

Baker, C. L. (1968) *Indirect questions in English*, PhD dissertation, University of Illinois.

—— (1970) 'Notes on the description of English questions. The role of an abstract question morpheme', *Foundations of Language* 6: 197–219.

Baker, M. (1988) *Incorporation: A theory of grammatical function changing*, Chicago: University of Chicago Press.

Baker, M., and Hale, K. (1990) 'Relativized Minimality and pronoun incorporation', *Linguistic Inquiry* 21: 289–97.

Barbiers, S. (1993) 'Modal verbs in Dutch: an LF analysis of the epistemic-root distinction' (MS., University of Leiden/ HIL).

—— (1995) *The syntax of interpretation*, doctoral dissertation, University of Leiden/ HIL.

—— (1998) 'English and Dutch as SOV languages and the distribution of CP complements', in R. van Bezooijen and R. Kager (eds), *Linguistics in the Netherlands*, Amsterdam: Benjamins.

Bauche, H. (1920) *Le langage populaire*, Paris: Payot.

Bec, P. (1967) *La langue occitane*, Paris: Presses Universitaires de France.

Belletti, A. (1990) *Generalized verb-movement: Aspects of verb syntax,* Turin: Rosenberg and Sellier.

Belletti, A., and Rizzi, L. (1988) 'Psych-verbs and θ-theory,' *Natural Language and Linguistic Theory* 6: 291–352.

Bellier, P. (1989) 'Mouvement et interprétation: les interrogatives indirectes en français', *Langages* 95: 23–34.

Bennis, H. (1986) *Gaps and dummies*, Dordrecht: Foris.

Bennis, H., and Haegeman, L. (1984) 'On the status of agreement and relative clauses in West Flemish', in W. de Geest and Y. Putseys (eds), *Sentential complementation*, Dordrecht: Foris, 33–54.

Benveniste, É. (1960) '"Être" et "avoir" dans leurs fonctions linguistiques,' *Bulletin de la société linguistique de Paris* LV.

—— (1966) *Problèmes de linguistique générale*, Paris: Gallimard.

Berman, S. (1989) 'An analysis of quantifier variability in indirect questions', in P. Branigan et al. (eds), *MIT working papers in linguistics vol. 11*, Cambridge, MA: MIT, 1–16.

Bernstein, J. (1991) 'DPs in French and Walloon: evidence for parametric variation in nominal head movement', *Probus* 3: 101–26.

Beukema, F., and Coopmans, P. (1989) 'A government-binding perspective on the imperative in English', *Journal of Linguistics* 25: 417–36.

Bogusławski, A. (1983) 'An analysis of *promise*', *Journal of Pragmatics* 7: 607–28.

Bok-Bennema, R., and Kampers-Manhe, B. (1993) 'Transparency effects in the Romance languages,' in M. Mazzola (ed.), *Issues and theory in romance linguistics: Selected papers from the Linguistic Symposium on Romance Languages XXIII*, Washington DC: Georgetown University Press, 199–219.

Bolinger, D. (1972) *That's that*, The Hague: Mouton.

Borer, H. (1989) 'Anaphoric AGR', in O. Jaeggli and K. Safir (eds), *The null subject parameter*, Dordrecht: Kluwer, 69–110.

Bouchard, D. (1985) 'PRO pronominal or anaphor?' *Linguistic Inquiry* 16: 471–7.

—— (1987) 'A few remarks on past participle agreement', *Linguistics and Philosophy* 10: 449–74.

Bouchard, D., and Hirschbühler, P. (1986) 'French *quoi* and its clitic allomorph *que*', in C. Neidle and R. Nuñez Cedeño (eds), *Studies in Romance languages*, Dordrecht: Foris, 39–60.

Bourciez, E. (1958) *Précis de phonétique française*, Paris: Klincksieck.

Bresnan, J. (1972) *Theory of complementation in English syntax*, PhD dissertation, Cambridge, MA: MIT.

—— (1982) 'Control and complementation', *Linguistic Inquiry* 13: 343–434.

Burzio, L. (1986) *Italian syntax: A government-binding approach*, Dordrecht: Reidel.

—— (1992) 'On the morphology of reflexives and impersonals,' in C. Laeufer and T. Morgan (eds), *Theoretical analyses in Romance linguistics, LSRL XIX*, Amsterdam: John Benjamins.

Cardinalletti, A. (1989) *Impersonal constructions and sentential arguments in German*, Padua: Unipress.

Carlson, G. (1984) 'On the role of thematic roles in linguistic theory', *Linguistics* 22: 259–79.

Castañeda, H.-N. (1966) '"He": a study in the logic of self-consciousness', *Ratio* 7: 130–57.

Chierchia, G., and Jacobson, P. (1986) 'Local and long distance control', *Proceedings of NELS 16*, Amherst: GLSA, 57–74.

Chomsky, N. (1965) *Aspects of the theory of syntax*, Cambridge, MA: MIT Press.

—— (1977) 'On *wh*-movement', in Peter Culicover, Thomas Wasow, and Adrian Akmajian (eds), *Formal syntax*, New York: Academic Press.

—— (1981) *Lectures on government and binding*, Dordrecht: Foris.

—— (1986a) *Barriers*, Cambridge, MA: MIT Press.

—— (1986b) *Knowledge of language*, New York: Praeger.

—— (1991) 'Some notes on the economy of derivation and representation', in R. Freidin (ed.), *Principles and parameters in comparative grammar*, Cambridge, MA: MIT Press, 417–54.

—— (1992) *A minimalist program for linguistic theory*, MIT Occasional Papers in Linguistics 1, Cambridge, MA: MIT.

—— (1995) *The minimalist program*, Cambridge, MA: MIT Press.

Chomsky, N, and Lasnik, H. (1991) 'Principles and parameters theory', in J. Jacobs, A. von Stechow, W. Sternefeld, and T. Vennemann (eds), *Syntax: An international handbook of contemporary research*, Berlin: de Gruyter.

Cinque, G. (1988) 'On *Si* constructions and the theory of *Arb*', *Linguistic Inquiry* 19: 521–81.

—— (1991) *Types of A´-dependencies*, Cambridge, MA: MIT Press.

Clark, R. (1985) *Boundaries and the treatment of control*, PhD dissertation, Los Angeles: UCLA.

Contreras, H. (1985) 'Clausal case-marking and the CRP', in L. D. King and C. A. Maley (eds), *Selected papers from the XIIIth Linguistics Symposium on Romance languages*, Amsterdam: John Benjamins.

Cornulier, B. de (1974) 'Sur une règle de déplacement de négation', *Le Français moderne*. 41: 43–57.

Corver, N., and Delfitto, D. (1993) 'Feature Asymmetry and the nature of Pronoun Movement', *OTS Working Papers*, Utrecht (OTS-WP-TL–93-013).

Costa, J. (1996) 'Adverb positioning and V-movement in English: some more evidence,' *Studia Linguistica* 50: 1–23.

—— (1998) *Word order variation: a constraint-based approach*, doctoral dissertation, Leiden University/HIL, LOT dissertation series 14, The Hague: HAG.

Costa, J., and Rooryck, J. (1996) 'On Pseudo-raising', in L. Nash, G. Tsoulas and A. Zribi-Hertz (eds), *Actes du second colloque Langues & Grammaire, Paris VIII*, 48–58.

Déchaine, R.-M. (1992) 'INFL in Ìgbo and Yorùbá', in C. Collins and V. Manfredi (eds), *MITWPL 17*, Cambridge, MA: MIT, 95–119.

—— (1994) 'Ellipsis and the position of subjects', in M. González (ed.), *Proceedings of NELS 24*, Amherst, MA: GLSA, 47–63.

den Dikken, M., and Mulder, R. (1992) 'Tough parasitic gaps', *Proceedings of NELS 22*, Amherst: GLSA, 303–17.

di Sciullo, A.-M., and Williams, E. (1987) *On the definition of word*, Cambridge, MA: MIT Press.

Dobrovie-Sorin, C. (1991) *The syntax of Romanian*, Comparative Studies in Romance, Paris: CNRS.

Doetjes, J. (1992) 'Rightward floating quantifiers float to the left,' *The Linguistic Review* 9: 313–32.

Dowty, D. (1991) 'Thematic proto-roles and argument selection', *Language* 67: 547–619.

Ewen, C., and van der Hulst, H. (1985) 'Single-valued features and the non-linear analysis of vowel harmony,' in H. Bennis and F. Beukema (eds), *Linguistics in the Netherlands 1985*, Dordrecht: Foris 317–36.

Faraci, R. (1974) *Aspects of the grammar of infinitives and* for- *phrases*, PhD dissertation, Cambridge, MA: MIT.

Fodor, J. (1975) *The language of thought*, Hassocks, Sussex: Harvester Press.

Foley, W., and van Valin, R., Jr. (1984) *Functional syntax and universal grammar*, Cambridge: Cambridge University Press.

Freeze, R. (1992) 'Existentials and other locatives', *Language* 68: 553–95.

Frei, H. (1929) *La grammaire des fautes*, Paris: Geuthner.

Friedemann, M.-A. (1989) 'Le *Que* interrogatif' (MS., University of Genève).

Grevisse, M. (1980) *Le bon usage*, 11th edn, Gembloux: Duculot.

—— (1986) *Le bon usage*, 12th edn, Gembloux: Duculot.

Grimshaw, J. (1979) 'Complement selection and the lexicon', *Linguistic Inquiry* 10: 279–326.

Grinder, J. (1970) 'Super Equi-NP deletion', *Papers from the sixth meeting of the Chicago Linguistics Society*, 297–317.

—— (1971) 'A reply to Super Equi-NP deletion as dative deletion', *Papers from the seventh meeting of the Chicago Linguistics Society*, 101–11.

Groos, A., and Van Riemsdijk, H. (1978) 'Matching effects in free relatives: a parameter of core grammar', in A. Belletti et al. (eds), *Theory of markedness in a generative grammar: Proceedings of the IV GLOW conference*, Pisa.

Gross, M. (1975) *Méthodes en syntaxe*, Paris: Hermann.

Guasti, M.-T. (1991) 'Incorporation, excorporation and lexical properties of causative heads', *The Linguistic Review* 8: 1–24.

Guéron, J. (1981) 'Logical operators, complete constituents, and extraction transformations', in R. May and J. Koster (eds), *Levels of syntactic representation*, Dordrecht: Foris, 65–142.

Guillaume, G. (1929) *Temps et verbe*, Paris: Masson.

Haegeman, L. (1983) '*Die* and *dat* in West-Flemish relative clauses', in H. Bennis and W.U.S. van Lessen Kloeke (eds), *Linguistics in the Netherlands*, Dordrecht: Foris, 83–92.

Haiman, J. (1988) 'Rhaeto-Romance', in M. Harris and N. Vincent (eds), *The Romance languages*, New York: Oxford University Press, 351–390.

Hajati, A. (1977) '*Ke' constructions in Persian: descriptive and theoretical aspects*, PhD dissertation: University of Illinois at Urbana-Champaign.

Hale, K. (1973) 'Person marking in Walbiri', in S. Anderson and P. Kiparsky (eds), *A Festschrift for Morris Halle*, New York: Holt, Rinehart, and Winston, 308–44.

Harbert, W. (1983) 'On the nature of the matching parameter', *The Linguistic Review* 2: 237–84.

Harmer, L. C. (1979) *Uncertainties in French grammar*, Cambridge: Cambridge University Press.

Haverkort, M. (1993) *Clitics and parametrization. Case studies in the interaction of head movement phenomena*, doctoral dissertation, Katholieke Universiteit Brabant, Tilburg.

Heim, I. (1982) *The semantics of definite and indefinite NPs*, PhD dissertation, Amherst, MA: GLSA.

Helke, M. (1979) *The grammar of English reflexives*, PhD MIT, New York: Garland.

Heycock, C. (1992) 'Layers of predication and the syntax of the copula', *Belgian Journal of Linguistics* 7: 95–123.

Higginbotham, J. (1989) 'Reference and control', in R. Larson, S. Iatridou, U. Lahiri, and J. Higginbotham (eds), *Control and grammar*, Dordrecht: Kluwer, 79–108.

Hirschbühler, P. (1976) 'Two analyses of free relatives in French', *Papers from the sixth meeting of the NELS*, Montréal papers in Linguistics III, 137–52.

—— (1978) *The syntax and semantics of Wh-constructions*, PhD dissertation, University of Massachusetts.

—— (1980) 'The French interrogative pronoun *que*', in W. Cressey and D. J. Napoli (eds), *Linguistic symposium on Romance languages 9*, Washington, DC: Georgetown University Press, 227–47.

Hoekstra, T. (1993) 'HAVE as BE plus or minus', (MS. HIL/Leiden University).

Horn, L. (1978) 'Remarks on Neg-Raising', in P. Cole (ed.), *Pragmatics*, Syntax and Semantics 9, New York: Academic Press, 129–220.

—— (1989) *A natural history of negation*, Chicago: University of Chicago Press.

Hulst, H. van der, and Smith, N. (1986) 'On neutral vowels', in K. Bogers, H. van der Hulst, and M. Mous (eds), *The representation of suprasegmentals*, Dordrecht: Foris, 233–79.

Hulst, H. van der, and van de Weijer, J. (1995) 'Vowel harmony', in J. Goldsmith (ed.), *A handbook of phonological theory*, Oxford: Basil Blackwell, 495–534.

Huot, H. (1979) *Recherches sur la subordination en français*, Thèse de doctorat d'Etat, Université de Lille III.

—— (1981) *Constructions infinitives du français: le subordonnant* de, Genève-Paris: Droz.

Jackendoff, R. (1972) *Semantic interpretation in generative grammar*, Cambridge, MA: MIT Press.

—— (1987) 'The status of thematic relations in linguistic theory', *Linguistic Inquiry* 18: 369–411.

Jacobson, P., and Neubauer, P. (1976) 'Rule cyclicity: evidence from the intervention constraint', *Linguistic Inquiry* 7: 429–62.

Jaeggli, O. (1986) 'Three issues in the theory of clitics: case, doubled NPs and extraction', in H. Borer (ed.), *The syntax of pronominal clitics*, New York: Academic Press, 15–42.

Johnson, K. (1991) 'Object positions', *Natural Language and Linguistic Theory* 9: 577–636.

Jones, C. (1985) *Syntax and the thematics of infinitival adjuncts*, PhD dissertation, Amherst: University of Massachusetts.

—— (1988) 'Thematic relations in control', in W. Wilkins (ed.), *Thematic relations*, Syntax and Semantics 21, New York: Academic Press, 75–90.

Jones, M. (1988) 'Sardinian', in M. Harris and N. Vincent (eds), *The Romance languages*, New York: Oxford University Press, 314–50.

Joseph, B. (1983) *The synchrony and diachrony of the Balkan infinitive, a study in areal, general, and historical linguistics*, Cambridge: Cambridge University Press.

Kamp, H. (1981) 'A theory of truth and semantic representation', in J. Groenendijk et al. (eds), *Truth, interpretation and information*, GRASS 2, Dordrecht: Foris, 1–42.

Kayne, R. (1975) *French syntax: The transformational cycle*, Cambridge, MA: MIT Press.

—— (1976) 'French relative *que*', in M. Luján and F. Hensey (eds), *Current studies in Romance linguistics*, Washington, DC: Georgetown University Press, 255–99.

—— (1981a) 'ECP extensions', *Linguistic Inquiry* 12: 93–133.

—— (1981b) 'On certain differences between French and English', *Linguistic Inquiry*, 12: 349–71.

—— (1983) 'Chains, categories external to S, and French complex inversion', *Natural Language and Linguistic Theory* 1: 107–39.

—— (1984) *Connectedness and binary branching*, Dordrecht: Foris.

—— (1985a) 'L'accord du participe passé en français et en italien', *Modèles linguistiques* VII: 73–90.

—— (1985b) 'Principles of particle constructions', in J. Guéron, H.-G. Obenauer, and J.-Y. Pollock, *Grammatical representation*, Dordrecht: Foris, 96–131.

—— (1986) 'Connexité et inversion du sujet', in Mitsou Ronat and Daniel Couquaux (eds), *La grammaire modulaire*, Paris: Editions de Minuit, 127–47.

—— (1989a) 'Facets of Romance past participle agreement,' in P. Benincà (ed.), *Dialect variation and the theory of grammar,* Dordrecht: Foris, 85–103.

—— (1989b) 'Notes on English agreement,' *C(entral) I(nstitute of) E(nglish and) F(oreign) L(anguages) Bulletin* 1:41–67 (Hyderabad, India).

—— (1989c) 'Null subjects and clitic climbing', in O. Jaeggli and K. Safir, *The null subject parameter*, Dordrecht: Kluwer, 239–61.

—— (1991a) 'Romance clitics, verb movement, and PRO', *Linguistic Inquiry* 22: 647–86.

—— (1991b) 'Italian negative infinitival imperatives and clitic climbing' (MS., CUNY Graduate Center).

—— (1993) 'Toward a modular theory of auxiliary selection,' *Studia Linguistica* 47: 3–31.

—— (1994) *The antisymmetry of syntax*, Cambridge, MA: MIT Press.

Kayne, R., and Pollock, J.-Y. (1978) 'Stylistic inversion, successive cyclicity, and Move-NP in French', *Linguistic Inquiry* 9: 595–621.

Keenan, E. (1976) 'Towards a universal definition of "subject",' in C. Li (ed.), *Subject and topic*, New York: Academic Press, 303–34.

—— (1984) 'Semantic correlates of the ergative/absolutive distinction', *Linguistics*, 22: 197–223.

Kerstens, J. (1993) *The syntax of number, person, and gender: A theory of phi-features*, Berlin: Mouton de Gruyter.

Khalaily, S. (1997) *One syntax for all categories*, Leiden: HIL dissertation 27.

Kimball, J. (1971) 'Super Equi-NP deletion as dative deletion', *Papers from the seventh meeting of the Chicago Linguistics Society*, 142–48.

Kiparsky, P., and Kiparsky, C. (1970) 'Fact', in M. Bierwisch and K. Heidolph (eds), *Progress in linguistics*, The Hague: Mouton, 143–73.

Koster, J. (1984) 'On binding and control', *Linguistic Inquiry*, 15: 417–59.

Kroch, A. (1989) 'Amount quantification, referentiality, and long *wh*-movement' (MS., University of Pennsylvania).

Kuno, S. (1972) 'Functional sentence perspective: a case study from Japanese and English', *Linguistic Inquiry* 3: 269–320.

Kuroda, S.-Y. (1968) 'English relativization and certain related problems', *Language* 44: 244–64.

Labelle, M. (1990) *Licensing of empty categories in child language*, (MS., UQAM).

Ladusaw, W., and Dowty, D., (1988) 'Toward a non-grammatical account of thematic roles', in W. Wilkins (ed.), *Thematic relations*, Syntax and Semantics 21, New York: Academic Press, 62–72.

Lahiri, U. (1990) 'The semantics of questions and the quantificational variability effect', in L. Cheng and H. Demirdache (eds), *MIT papers in linguistics 13*, Cambridge, MA: MIT, 163–78.

—— (1991) 'Questions, answers and selection', in T. Sherer (ed.), *Proceedings of NELS 21*, Amherst, MA: GLSA, 233–46.

Lakoff, G. (1970) 'Pronominalization, negation and the analysis of adverbs', in R. Jacobs and P. Rosenbaum (eds), *Readings in English transformational grammar*, Waltham, MA: Ginn, 145–65.

Lappin, S. (1983) 'Theta-roles and NP movement', in P. Sells and C. Jones (eds), *Proceedings of NELS 13*, Amherst, MA: GLSA, 121–8.

—— (1984) 'Predication and raising', in C. Jones and P. Sells (eds), *Proceedings of NELS 14*, Amherst, MA: GLSA, 237–52.

Larson, R. (1990) '*Promise* and the theory of control', *Linguistic Inquiry* 21: 103–40.

Lasnik, H. (1992) 'Case and expletives: notes toward a parametric account', *Linguistic Inquiry* 23: 381–405.

——(1994) 'Lectures on minimalist syntax' (MS., University of Connecticut).

——and Fiengo, R. (1975) 'Complement object deletion', *Linguistic Inquiry* 5: 535–72.

Lebeaux, D. (1984) 'Anaphoric binding and the definition of PRO', in C. Jones and P. Sells (eds), *Proceedings of NELS 14*, Amherst, MA: GLSA, 253–74.

Long, M. (1974) 'French infinitival complementizers and their place in a generative grammar', in M. Luján and F. Hensey (eds), *Current studies in Romance linguistics*, Washington, DC: Georgetown University Press, 205–20.

Longobardi, G. (1995) 'Reference and proper names', *Linguistic Inquiry* 26: 609–66.

Lyons, J. (1977) *Semantics*, Cambridge: Cambridge University Press.

Manzini, M.-R. (1983) 'On control and control theory', *Linguistic Inquiry* 14: 421–67.

Martineau, F. (1991) 'Clitic climbing in infinitival constructions in Middle French', in D. Wanner and D. Kibbee (eds), *New analyses in Romance linguistics*, Amsterdam: John Benjamins.

May, R. (1985) *Logical form*, Cambridge, MA: MIT Press.

Melis, L. (1988) 'Les propositions enchevêtrées, des complétives ou des relatives-interrogatives?' *Neuphilologische Mitteilungen* 67: 189–96.

Menuzzi, S. (1995) '1st person plural anaphora in Brazilian Portuguese and the Chain Condition', in M. den Dikken and K. Hengeveld (eds), *Linguistics in the Netherlands 1995*, Amsterdam: John Benjamins, 151–62.

Meulen, A. ter (1990) 'Aspectual verbs as generalized quantifiers', in A. Halpern (ed.), *The proceedings of the ninth West Coast Conference on Formal Linguistics*, Stanford, CA: CSLI, 374–60.

Miller, P. (1991) *Clitics and constituents in phrase structure grammar*, PhD dissertation, Utrecht.

Mohanan, K. (1983) 'Functional and anaphoric control', *Linguistic Inquiry* 14: 641–74.

Moore, J. (1991) *Reduced constructions in Spanish*, doctoral dissertation, University of California, Santa Cruz.

Moreau, M.-L. (1971) 'L'homme que je crois qui est venu; *qui, que*: relatifs et conjonctions', *Langue Française* 11: 77–90.

Moro, A. (1992) *I predicati nominali e la struttura della frase*, doctoral dissertation, Università di Venezia.

Motapanyane, V. (1994) 'An A- position for Romanian subjects', *Linguistic Inquiry* 25: 729–34.

Mulder, R. (1992) *On the aspectual nature of syntactic complementation*, Leiden: HIL dissertations 3.

Napoli, D. J. (1981) 'Semantic interpretation vs. lexical governance', *Language* 57: 841–87.

Newmark, L., Hubbard, P., and Prifti, P. (1982) *Standard Albanian*, Stanford, CA: Stanford University Press.

Nishigauchi, T. (1984) 'Control and the thematic domain', *Language* 60: 215–50.

Obenauer, H.-G. (1976) *Etudes de syntaxe interrogative du français: quoi, combien et le complémenteur*, Tübingen: Niemeyer.

——(1977) 'Syntaxe et interprétation: *que* interrogatif', *Le Français Moderne* 45.

Palmer, F. R. (1974) *The English verb*, London: Longman.

Partee, B. (1991) 'Topic, focus, and quantification', *Proceedings of SALT 1*, 159–87.

Pearce, E. (1990) *Parameters in Old French syntax: Infinitival complements*, Dordrecht: Kluwer.

Pernot, H. (1934) *Introduction à l'étude du dialecte tsakonien*, Paris: Les Belles Lettres.

Pesetsky, D. (1982a) *Paths and categories*, PhD dissertation, Cambridge, MA: MIT.

—— (1982b) 'Complementizer-trace phenomena and the nominative island condition', *The Linguistic Review* 1: 297–43.

—— (1989) 'Language-particular processes and the earliness principle' (MS., Cambridge, MA: MIT).

—— (1990) 'Experiencer predicates and universal alignment principles' (MS., Cambridge, MA: MIT).

—— (1994) *Zero syntax*, Cambridge, MA: MIT Press.

Pica, P. (1987) 'On the nature of the reflexivization cycle', in J. McDonough and B. Plunkett (eds), *Proceedings of NELS 17*, Amherst, MA: GLSA, 483–500.

—— (1991) 'On the relationship between binding and antecedent-government: the case of long-distance reflexives', in J. Koster and E. Reuland (eds), *Issues in long-distance anaphora*, Cambridge: Cambridge University Press, 119–35.

Pica, P. and Rooryck, J. (1995) 'Configurational attitudes'. Talk presented at LSRL XXVI, Mexico City, March 1995. To appear in J. Lema and E. Trevi *Theoretical research on Romance languages, Proceedings of the LSRL XXVI Symposium*, Amsterdam: John Benjamins.

Picallo, C. (1985) *Opaque domains*, PhD dissertation, CUNY.

—— (1991) 'Nominals and nominalization in Catalan', *Probus* 3: 279–316.

Pizzini, Q. (1981) 'The placement of clitic pronouns in Portuguese', *Linguistic Analysis* 5: 293–312.

Plann, S. (1986) 'On case-marking clauses in Spanish: evidence against the Case Resistance Principle', *Linguistic Inquiry* 15: 75–102.

Pollock, J.-Y. (1985) 'On case and the syntax of infinitives in French', in J. Guéron, H.-G. Obenauer, and J.-Y. Pollock (eds), *Grammatical representation*, Dordrecht: Foris, 293–326.

—— (1989) 'Verb movement, universal grammar, and the structure of IP', *Linguistic Inquiry* 20: 365–424.

—— (1992) 'Opérateurs nuls, *dont*, questions indirectes et théorie de la quantification', in L. Tasmowski and A. Zribi-Hertz (eds), *Hommages à Nicolas Ruwet*, Gent: Communication and Cognition, 440–63.

Pope, M. (1966) *From Latin to Modern French, with especial consideration of Anglo-Norman*, Manchester: Manchester University Press.

Postal, P. (1970) 'On coreferential complement subject deletion', *Linguistic Inquiry* 1: 439–500.

—— (1974) *On raising*, Cambridge, MA: MIT Press.

—— (1993) 'Some defective paradigms', *Linguistic Inquiry* 24: 347–64.

Postma, G. (1994) *Zero-semantics. A study of the syntactic construction of quantificational meaning*, doctoral dissertation, Leiden University/HIL.

—— (1995) 'Zero-semantics: the syntactic encoding of universal quantification', in M. den Dikken (ed.), *Linguistics in the Netherlands 1995*, Amsterdam: John Benjamins.

Progovac, L. (1988) *A binding approach to polarity sensitivity*, PhD dissertation, University of Southern California, Los Angeles.

—— (1991) 'Polarity in Serbo-Croatian: anaphoric NPIs and pronominal PPIs', *Linguistic Inquiry* 22: 567–72.

Pustejovsky, J. (1988) 'The geometry of events', in C. Tenny (ed.), *Studies in generative approaches to syntax*, Lexicon Project Working Papers 24, Cambridge, MA: MIT, 19–40.

Radford, A. (1988) *Transformational grammar*, Cambridge: Cambridge University Press.

Raposo, E. (1987) 'Romance infinitival clauses and Case theory', in C. Neidle and R. Nuñez-Cedeño (eds), *Linguistic studies in Romance languages*, Dordrecht: Foris.

Remacle, L. (1952) *Syntaxe du parler wallon de la Gleize*, Tome 1, Paris: Les Belles Lettres.

Rennison, J. (1986) 'On tridirectional feature systems for vowels', in J. Durand (ed.), *Dependency and non-tier phonology*, London: Croom Helm, 281–303.

Rézean, P. (1976) *Un patois de Vendée, le parler rural de Vouvant*, Paris: Klincksieck.

Ritter, E. (1991) 'Two functional categories in noun phrases: evidence from Modern Hebrew', in S. Rothstein (ed.), *Syntax and Semantics 26*, San Diego: Academic Press, 37–62.

Rivero, M.-L. (1988) 'The structure of IP and V-movement in the languages of the Balkans' (MS., University of Ottawa).

Rizzi, L. (1982) *Issues in Italian syntax*, Dordrecht: Foris.

—— (1986) 'Null objects in Italian and the theory of *pro*', *Linguistic Inquiry* 17: 501–58.

—— (1990a) *Relativized minimality*, Cambridge, MA: MIT Press.

—— (1990b) 'Speculations on verb second', in J. Mascaró and M. Nespor (eds), *Grammar in progress: GLOW essays for Henk Van Riemsdijk*, Dordrecht: Foris, 375–86.

—— (1991) 'Residual verb second and the *Wh*-criterion', Technical reports in formal and computational linguistics 2, Université de Genève.

Rizzi, L., and Roberts, I. (1989) 'Complex inversion in French', *Probus* 1: 1–30.

Roberge, Y. (1986) 'On doubling and null argument languages', *Proceedings of NELS 16*, Amherst, MA: GLSA.

Roberts, I. (1991) 'Excorporation and minimality', *Linguistic Inquiry* 22: 209–18.

Rochette, A. (1988) *Semantic and syntactic aspects of Romance sentential complementation*, PhD dissertation, Cambridge, MA: MIT.

Rohlfs, G. (1977) *Le gascon: études de philologie pyrénéenne*, Tübingen: Niemeyer/Pau: Marrimpouey Jeune.

Rooryck, J. (1987) *Les verbes de contrôle: une analyse de l'interprétation du sujet non exprimé des constructions infinitives en français*, doctoral dissertation: KULeuven.

—— (1992a) 'Negative and factive islands revisited', *Journal of Linguistics* 28: 343–74.

—— (1992b) 'Romance enclitic ordering and Universal Grammar', *The Linguistic Review* 9: 219–50.

—— (1992c) 'On the distinction between raising and control', in *Romance Languages and Modern Linguistic Theory*, P. Hirschbühler and Konrad Koerner, (eds), Amsterdam: John Benjamins 225–50.

—— (1992d) 'On control and binding by null arguments', Paper presented at *Going Romance* 1992, Utrecht.

—— (1994a) 'On two types of underspecification: towards a feature theory shared by syntax and phonology', *Probus* 6: 207–33.

—— (1994b) 'Against optional movement for clitic climbing', in M. Mazzola (ed.), *Issues and theory in Romance linguistics: Selected papers from the Linguistic Symposium on Romance Languages XXIII*, Washington, DC: Georgetown University Press, 417–43.

—— (1995) 'On passive as partitive quantification', in Anna-Maria di Sciullo (ed.), *Projections and Interface Conditions*, Oxford: Oxford University Press, 201–34.

—— (1997) 'On the interaction between Raising and Focus in sentential complementation', *Studia Linguistica* 50: 1–49.

Rosen, S. (1990) 'Restructuring verbs are light verbs', in A. Halpern (ed.), *The Proceedings of the Ninth West Coast Conference on Formal Linguistics*, Stanford, CA: CLSI, 477–92.

Rosenbaum, P. (1967) *The grammar of English predicate complement constructions*, Cambridge, MA: MIT Press.

Ross, J. (1984) 'Inner islands', in C. Brugman and M. Macaulay (eds), *Proceedings of the 10th Annual Meeting of the Berkeley Linguistics Society*, 258–65.

Rouveret, A. (1980) 'Sur la notion de proposition finie: gouvernement et inversion', *Langages* 60: 61–88.

—— (1989) 'Cliticisation et temps en portugais européen', *Revue des langues romanes* XCIII.2: 337–72.

Rudanko, J. (1985) 'Towards classifying verbs governing object-controlled infinitival Equi in Modern English', *Studia Neophilologica* 57: 145–55.

—— (1989) *Complementation and case grammar*, Albany: SUNY Press.

Ruwet, N. (1982) *Grammaire des insultes et autres études*, Paris: Seuil.

—— (1983) 'Montée et contrôle: une question à revoir?' *Revue Romane (numéro spécial)* 24: 17–37.

Růžička, R. (1983a) 'Autonomie und Interaktion in Syntax und Semantik', in R. Růžička and W. Motsch (eds), *Untersuchungen zur Semantik*, Berlin: Akademie Verlag, Studia Grammatica XXV: 15–60.

—— (1983b) 'Remarks on control', *Linguistic Inquiry* 14: 309–24.

Sag, I., and Pollard, C. (1991) 'An integrated theory of complement control', *Language* 67: 63–113.

Sandfeld, K. (1943) *Syntaxe du français contemporain: III L'infinitif*, Copenhague: Gyldendalske boghandel Nordisk forlag.

Sauzet, P. (1986) 'Les clitiques occitans: analyse métrique de leur variation dialectale', *Morphosyntaxe des langues romanes, Actes du XVIIe congrès international de linguistique et de philologie romanes*, Vol. 4, Aix-en-Provence: Université de Provence, 153–80.

Scobbie, J. (1991) *Attribute value phonology*, PhD dissertation: Edinburgh.

Searle, J. (1969) *Speech acts: An essay in the philosophy of language*, Cambridge: Cambridge University Press.

Siebert-Ott, G. (1983) *Kontroll-Probleme in infinitiven Komplementkonstruktionen*, Tübingen: Gunter Narr Verlag.

—— (1985) 'Bemerkungen zu den Elementen einer Theorie der Kontrolle', in W. Abraham (ed.), *Erklärende Syntax des Deutschen*, Tübingen: Gunter Narr Verlag, 255–70.

Sigurdsson, H. (1989) *Verbal syntax and case in Icelandic in a comparative GB approach*, doctoral dissertation, University of Lund.

Sportiche, D. (1995) 'Clitic constructions', in J. Rooryck and L. Zaring (eds), *Phrase structure and the lexicon*, Dordrecht: Kluwer, 213–76.

Stowell, T. (1981) *Origins of phrase structure*, PhD dissertation, Cambridge, MA: MIT Press.

—— (1982) 'The tense of infinitives', *Linguistic Inquiry* 13: 561–70.

Suñer, M. (1984) 'Free relatives and the matching parameter', *The Linguistic Review* 3: 363–87.

Szabolcsi, A., and Zwarts, F. (1993) 'Weak islands and an algebraic semantics for scope taking', *Natural Language Semantics* 1: 235–84.

Tancredi, C. (1997) Pronouns and perspectives', in H. Bennis, J. Rooryck, and P. Pica (eds), *Atomism and binding*, Dordrecht: Foris, 381–407 (distributed by HAG Publications, The Hague).

Tenny, C. (1987) *Grammaticalizing aspect and affectedness*, PhD dissertation: Cambridge, MA: MIT.

—— (1988) 'The aspectual interface hypothesis: the connection between syntax and lexical semantics', in C. Tenny (ed.), *Studies in generative approaches to syntax*, Cambridge, MA: MIT, Lexicon Project Working Papers 24: 1–19.

Thompson, S. (1973) 'On subjectless gerunds in English', *Foundations of Language* 9: 374–83.

Torrego, E. (1985) 'On empty categories in nominals' (MS., Boston: University of Massachusetts).

Tranel, B. (1981) *Concreteness in generative phonology*, Berkeley: University of California Press.

Travis, L. (1984) *Parameters and effects of word order variation*, PhD dissertation, MIT.

Vanden Wyngaerd, G. (1989) 'Raising to object in English and Dutch', *Dutch working papers in English language and linguistics 14*, Leiden University: Department of English.

—— (1990) *PRO-legomena. An investigation into the distribution and the referential properties of the empty category PRO*, doctoral dissertation, UIA (Universitaire Instelling Antwerpen).

—— (1994) *PRO-legomena. An investigation into the distribution and the referential properties of the empty category PRO*, revised version, Berlin: Mouton de Gruyter.

Van Gelderen, E. (1992) 'Arguments without number: the case of *it* and *het*', *Linguistics* 30: 381–7.

Van Haaften, T. (1982) 'Interpretaties van begrepen subjecten', *Glot* 5: 107–22.

Vendler, Z. (1967) *Linguistics and philosophy*, Ithaca, NY: Cornell University Press.

Visser, F. (1972) *An historical syntax of the English language* Part 2. *Syntactical units with one verb*, Leiden: E.J. Brill.

—— (1973) *An historical syntax of the English language* Part 3. second half. *Syntactical units with two and with more verbs*, Leiden: E.J. Brill.

—— (1978) [1969¹] *An historical syntax of the English language* Part 3. first half. *Syntactical units with two verbs*, Leiden: E.J. Brill.

Weerman, F. (1989) *The V2 conspiracy: A synchronic and diachronic analysis of verbal positions in Germanic languages*, Dordrecht: Foris.

Wegener, H. (1989) '"Kontrolle" semantisch gesehen. Zur Interpretation von Infinitivkomplementen im Deutschen', *Deutsche Sprache* 17: 206–28.

Wierzbicka, A. (1987) *English speech act verbs: A semantic dictionary*, Sydney: Academic Press.

Williams, E. (1980) 'Predication', *Linguistic Inquiry* 11: 203–38.

—— (1981) 'Argument structure and morphology', *The Linguistic Review* 1: 81–114.

Zanuttini, R. (1991) *Syntactic properties of sentential negation: a comparative study of Romance languages*, PhD dissertation, University of Pennsylvania, IRCS Report No. 91–26.

Zribi-Hertz, A. (1989) 'Anaphoric binding and narrative point of view: English reflexive pronouns in sentence and discourse', *Language* 65: 695–728.

—— (1994) 'The syntax of nominative clitics in Standard French and in Advanced French', in G. Cinque, J. Koster, J.-Y. Pollock, and R. Zanuttini (eds), *Paths towards Universal Grammar*, Washington, DC: Georgetown University Press, 453–72.

Zubizarreta, M.-L. (1982) 'Theoretical implications of subject extraction in Portuguese', *The Linguistic Review* 2: 79–96.

INDEX